Study Guide

for use with

Marketing

Eighth Edition

Roger A. Kerin
Southern Methodist University

Steven W. Hartley
University of Denver

Eric N. Berkowitz
University of Massachusetts

William Rudelius
University of Minnesota

Prepared by
William J. Carner, PH.D.
University of Texas

 **McGraw-Hill
Irwin**

*Boston   Burr Ridge, IL   Dubuque, IA   Madison, WI   New York   San Francisco   St. Louis
Bangkok   Bogotá   Caracas   Kuala Lumpur   Lisbon   London   Madrid   Mexico City
Milan   Montreal   New Delhi   Santiago   Seoul   Singapore   Sydney   Taipei   Toronto*

McGraw-Hill
Irwin

Study Guide for use with
MARKETING
Roger A. Kerin, Steven W. Hartley, Eric N. Berkowitz, William Rudelius

Published by McGraw-Hill/Irwin, an imprint of The McGraw-Hill Companies, Inc., 1221 Avenue of the Americas, New York, NY 10020. Copyright © 2006, 2003, 2000, 1997, 1994, 1992, 1989, 1986 by The McGraw-Hill Companies, Inc. All rights reserved.

1 2 3 4 5 6 7 8 9 0 CUS/CUS 0 9 8 7 6 5

ISBN 0-07-282891-9

www.mhhe.com

Introduction

As I tell my students, business can be defined by its two most vital functions – production and marketing. You have to make something and you have to be able to sell it. What makes marketing the best part of business is that it is also the fun part. Figuring out why people buy what they do and using that information to sell your product is a creative endeavor that should be enjoyed. With that in mind, this study guide has been designed not only to help you succeed in this course, but to increase your enjoyment of it as well.

The format of this study guide has come from the input of students just like yourself who want to do their best in every course they take. Focus groups with Business and Marketing majors have showed that they wanted a study guide designed to enhance their existing study habits. These students reported that as they study their first task was most often to outline the chapter. Their next step was then to relate the material in the book to real life situations. Some used flashcards to remember terms, definitions, and concepts while others wanted to use realistic sample tests to help their learning process. These approaches to learning form the basis of what I hope will be your best study guide in your favorite course.

This study guide is a direct response to what students have said they do to learn better. It comprehensively approaches the ways in which we learn and is an intensely efficient companion to the text. Using the study guide along with the book maximizes both the amount of what you learn and the effectiveness of the time you spend studying. You will find that as you begin to use the study guide, you'll be almost effortlessly reinforcing what you learn in the book in a myriad of ways. Here's how it works. First and foremost, read the assigned chapter in the text. Read it straight through as you might read a magazine article, or a chapter of a novel. Remember to pay particular attention to the examples, especially the ones in the boxes. Once you have read an entire chapter, grab the study guide and go back over the material using the chapter outlines. This is a good way to pick up the terms and concepts that may have slipped past you in the first reading. Next, to remember the relevant cases in the book, you should answer the discussion questions. By answering these questions in the study guide you can better relate the material in the book to real life situations. Finally, take the sample tests in the study guide to simulate a testing situation and also to approach learning the material in still another way. Using the flash cards is another good way to remember the terms and concepts for your exams.

Good luck and remember to enjoy what you do.

William J. Carner, Ph.D.
Director, Business Foundations Program
University of Texas at Austin

TABLE OF CONTENTS

FLASH CARDS

CHAPTER 1

DEVELOPING CUSTOMER RELATIONSHIPS AND VALUE THROUGH MARKETING

<u>Why is Chapter 1 important</u>? This is the overview, the chapter to let you know what this term is going to cover. What is marketing? Why is it important to business and consumers? What are the components of marketing? How did it begin and how has it progressed? What affects marketing? What are the benefits of good marketing programs? You will see examples of how marketing affects everything you do—from marketing yourself to get a date or a job to the reputation of the school you are attending.

Marketing: An organizational function and a set of processes for creating, communicating, and delivering value to customers and for managing customer relationships in ways that benefit the organization and its stakeholders.

CHAPTER OUTLINE

I. WHAT IS MARKETING?

    A. Definition
        1. Exchange
        2. Need Satisfaction

    B. Influencing Factors
        1. Organizational Factors
            a. Management
            b. Human Resources
            c. Information Systems
            d. Marketing
            e. Finance
            f. Manufacturing
            g. Research and Development
        2. Environmental Factors
            a. Social
            b. Economic
            c. Technological
            d. Competitive
            e. Regulatory
        3. Societal Factors
            a. Shareholders (owners)
            b. Customers
            c. Suppliers
            d. Other Organizations

C. Requirements
1. Two or more parties with unsatisfied needs.
2. Desire and ability to satisfy these needs.
3. A way for the parties to communicate.
4. Something to exchange.

II. HOW MARKETING DISCOVERS AND SATISFIES CONSUMER NEEDS

A. Discovering Consumer Needs
1. Customer needs and wants
2. Market
   a. People
   b. Desire
   c. Ability to buy

B. Satisfying Consumer Needs
1. The Four P's: Controllable Factors--Marketing Mix
   a. Product
   b. Price
   c. Promotion
   d. Place
2. Uncontrollable Factors--Environmental Factors
   a. Social
   b. Technological
   c. Economic
   d. Competitive
   e. Regulatory

III. THE MARKETING PROGRAM: HOW CUSTOMER RELATIONSHIPS ARE BUILT

A. Relationship Marketing
1. Easy to understand
2. Difficult to implement

B. The Marketing Program

IV. HOW MARKETING BECAME SO IMPORTANT

A. Evolution of the Marketing Orientation
1. Production Era
2. Sales Era
3. Marketing Concept Era
4. Customer Era
   a. Continuously collecting information about customers' needs.
   b. Sharing this information across departments.
   c. Using the information to create customer value.
B. Ethics and Social Responsibility: Balancing the Interest of Different Groups
1. Ethics
2. Social Responsibility
   a. Societal Marketing Concept
   b. Micromarketing
   c. Micromarketing

C. Breadth and Depth of Marketing
    1. Who Markets?
        a. Organizations
            i.   For profit
            ii.   Non-profit
        b. Places
        c. Individuals
    2. What is Marketed?
        a. Goods
        b. Services
        c. Ideas
    3. Who Buys and Uses What is Marketed?
        a. Ultimate consumers
        b. Organizations
    4. Who Benefits?
        a. Consumers who buy
            i.   Form utility
            ii.   Place utility
            iii.   Time utility
            iv.   Possession utility
        b. Organizations who sell
        c. Society as a whole.

You should be able to place these key terms in the outline and be able to discuss them.

customer relationship management (CRM)	marketing mix
customer value	marketing program
environmental factors	micromarketing
exchange	organizational buyers
macromarketing	relationship marketing
market	societal marketing concept
market orientation	target market
marketing	ultimate consumers
marketing concept	utility

QUESTIONS & PROBLEMS

MARKETING: A DEFINITION TO FOCUS ON NEEDS

To serve both buyers and sellers, marketing seeks (1) to discover the needs and wants of prospective customers and (2) to satisfy them.

Decide which of the following statements demonstrate discovering needs, and which statements demonstrate satisfying needs:

1. A restaurant designates part of its seating as a "nonsmoking" section._____

2. A dentist starts office hours at 6:30 a.m. for patients who work "nine to five"._____

3. A new laundry product comes with the offer of a 50 cents-off coupon upon the completion of a mail-in questionnaire._____

4. An ice cream parlor has its patrons vote for their favorite ice cream flavor._____

5. A major studio looks at the most popular television series this season to decide what type of television shows to produce for next season._____

REQUIREMENTS FOR MARKETING TO OCCUR

List the four elements necessary for marketing to occur:

1._____

2._____

3._____

4._____

Identify how each requirement is being met when a consumer buys a new car. When a citizen votes for a political candidate. When a person chooses where to vacation.

TARGET MARKETS

List at least two possible target markets and the need or want to be satisfied for each product below:

1. Low-salt, low-fat baked potato chips.

Target markets: (for example: wives who want their husbands to lose weight)

Needs:_____

Wants:_____

2. Hotels rooms with computer terminals and hookups for modems and printers.

Target markets:_____

Needs:_____

Wants:_____

List at least two products (goods or services) that can satisfy these target markets:

1. Market: people who exercise
Target market: young mothers with small children

Products: (for example: in-house trainers)
_____
_____

2. Market: pet owners
Target market: extensive travelers

Products
_____
_____

MARKETING MIX - FOUR Ps

"The marketing mix elements are called controllable factors because they are under the control of the marketing department in an organization." The four elements of marketing mix include: Product, Price, Promotion, and Place.

Hamburger restaurants have dominated the fast-food business since its inception. Over the last ten years, inroads have been made by fast food franchises specializing in chicken, Mexican food, pizza, and "deli" sandwiches. The chicken and "deli" restaurants have emphasized their healthy menus, while the Mexican restaurants have emphasized the different taste of their product plus its low cost and the pizza franchises have made their entry with home delivery. Meanwhile, McDonald's and Burger King have run large ad campaigns and signed with Disney and other entertainment companies for special giveaways and events. Identify and discuss the 4 P's as they relate to the fast food industry.

UNCONTROLLABLE ENVIRONMENTAL FACTORS

Assume you are the head of a major television network. Social trends indicate that the public is becoming more and more concerned with sex and violence on television. If you don't do something to react to this trend, chances are that the government will come in and regulate the industry for you. In addition, certain groups are organizing boycotts against your sponsors and many major sponsors are threatening to pull advertising on some of your most popular programs. At the same time, more viewers are moving to cable TV, which offers more variety and less "censorship." What environmental factors are involved here and how would you respond?

MARKETING PROGRAM

After discovering what prospective customers need, the marketing manager must translate the ideas from consumers into some concepts for products that the firm might develop. These ideas must then be converted into a tangible marketing program - a plan that integrates the marketing mix to provide a good, service, or idea to prospective buyers.

Assume you are an intelligent, enterprising ten-year-old. You have been asked by Major League Baseball to identify the needs of their customers and design a program to meet those needs.

Use the following grid to design a simple but thorough marketing program to meet at least three identified customer needs or wants.

Customer Need or Want	Product	Promotion	Place	Price
1._____	_____	_____	_____	_____
2._____	_____	_____	_____	_____
3._____	_____	_____	_____	_____

EVOLUTION OF MARKETING

Identify the marketing era represented in each of the following:

1. First era of American marketing history, which extended into the 1920's._____

2. Began in the 1980's and is apparent today._____

3. This era began in the 1920's and extended for many firms into the 1960's._____

4. This era began in the late 1950's and continues today for many American firms._____

5. We are in the business of satisfying needs and wants of consumers (but firms may not specifically have departments designed to discover these needs)._____

6. Production capabilities exceeded regular demand, competition increased, and reaching new markets became more complex._____

7. Businesses have one or more departments specifically designed to understand consumers' needs and readily share this knowledge across departments._____

8. Goods were scarce and buyers were willing to accept virtually any goods that were produced and make do with them as best they could._____

BENEFITS OF MARKETING

1. A retail outdoor store decides to offer its full line on the Internet so consumers can order at home. This represents the utility of _____

2. Southwest Airlines has a major competitive advantage in the Dallas market by offering multiple flights throughout the day to Houston. This represents the utility of _____

3. Burger King's most famous promotion was "Have it your way!" This represents the utility of

_____

4. Little Caesar's offers your choice of pizza delivered directly to you at your home in 30-45 minutes. This represents the utility of _____.

CAN YOU PASS THE TEST?
Sample Multiple Choice Questions

1. *All You* is a new magazine published by Time Inc. that is sold only in discount superstores like Wal-Mart. The women who shop at Wal-Mart wanted to see models of all shapes and skin tones wearing clothes from stores like Kmart, Wal-Mart and Sears. The magazine is striving to do this. These women are the _____ for *All You.*
   - a. marketers
   - b. low cost market
   - c. target market
   - d. representative market
   - e. exclusive marketers

2. *All You*, a new magazine published by Time Inc. is an example of which of the Four Ps?
   - a. price
   - b. product
   - c. partnering
   - d. promotion
   - e. place

3. Prospective customers for a printer that can print photographs in addition to documents include:
   - a. schools who take digital pictures of students and use them on identification cards.
   - b. students who are making signs for a group project.
   - c. businesspeople who need to print invoices.
   - d. individuals who want to print email they have received.
   - e. all of the above

4. Which of the following statements about marketing activities is true?
   - a. Marketing is not affected by society and in return affects society as a whole
   - b. The marketing department never works with other departments and employees to implement marketing activities.
   - c. Marketing activities provide the customer-satisfying products required for the organization to survive and prosper.
   - d. Environmental factors do not affect marketing activities.
   - e. All of the above statements about marketing activities are true.

5. Which of the following factors is necessary for marketing to occur?
   - a. two or more parties with satisfied needs
   - b. something to exchange
   - c. a one-way communication channel
   - d. a transactional partnership
   - e. all of the above

6. The Peabody Hotel in Orlando is setting up a clinic where visiting executives can get a top-to-bottom physical while attending conventions. The largest anticipated problem is the unwillingness for people to go to doctors that they don't know. Marketing may fail to occur here because:
   - a. two or more parties have unsatisfied needs.
   - b. there may be no desire on the part of the executive to satisfy this need.
   - c. there is nothing to exchange.
   - d. there is no way for the parties involved to communicate.
   - e. there has been no assessment of consumers' wants and needs.

7. The first objective in marketing is:
   a. brainstorming.
   b. promotion of product to make consumers aware of its existence.
   c. product innovation.
   d. creating a mission statement.
   e. discovering the needs of prospective consumers.

8. Which of the following represents an example of an exchange?
   a. A student pays tuition at the local university.
   b. An attorney receives a fee from a client for whom she has done legal work.
   c. A retailer sells a DVD to a customer who used the Discover card.
   d. A homeowner pays her mortgage.
   e. All of the above are examples of exchange.

9. Which of the following statements accurately describes a need?
   a. Tiffany needs a new dress to wear to the Spring Fling dance.
   b. Ambrose needs the latest edition of his favorite video game.
   c. Georgia needs a drink of water.
   d. Robin needs a laser printer.
   e. Tyler needs a pair of Avia running shoes.

10. The intended _____ for "Sesame Street" is preschoolers learning language skills.
    a. target market.
    b. marketing mix.
    c. competitive advantage.
    d. distinctive competence.
    e. informational utility.

11. The market for cosmetic dentistry (which can cost $15,000 for straightening and whitening) is:
    a. children with crooked teeth.
    b. all former smokers.
    c. any adult who has the time, the money, and the desire to undergo the procedures.
    d. anyone that has ever had any plastic surgery.
    e. adults who rely on making a good first impression for job success.

12. Which of the following would be the BEST target market for tickets to the home games of the Dallas Cowboys professional football team?
    a. all people in the Dallas area
    b. all people in the U.S.
    c. all men in the U.S.
    d. people in the Dallas area with an interest in professional football
    e. all people in the U.S. with an interest in professional football

13. The marketing mix is composed of:
    a. micromarketing and macromarketing factors.
    b. product, place, price, and promotion.
    c. target markets and exchanges.
    d. what the consumer values.
    e. none of the above.

14. The four Ps of the marketing mix are:
    a. personnel, priorities, placement, and profits.
    b. promotion, product, personnel, and place.
    c. product, place, distribution, and advertising.
    d. product, promotion, price, and place.
    e. profitability, productivity, personnel, and packaging.

15. To attend the winter concert presented by the community chorus, every person had to donate one unwrapped toy at the concert hall door. This statement is most closely related to the _____ element of the market mix.
    a. product
    c. process
    c. price
    d. production
    e. promotion

16. Which of the following is an example of a factor that can be controlled by a marketing manager?
    a. distribution
    b. technology
    c. laws and regulations
    d. competition
    e. the economy

17. After years of resistance, the People's Republic of China finally allowed Coca-Cola to import soft drinks into the country. The import restriction was an example of what is called in marketing an uncontrollable, or _____ factor because it relates to forces outside the marketing company.
    a. environmental
    b. technological
    c. epistemological
    d. heuristic
    e. synergistic

18. _____ is the unique combination of benefits received by targeted buyers that include quality, price, convenience and both before-sale and after-sale service.
    a. Transactional exchange
    b. Partnering
    c. Customer value
    d. Transaction quality
    e. Relationship marketing

19. If you ever talked to anyone who has flown on Singapore Air, you will no doubt hear that individual praise the food that was served during the flight, the friendliness of the air stewards, and the comfortable surroundings. From this description, you can surmise Singapore Air creates customer value by providing its customers with:
    a. the best service.
    b. the most convenient flight schedules.
    c. the best price.
    d. the best airport experience.
    e. all of the above

20. Relationship marketing:
        a. was most popular in the sales era.
        b. emphasizes the product over the competitor.
        c. creates short-term relationships.
        d. links the organization to its customers for their mutual long-term benefit.
        e. is also called a transactional exchange arrangement.

21. A _____ is a plan that integrates elements of the marketing mix to provide goods, services, or ideas to prospective buyers.
        a. marketing strategy
        b. marketing program
        c. macromarketing program
        d. micromarketing program
        e. sales promotion

22. During the _____ in the United States, goods were scarce, and buyers were willing to accept virtually any goods that were produced.
        a. sales era
        b. relationship era
        c. marketing concept era
        d. production era
        e. market orientation era

23. The _____ is the idea that an organization should strive to satisfy the needs of consumers while also trying to achieve the organization's goals.
        a. macromarketing concept.
        b. marketing concept.
        c. target marketing strategy.
        d. concept of transactional marketing
        e. micromarketing philosophy.

24. During the _____ era in U.S. business history, the primary function of the Pillsbury Company was to mill quality flour.
        a. production
        b. sales
        c. marketing concept
        d. societal marketing concept
        e. market orientation

25. During the marketing concept era in the United States:
        a. goods were scarce, and buyers were willing to accept virtually any goods that were produced.
        b. marketing became the motivating force among many U.S. firms.
        c. companies discovered they could produce more goods than consumers could buy.
        d. there was little competition.
        e. companies believed that products would sell themselves.

26. In the 1960s, Pillsbury defined its mission as, "We are in the business of satisfying needs and wants of customers." This is a brief statement of what has come to be known as the:
        a. hard-sell strategy.
        b. soft-sell strategy.
        c. selling concept.
        d. marketing concept.
        e. marketing mix.

27. The often used solution during the _____ era was to hire more salespeople to find new buyers.
   a. production
   b. sales
   c. marketing concept
   d. industrial revolution
   e. micromarketing

28. During the _____ era organizations would likely have a market orientation focusing its efforts on colleting information about customers' needs and using the information to create customer value.
   a. production
   b. sales
   c. customer
   d. competitive intelligence
   d. marketing concept

29. Many marketing issues are not specifically addressed by existing laws and regulations, so companies, industries, and professional associations develop _____ to help managers deal with such issues.
   a. manuals
   b. theories
   c. explanations
   d. codes of ethics
   e. approaches

30. The water supply in many villages in Bangladesh is contaminated with heavy concentrations of arsenic. When it learned of this problem, Apyron Technology developed an innovative water purification device that removes all traces of arsenic from the water. Working with UNICEF, Apyron Technology has installed its system in 50 villages. Apyron Technology is acting in accordance with the:
   a. macromarketing concept.
   b. societal marketing concept.
   c. target marketing strategy.
   d. concept of transactional marketing
   e. micromarketing philosophy.

31. ScotchBrite Never Rust Soap Pads from 3M are made from recycled plastic bottles and are more expensive than competitive soap pads because they will not rust or scratch. This is an example of:
   a. micromarketing.
   b. the societal marketing concept.
   c. reverse marketing.
   d. consumer advocacy.
   e. repositioning by 3M.

32. The study of the aggregate flow of a nation's goods and services to benefit society is called:
   a. micromarketing.
   b. macromarketing.
   c. societal marketing.
   d. financial marketing.
   e. the marketing concept.

33. The paper manufacturer sells rolls of paper to the newspaper publishing company so that the newspaper can publish a daily paper. The newspaper publishing company is an example of what type of buyer?
   a. ultimate consumer
   b. institutional market
   c. organizational buyer
   d. government market
   e. reseller

34. The paper manufacturer sells rolls of paper to the soda bottler so that the bottler can manufacture boxes for cans of soda. These boxes of soda are then sold to the grocery store, which then resells the sodas to grocery shoppers. The people who buy the sodas to consume at home are examples of what types of buyers?
   a. ultimate consumers
   b. institutional markets
   c. organizational buyers
   d. government markets
   e. resellers

35. The paper manufacturer sells rolls of paper to the soda bottler so that the bottler can manufacture boxes for cans of soda. These boxes of soda are then sold to the grocery store, which then resells the sodas to grocery shoppers. The grocery store buyers who buy the boxes of soda for resale are examples of what types of buyers?
   a. ultimate consumers
   b. institutional markets
   c. organizational buyers
   d. government markets
   e. consumer markets

36. Which of the following statements is an example of time utility?
   a. A new motor oil container comes equipped with a disposable pouring spout.
   b. Stamp vending machines are located in drug stores.
   c. A service station has a 24-hour ice machine available for use even when the station is closed.
   d. A waterbed company offers six-month financing, same as cash.
   e. A gourmet shop offers a home delivery service.

37. In the Dallas area, Southwest Airlines has a major competitive advantage over other airlines because it offers multiple flights throughout the day to Houston. Southwest Airlines is providing _____ utility to consumers.
   a. form
   b. product
   c. possession
   d. space
   e. time

38. The transformation of sheep wool into soft wool sweaters constitutes _____ utility.
   a. form
   b. place
   c. possession
   d. space
   e. time

39. A seamstress who custom-makes a suit from bolts of fabric creates _____ utility.
    a. product
    b. price
    c. possession
    d. form
    e. market

40. A pizza delivery service creates _____ utility because the pizza is brought to you to consume.
    a. form
    b. place
    c. possession
    d. space
    e. time

41. Wal-Mart displays a new magazine, *All You* targeted at their female customers by the cash registers. Based only on this, has marketing occurred?
    a. No, because there is only one party with unsatisfied needs.
    b. No, because there is nothing to exchange.
    c. Yes, because Wal-Mart is communicating that they have a magazine for sale.
    d. Yes, because there is one party with unsatisfied needs.
    e. Yes, because people buy anything from Wal-Mart.

42. The goal of the _____ era is to integrate marketing into all phases of the business process.
    a. production
    b. sales
    c. marketing concept
    d. industrial revolution
    e. micromarketing

43. Every day, buyers from large utility companies and sellers from energy companies visit an online exchange dealing in wholesale electricity and gas to negotiate prices for the energy that heats and lights many homes and businesses. The exchange knows there are competitors vying for its customers so it relies heavily on technology to build and retain strong, one-on-one relationships with each customer. The exchange uses _____ to know its customer and to win their allegiance.
    a. a flexible marketing system
    b. a database warehouse
    c. customer relationship management
    d. competitive intelligence
    e. a customer-oriented marketing mix

44. In the past, Burger King, Wendy's, and McDonald's used to market their burgers in non-biodegradable Styrofoam containers. In response to calls from the public to use more environmentally-friendly materials, most fast food marketers use paper containers for their burgers. Indeed, many such containers are made from recycled materials. This is an example of:
    a. macromarketing by the fast food chains.
    b. societal marketing.
    c. reverse marketing.
    d. consumer advocacy.
    e. repositioning by the fast food chains.

45. Which of the following is an example of an ultimate consumer?
    a. a woman buying a new car
    b. a mom purchasing peanut butter
    c. a retired steelworker taking a cruise
    d. a doctor buying a piano
    e. all of the above

46. Which is an example of an environmental factor?
    a. place
    b. product
    c. price
    d. competitors
    e. promotion

47. A consumer purchases a new digital camera from Circuit City. The purchase provides customer value for which of the following reasons?
    a. the price is reasonable
    b. the name brand of the camera represents quality to the buyer
    c. the Circuit City store was located just five minutes from the buyer's home
    d. Because the buyer also bought an extended warranty, Circuit City will repair the camera for up to one year after the purchase for free.
    e. All of the above provide value to the buyer.

48. For which of the following reasons is relationship marketing difficult to implement between companies and customers?
    a. Orders placed over the internet may be tailored to exact customer specifications and delivered in just a few days at a low cost.
    b. It is difficult for a customer to maintain a personal relationship with an internet organization.
    c. Many organizations are offering to develop relationships with a single consumer.
    d. Maintaining relationships with many organizations is difficult.
    e. All of the above are reasons why relationship marketing is difficult to implement.

49. Rollerblade has developed a marketing program to reach several segments. Offering Zetrablade in-line skates for beginning and intermediate skaters wanting fun and exercise, and offering the Microblade XT for children that extends in size as their feet grow are examples of which element of the marketing mix?
    a. segmentation
    b. place
    c. product
    d. price
    e. promotion

50. Customer relationship management is most closely identified with which orientation in the history of American business?
    a. production
    b. sales
    c. marketing concept
    d. customer
    e. macromarketing

ANSWER KEY

Answers to Questions & Problems

Marketing: A Definition to Focus on Needs

1. Satisfying needs
2. Satisfying needs
3. Discovering needs
4. Discovering needs
5. Discovering needs

Requirements for Marketing to Occur

1. Two or more parties with unsatisfied needs
2. Desire and ability to be satisfied
3. Way to communicate
4. Something to exchange

Example: New car

1. Buyer and dealer
2. Buyer has desire for new car and dealer has new cars to sell
3. Advertising communicates "deal" Dealer communicates personal sales pitch
4. Buyer exchanges money and trade-in; dealer exchanges new car

Target Markets

Example: Low salt, low fat baked potato chips

Target market: health conscious consumers
Need: healthy foods including snacks
Wants: healthy snack food without guilt

Marketing Mix-4 P's

Product--sandwiches
Place--convenient location
Price--low
Promotion--advertising, sales promotion

Uncontrollable Environmental Factors

Social culture environment
Legal/political environment
Separate "adult" themes to later in evening

Baseball: (example)

Need or want--entertainment
Product--more exciting games
Promotion--prizes for home runs
Place--at the park or on TV or radio

Price--grandstand prices

Evolution of Marketing

1. Production era
2. Marketing orientation era
3. Sales era
4. Marketing concept era
5. Marketing concept era
6. Sales era
7. Marketing orientation era
8. Production era

Benefits of Marketing

1. Place
2. Time
3. Form
4. Place

Answers to Sample Multiple Choice Questions

1. c p. 14 LO 2	13. b p. 14 LO 3	26. d p. 20 LO 5	38. a p. 23 LO 6
2. b p. 14 LO 3	14. d p. 14 LO 3	27. b p. 19 LO 5	39. d p. 23 LO 6
3. e p. 8 LO 1	15. c p. 14 LO 3	28. c p. 20 LO 5	40. b p. 23 LO 6
4. c p. 9 LO 1	16. a p. 14 LO 3	29. d p. 21 LO 5	41. a p. 9-10 LO 2
5. b p. 9 LO 1	17. a p. 14-15 LO 3	30. b p. 21 LO 5	42. c p. 20 LO 5
6. b p. 10 LO 1	18. c p. 15 LO 4	31. b p. 21 LO 5	43. c p. 20 LO 5
7. e p. 10 LO 2	19. a p. 15 LO 4	32. b p. 21 LO 5	44. b p. 21 LO 5
8. e p. 8 LO 2	20. d p. 16 LO 4	33. c p. 22 LO 2	45. e p. 22 LO 6
9. c p. 12 LO 2	21. b p. 16 LO 4	34. a p. 22 LO 2	46. d p. 14 LO 3
10. a p. 14; LO 3	22. d p. 19 LO 5	35. c p. 22 LO 2	47. e p. 15 LO 4
11. c p. 13 LO 2	23. b p. 20 LO 5	36. c p. 23 LO 6	48. e p. 16 LO 4
12. d p. 14 LO 2	24. a p. 19 LO 5	37. e p. 23 LO 6	49. c p. 18 LO 3
	25. b p.20 LO 5		50. d p. 20 LO 5

Note: LO indicates learning objective.

CHAPTER 2

DEVELOPING SUCCESSFUL MARKETING AND CORPORATE STRATEGIES

<u>Why is Chapter 2 important?</u> This chapter will show you how a company decides which products to offer and to whom. You will see why marketing planning is important, what the planning process consists of, and how each part of the organization is involved. You will learn how marketing strategies are determined, measured, and adjusted. It will show you what to expect from each product based on its market position and how not to have surprises like Crystal Pepsi.

Marketing Strategy: The means by which a marketing goal is to be achieved, usually characterized by a specified target market and a marketing program to reach it.

CHAPTER OUTLINE

I. LEVELS OF STRATEGY IN ORGANIZATIONS

    A. Kinds of Organizations
        1. Profit
        2. Non-profit

    B. Levels in Organizations
        1. Corporate Level Strategy
            a. Corporate mission
            b. Corporate values and culture
            c. Corporate goals
                i.   profit
                ii.   sales revenue
                iii.   market share
                iv.   unit sales
                v.   quality
                vi.   customer satisfaction
                vii.   employee welfare
                viii. social responsibility
        2. Functional Level Strategy
            a. Information systems
            b. Finance
            c. Research and development
            d. Marketing
            e. Manufacturing
            f. Human Resources
            g. Cross-functional

II. SETTING STRATEGIC DIRECTIONS

    A. Customers
    B. Competencies
          1. Competitive advantage
          2. Quality
    C. Competitors
    D. Growth Strategies
          1. Boston Consulting Group (BCG) business portfolio analysis
               a.   cash cow
               b.   star
               c.   question mark (problem children)
               d.   dogs
          2. Market-Product Analysis
               a.   Market penetration
               b.   Market development
               c.   Product development
               d.   Diversification
    E. Building Blocks for an Organization's Success
          1. Customer relationships
          2. Innovation
          3. Quality
          4. Efficiency

III. STRATEGIC MARKETING PROCESS--MARKETING PLAN

    A. Situation Analysis (SWOT Analysis)
          1. Strengths
          2. Weaknesses
          3. Opportunities
          4. Threats

    B. Market-Product Focus and Goal Setting
          1. Market Segmentation
          2. Measurable Marketing Objectives

    C. Marketing Program
          1. Product Strategy
          2. Price Strategy
          3. Promotion Strategy
          4. Place (Distribution) Strategy

    D. Implementation
          1. Obtaining Resources
          2. Designing Marketing Organization
          3. Developing Schedules
          4. Executing Marketing Program—Marketing Tactics

    E. Control
          1. Comparing Results with Plan to Identify Deviations
          2. Acting on Deviations
                a. exploiting positive deviations
               b. correcting negative deviations

You should be able to place these key terms in the outline and be able to discuss them.

benchmarking	goals	organizational culture
business unit	market segmentation	points of difference
business unit level	market share	profit
competencies	marketing plan	quality
competitive advantage	marketing strategy	situation analysis
corporate level	marketing tactics	stakeholders
cross-functional team	mission	strategic marketing process
functional level	objectives	SWOT analysis

QUESTIONS & PROBLEMS

STRATEGIC MARKETING PROCESS

There are three main phases in the strategic marketing process:

Planning
Implementation
Control

Match the proper phase of the strategic marketing process with the situations below:

1. The three steps of situation analysis, goal setting, and marketing program development are highly interrelated._____

2. In this phase, the marketing manager compares the results of the marketing program with the goals in the written plan to identify deviations and to act on deviations—correcting negative deviations and exploiting positive ones._____

3. This phase includes executing the program described in the marketing plan and designing the marketing organization needed._____

4. Pillsbury assigns the responsibility for a new Hungry Jack Biscuit promotion to a marketing manager. Above him in the chain of command is the Group Marketing Manager for biscuits. Below him are the Associate Marketing Manager and the Marketing Assistant._____

5. Coca-Cola decides to produce products for target markets wanting sugar and/or non-sugar and caffeine and/or non-caffeine products._____

MARKETING PLAN

There are three steps in the planning phase of the strategic marketing process:

Situation analysis
Goal setting
Marketing program

Match the correct term with the statements listed below:

1. Organizing potential resources into a coherent marketing program that uses the four marketing mix elements (4Ps) to reach the targeted goal._____

2. Taking stock of where the firm or product has been recently, where it is now, and where it is likely to end up using present plans._____

3. Setting measurable marketing objectives to be achieved._____

BUSINESS MISSION

An organization's business, or mission, is a statement that specifies the markets and product lines in which the business will compete, i.e., the scope of the business unit. The "mission" can dramatically narrow or broaden the range of marketing opportunities available.

Give a possible "business" or "mission" statement for each of the companies below:

1. SBC (Southwestern Bell Corporation)
2. Anheuser-Busch
3. Xerox
4. NBA (National Basketball Association)
5. Nabisco

SITUATION ANALYSIS

The letters in the SWOT acronym stand for:

1. S = _____

2. W = _____

3. 0 = _____

4. T = _____

Using the Ben & Jerry's example in the text, write out a SWOT analysis for Ben & Jerry's.

THE BCG GROWTH SHARE MATRIX

The growth-share matrix helps in evaluating individual SBUs (strategic business units) as if they were separate, independent businesses. They are plotted on a matrix with market growth rate on the vertical axis and relative market share on the horizontal axis. The matrix is divided into four quadrants based on the amount of cash each generates for the firm or requires from it. The quadrants are called:

Cash cows
Stars
Question marks (or problem children)
Dogs

Match the correct BCG quadrant name to the products listed below:

1. Coca-Cola_____
2. Netscape_____
3. Crystal Pepsi_____
4. Gillette Sensor_____
5. AOL_____
6. Kellogg's Frosted Flakes_____
7. iPod_____
8. Windows XP_____

MARKET-PRODUCT FOCUS AND GOAL SETTING

There are four market-product strategies:

Market penetration
Market development
Product development
Diversification

Match the correct product strategy to the statements below:

1. There is no change in product line offered but increased sales are made possible through better advertising, more retail outlets, and/or lower prices._____

2. The sale of existing products to new markets._____

3. This involves developing new products and selling them in new markets._____

4. The product changes, but it is sold to existing markets._____

5. Tide laundry detergent, sold for years in powder form, now is available in liquid laundry detergent.
_____

6. Proctor & Gamble now manufactures diaper products for adults, as well as for babies.
_____

7. White Castle Hamburgers had an ad campaign, "Hamburgers for breakfast? Why not?"
_____

8. Sara Lee Corporation has a division that includes "non-edibles" such as Bali, Hanes, and L'eggs products._____

MARKETING PROGRAM

Using the Ben and Jerry's example in the text, develop a strategy for each of the elements of the Marketing Mix (examples of items to be considered below):

<u>Product</u>	<u>Price</u>	<u>Promotion</u>	<u>Place</u>
Features	List price	Advertising	Outlets
Accessories	Discounts	Personal selling	Channels
Options	Allowances	Sales promotion	Coverage
Line breadth	Credit terms	Publicity	Transportation
Brand name	Payment period		Stock level
Service			
Warranty			
Returns			

IMPLEMENTATION

Two key elements of the implementation stage are (1) executing the program described in the marketing plan, and (2) designing the marketing organization needed.

There are two main aspects to executing the marketing program:

Marketing strategies
Marketing tactics

Which of the following would most likely be a marketing strategy decision and which would be a marketing tactic decision?

1. The best way to reach our target market will be to advertise on country western radio stations._____

2. Select the best country western station in the metropolitan listening area._____

CONTROL

The control phase of the strategic marketing process seeks to keep the marketing program moving in the direction set for it. Accomplishing this requires the marketing manager (1) to compare the results of the marketing program with the goals in the written plans to identify deviations, and (2) to act on these deviations - correcting negative deviations and exploiting positive ones.

The Ocean Spray Cranberries Company has to decide whether to sell its new Mauna La'i Hawaiian Guava Drink nationally or not. The marketing plan target market was older children through older adults with average income and education. Goals were set for both "first trial" and "repeat purchases." Although "first trial" results were good, "repeat purchase" results were not. Research showed that the highest buying group was not the targeted market but young (18-29) upscale buyers. Research also showed that upscale buyers consumed larger quantities than expected.

Using the information above, demonstrate your knowledge of the control phase of the strategic marketing process. Describe which steps you would take next:

CAN YOU PASS THE TEST?
Sample Multiple Choice Questions

1. _____ is the reward to a business firm for the risk it undertakes to market a product for sale.
   a. Net equity
   b. Profit
   c. Sales revenue
   d. Liquidity
   e. Gross margin

2. Which of the following is the BEST example of a nonprofit organization?
   a. UPS, an international delivery service
   b. Big Bob's, a local restaurant
   c. Ben and Jerry's, ice cream and frozen yogurt manufacturer
   d. American Red Cross, an organization that helps people in need
   e. Cybelore Studios, a producer of computer games

3. Large organizations are often extremely complex. To deal with them, it's useful to understand:
   a. the two basic kinds of organizations.
   b. the levels that exist in them.
   c. the functional areas.
   d. cross-functional teams.
   e. all of the above.

4. A business unit refers to an organization that:
   a. directs overall strategy for the organization.
   b. markets a set of related products to a clearly defined group of customers.
   c. has marketing and other specialized activities.
   d. also has a comparable non-business unit.
   e. is usually nonprofit.

5. The R & D, finance, and human resources department operate at the _____ level.
   a. business unit
   b. corporate
   c. functional
   d. divisional
   e. tactical

6. At the business unit level, the marketing department provides leadership for the other functional activities in:
   a. maintaining discipline.
   b. creating fiscal restraint.
   c. developing integrated customer service programs.
   d. creating the corporate culture.
   e. sustaining the means-end chain.

7. _____ are made up of a small number of people from different departments in an organization who are mutually accountable to a common set of performance goals.
   a. Cross-functional teams
   b. Ad hoc groups
   c. De facto teams
   d. Focus groups
   e. Multi-specialty teams

8. PeopleSoft designs, produces, and markets software that enables companies to automate basic human-resources functions such as payroll. At its inception, the company's leaders created a _____ that encouraged employees to get in touch with their feelings. The work environment was laid back, employees' dogs roamed the halls, and sunny days found employees playing Frisbee on the corporate lawns.
     a. corporate philosophy
     b. benefits statement
     c. organizational culture
     d. corporate profile
     e. business edge

9. A _____ is a statement of an organization's scope. It often identifies its customers, markets, products, technology, and values.
     a. mission
     b. core competency
     c. business analysis
     d. situation analysis
     e. corporate vision

10. Often used interchangeably with "vision," a _____ statement frequently has an inspirational theme:
     a. a point of difference.
     b. a corporate vision.
     c. a business portfolio.
     d. corporate marketing.
     e. an annual report.

11. Ampco Metal is a company that specializes in making copper alloy maintenance tools that are non-sparking, non-magnetic, and corrosion-resistant. Who would be the stakeholders for this company?
     a. Lab Safety Supply Company, its distributor
     b. investors in the company
     c. manufacturers that buy the tools as one way to protect their employees
     d. the company that supplies the copper alloy Ampco Metal uses in its tools
     e. all of the above

12. If profits are acceptable, a firm may elect to _____ even though profitability may not be maximized.
     a. abandon green marketing
     b. decrease employee loyalty
     c. maintain or increase sales
     d. decrease social responsibility
     e. buy company stock

13. Which of the following is an example of a business goal?
     a. to maintain market share
     b. to seek maximum, long-term profit
     c. to promote overall welfare of its stakeholders even at the expense of profits
     d. to target the highest possible quality levels
     e. all of the above

14. _____ is the ratio of a firm's sales revenue to the total sales revenue of all firms in the industry, including the firm itself.
      a. Profit margin
      b. Contribution margin
      c. Industry attractiveness
      d. Market share
      e. Sales forecast

15. A firm may choose to maintain or increase its market share, sometimes at the expense of greater profits if:
      a.   there are poor sales databases.
      b.   there are fluctuations in inventory.
      c.   there are unpredictable sales expenses.
      d.   industry status or prestige is at stake.
      e.   inflation is present.

16. The business goal of a company that is trying to balance conflicting goals of consumers, employees, and stockholders even at the expense of profits is referred to as a _____ goal.
      a. return on investment
      b. market share
      c. sales revenue
      d. unit sales
      e. social responsibility

17. A company that is trying to answer the following questions about itself: "What are we now?" and "Where do we want to go?" is:
      a. setting its strategic direction.
      b. planning to modify its mission.
      c. emphasizing tactical plans over strategic plans.
      d. more concerned with setting goals than developing plans.
      e. using cross-functional teams to conduct a SWOT analysis.

18. Atrix is a company that manufactures waterless hand cleaners that are gentle on the skin. It allows the user to clean up anytime and anyplace. The patents it holds on this waterless cleaning solution gives it a _____ over companies that manufacture other types of hand cleaners.
      a. non-sustainable advantage
      b. competitive advantage
      c. synergistic differentiation
      d. competitive synergy
      e. competitive mission

19. _____ means those features and characteristics of a product that influence its ability to satisfy customer needs.
      a. Product concept
      b. Core benefit proposition
      c. Prototype
      d. Quality
      e. Core competency

20. _____ is the process of discovering how other firms do something better than your firm so you can imitate, or leapfrog competition.
    a. Product emulation
    b. Research straddling
    c. Benchmarking
    d. Reverse engineering
    e. Demarketing

21. A hotel owner who determines what amenities are offered at competitors' hotels is engaged in:
    a. mirroring.
    b. leapfrogging.
    c. benchmarking.
    d. echoing.
    e. synergistic imitation.

22. The vertical axis of the Boston Consulting Group growth-share matrix shows:
    a. relative market share.
    b. industry forecast.
    c. the contribution margin.
    d. size of business in terms of units sold.
    e. none of the above.

23. Gillette continues to manufacture Liquid Paper correction fluid for use with typewriters even though most of the world uses word processors. It is a small market that has little growth, but Liquid Paper has the largest market share, and Gillette invests no promotional monies in maintaining the declining product. Liquid Paper is an example of a:
    a. star.
    b. cash cow.
    c. question mark.
    d. exclamation mark.
    e. shooting star.

24. According to the BCG growth-share matrix, _____ are SBUs with a high share of a high-growth market. These SBUs may not generate enough cash to support their own demanding needs for future growth.
    a. problem children
    b. cash cows
    c. question marks
    d. stars
    e. dogs

25. The market for the fast car with so much horsepower that handling becomes an issue is decreasing. People are more interested in buying SUVs and pickups. As a result, General Motors is stopping production of its Camaro, a car that has had limited sales recently. Since the Camaro can no longer generate enough cash to sustain its manufacture, the BCG portfolio would classify it as a:
    a. dog.
    b. cash cow.
    c. question mark.
    d. star.
    e. bonanza.

26. New fiberglass bathtubs and sinks do not require the abrasive cleansers that were popular for many years. Manufacturers of bathroom and kitchen cleaners have developed gentler cleansers, but some consumers still prefer the older abrasive cleansers. For this small market that is not growing, Procter & Gamble makes Comet powder scrubbing agent.   According to the Boston Consulting Group growth-share matrix, Comet would be classified as a _____ because the product has a large share of abrasive cleanser market.
    a. cash cow
    b. dog
    c. question mark
    d. problem child
    e. fading star

27. The primary strength of the Boston Consulting Group growth-share matrix includes:
    a. the ease with which information can be determined in order to locate each SBU on the matrix.
    b. the ease with which people who are in SBUs labeled as dogs or cash cows can be motivated to strive for even greater results.
    c. the fact that the matrix considers synergies that can exist among the various SBUs.
    d. the fact that it forces the firm to assess each of its SBUs in terms of relative market share and industry growth rate.
    e. all of the above.

28. In the 2001 television season, the producers of the television show *Law & Order* introduced two new versions of the show—*Law & Order: Criminal Intent* and *Law & Order: Special Victims Unit*. The producers were implementing a _____ strategy and hoping that viewers of the original *Law & Order* series would watch and enjoy the newer versions.
    a. market penetration
    b. product development
    c. market development
    d. product penetration
    e. diversification

29. After late spring freezes, orange growers in Florida lost millions of dollars. As a result, some growers bulldozed their orange groves and put in freshwater lakes for raising shrimp, a product that is also popular with growers' customers and is more weather resistant. Former orange growers who are now raising shrimp have selected a _____ strategy.
    a. market penetration
    b. product development
    c. market development
    d. product penetration
    e. diversification

30. Massachusetts-based BJs Wholesale (third in sales among member-only retail chains) recently opened its first stores in Georgia in 2002. This is an example of:
    a. market penetration.
    b. market development.
    c. product development.
    d. diversification.
    e. product dissemination.

31. Matsura Industries distributes candy and coffee through its vending machines in Tokyo. The addition of sandwich vending machines to the same market is an example of a _____ strategy.
    a. market penetration
    b. market development
    c. product development
    d. diversification
    e. divestment

32. NDCHealth Corp. is a U.S.-based company that provides pharmaceutical manufacturers with market research on prescription drug sales. It recently started distributing commonly-used prescription drugs in the United Kingdom. Since it was new to the wholesaling end of the pharmaceutical business, NDCHealth was implementing a _____ strategy.
    a. market penetration
    b. market development
    c. product development
    d. diversification
    e. product penetration

33. All of the following are examples of growth strategies that can be used to increase revenues EXCEPT:
    a. market penetration.
    b. product development.
    c. market development.
    d. product penetration.
    e. diversification.

34. If the Hong Kong Bank opened a branch in Vancouver to target Chinese-Canadians, its new bank would be an example of which of the following market-product strategies?
    a. market penetration
    b. product development
    c. market development
    d. product penetration
    e. diversification

35. The _____ consists of the steps taken at the product and market levels to allocate marketing resources to viable marketing positions and programs. It involves planning, implementation, and control.
    a. diversification strategy
    b. business analysis
    c. market development strategy
    d. strategic marketing process
    e. market segmentation process

36. The _____ is a written statement that identifies a company's target market, its specific marketing goals, its budget, and its marketing mix elements.
    a. action program
    b. tactical program
    c. business analysis
    d. SWOT analysis
    e. marketing plan

37. In design, a marketing plan is most closely related to a:
    a. novel.
    b. pyramid.
    c. road map.
    d. circle.
    e. cloverleaf shape.

38. A television production company was looking for an idea for a new show and approached Emeril Lagasse, a charismatic Cajun chef that frequently appears on the Food Channel. It was decided that the production company would build a show based around Lagasse's life. While the casting of the popular Lagasse insured that people would watch the first couple shows, poor scripts led to the cancellation of the show. In terms of the SWOT analysis, the casting of Lagasse was a _____, and the poor scripts were a _____.
>   a. strength; weakness
>   b. weakness; threat
>   c. threat; opportunity
>   d. opportunity; threat
>   e. opportunity; strength

39. The goal of a SWOT analysis is to:
>   a. identify those critical factors that can have a major effect on the firm.
>   b. keep top management placated.
>   c. discover areas for diversified investment outside the firm's marketing areas.
>   d. develop new products for new market segments.
>   e. allocate financial resources across the industry.

40. There are a number of farms in Mississippi that produce about 300 million pounds of catfish annually. The home-grown catfish is more expensive than the 16 million pounds of catfish imported from Vietnam. A catfish farmer conducting a SWOT analysis would view the imported catfish as a(n) _____ .
>   a. threat
>   b. strength
>   c. competitive advantage
>   d. opportunity
>   e. weakness

41. _____ involves aggregating prospective buyers into groups that have common needs and will respond similarly to a marketing action.
>   a. Market aggregation
>   b. Mass marketing
>   c. Market segmentation
>   d. Market penetration
>   e. Market development

42. At which step of the planning stage of the strategic marketing process does a firm develop the program's marketing mix?
>   a. situation analysis
>   b. goal setting
>   c. marketing program
>   d. sales forecasting
>   e. market segmentation

43. When BellSouth made plans to increase its presence in the lucrative Latin American market, some of its employees decided BellSouth needed to acquire the rest of Telefonia Cellular de Nicaragua, one of its subsidiaries in Latin America. To do so, they paid a substantial sum to the wife of a Nicaraguan legislator who was responsible for legal changes that were needed to allow Telefonia to become completely owned by BellSouth. This payment was in direct violation of U.S. law, and BellSouth had to pay a hefty fine and divest itself of its illegal acquisition. In which phase of the strategic marketing process did the BellSouth strategy fail?
      a. the goal-setting phase
      b. the implementation phase
      c. the control phase
      d. the strategic development phase
      e. the resource administration phase

44. David and Cecilia Stanford, owners of Prairie Herb vinegars, decided to offer the product in 5-ounce and 13-ounce sizes as well as in a 16-ounce European glass bottle. They decided to sell the vinegar only through the mail and to price the smaller bottles at $4.45 and the largest bottles at $13.25. They were determining its:
      a. tactics.
      b. missions.
      c. visions.
      d. strategies.
      e. operational procedures.

45. The detailed day-to-day operational decisions, or _____ are essential to the overall success of marketing strategies.
      a. functional goals
      b. strategic plans
      c. business-level competency
      d. marketing tactics
      e. tactical goals

46. During the _____ phase of the strategic marketing process, a company compares the results of its marketing programs with the goals in its written plans to identify deviations.
      a. staffing
      b. implementation
      c. control
      d. planning
      e. motivating

47. After examining a planning gap, firms typically attempt to:
      a. decide if the time horizon should be increased or decreased.
      b. perform a SWOT analysis with their major competitor as the focus.
      c. use statistical trend analysis to interpret the results.
      d. exploit a positive deviation and correct a negative deviation.
      e. adopt a product-market focus.

48. The channel of distribution used for the sale of airline tickets is which element of the marketing mix?
      a. product
      b. place
      c. promotion
      d. price
      e. production

49. Airline tickets represent which element of the marketing mix for an airline?
    a. product
    b. place
    c. promotion
    d. price
    e. production

50. Business travelers may have to spend over $1000 to fly from Denver to New York, while pleasure travelers may purchase the ticket for much less. Which element of the marketing mix does this describe?
    a. product
    b. place
    c. promotion
    d. price
    e. segments

ANSWER KEY

Answers to Questions & Problems

Strategic Marketing Process

1. Planning
2. Control
3. Implementation
4. Implementation
5. Planning

Marketing Planning

1. Marketing program
2. Situation analysis
3. Goal setting

Business Mission

1. Communication (example)

Situation Analysis

S = strengths
W = weaknesses
O = opportunities
T = threats

The BCG Growth Share Matrix

1. Cash cow
2. Stars
3. ?
4. Stars
5. Dogs
6. Cash cow
7. ?
8. Star

Market-Product Focus and Goal Setting

1. Market penetration
2. Market development
3. Diversification
4. Product development
5. Product development
6. Market development
7. Market penetration
8. Diversification

Marketing Program

Example:

Product: feature flavors
Price: premium
Promotion: advertising
Place: grocery outlets

Implementation

1. Marketing strategies
2. Marketing tactics

Control

Example: Adjust target market to upscale buyers and retest.

Answers to Sample Multiple Choice Questions

1. b p. 30 LO 1	14. d p. 34 LO 2	26. a p. 38 LO 3	38. a p. 43 LO 4
2. d p. 30 LO 1	15. d p. 34 LO 2	27. d p. 40 LO 3	39. a p. 44 LO 4
3. e p. 30 LO 1	16. e p. 34 LO 2	28. a p. 40 LO 3	40. a p. 44 LO 4
4. b p. 31 LO 1	17. a p. 35 LO 3	29. b p. 40 LO 3	41. c p. 44 LO 4
5. c p. 31 LO 1	18. b p. 36 LO 3	30. b p. 40 LO 3	42. c p. 42 LO 4
6. c p. 31 LO 1	19. d p. 36 LO 3	31. c p. 40 LO 3	43. b p. 42 LO 4
7. a p. 31 LO 1	20. c p. 36 LO 3	32. d p. 41 LO 3	44. a p. 48 LO 4
8. c p. 33 LO 2	21. c p. 36 LO 3	33. d p. 41 LO 3	45. d p. 48 LO 4
9. a p. 33 LO 2	22. e p. 38 LO 3	34. c p. 40 LO 3	46. c p. 48 LO 4
10. b p. 33 LO 2	23. b p. 38 LO 3	35. d p. 42 LO 4	47. d p. 49 LO 4
11. e p. 33 LO 2	24. d p. 38 LO 3	36. e p. 42 LO 4	48. b p. 46 LO 5
12. c p. 34 LO 2	25. a p. 38 LO 3	37. c p. 42 LO 4	49. a p. 46 LO 5
13. e p. 34 LO 2			50. d p. 46 LO 5

Note: LO indicates learning objective.

CHAPTER 3

SCANNING THE MARKETING ENVIRONMENT

<u>Why is Chapter 3 important</u>? This chapter illustrates all of the environmental factors that affect the marketing of products. It will show you how changes in the external environments dictate changes in the marketing mix.

Environmental Scanning: The process of continually acquiring information on events occurring outside the organization in order to identify and interpret potential trends.

CHAPTER OUTLINE

I. ENVIRONMENTAL SCAN

    A. Social Forces
        1. Demographics
            a. population trend
            b. Baby Boom, Generation X and Generation Y
            c. American family
            d. population shifts
            e. racial and ethnic diversity
            f. regional marketing
        2. Culture
            a. changing attitudes and roles of women
            b. changing values

    B. Economic Forces
        1. Macroeconomic conditions
            a. inflation
            b. recession
         2. Consumer Income
            a. gross income
            b. disposable income
            c. discretionary income

    C. Technological Forces
        1. Impact on customer value
        2. Electronic business technologies

    D. Competitive Forces
        1. Alternative forms of competition
            a. pure competition
            b. monopolistic competition
            c. oligopoly
            d. monopoly

   2. Components of competition
        a. entry
        b. power of buyers and suppliers
        c. existing competitors and substitutes
        d. start-ups, entrepreneurs, and small business

   E. Regulatory Forces
        1. Protecting competition
        2. Product-related legislation
             a. company protection
             b. consumer protection
             c. both company and consumer protection
        3. Pricing-related legislation
        4. Distribution-related legislation
             a. exclusive dealing
             b. requirement contracts
             c. exclusive territory distributorship
             d. tying arrangements
        5. Advertising- and promotion-related legislation
        6. Control through self-regulation

You should be able to place these key terms in the outline and be able to discuss them.

baby boomers	disposable income	Intranet
barriers to entry	economy	marketspace
blended family	electronic commerce	multicultural marketing
competition	environmental scanning	regulation
consumerism	Extranets	self-regulation
culture	Generation X	social forces
demographics	Generation Y	technology
discretionary income	gross income	value consciousness

QUESTIONS & PROBLEMS

SOCIAL FORCES

Demographics

Grocery stores have progressed from general stores to Mom-and-Pop neighborhood stores to giant supermarkets. Now, the trends in grocery stores include operating 24 hours a day, ethnic foods, fresh bakeries, deli's, salad bars and pre-prepared meals, plus delivery, acceptance of credit cards and specialization in exotic or natural foods. Discuss how these changes have been influenced by demographics and what current or future changes could be in store.

Culture

Which of the three cultural influences, changing role of women and men, changing attitudes, or changing values is best demonstrated by the statements below?

1. They purchase 49 percent of all new cars and 23 percent of new trucks, spend $65 billion a year on vehicles for their personal use and influence 80 percent of all new car sales._____

2. Nestle replaces a picture of a woman with that of a man on the label of Taster's Choice decaffeinated coffee._____

3. Del Monte has added a 14-item product line of no-salt vegetables to appeal to the more health-conscious consumer._____

4. Work is seen as a means to an end—recreation, leisure, and entertainment—which has contributed to a growth in sales of products such as videocassette recorders, sports equipment, and easily prepared meals.

ECONOMIC FORCES

Ted Jones earns $36,000 a year and his wife Rebecca earns $30,000 a year. Both are paid monthly and have the following deductions:

Federal taxes	$550
State taxes	$150
Social security	$400

Their average monthly bills and expenses:

Rent	$900
Food	$350
Utilities	$150
Clothing	$100
Medical	$50
Insurance	$50
Transportation	$100
Car payment	$350

Using the information above answer the following questions:

1. What is their gross monthly income?_____

2. What is their monthly disposable income?_____

3. What is their monthly discretionary income?_____

4. What percent of their gross income does their discretionary income represent?_____

TECHNOLOGY

What technological development(s) affected the following products?

1. Straight razor_____

2. Slide rule_____

3. 8-track tapes_____

4. Atari Video games_____

5. Vinyl records (LPs)_____

6. Typewriters_____

REGULATORY FORCES

Consumerism is a movement to increase the influence, power, and rights of consumers in their dealings with institutions of all types. This movement was responsible for the creation of many of the laws. Interestingly, much of the momentum for these laws was generated by popular literature (fiction, non-fiction, and speeches). Examples include: *The Jungle, Silent Spring, The Elixir*, the "Consumer Bill of Rights," and television shows like *Frontline* and *60 Minutes*. What current regulation of business (proposed regulation) can you name that has been influenced by the popular culture?

CAN YOU PASS THE TEST?
Sample Multiple Choice Questions

1. Environmental trends typically arise from five sources. They are _____ forces.
   - a. economic, social, cultural, demographic, and technological
   - b. demographic, internal, social, economic, and external
   - c. regulatory, managerial, competitive, social, and economic
   - d. social, economic, regulatory, technological, and competitive
   - d. economic, regulatory, innovative, internal, and cultural

2. Environmental scanning:
   - a. is a continuous process.
   - b. is a method for tracking trends.
   - c. is used to explain why trends occur.
   - d. can be used as an interpretive tool.
   - e. is accurately described by all of the above.

3. In a recent survey consumers indicated that they plan to do more volunteering. This type of information is the result of:
   - a. social needs forecasting.
   - b. environmental scanning.
   - c. macroeconomic analysis.
   - d. transactional exchange.
   - e. futuristic marketing.

4. The Lemon Tree is a high-fashion boutique selling top-of-the-line women's clothing and accessories. The keys to The Lemon Tree's success include knowing the customers' changing tastes and providing something different from other retailers. In addition, because of the high value of the merchandise, The Lemon Tree's management is searching for information on available computerized inventory controls and sales order processing. From this description, one can infer that the environmental category of least importance to The Lemon Tree is:
   - a. economic.
   - b. regulatory.
   - c. technological.
   - d. social.
   - e. competitive.

5. Social forces:
   - a. include demographics and values.
   - b. usually have little impact on marketing strategy.
   - c. include reduced emphasis on trade regulation.
   - d. empower workers to improve their performances.
   - e. encourage international trade.

6. According to the 2000 Census, the U.S. population is growing older and becoming more ethnically diverse. This represents _____ forces that will affect future marketing.
      a. economic
      b. regulatory
      c. social
      d. competitive
      e. internal

7. U.S. baby boomers will be over age 55 by 2020. This will impact the types of products purchased. This is an example of how _____ forces affect the marketplace.
      a. social
      b. ecological
      c. psychographic
      d. competitive
      e. technological

8. The fastest growing age segment in America is composed of:
      a. infants.
      b. people over 50 years of age.
      c. children of baby boomers.
      d. teens.
      e. people in their early 30s.

9. Baby boomers will all be over age 55 by 2020. This will impact the types of products purchased. This is an example of a _____ change.
      a. cultural
      b. psychographic
      c. economic
      d. demographic
      e. competitive

10. The generation often referred to as the echo-boom is:
      a. Generation X.
      b. Generation Y.
      c. Generation Z.
      d. the new parent market.
      e. is accurately described by none of the above.

11. Which of the following statements about Generation X is true?
      a. Generation Xers are becoming less fiscally conservative.
      b. Generation Xers are self-reliant.
      c. Generation Xers will change their buying behavior to reflect concern about their children and future retirement issues.
      d. Generation Xers are those people who were born between 1946 and 1965.
      e. All of the above statements about Generation Xers are true.

12. _____ is the name for the group of consumers who are self-reliant, entrepreneurial, supportive of racial and sexual diversity, and not prone to extravagance.
    a. Generation X
    b. Generation Y
    c. Baby boomer
    d. A liberal cohort
    e. A postwar cohort

13. In the United States, the fastest growing type of household consists of:
    a. married people with children.
    b. married couples with no children living at home.
    c. single parents.
    d. immigrant parents with naturalized children.
    e. unrelated people living under one roof.

14. A _____ is formed by the merging of two previously separated units into a single household.
    a. mature household
    b. shifting family unit
    c. merging household
    d. blended family
    e. traditional household

15. From the 1930s through the 1980s, Americans moved from the cities to the suburbs. During the 1990s and 2000s, the population began to shift again, from the suburbs to:
    a. the exurbs.
    b. working farms.
    c. states like North Dakota and West Virginia.
    d. Canada.
    e. a metropolitan statistical area (MSA).

16. There are approximately 6.3 billion people in the world today. By 2050 it is expected there will be:
    a. 9 billion people in the world.
    b. 12 billion people in the world.
    c. 15 billion people in the world.
    d. 18 billion people in the world.
    e. 7 billion people in the world.

17. HSBC Bank International Ltd. (Europe's largest bank) selected its advertising agency because that agency was "always sensitive to the possibility that something might not translate well or may offend superstitions about colours or numbers." This is an example of how _____ forces affect marketing.
    a. social
    b. technological
    c. economic
    d. competitive
    e. regulatory

18. Multicultural marketing programs:
    a. are combinations of the marketing mix that reflect unique attitudes of different races.
    b. are combinations of the marketing mix that reflect unique lifestyles of different races.
    c. are combinations of the marketing mix that reflect unique communication preferences of different races.
    d. are combinations of the marketing mix that reflect unique ancestry of different races.
    e. are all of the above.

19. Which of the following factors can be used to help explain why Generation Y women no longer feel the need to be feminists?
    a. The television industry eliminated all shows where the woman was portrayed as a stay-at-home mother.
    b. The movie industry stopped making films about dependent women.
    c. They were able to shop freely on the Internet.
    d. Their mothers worked and gave them a reference point for lifestyle choices.
    e. All of the above are factors that can be used to help explain why Generation Y women no longer feel the need to be feminists.

20. In his first job after college, Mike sits at a computer. To maintain his health and fitness, Mike decides to join a gym. This decision reflects which of the following cultural elements?
    a. quality-price duality
    b. price-based marketing
    c. cocooning
    d. price synergy
    e. values

21. Technology can:
    a. reduce the cost of technology-based products.
    b. provide value through the development of new products.
    c. change existing products.
    d. change the way products are produced.
    e. do all of the above.

22. In 1960 the average annual tuition was the equivalent of 110 hours of pay for an average worker. Today it is 250 hours. This is an example of _____ forces.
    a. economic
    b. regulatory
    c. competitive
    d. social
    e. ecological

23. Coffee is a major export in many nations. A glut in the market has caused prices for coffee beans to plummet by 50 percent. As a result, coffee farmers would have:
    a. more disposable income but less gross income.
    b. more discretionary income but less gross income.
    c. less gross, disposable, and discretionary incomes.
    d. more gross income but less disposable income.
    e. more gross and disposable but less discretionary income.

24. _____ income is the money a consumer has left after paying taxes to use for food, clothing, and shelter.
     a. Net
     b. Discretionary
     c. Disposable
     d. Household
     e. Gross

25. Emily had an excellent year as a saleswoman in 2005. She earned $97,000. She paid $17,000 for "necessities" such as mortgage, food, and clothing. She was given a six-week all expenses paid vacation by the company for her sales performance that had a value of $9,000. Her state and federal income taxes totaled $24,000. What was her discretionary income?
     a. $56,000
     b. $73,000
     c. $80,000
     d. $88,000
     e. There is not enough data provided to calculate her discretionary income.

26. The U.S. Treasury Department developed and operates a website called www.pay.gov. This site is designed to provide U.S. agencies with the ability to process payments for fines, licenses, taxes, etc. from individuals and businesses. The Treasury Department is hoping that use of this site will standardize how U.S. agencies collect money and reduce paperwork by streamlining the payment process. This is best described as a way that _____ forces have changed how business is conducted.
     a. economic
     b. regulatory
     c. competitive
     d. social
     e. technological

27. Which of the following statements concerning technological forces is true?
     a. A new wave of technological innovation will not replace existing products and companies.
     b. Because technological change is the result of research, it is highly predictable.
     c. An advantage of technology is that advances can in no way harm an industry's growth.
     d. The cost of technology is increasing.
     e. Advances in technology are having important effects on marketing because they allow marketers to better understand and serve consumers.

28. Some cereal manufacturers are selling cereals in plastic bags rather than cardboard boxes with cellophane inserts. Cereal packed in bags requires less packing material than cereal packaged in traditional boxes. This example reflects the use of:
     a. green marketing.
     b. the green initiative.
     c. recycling.
     d. pre-recycling.
     e. precycling.

29. _____ can be defined as the electronic equivalent of a physical-world marketplace.
     a. Intranet exchange
     b. Marketspace
     c. An extranet
     d. A commercial online server
     e. An Internet browser

30. Office Depot has developed wireless, handheld computers for staff. When customers inquire about a product, a computer-equipped sales associate can pull detailed information on products right out of the corporate database. Employees at one store can contact employees at another store for advice or information. This is an example of how _____ can be used to enhance marketing.
     a. intranets
     b. partnering software
     c. extranets
     d. Internet servers
     e. electronic data interchangeable browsers

31. Which of the following statements about electronic business technologies is true?
     a. Electronic commerce does not occur in marketspace.
     b. The Internet is distinct and separate from the World Wide Web.
     c. Ordering a parka from a Lands' End catalog exemplifies electronic commerce.
     d. Purchasing a book from Amazon.com is an example of electronic commerce.
     e. All of the above statements about electronic business technologies are true.

32. Blimpie and Quizno's, sandwich chains based in Atlanta and Denver, respectively, both face threats from Subway, national maker of sub sandwiches. Subway represents a(n) _____ forces for them.
     a. ecological
     b. technological
     c. competitive
     d. cultural
     e. economic

33. Which of the following products would most likely be sold through pure competition?
     a. vacation cruises
     b. wheat
     c. musical instruments
     d. electricity
     e. magazines

34. Coupons and sales are frequently used marketing tactics in which form of competition?
     a. pure competition
     b. cross-market competition
     c. oligopoly
     d. monopolistic competition
     e. monopoly

35. A(n) _____ occurs when a few companies control the majority of industry sales.
     a. monopolistic competition
     b. pure competition
     c. oligopoly
     d. oligopolistic monopoly
     e. marketspace

36. Since _____ is regulated by the state or federal government, marketing plays a small role in this setting.
     a. pure competition
     b. cross-market competition
     c. an oligopoly
     d. monopolistic competition
     e. a monopoly

37. Lucent Technologies is the largest supplier of phone network equipment in the world. Its past customers find it less expensive to upgrade equipment rather than switch to another supplier. This is an example of a(n):
　　a. oligopolistic monopoly.
　　b. monopolistic competition.
　　c. barrier to entry.
　　d. pure competition.
　　e. ethical dilemma

38. Although in the United States reasonable efforts are made to provide a "level playing field" in business, it would be difficult for a new American automobile company to be established today, primarily because of:
　　a. barriers to entry.
　　b. corporate prejudices.
　　c. government regulations of competitive practices.
　　d. lower standards of living.
　　e. consumer apathy and ignorance.

39. In the 1930s small businesses were threatened by early chain stores and lobbied for the Robinson-Patman Act (1936). This act is an example of how _____ forces have a powerful influence on the marketing environment.
　　a. economic
　　b. competitive
　　c. ecological
　　d. regulatory
　　e. technological

40. A car collector, Mr. F. Hanson, who said his 1975 Chevrolet Corvette was certified as the last Corvette convertible to be produced, sued General Motors to stop it from manufacturing any more of the convertible sports cars. The suit also requested $1.5 million in damages. Hansen claimed he bought the car for its collector's value. It came with a letter from GM dated Aug. 25, 1975, that said the car was "the last Corvette convertible that General Motors Corp. would ever manufacture." But GM and Hansen said the value of his car has been decreasing ever since GM resumed manufacturing convertibles in 1985. If the court ruled in favor of Mr. Hansen, what general type of regulation would such a ruling represent?
　　a. protecting companies from one another
　　b. protecting people from unfair business practices
　　c. protecting the future interests of society from dangerous business practices
　　d. protecting consumers from one another
　　e. protecting businesses from unfair consumer practices

41. The _____ makes it unlawful to discriminate in prices charged to different purchasers of the same product, where the effect may substantially lessen competition or help to create a monopoly.
　　a. Fair Packaging and Labeling Act
　　b. Sherman Antitrust Act
　　c. Telephone Consumer Protection Act
　　d. Robinson-Patman Act
　　e. Clayton Act

42. Laws governing _____ are examples of legislation designed to protect companies.
　　a. consumer product safety
　　b. trademarks
　　c. copyrights and patents
　　d. packaging and labeling
　　e. clean air and water

43. The Infant Formula Act, the Nutritional Labeling and Education Act, and the Fair Packaging and Labeling Act are all examples of _____ legislation.
   a. company protection
   b. ecological
   c. distributed-related
   d. value-related
   e. consumer protection

44. Consumerism:
   a. is a movement by industry to gain a more ethical image.
   b. started in the 1960s.
   c. supports the use of patents, copyrights, and trademarks to protect assets.
   d. is referred to as a grassroots movement because it must be controlled by federal agencies.
   e. is accurately described by all of the above.

45. Coca-Cola has hired brand cops to make sure that the Coca-Cola brand name and logo are not used without written permission. Why is Coca-Cola so rigorous in protecting its trademark?
   a. Coke risks losing its generic status.
   b. The government will file charges for trademark infringement only if the owner of the trademark has documented proof of wrongdoing.
   c. The Lanham Act conferred ownership of the Coke name and other trademarked property to the Coca-Cola Company.
   d. In order to maintain the use of its widely recognizable trademark, Coca-Cola must prevent the name from becoming generic.
   e. By protecting its trademark, Coca-Cola is protecting the entire soft drink industry from indirect competition.

46. The government has four concerns with regard to distribution and the maintenance of competition. Which of the following is NOT one of those four concerns?
   a. exclusive dealing
   b. requirement contracts
   c. inventory maintenance agreements
   d. exclusive territorial distributorship
   e. tying arrangements

47. A situation in which a manufacturer grants a distributor the sole right to sell a product in a specific geographic area is called:
   a. exclusive dealing.
   b. a geographic shift.
   c. a preferential promotions contract.
   d. an exclusive territorial distributorship.
   e. monopolistic competition.

48. _____ is an FTC action that requires a company to spend money on advertising to correct previous misleading ads.
   a. Comparative advertisement
   b. Corrective advertising
   c. Competitive advertising
   d. Truth in advertising
   e. Promotional monitoring

49. The Better Business Bureau is a voluntary alliance of companies whose goal is to help maintain fair practices. This is an example of:
     a. self-regulation
     b. federal regulation
     c. industrial action
     d. fair trade
     e. exclusive dealing

50. The Better Business Bureau:
     a. is the best-known federal agency involved in monitoring self-regulation of competing businesses.
     b. has a great deal of legal power to force a company to comply with regulations.
     c. is not involved with Internet commerce.
     d. is a voluntary alliance of companies whose goal is to help maintain fair practices.
     e. oversees the content of television shows and advertising that runs on those programs.

ANSWER KEY

Answers to Questions & Problems

Social Forces--Culture

1. Role of men and women
2. Changing attitudes
3. Changing values
4. Changing values

Economic Forces

1. $5500
2. $4400
3. $2350
4. 42.7%

Technology

Example:

1. Straight razor—safety razor (currently like Sensor) or electric razor

Regulatory Forces

Example: Regulation and trace elements required for large fertilizer sales (due to Oklahoma City bombing).

Answers to Sample Multiple Choice Questions

1. d p. 72; LO 1	14. d p. 77; LO 2	26. e p. 83; LO 3	38. a p. 87; LO 4
2. e p. 72; LO 1	15. a p. 77; LO 2	27. e p. 84; LO 3	39. d p. 88; LO 5
3. b p. 72; LO 1	16. a p. 74; LO 2	28. e p. 84; LO 3	40. b p. 88-89; LO 5
4. b p. 73; LO 1	17. a p. 77; LO 2	29. b p. 85; LO 3	41. d p. 88; LO 5
5. a p. 74; LO 2	18. e p. 78; LO 2	30. a p. 85; LO 3	42. c p. 88; LO 5
6. c p. 75; LO 2	19. d p. 79; LO 2	31.d p. 85; LO 3	43. e p. 88; LO 5
7. a p. 75; LO 2	20. e p. 80; LO 2	32. c p. 85; LO 4	44. b p. 88; LO 5
8. e p. 76; LO 2	21. e p. 84; LO 3	33. b p. 85-86; LO 4	45. d p. 89; LO 5
9. d p. 76; LO 2	22. a p. 80; LO 2	34. d p. 86; LO 4	46. c p. 90; LO 5
10. b p. 76; LO 2	23. c p. 81; LO 2	35. c p. 86; LO 4	47. d p. 90; LO 5
11. b p. 75; LO 2	24. c p. 82; LO 2	36. e p. 86; LO 4	48. b p. 90; LO 5
12. a p. 75; LO 2	25. a p. 82-83; LO 2	37. c p. 87; LO 4	49. a p. 91; LO 5
13. c p. 76; LO 2			50. d p. 91; LO 5

Note: LO indicates learning objective.

CHAPTER 4

ETHICS AND SOCIAL RESPONSIBILITY IN MARKETING

<u>Why is Chapter 4 important</u>? This chapter illustrates the necessity of operating a business in an ethical fashion. It also shows the rewards of exercising social responsibility in the workings of a business enterprise.

Ethics: The moral principles and values that govern the actions and decisions of an individual or group.

CHAPTER OUTLINE

I. NATURE AND SIGNIFICANCE OF MARKETING ETHICS

    A. Ethical/Legal Framework
        1. Ethics
        2. Laws

    B. Current Perceptions of Ethical Behavior

II. UNDERSTANDING ETHICAL MARKETING BEHAVIOR

    A. Societal Culture and Norms

    B. Business Culture and Industry Practices
        1. Ethics of exchange
            a. caveat emptor
            b. Consumer Bill of Rights
                i. safety
                ii. be informed
                iii. choice
                iv. be heard
        2. Ethics of competition
            a. economic espionage
            b. bribery

    C. Corporation Culture and Expectations
        1. Code of ethics
        2. Ethical behavior of top management and co-workers

    D. Personal Moral Philosophy and Ethical Behavior
        1. Moral idealism
        2. Utilitarianism

III. UNDERSTANDING SOCIAL RESPONSIBILITY IN MARKETING

    A. Concepts of Social Responsibility
        1. Profit responsibility
        2. Stakeholder responsibility
        3. Societal responsibility
            a. green marketing
            b. ISO 14000
            c. cause marketing

    B. Social Audit
        1. Recognition and rationale
        2. Identification
        3. Determination
        4. Specification
        5. Evaluation

    C. Consumer Ethics and Social Responsibility

You should be able to place these key terms in the outline and be able to discuss them.

cause marketing	**economic espionage**	**laws**	**sustainable development**
caveat emptor	**ethics**	**moral idealism**	**utilitarianism**
code of ethics	**green marketing**	**social audit**	**whistle blowers**
Consumer Bill of Rights	**ISO 14000**	**social responsibility**	

QUESTIONS & PROBLEMS

ETHICAL/LEGAL FRAMEWORK IN MARKETING

1. What is the key difference between legality and ethically?_____

2. Using Enron as an example, discuss the conduct of the officers in relation to ethical and legal behavior.
_____

CURRENT STATUS OF ETHICAL BEHAVIOR

List four possible reasons and cite examples of why the state of perceived ethical business conduct is at its present level.

1._____

2._____

3._____

4._____

ETHICS OF EXCHANGE

1. Many discount and commuter airlines regularly contract with outside companies for maintenance and training to save money. They also buy older airplanes that are far cheaper than newer more up to date equipment. When asked about safety concerns they respond that the safety record of discount and commuter airlines is comparable to that of the major airlines. This is true only when you include Southwest Airlines, which leads the entire airline industry, major and discount, with its safety record. Without Southwest, the other discount airlines are up to four times higher in "incidents" than major airlines. Which of the rights of the consumer are the discount and commuter airlines violating? How would you remedy this situation?_____
_____
_____
_____

2. The US Post Office has the sole authority to deliver first class mail in the United States. Over the last several years its inspectors have audited companies who utilize overnight delivery services to see if the packages sent really warranted overnight service. Many were judged not to be "urgent" and the companies had to pay the first class postage plus a fine. How is this violated consumer rights?_____
_____
_____
_____

ETHICS OF COMPETITION

Two kinds of unethical behaviors among competitors are most common: industrial espionage and bribery.

1. Many companies regularly buy the products of their competitors or ask their customers to buy them so they can test and evaluate the products. In a slightly different version, an employee of a competitor will pose as a potential customer to receive literature and other sales information. A major consumer products company monitors the test markets of its largest competitor and rolls nationally with the product months before the competitor without doing test marketing of their own. Are these examples ethical? How can you ethically get information on your competitors?_____
_____
_____

2. General Motors charged Volkswagen with hiring away one of its top executives and receiving privileged information he had taken with him. A regional bank had spent eighteen months and several million dollars planning a new product when their executive vice president in charge of the product development left, taking the information to a major competitor who then introduced the product first. How do you protect yourself against this type of industrial espionage?_____
_____
_____

3. Foreign makers of defense related material regularly bribe government officials in third world countries to sell their products. Under the Foreign Corrupt Practices Act, US companies cannot legally do this. How do you compete against this type of competition?_____
_____
_____

PERSONAL MORAL PHILOSOPHY AND ETHICAL BEHAVIOR

Ultimately, ethical choices are based on the moral philosophy of the decision maker.
Moral philosophy consists of two major types:

Moral idealism
Utilitarianism

Match the correct moral philosophy to the example or statement below:

_____1. In 1991 there was a major controversy over the drug Prozac. In some cases there were reports of extremely dangerous side effects. However, the company did not withdraw the drug because of the extremely effective job it did with most patients.

_____2. This philosophy exists in the Consumer Bill of Rights.

_____3. This philosophy is favored by moral philosophers.

_____4. When several people died as the result of the tampering of a handful of Tylenol bottles, literally millions of bottles were withdrawn from shelves to avoid even the slightest risk of endangering anyone else.

_____5. This philosophy considers certain individual rights or duties to be universal.

_____6. A personal moral philosophy that focuses on "the greatest good for the greatest number."

_____7. In this philosophy, if the benefits exceed the costs, the behavior is considered ethical.

SOCIAL AUDIT

A social audit is a systematic assessment of a firm's objectives, strategies, and performance in the domain of social responsibility.

List the five basic steps in a social audit:

1._____

2._____

3._____

4._____

5._____

SOCIETAL RESPONSIBILITY

Two aspects of societal marketing include:

Green marketing
Cause-related marketing

Match the correct term to the definition or statement below:

_____1. Oxydol laundry detergent now comes in a highly concentrated form in order to reduce waste in packaging.

_____2. Every time you buy Daily's frozen yogurt pops money is donated to save the penguins.

_____3. Tying the charitable contributions of a firm directly to the customer revenues produced through the promotion of one of its products

_____4. Marketing efforts to produce, promote, and redeem environmentally sensitive products

CONSUMER ETHICS AND SOCIAL RESPONSIBILITY

1. There is a practice that many retailers are familiar with but seldom do very much about. A consumer will come into a store and ask to take an expensive evening outfit out on approval or will actually buy it. After wearing it to the "event," it will be returned as "unacceptable." The store is then stuck with a garment that has been worn. The store usually does nothing about this because the consumer is a good customer throughout the year. How would you handle this situation?_____
_____

2. Some consumers will shop establishments for deals directed towards new customers. An example would be a free cellular phone and one month's service with the sign-up for one year of service. Shortly after they get the free phone, they cancel the service saying they are moving and repeat the process with another company. Most times they end up with the phone and the first month's service. How should this be handled?_____
_____

CAN YOU PASS THE TEST?
Sample Multiple Choice Questions

1. _____ are the moral principles and values that govern the actions and decisions of an individual or group.
>   a. Laws
>   b. Corporate policies
>   c. Ethics
>   d. Heuristics
>   e. Judicial rulings

2. Robin is a research engineer for a company that manufactures industrial equipment. Her department has recently developed an unpatentable technique that speeds processing by 20 percent. A competitive firm has approached Robin and offered to double her salary to work for them and share her knowledge about the technique. As a result of _____, Robin turns down the job offer.
>   a. laws
>   b. state policies
>   c. ethics
>   d. heuristics
>   e. judicial rulings

3. Laws are:
>   a. a specific set of behaviors a given society considers to be ethical.
>   b. society's values and standards that are enforceable in the courts.
>   c. the agreed upon code of behavior for a given nation, community, religious group, or family unit.
>   d. written documentation of a prescribed set of behaviors.
>   e. a legislated code of ethics defining both what may and may not be done in specific circumstances.

4. A computer program aimed at car dealers shows financing outcomes that misstate taxes and interest. The computer company agrees the program misleads buyers, but says it will provide what dealers want as long as it is not against the law. This is an example of an act that is:
>   a. ethical but illegal.
>   b. ethical and legal.
>   c. unethical and illegal.
>   d. unethical but legal.

5. Which of the following statements can be used to explain why the state of perceived ethical business conduct is at its present level?
>   a. There is increased pressure on businesspeople to make decisions in a society characterized by a diverse value system.
>   b. There is a growing tendency for business decisions to be judged publicly by groups with different values and interests.
>   c. Ethical business conduct may have declined.
>   d. The public's expectations of ethical business behavior has increased.
>   e. All of the above statements can be used to explain why the state of perceived ethical business conduct is at its present level.

6. Ethical business behavior is influenced by:
   - a. industry practices.
   - b. societal norms.
   - c. the organizational culture.
   - d. organizational expectations.
   - e. all of the above.

7. Culture serves as a socializing force that dictates what:
   - a. is the will of the largest minority in a society.
   - b. is morally right and just.
   - c. is the considered opinion of a society's elders.
   - d. is exclusively the law of the land.
   - e. expresses the diverse backgrounds of a nation's subcultures.

8. Levi Strauss decided to end much of its business dealings in China because of what the company called "pervasive human rights abuses." This is an example of how _____ affect ethical standards.
   - a. organizational cultures
   - b. societal culture and norms
   - c. organizational expectations
   - d. ethical ombudsmen
   - e. all of the above

9. A large investment bank has been notified by the Securities and Exchange Commission that several of its sales and trading officials may face charges for taking inflated commissions in exchange for providing information on IPO shares in 1999 and 2000. This plus many other allegations caused the bank to release the following statement: "Our bank dealing follow an accepted code of conduct in our industry." This statement means the bank executives:
   - a. are taking full blame for its actions.
   - b. will accept punishment for their actions if the punishment is determined by members of their industry.
   - c. believe they should be punished only if everyone else in their industry is.
   - d. attribute the bank's actions to business culture.
   - e. have decided to act socially responsible.

10. The legal concept of *caveat emptor* means:
   - a. having a good self concept.
   - b. telling the whole truth and nothing but the truth.
   - c. requiring full disclosure by the seller.
   - d. telling the buyer to beware.
   - e. avoiding nondiscriminatory pricing practices.

11. When Sam went to buy an engagement ring, he decided to buy it from a friend of his cousin's wife rather than a jewelry store. He congratulated himself when he saw the size of the stone he had purchased for $400. The ring turned his fiancée's finger green, and the "diamond" turned out to be zirconium. Sam should have remembered:
   - a. the iceberg principle.
   - b. *e pluribus unum.*
   - c. *de facto* marketing.
   - d. the marketing concept.
   - e. *caveat emptor.*

12. Which president is given credit for the Consumer Bill of Rights?
   - a. Ronald Reagan
   - b. John Kennedy
   - c. George Bush
   - d. Gerald Ford
   - e. Jimmy Carter

13. When shopping on the Internet, most consumers assume the personal information they give out is confidential. Subscribers to America Online (AOL) were upset when AOL proposed giving member information to partners without telling the subscribers. This is related most directly to the consumer's:

      a. right to choose.

      b. right to be informed.

      c. right to be treated courteously.

      d. right to safety.

      e. right to happiness.

14. According to the text, the two most common types of unethical behavior in competition are:

      a. price fixing and copyright infringement.

      b. economic espionage and bribery.

      c. bribery and extortion.

      d. price fixing and economic espionage.

      e. economic espionage and anti-trust infractions.

15. _____ is the clandestine collection of trade secrets or proprietary information about a company's competitors.

      a. Economic espionage

      b. Environmental spying

      c. Covert spying

      d. Covert corporate scrutiny

      e. Fiscal impropriety

16. Proctor & Gamble charged that competitors photographed its production line and infiltrated a confidential sales presentation. This is an example of:

      a. economic espionage.

      b. environmental spying.

      c. covert spying.

      d. covert corporate scrutiny.

      e. fiscal impropriety.

17. Corporate culture:

      a. is a formalized method for controlling the marketing environment.

      b. is the set of accepted standards and practices within a given industry by its principal members.

      c. is the description of both ethical and behavioral attributes of "white collar" versus "blue collar" workers in the United States business environment.

      d. is a set of values, ideas and attitudes that is learned and shared among members of an organization.

      e. is the formal statement of ethical principles and rules of conduct adopted by an organization.

18. Employees' dress ("We don't wear ties") and manner of work (team style) demonstrate:

      a. ethnocentricity

      b. corporate culture

      c. industry icon

      d. sociocultural environment

      e. industry norms

19. A code of ethics:

      a. is typically informal.

      b. is not needed by large companies who are monitored by their stakeholders.

      c. is unrelated to the corporate culture.

      d. typically provides guidelines for dealing with suppliers, competitors, and customers.

      e. is accurately described by all of the above.

20. Which of the following statements describes shortcomings associated with codes of ethics?
    a. Most companies do not have a formal code of ethics and for those that do, there is no way for the codes to be enforced.
    b. Most companies overlook infractions if the action is unethical but legal, and little action is taken if the unethical behavior results in a profit for the firm.
    c. Many codes of ethics lack specificity, and a problem exists with the perceived behavior of top management and coworkers.
    d. There is often a discrepancy between the code of ethics of a firm and the code of ethics of labor unions, and there is often a discrepancy between the code of ethics of a firm and the personal and moral beliefs of an individual employee.
    e. There are very few violations in firms with written codes of ethics.

21. In 2002, six executives of Tyson Foods, one of the world's largest poultry, beef, and pork processors, were arrested for illegal smuggling of undocumented foreign workers into the U.S. to work at Tyson plants. Tyson's violations are the result of _____, one of the major reasons why some companies fail to establish ethical behavior.
    a. too ambiguous a mission statement
    b. the absence of an executive summary
    c. anti-whistleblowing
    d. top management's behavior
    e. poor marketing research

22. _____ are employees who make public the unethical or illegal actions of their employees.
    a. Tattletales
    b. Ethical ombudsmen
    c. Ethical liaisons
    d. Situation managers
    e. Whistleblowers

23. An employee who reports illegal accounting procedures is an example of a(n):
    a. corporate proctor.
    b. ethical ombudsman.
    c. whistleblower.
    d. ethical poacher.
    e. scab.

24. Two personal moral philosophies have a direct bearing on marketing practices. They are:
    a. moral piety and pragmatism.
    b. moral idealism and utilitarianism.
    c. overt morality and moral sentiment.
    d. codes of ethics and ethical committees.
    e. pragmatism and utilitarianism.

25. 3M stopped production of a chemical made nearly 40 years when tests showed the chemical could be harmful in large doses, even though the products in which it was used had no known harmful health or environmental effect. This is an example of:
    a. a code of ethics violation.
    b. moral idealism.
    c. utilitarianism.
    d. cultural and corporate ethics.
    e. internal economic espionage.

26. Utilitarianism:
        a. focuses on the greatest good for the greatest number.
        b. supports the concept that a product, service, or idea is immoral if it is not accessible to every individual.
        c. focuses on the greatest good possible for each individual.
        d. supports an ethnocentric view of the world.
        e. considers the welfare of the individual more important than that of the group.

27. In the late 18th century, English jurist Jeremy Bentham systematically analyzed law and legislation, laying the foundation for utilitarian philosophy. Which of the following statements about his philosophy is true today?
        a. This philosophy exists in the Consumer Bill of Rights.
        b. This philosophy considers certain individual rights or duties as universal, regardless of the outcome.
        c. Moral philosophers and consumer interest groups favor this philosophy.
        d. This philosophy focuses on the greatest good for the greatest number by assessing the costs and benefits of the consequences of ethical behavior.
        e. All of the above statements about Bentham's philosophy are true today.

28. The three concepts of social responsibility are:
        a. cultural responsibility, national responsibility, and local responsibility.
        b. utilitarian responsibility, moral responsibility, and pragmatic responsibility.
        c. profit responsibility, societal responsibility, and stakeholder responsibility.
        d. fiscal responsibility, legal responsibility, and monetary responsibility.
        e. supplier responsibility, customer responsibility, and distributor responsibility.

29. Florida Gas Service Co. has put large stickers on all of its vehicles designating them as safety watch vehicles. Employees are trained to help children, older citizens, and others in need of help. This safety watch program is demonstrating:
        a. the Golden Rule.
        b. social responsibility.
        c. profit responsibility.
        d. utilitarianism.
        e. the Valdez Principle.

30. Glock, Inc. has set up a voluntary program that "fingerprints" every gun the company assembles. The program enables police to trace the owners of guns used in crimes when only the bullets or casings are recovered. This plan received praise from law enforcement officials, and the company is pleased to support it. This plan is an example of how a company practices:
        a. profit responsibility.
        b. mission synergy.
        c. transactional marketing.
        d. mass marketing.
        e. stakeholder responsibility.

31. Xerox's "Design for the Environment" program focuses on ways to make its equipment recyclable and remanufacturable. This is an example of:
        a. the concept of technological responsibility.
        b. the caveat emptor concept.
        c. cause marketing.
        d. green marketing.
        e. the concept of profit responsibility.

32. Which of the following is an example of green marketing?
    a. The Anheuser-Busch Corporation added green colors to its labels.
    b. 3M created a new fertilizer for trees.
    c. Boise Cascade, Lowe's and Home Depot discontinued the sale of wood products made from the world's endangered forests.
    d. Levi-Strauss markets pre-washed jeans.
    e. Joe's Lawn Service is offering a special spring promotion.

33. ISO 14000 is most closely related to:
    a. the concept of profit responsibility.
    b. green marketing.
    c. ethnocentric marketing.
    d. whistleblowing.
    e. an international code of ethics.

34. Menlo Park, Calif.-based Schoolpop.com launched in June 1999 as an online shopping mall, where consumers could make purchases from Amazon and similar online retailers and designate a portion of the proceeds to a K-12 school of their choice. In its first year of operation Schoolpop raised over $1 million for education. It is using _____ to attract customers to the intermediary website.
    a. the concept of stakeholder responsibility.
    b. the caveat emptor concept.
    c. cause marketing.
    d. green marketing.
    e. the concept of profit responsibility.

35. Cause marketing refers to:
    a. marketing efforts made on behalf of a nonprofit organization.
    b. marketing services provided at little or no cost for the purpose of promoting or supporting a worthy cause.
    c. charitable contributions tied directly to the customer revenues produced through the promotion of one of a firm's products.
    d. marketing efforts specifically taken to counteract negative publicity based on a firm's involvement in environmentally sensitive issues.
    e. all of the above.

36. American Express Company pioneered _____ when it raised the funds for the renovation of the Statue of Liberty.
    a. philanthropic marketing
    b. goodwill marketing
    c. public relations marketing
    d. transactional marketing
    e. cause marketing

37. According to the text, the first step in a social audit is to:
    a. specify the type and amount of resources needed for social programs.
    b. identify social responsibility causes.
    c. determine organizational objectives for social programs.
    d. evaluate ongoing social programs.
    e. recognize the firm's social expectations.

38. Environmentalists who are concerned about preserving the Amazon rain forest would be in support of:
    a. national competitive advantages.
    b. using whatever resources are available to improve a nation's quality of life.
    c. economic hegemony.
    d. sustainable development.
    e. uncontrolled economic growth.

39. _____ involves conducting business in a way that protects the natural environment while making economic progress.
        a. Sustainable development
        b. Maximizing profit
        c. Concentrating on stakeholder responsibility
        d. The economic model
        e. Natural marketing

40. Practices that include filing warranty claims after the claim period, misredeeming coupons, making fraudulent returns of merchandise, providing inaccurate information on credit applications, tampering with utility meters, tapping cable TV lines, duplicating copyrighted music and software, and submitting phony insurance claims are examples of:
        a. normal and reasonable consumer behavior.
        b. unethical practices of consumers.
        c. acceptable business costs.
        d. costs to be passed along to shareholders.
        e. violations of the Consumer Bill of Rights.

ANSWER KEY

Answers to Questions & Problems

Ethical/Legal Framework in Marketing

1. Legality is required by law and ethically is required by consumers.

Current Status of Ethical Behavior

1. Increased pressure for diverse value systems
2. Public judgment
3. Increased expectations
4. Ethical business conduct declining

Ethics of Exchange

1. Safety
2. Choice

Ethics of Competition

1. Yes, these are ethical and utilized frequently.
2. Employment contracts are the most common protection.
3. High quality products with superior performance.

Personal Moral Philosophy and Ethical Behavior

1. Utilitarianism
2. Moral idealism
3. Moral idealism
4. Moral idealism
5. Utilitarianism
6. Utilitarianism
7. Utilitarianism

Social Audit

1. Recognition and rationale
2. Identification
3. Determination
4. Specification
5. Evaluation

Societal Responsibility

1. Green marketing
2. Cause-related marketing
3. Cause-related marketing
4. Green marketing

Consumer Ethics and Social Responsibility

1. Possibly develop a rental section of your formal wear.
2. Monitor and require deposit that is returned at the end of trial contract.

Answers to Sample Multiple Choice Questions

1. c p. 98; LO 1	11. e p. 101; LO 2	21. d p. 104-5; LO 2	31. d p. 108; LO 3
2. c p. 98; LO 1	12. b p. 101; LO 2	22. e p. 105; LO 2	32. c p. 108; LO 3
3. b p. 98; LO 1	13. b p. 101; LO 2	23. c p. 105; LO 2	33. b p. 108; LO 3
4. d p. 98; LO 1	14. b p. 102; LO 2	24. b p. 105: LO 2	34. c p. 108; LO 3
5. e p. 99; LO 1	15. a p. 102; LO 2	25. b p. 106; LO 2	35. c p. 108; LO 3
6. e p. 100; LO 2	16. a p. 102; LO 2	26. a p. 106; LO 2	36. e p. 109; LO 3
7. b p. 100; LO 2	17. d p. 103; LO 2	27. d p. 106; LO 2	37. e p. 109; LO 3
8. b p. 100; LO 2	18. b p. 102; LO 2	28. c p. 107; LO 3	38. d p. 110; LO 3
9. d p. 100; LO 2	19. d p. 103; LO 2	29. b p. 107; LO 3	39. a p. 110; LO 3
10. d p. 101; LO 2	20. c p. 104; LO 2	30. e p. 107; LO 3	40. b p. 110; LO 4

Note: LO indicates learning objective.

CHAPTER 5

CONSUMER BEHAVIOR

<u>Why is Chapter 5 important</u>? This chapter illustrates why consumers buy. Understanding consumer behavior is vital to the successful implementation of the marketing mix. This chapter outlines the consumer decision process and shows how the marketing mix can relate to each step. It also shows the external and internal influences on that buying process and how they can be influenced.

Consumer Behavior: The actions a person takes in purchasing and using products and services, including the mental and social processes that precede and follow these actions.

CHAPTER OUTLINE

I. CONSUMER PURCHASE DECISION PROCESS

    A. Problem Recognition: Perceiving a Need

    B. Information Search: Seeking Value
        1. Internal sources
        2. External information
            a. personal sources
            b. public sources
            c. market-dominated sources

    C. Alternative Evaluation: Assessing Value
        1. Suggesting criteria to use for purchase
        2. Yielding brand names that might meet the criteria
        3. Develop consumer value perceptions

    D. Purchase Decision: Buying Value
        1. From whom to buy
        2. When to buy

    E. Postpurchase Behavior: Value in Consumption or Use

    F. Involvement and Problem Solving Variation
        1. Involvement
            a. high involvement
               1. expensive
               2. can have serious personal consequence
               3. could reflect on one's social image
            b. low involvement
            c. involvement and marketing strategy
               1. maintaining product quality
               2. avoiding stock-out situations
               3. advertising messages that reinforce knowledge or reassure choices
        3. Routine problem solving
        4. Limited problem solving
        5. Extended problem solving

    G. Situational Influences
       1. Purchase task
       2. Social surroundings
       3. Physical surroundings
       4. Temporal effects
       5. Antecedent states

II. PSYCHOLOGICAL INFLUENCES

    A. Motivation
       1. Physiological needs
       2. Safety needs
       3. Social needs
       4. Personal needs
       5. Self-actualization needs

    B. Personality
       1. National character
       2. Self-concept

    C. Perception
       1. Selective perception
          a. selective exposure
          b. selective comprehension
          c. selective retention
          d. subliminal perception
       2. Perceived risk

    D. Learning
       1. Behavioral learning
          a. drive
          b. response
          c. reinforcement
          d. stimulus generalization
          e. stimulus discrimination
       2. Cognitive Learning
       3. Brand Loyalty

    E. Values, Beliefs and Attitudes
       1. Values
       2. Beliefs
       3. Attitudes
          a. attitude formation
          b. attitude change
             i. changing beliefs about brand attributes
             ii. changing perceived importance of attributes
             iii. adding new attributes to the product
       4. Lifestyle
          a. self-concept
          b. VALS 2 system
             i. Principle-oriented consumers
             ii. Status-oriented consumers
             iii. Action-oriented consumers

III. SOCIOCULTURAL INFLUENCES

A. Personal Influences
      1. Opinion leadership
      2. Word-of-mouth

B. Reference Groups
      1. Membership group
      2. Aspiration group
      3. Dissociative group

C. Family Influences
      1 Consumer socialization
      2. Family Life Cycle
      3. Family decision making
            a. information gatherer
            b. influencer
            c. decision maker
            d. purchaser
            e. user

D. Social Class

E. Culture and Subculture
      1. African-American
      2. Hispanic-American
      3. Asian-Pacific American

You should be able to place these key terms in the outline and be able to discuss them.

attitude	opinion leaders
beliefs	perceived risk
brand loyalty	perception
cognitive dissonance	personality
consideration set	purchase decision process
consumer behavior	reference groups
consumer socialization	self-concept
evaluation criteria	situational influences
family life cycle	social class
involvement	subcultures
learning	subliminal perception
lifestyle	word of mouth
motivation	

QUESTIONS & PROBLEMS

PROBLEM RECOGNITION

Problem recognition, the initial step in the purchase decision, is perceiving a difference between a person's ideal and actual situations big enough to trigger a decision. There are many ways a marketer can "activate" a consumer's decision process.

Discuss how problem recognition occurs (and which ones are aided by the marketer) for each of the following:

1. Gasoline_____

2. A new Mustang convertible_____

3. A birthday card_____

4. Lunch at Burger King_____

5. A Broadway play_____

6. A new Visa card_____

INFORMATION SEARCH

The information search stage clarifies the problem for the consumer by (1) suggesting criteria to use for the purchase, (2) yielding brand names that might meet the criteria, and (3) developing consumer value perceptions.

An information search can be internal (personal experience) or external (personal sources, public sources or marketer-dominated sources).

1. If you were looking for a fun time in New Orleans, including meals, nightlife, and hotels plus shopping and sightseeing, trace your information search, both internal and external. Did it yield a criteria for selection and a list of items meeting that criteria?_____
_____
_____

2. Repeat the above exercise for buying a long distance service._____
_____
_____

ALTERNATIVE EVALUATION

Complete the following exercise for each of the following items:

coffee
personal computer
restaurant (evening meal)
running shoes
college

1. Select criteria to be used for the purchases (evaluative criteria):_____
_____

2. Select brands that might meet your criteria (evoked set):_____
_____

3. Develop consumer value perceptions; decide where and when to buy:_____
_____

4. Evaluate (hypothetically) your decision (How would you do this?):_____
_____

5. In what ways could the company manufacturer reduce your cognitive dissonance?_____
_____

PURCHASE DECISION

During the purchase decision, "two choices remain: (1) from whom to buy and (2) when to buy. These two issues can be affected by many factors, whether your preferred brand is on sale, whether you've just won the lottery, whether you're making a purchase in the company of a friend, whether the sales staff is rude, etc.

Think of the last time you purchased a CD, a computer (or other major purchase), and an airline ticket. Discuss what influenced your decision of when to buy and from whom to buy._____
_____
_____

POST PURCHASE BEHAVIOR

After buying a product, the consumer compares it with his or her expectations and is either satisfied or dissatisfied. If the consumer is dissatisfied, marketers must decide whether the product was deficient or if consumer expectations were too high.

List three ways each of these types of marketers can attempt to reduce cognitive dissonance in the postpurchase stage:

1. Automobile dealer_____

2. Expensive restaurant_____

3. Hotel_____

4. Clothing store_____

5. University_____

INVOLVEMENT

Involvement refers to "... the personal, social, and economic significance of the purchase to the consumer."

Discuss the difference, in terms of personal, social, and economic significance, the amount of involvement in buying gas for your car, purchasing a T-shirt, and selecting a college to attend.

SITUATIONAL INFLUENCES: MOTIVATION

Motivation is the energizing force that causes the behavior that satisfies a need. There are five need classes:

physiological
safety
social
personal
self-actualization

Which needs do the following products meet?

1. LA Gear apparel_____

2. Dr. Pepper_____

3. First Alert smoke detectors_____

4. milk_____

5. Ph.D._____

PERCEPTION

There are three types of selective perception:

Selective exposure
Selective comprehension
Selective retention

Match the type of selective perception with the statements below:

_____1. Consumers do not remember all the information they see, read, or hear.

_____2. Consumers pay attention to messages that are consistent with their attitudes and beliefs and ignore messages that are inconsistent.

_____3. The ad said something about a warranty, but I'm not sure if they said they had one or didn't have one.

_____4. The consumer interprets information so it is consistent with her attitudes or beliefs.

_____5. People thought Toro's SnowPup was a toy or too lightweight to do snow blowing even though it could do the job.

_____6. I'm glad I bought my home through this realty company; I see their signs everywhere.

LEARNING

Learning refers to those behaviors that result from repeated experience and thinking. Five variables are linked to learning:

Drive
Response
Reinforcement
Stimulus generalization
Stimulus discrimination

Match the learning variable to the correct statement:

_____ A person fires up the grill and throws on a steak.

_____ A person is hungry.

_____ A person slices into a thick, juicy, rare steak, eats it, and smiles.

_____ Weight Watchers, in addition to having a well-known weight loss program, also distributes a line of frozen foods, desserts, and cookbooks.

_____ Trident gum used an advertising slogan, "... the ONLY gum my mom lets me chew."

VALUES, BELIEFS, AND ATTITUDES

An attitude is a "learned" predisposition to respond to an object or class of objects in a consistently favorable or unfavorable way. Beliefs are a consumer's subjective perception of how well a product or brand performs on different attributes. Personal values affect attitudes by influencing the importance assigned to specific product attributes.

Match the correct term to the statements listed below:

_____1. My mother always said Hellmann's was the smoothest mayonnaise.

_____2. Reliability, not style, is the most important function of a good watch.

_____3. All female doctors are more caring.

LIFESTYLE

VALS 2 System has identified eight interconnected categories of adult lifestyles based on a person's self-orientation and resources. Three patterns have been uncovered. Consumer patterns are oriented towards principles, status, and action. They are categorized as:

Principle-oriented consumers
Status-oriented consumers
Action-oriented consumers

Describe the consumer category at which each of the following products directs its appeal:

1. Quaker Oats_____

2. Rolex watches_____

3. Mountain Dew_____

4. BMW_____

5. Volvo_____

6. Nike_____

7. Bayer Aspirin_____

SOCIOCULTURAL INFLUENCES ON CONSUMER BEHAVIOR

The effects of sociocultural influences are examined in terms of personal influence, reference groups, the family, social class, and culture and subculture.

PERSONAL INFLUENCE

Two aspects of personal influence are important to marketing:

Opinion leadership
Word-of-mouth activity

Match the type of personal influence to the correct statement below:

_____ This type of influence is more likely to be important for products that provide a form of self-expression.

_____ Celebrities and sports figures are often used as spokespeople.

_____ This is perhaps the most powerful information source for consumers.

_____ This is a form of one-way directed influence.

_____ This form of influence often uses "teaser" advertising and toll-free numbers are sometimes used.

REFERENCE GROUPS

Reference groups are people to whom an individual looks as a basis for self-appraisal or as a source of personal standards. There are three important reference groups with marketing implications:

Membership group
Aspiration group
Dissociative group

Discuss which reference group relates to each of these examples.

1. A junior high school student buying an Atlanta Braves cap and shirt._____

2. A person wearing his Phi Beta Kappa key._____

3. An environmentalist not buying Exxon products._____

FAMILY INFLUENCE

Discuss the stage of the family life cycle for yourself, your parents, and your grandparents. When you graduate, how will this change your stage and the stage of your parents within the cycle?_____

_____

Five roles exist in the family decision-making process: Information gatherer, influencer, decision maker, purchaser, and user.

The Nelson family has decided to take a vacation this year. Mrs. Nelson looks in National Geographic Traveler and sends in the reply card for brochures from all 50 states. Mr. Nelson and son, John, want to see a baseball game, while daughter, Kimberly, wants to go to the beach. Mrs. Nelson rules out any destination north of Dallas that isn't on a coastline. After comparing prices, Mr. Nelson makes reservations for San Diego on the Internet and calls a friend in California to secure good seats at a Padres game. Which roles did each family member play? (Multiple roles expected)_____

_____

_____

SOCIAL CLASS, CULTURE AND SUBCULTURE

Cigarette companies got into trouble several years ago by testing cigarettes targeted toward poor rural white women and another brand targeted at inner city blacks. At the same time Benson and Hedges had the reputation of being a fine upscale cigarette. People sharing similar values, interests, and behavior can be grouped. Malt liquor has long been targeted toward the lower class and inner city residents, while the new "micro-brewery" beers target upper income urban residents. Pick a consumer product category and discuss which brands target which of the classes and cultures.

CAN YOU PASS THE TEST?
Sample Multiple Choice Questions

1. Kevin has just been overheard saying, "I'm tired of wearing my old clothes. I need something more up to date." In which stage of the purchase decision process is Kevin?
        a. problem recognition.
        b. information search.
        c. alternative evaluation.
        e. purchase decision.
        e. postpurchase behavior.

2. Assume Nike has developed a new cushioning substance for use in the sole portions of athletic shoes. The new substance not only absorbs shocks better, it rebounds more completely, thereby improving the wearer's speed and jumping ability. Nike believes this new characteristic—promoted as *reflex response*—will make the new shoe a superior product. Due to increased costs of materials and production, the price will be about $150. Based on responses of people who have tried the new product, Nike is confident consumers will have a relatively favorable evaluation of the shoe. To have a favorable evaluation consumers must first:
        a. experience problem recognition.
        b. consult a public source of information.
        c. consult a personal source of information.
        d. make a purchase decision.
        e. experience cognitive dissonance.

3. Kevin is experiencing a bad case of hay fever. He wants to buy some tissues. but before he does, he calls his mother and asks, "What kind of tissues did you buy for me in the past?" In which stage of the purchase decision process is Kevin?
        a. problem recognition.
        b. information search.
        c. alternative evaluation.
        d. purchase decision.
        e. postpurchase behavior.

4. Eddie, an avid football fan, is glued to the television every Sunday afternoon as he watches his favorite teams. He thinks games would be more enjoyable on a big screen television. Eddie has begun talking with friends to learn more about the various brands of big screen televisions available. In which step of the purchase decision making process is Eddie engaged?
        a. problem recognition.
        b. evaluation of alternatives.
        c. purchase decision.
        d. information search.
        e. post purchase evaluation.

5. Emily wants to purchase a new computer. She is unsure about what hardware and software she will need. As a result, she has begun asking for advice from friends and relatives. In addition, she has talked to several computer salespeople and has looked at some websites. Emily is engaging in:
        a. problem recognition.
        b. an internal search.
        c. an external search.
        d. a purchase task.
        e. the creation of an antecedent state.

6. Kevin has just been overheard saying, "I know I want to buy some tissues, but there are so many choices. Do I choose the designer box or the convenience pack? Should I buy scented or unscented?" Should I buy the kind with lotion in them?" In which stage of the purchase decision process is Kevin?
    a. problem recognition.
    b. information search.
    c. alternative evaluation.
    d. purchase decision.
    e. postpurchase behavior.

7. When Judy decided to buy an electric can opener as a wedding present, she wanted to buy a brand name opener that attached under a cabinet and that had sleek styling. These are _____ used during the alternative evaluation stage of the purchase decision process.
    a. hot buttons
    b. informational alternatives
    c. evaluative criteria
    d. buying decision-makers
    e. consumer attributes

8. When Kevin took the unscented, convenience pack of tissues to the counter and announced, "I'd like to buy these, please," he was in which stage of the purchase decision process?
    a. problem recognition
    b. information search
    c. alternative evaluation
    d. purchase decision
    e. postpurchase behavior

9. Kevin has just been overheard saying, "I'm glad I bought a sweatshirt with the university logo. The football team is doing well, and it'll look good at basketball games too." In which stage of the purchase decision process is Kevin?
    a. problem recognition
    b. information search
    c. alternative evaluation
    d. purchase decision
    e. postpurchase behavior

10. Customer satisfaction is an important focus for marketers because:
    a. marketing research is an inexpensive process.
    b. the financial value of a retained customer can be significant.
    c. customer value is a non-quantifiable statistic.
    d. attracting new customers is easier than keeping old ones.
    e. a market development strategy is preferable to a market penetration strategy.

11. _____ is the feeling of postpurchase psychological tension or anxiety.
    a. Cognitive dissonance
    b. Seller remorse
    c. A negative antecedent state
    d. Subliminal anxiety
    e. Perceived risk

12. A consumer's _____ refers to the personal, social, and economic significance of the purchase to the consumer.
> a. involvement
> b. aspiration
> c. acculturative response
> d. motivation
> e. selective perception

13. Which problem solving variation would likely be used for real estate, automobiles, or personal computers?
> a. routine response behavior
> b. limited problem solving
> c. extended problem solving
> d. simulated selection
> e. integrated problem solving

14. Which situational influence is impacting your purchase decision when you decide to not purchase your marketing text today because the bookstore lines are so long?
> a. temporal effects
> b. antecedent states
> c. purchase task
> d. social surroundings
> e. physical surroundings

15. As she hunted for tomato juice, Sally thought, "Nothing in this store is logically arranged." Then she ran her cart into the side of a display because the aisle was so crowded. As a result of _____, she has vowed never to shop at that store again.
> a. purchase task
> b. social surroundings
> c. physical surroundings
> d. temporal effects
> e. spatial surroundings

16. Marlowe's mother sent her to the department store with instructions to buy her the very best set of four steak knives she could find for $20. Marlowe knows that it will be difficult to please her mother. Which situational influence would most likely be affecting her purchase decision?
> a. temporal effects
> b. antecedent states
> c. purchase task
> d. social surroundings
> e. physical surroundings

17. When Bart went to pay for the table he'd spotted at a secondhand store, he was surprised to learn the store did not accept credit cards; he did not have enough cash to make the purchase. Which situational influence would most likely be affecting his purchase decision?
> a. temporal effects
> b. antecedent states
> c. purchase task
> d. social surroundings
> e. physical surroundings

18. Because of traffic problems, Robin got to the store just minutes before it closed and had to select a gift for her son quickly. Which situational influence would most likely be affecting her purchase decision?
>   a. temporal effects
>   b. antecedent states
>   c. purchase task
>   d. social surroundings
>   e. physical surroundings

19. Katherine was glad that Megan and Nikki were with her when she went to buy curtains. They advised her which would look best in her new apartment and helped her choose the length and style. Which situational influence would most likely be affecting Katherine's purchase decisions?
>   a. temporal effects
>   b. antecedent states
>   c. purchase task
>   d. social surroundings
>   e. physical surroundings

20. According to the hierarchy of needs, which type of needs must be satisfied first?
>   a. self-actualization needs
>   b. psychological needs
>   c. physiological needs
>   d. personal needs
>   e. social needs

21. The slogan for Allstate Insurance is "You're in good hands with Allstate." This slogan is designed to appeal to consumers' _____ needs.
>   a. social
>   b. safety
>   c. physiological
>   d. self-actualization
>   e. personal

22. The slogan for Hallmark cards is "When you care enough to send the very best."
This slogan is designed to appeal to consumers' _____ needs.
>   a. social
>   b. safety
>   c. physiological
>   d. self-actualization
>   e. personal

23. The slogan for Olive Garden restaurants is "When you're here, you're family." This slogan is designed to appeal to consumers' _____ needs.
>   a. psychological
>   b. safety
>   c. physiological
>   d. self-actualization
>   e. personal

24. Which of the following statements about subliminal messages is true?
>   a. The use of subliminal messages is an ethical tactic.
>   b. The use of subliminal messages is illegal in the United States.
>   c. There is a vast amount of scientific research that proves the effectiveness of subliminal messages.
>   d. Amost 2/3 of U.S. consumers think subliminal messages are present in commercials.
>   e. None of the above statements about subliminal messages is true.

25. In the hierarchy of needs water, food, and sex would be considered _____ needs.
   a. physiological
   b. safety
   c. social
   d. personal
   e. psychological

26. An ad for The King's Daughters' School, a private academy for children has the headline, "Living Up to Their Potential." This ad is appealing to the parents' desire to satisfy their children's:
   a. physiological needs.
   b. safety needs.
   c. social needs.
   d. personal needs.
   e. self actualization needs.

27. An ad for Dove body wash asks the question, "How old will you be when you stop feeling 29?" The ad is using the _____ to appeal to its target market.
   a. self-concept
   b. greed
   c. lust
   d. avarice
   e. hedonism

28. _____ refers to a consumer's ability to tell the difference among Coca-Cola, Pepsi Cola, Royal Crown cola, and Sam's cola.
   a. Stimulus discrimination
   b. Responsive differentiation
   c. Source distinction
   d. Cognitive differentiation
   e. Selective differentiation

29. The tendency to pay attention to messages consistent with one's attitudes and beliefs and to ignore messages that are inconsistent is called:
   a. selective retention.
   b. selective comprehension.
   c. selective exposure.
   d. selective perception.
   e. stimulus discrimination.

30. The process of seeing or hearing messages without being aware of them is called:
   a. selective retention.
   b. subliminal perception.
   c. selective perception.
   d. selective attention.
   e. indifference.

31. Companies develop strategies to reduce perceived risk. Which types of perceived risk is Black & Decker trying to reduce when it places the Underwriter's Laboratory seal on its circular saws?
   a. financial outlay and psychosocial
   b. psychosocial and physical harm
   c. physical harm and financial outlay
   d. product performance and physical harm
   e. psychosocial and product performance

32. Companies develop strategies to reduce perceived risk. Which types of perceived risk did Clairol try to reduce when it sent prospective customers samples of its shampoo Herbal Essences?
   a. physical harm, psychosocial, and product performance
   b. psychosocial, financial outlay, and customer performance
   c. product performance and psychosocial
   d. customer performance, psychosocial, and physical harm
   e. financial outlay and customer performance

33. The ad for Redwood Springs Academy reads, "Redwood Springs offers scholarships to all qualified students, and a tuition-refund guarantee if you are not completely satisfied." What type of perceived risk was this ad most likely trying to reduce in parents who send their children to the academy?
   a. customer preference
   b. physical harm
   c. psychographic
   d. financial outlay
   e. none of the above

34. A component supplier needs a fast way to send an urgently needed part to a manufacturer in Illinois. If the part does not reach the manufacturer, the supplier stands to lose thousands of dollars in business. The Emery Air Freight slogan, "It's as good as there!" should reduce which type of perceived risk for the supplier?
   a. customer preference
   b. antecedent
   c. psychosocial
   d. product performance
   e. none of the above

35. _____ learning is the process of developing an automatic response to a situation built up through repeated exposure to the situation.
   a. Perceptual
   b. Retentive
   c. Functional
   d. Motivated
   e. Behavioral

36. Joan is hungry (drive); she sees an advertisement (cue); goes to the store and buys the product (response); in terms of behavioral learning the great taste of the food is a(n):
   a. achievement
   b. drive.
   c. reinforcement.
   d. prestige.
   e. preference.

37. In the first chapter of this text, the authors describe how marketing is not something alien to you like Shakespeare or physics—it is something you are already very familiar with because you observe marketing throughout many different facets of life. The authors hoped you would use _____ to conclude marketing is an interesting subject and worthy of your time and effort.
   a. cognitive learning
   b. cognitive dissonance
   c. behavioral learning
   d. functional adaptation
   e. selective learning

38. A(n) _____ is a learned predisposition to respond to an object or class of objects in a consistently favorable or unfavorable way.
        a. belief
        b. value
        c. attitude
        d. motivation
        e. perception

39. A _____ is a mode of living that is identified by how people spend their time and resources; what they consider important in their environment; and what they think of themselves and the world around them.
        a. culture
        b. subculture
        c. social class
        d. lifestyle
        e. reference group

40. Consumers who are motivated by _____ look for products and services that demonstrate success to their peers.
        a. ideals
        b. achievement
        c. self-expression
        d. rewards
        e. success

41. Sociocultural influences on consumer behavior include:
        a. the temporal effect and physical surroundings.
        b. motivation and personality.
        c. values, beliefs, and attitudes.
        d. antecedent states and social surroundings.
        e. social class, subculture, and culture

42. Individuals who exert direct or indirect social influence over others are called:
        a. decision makers.
        b. achievers.
        c. brand loyal consumers.
        d. a reference group.
        e. opinion leaders.

43. _____ affect consumer purchases because they influence the information, attitudes and aspiration levels that help set a consumer's standards.
        a. Reference groups.
        b. Economic classes.
        c. Inspirational groups.
        d. Associative groups.
        e. Acculturated groups.

44. A reference group to which a person actually belongs is called a(n) _____ group.
        a. primary reference
        b. membership
        c. aspiration
        d. disassociative
        e. integrated

45. Frank Wright believes having the right sound system is important because many people will see and hear it when they visit his home. If you were the marketing VP for Quality Electronics and your market was made up of people just like Wright, which influence source would you most likely build into your promotional messages?
     a. situational influences
     b. perceptual risk influences
     c. self-concept influences
     d. reference group influences
     e. cognitive dissonance influences

46. Which of the following statements about the family life cycle is true?
     a. The family life cycle concept describes a continuum along which developing families can be arbitrarily placed.
     b. Young singles represent a target market for recreational travel, automobiles, and consumer electronics.
     c. The majority of households today are composed of traditional families.
     d. Young singles are more likely to buy life insurance than any other group.
     e. The most financially secure of any of the family groups is singles with children.

47. Which of the following is NOT one of the roles typically played by a family member during the purchase process?
     a. influencer
     b. gatekeeper
     c. user
     d. decision maker
     e. information gatherer

48. The Lee family is composed of five children, a mother, a father, and one set of grandparents. The family has to decide whether to move the grandparents to an assisted living facility. In terms of the roles played by individual family members, the grandparents are the only family members who will have the role of:
     a. user.
     b. influencer.
     c. gatekeeper.
     d. decision maker.
     e. information gatherer.

49. Which of the following statements about African-American buying patterns is true?
     a. African-Americans spend far more on boy's clothing, rental goods and audio equipment.
     b. Differences in buying patterns are greater within the African-American subculture than between African-Americans and whites of similar status.
     c. While African-Americans are price conscious, they are strongly motivated by quality and choice.
     d. Adult African-Americans spend twice as much on online services.
     e. All of the above statements about African-American buying patterns are true.

50. Which of the following statements about Hispanic buying patterns is true?
     a. Hispanic buying preferences are strongly influenced by family and peers.
     b. Hispanics are quality and brand conscious.
     c. Convenience is not an important product attribute to Hispanic homemakers with respect to food preparation or consumption.
     e. Hispanics prefer to buy American-made products.
     e. All of the above statements correctly describe Hispanic buying patterns.

ANSWER KEY

Answers to Questions & Problems

Problem Recognition

Example:
1. Gasoline—gas gauge in car or the car sputtering and rolling to a stop

Information Search

Example:
1. New Orleans—internal—memory, experience; external—brochures, travel agents, friends

Alternative Selection

Example:
1. Coffee—criteria—strong and dark
        —brands—Starbucks, Gevalia
        —where and when to buy—now, Starbucks
        —evaluation—outstanding
        —cognitive dissonance—add value by including frequent buyer incentives

Post Purchase Behavior

Example:
1. Automobile dealer—follow-up; good service; communication

Motivation

1. Personal
2. Social
3. Safety
4. Physiological
5. Self-actualization

Perception

1. Selective retention
2. Selective exposure
3. Selective retention
4. Selective comprehension
5. Selective comprehension
6. Selective exposure

Learning

1. Response
2. Drive
3. Reinforcement
4. Stimulus generalization
5. Stimulus discrimination

Values, Beliefs, and Attitudes

1. Belief
2. Value
3. Attitude

Lifestyle

1. Principle-oriented consumers
2. Status-oriented consumers
3. Action-oriented consumers
4. Status-oriented consumers
5. Principle-oriented consumers
6. Action-oriented consumers
7. Principle-oriented consumers

Personal Influence

1. Opinion leadership
2. Opinion leadership
3. Word-of-mouth
4. Word-of-mouth
5. Word-of-mouth

Reference Groups

1. Aspiration group
2. Membership group
3. Disassociative group

Family Influence

Mrs. Nelson—information gather; influencer
Mr. Nelson—purchaser; influencer; decision maker
John—influencer
Kimberly—influencer

All are users

Answers to Sample Multiple Choice Questions

1. a p. 120 LO1	14. e p. 125 LO 2	26. e p. 127 LO 3	38. c p. 131 LO 3
2. a p. 120 LO 1	15. c p. 125 LO 2	27. a p. 127 LO 3	39. d p. 132 LO 3
3. b p. 120 LO 1	16. c p. 125 LO 2	28. a p. 130 LO 3	40. b p. 133 LO 3
4. d p. 120 LO 1	17. b p. 125 LO 2	29. c p. 128 LO 3	41. e p. 134 LO 4
5. c p. 120 LO 1	18. a p. 125 LO 2	30. b p. 129 LO 3	42. e p. 134 LO 4
6. c p. 121 LO 1	19. d p. 125 LO 2	31. d p. 130 LO 3	43. a p. 136 LO 4
7. c p. 121 LO 1	20. c p. 126-127 LO 3	32. a p. 130 LO 3	44. b p. 136 LO 4
8. d p. 122 LO 1	21. b p. 127 LO 3	33. d p. 129 LO 3	45. d p. 136 LO 4
9. e p. 122 LO 1	22. e p. 127 LO 3	34. d p. 129 LO 3	46. b p. 136 LO 4
10. b p. 122 LO 1	23. a p. 127 LO 3	35. e p. 130 LO 3	47. b p. 137 LO 4
11. a p. 123 LO 1	24. d p. 128 LO 3	36. c p. 130 LO 3	48. a p. 137 LO 4
12. a p. 124 LO 2	25. a p. 126-127 LO 3	37. a p. 130 LO 3	49. e p. 139 LO 4
13. c p. 124 LO 2			50. e p. 140 LO 4

Note: LO indicates learning objective.

CHAPTER 6

ORGANIZATIONAL MARKETS AND BUYER BEHAVIOR

<u>Why is Chapter 6 important?</u> Just like the consumer market, the business-to-business market has a buying process that marketers must know and utilize. This chapter illustrates how that process works and the differences between it and the consumer buying process. It shows who the participates are and what influences their behavior.

Business Marketing: The marketing of goods and services to commercial enterprises, governments, and other profit and not-for-profit organizations for use in the creation of goods and services that they then produce and market to other business customers, as well as individuals and ultimate consumers.

CHAPTER OUTLINE

I. NATURE AND SIZE OF ORGANIZATIONAL MARKETS

    A. Industrial Markets
        1. Manufacturers
        2. Mining
        3. Construction
        4. Farms, forestry and fisheries
        5. Services

    B. Reseller Markets
        1. Wholesalers
        2. Retailers

    C. Government and Government Agency Markets
        1. Federal
        2. State
        3. Local

    D.   Global Organizational Markets

II. MEASURING DOMESTIC AND GLOBAL INDUSTRIAL, RESELLER, AND GOVERNMENT MARKETS

    A. North American Industry Classification System (NAICS)

III. CHARACTERISTICS OF ORGANIZATION BUYING

    A. Demand Characteristics

    B. Size of Order or Purchase

C. Number of Potential Buyers

D. Organizational Buying Objections

E. Organizational Buying Criteria
    1. Price
    2. Ability to meet quality specifications
    3. Ability to meet required delivery schedules
    4. Technical capability
    5. Warranties and claim policies
    6. Past performances on previous contracts
    7. Production facilities and capacity

F. Buyer-Seller Relationship and Supply Partnership
    1. Complex and lengthy negotiations
    2. Reciprocity
    3. Long-term relationships
    4. Supply partnerships

G. The Buying Center: A Cross-Functional Group
    1. People in the Buying Center
    2. Roles in the Buying Center
        a. Users
        b. Influences
        c. Buyers
        d. Deciders
        e. Gatekeepers
    3. Buying Situations in the Buying Center
        a. Straight rebuy
        b. Modified rebuy
        c. New buy

IV. CHARTING THE ORGANIZATIONAL BUYING PROCESS

A. Stages in an Organizational Buyers Decision
    1. Problem recognition
    2. Information search
    3. Alternative evaluation
    4. Purchase decision
    5. Postpurchase behavior

V. ONLINE BUYING IN ORGANIZATIONAL MARKETS

A. Prominence of Online Buying in Organizational Markets
B. E-Marketplaces: Virtual Organizational Markets
C. Online Auctions in Organizational Markets
    1. Traditional auctions
    2. Reverse auctions

You should be able to place these key terms in the outline and be able to discuss them.

bidder's list	industrial firms	reciprocity
business marketing	ISO 9000	resellers
buy classes	make-buy decision	reverse auction
buying center	NAICS	reverse marketing
derived demand	organizational buyers	supply partnership
e-marketplaces	organizational buying behavior	traditional auction
government units	organizational buying criteria	value analysis

QUESTIONS & PROBLEMS

ORGANIZATIONAL BUYERS

Industrial markets
Reseller markets
Government markets
Global markets

Match the correct organizational buyer market with the statements below:

_____1. Wholesalers and retailers who buy physical products and resell them again without any reprocessing.

_____2. Federal, state, and local agencies that buy goods and services for the constituents they serve.

_____3. They in some way reprocess a product or service they buy before selling it again to the next buyer.

_____4. Montgomery Ward purchases food dehydrators from Alternative Pioneer Systems.

_____5. The Illinois Department of Commerce places an order with Scott for over 100,000 rolls of toilet tissue.

_____6. A large metropolitan firm hires Arthur Young to do its accounting.

_____7. Dell Computer buys memory chips from Intel which are made in Asia, assembles computers in Texas and Tennessee, then sells them in Europe.

DERIVED DEMAND CHARACTERISTICS

Explain how derived demand is a factor for the following and what product(s) from which the demand could be derived:

Intel's Pentium Chip_____

Hot dogs_____

Liquid Paper Correcting Fluid_____

Windows 95_____

Refrigerators, Stoves, and Dishwashers_____

CHARACTERISTICS OF ORGANIZATIONAL BUYING BEHAVIOR - BUYING CRITERIA

There are seven important buying criteria most organizations use. The criteria may change from situation to situation even with the same product.

Rank the following purchase criteria for Personal Computers for the three different buying situations listed below. Be able to explain your rationale:

<u>College student</u>	<u>**Rank**</u>
Price	_____
Quality	_____
Delivery	_____
Technical capability	_____
Warranties	_____
Past performance	_____
Production facilities and capacity	_____

<u>Small Business (under 10 employees)</u>	<u>**Rank**</u>
Price	_____
Quality	_____
Delivery	_____
Technical capability	_____
Warranties	_____
Past performance	_____
Production facilities and capacity	_____

<u>General Motors</u>	<u>**Rank**</u>
Price	_____
Quality	_____
Delivery	_____
Technical capability	_____
Warranties	_____
Past performance	_____
Production facilities and capacity	_____

ROLES IN THE BUYING CENTER

John Wilson, a salesman for the Greater Copier Company, has just finished a successful sales call on Acme Structural Corporation. He had tried to make an appointment with the company president, Bob Miller, but was put off by Ms. Browne, his executive assistant. When he tried to leave material, Ms. Browne said she would look at it and forward it on to the appropriate people. After several weeks of hearing nothing and still unable to see Mr. Miller, he called on the office manager, Tom Watson. Mr. Watson said they were dissatisfied with their present copier and were in the market for a new one. As he left his brochures with Mr. Watson, he was surprised to see Rebecca Nelson, an old customer form Giant Steel, Inc. walk in. "I am now the purchasing manager for Acme," she said. "I will put in a good word for you because you gave us the best product with the best service we ever had." Later that day, Ms. Browne called and said Mr. Miller wanted a full presentation. At the end of the presentation, Mr. Miller signed a contract for a new high-speed copier and Ms. Nelson issued a purchase order. What roles did each of the people above play in the buying process?

STAGES IN AN ORGANIZATIONAL BUYING DECISION

There are five stages in an organizational buying decision:

Problem recognition
Information search
Alternative evaluation
Purchase decision
Postpurchase behavior

Use common sense and your text to answer the following questions:

1. What situations are likely to make an organization recognize a problem?_____

2. What sources might an organization use to seek out information?_____

3. What forms of alternative evaluation do organizational buyers use?_____

4. What are likely differences between the purchase decision of an ultimate consumer and an organizational buyer?_____

5. What are likely differences between the postpurchase behavior of an ultimate consumer and an organizational buyer?_____

BUY CLASSES

There are three buy classes:

Straight rebuy
Modified rebuy
New buy

Match the correct buy classes with the statements below:

_____ 1. The buyer or purchasing manager reorders a replacement ball bearing from the organization's list of ten acceptable suppliers on the bidders list.

_____ 2. Montgomery Wards is considering a line of food dehydrators and is approached by Alternative Pioneering Systems. Wards has not carried this type of product before.

_____ 3. Engineering has come up with a new design for the motor's cooling system that can save $20 per unit in assembly costs. I wonder if our current supplier can meet the tolerances for the new design.

E-MARKETPLACE

Metalsite.com is a web site that brings together buyers, sellers, and other industry users of basic metals. Visit the site and then suggest other industries or organizational products that could benefit from a site with similar characteristics.

CAN YOU PASS THE TEST?
Sample Multiple Choice Questions

1. _____ is the marketing of goods and services to companies, governments, or not-for-profit organizations for use in the creation of goods and services that they can produce and market to others.
   a. A relational enterprise
   b. Institutional marketing
   c. Business marketing
   d. Reseller marketing
   e. Agricultural marketing

2. Organizational buyers are divided into three different markets. They are _____ markets.
   a. wholesaler, retailer, and distributor
   b. agricultural, industrial, and service
   c. service, manufacturing, and reseller
   d. government, institutional, and reseller
   e. industrial, reseller, and government

3. The purchase of the fruits to go into Welch's Country Pear and Welch's Wild Raspberry flavored fruit drinks would take place in the _____ market.
   a. institutional
   b. governmental
   c. industrial
   d. retailer
   e. consumer

4. An industrial firm is a firm that:
   a. is distinguished by the amount of energy it uses and potential for pollution to the environment.
   b. employs more than 500 people, who are paid minimum wage with few or no benefits.
   c deals exclusively with federal, state, and local governments, and often mediates governmental agency disputes.
   d. in some way reprocesses a good or service it buys before selling the product again to the next buyer.
   e. is most likely to be located in the eastern U.S., and operates out of what is called a factory.

5. A manufacturer of consumer food products for the Chinese market in the U.S. buys several tons of camellia nuts annually. It converts those nuts into a cooking oil that is popular among the Chinese population because it has a milder taste than olive oil and a higher burning point. The oil is sold to supermarkets. The pulp from which the oil is extracted is sold to beef cattle farmers who use it to fatten their cattle. These transactions occur in the _____ market.
   a. reseller
   b. government
   c. institutional
   d. psychographic
   e. industrial

6. When Welch Foods sells Welch's Country Pear and Welch's Wild Raspberry flavored fruit drinks to supermarkets, the transactions occur in the _____ market.
        a. reseller
        b. agricultural
        c. institutional
        d. industrial
        e. manufacturing

7. Which of the following is the BEST example of a reseller?
        a. Kansas State University
        b. JCPenney
        c. FedEx
        d. a tax accountant
        e. WABC, a television station

8. _____ are federal, state, and local agencies that buy goods and services for the constituents they serve.
        a. Industrial markets
        b. Reseller markets
        c. Cooperative markets
        d. Government units
        e. Facilitating agents

9. The letters NAICS is an acronym for:
        a. National Association of Internet Communities and Societies.
        b. National Association for Innovative Customer Service.
        c. North American Industry Classification System.
        d. North American Institute for Customer Service.
        e. National Agency for the Integrating of Collaborative System.

10. A disadvantage of the North American Industry Classification System (NAICS) systems is that:
        a. it only lists the top ten firms in any particular industry.
        b. it is too difficult and confusing to read.
        c. it assigns one code to each organization based on its major economic activity, so large firms that engage in many different activities are given only one code.
        d. it only covers organizations with sales in excess of (US) $1 million.
        e. it makes it possible to find how the firm's customers are coded.

11. Which of the following statements describes a characteristic of organizational buying behavior?
        a. In organizational buying, demand for industrial products and services is derived.
        b. The size of the order in organizational buying is typically large.
        c. The number of potential buyers engaged in organizational buying is small.
        d. Direct selling is commonplace in organizational buying.
        e. All of the above statements describe a characteristic of organizational buying behavior.

12. The demand for industrial products and services that is driven by demand for consumer products and services is called:
        a. Gross National Product.
        b. derived demand.
        c. the Consumer Price Index.
        d. break-even demand.
        e. high-risk demand.

13. Silicate particulate is used to clean up caustic acid spills in industrial settings. Its demand is dependent upon how many spills occur and how large the spills are. The demand for silicate particulates is:
     a. contiguous.
     b. pooled.
     c. conjoint.
     d. congruent.
     e. derived.

14. Andersen Windows is the manufacturer of high-quality, energy-efficient windows for homes and offices. The number of windows sold is directly linked to the number of new homes being built. When the economy is strong and many homes are being built, Andersen sells lots of windows; when few homes are being built, few windows are sold. This is an example of:
     a. derived demand.
     b. the price-quality relationship.
     c. the acceleration principle.
     d. price-elasticity.
     e. price-inelasticity.

15. When compared to consumer marketing, industrial marketing is simpler because:
     a. firms have buying centers.
     b. it is easy to forecast derived demand.
     c the buying objectives of industrial buyers are easily identifiable.
     d. industrial orders are smaller.
     e. industrial products involve fewer services and types of customer assistance.

16. An Illinois-based company that runs its trucks on a mixture of petroleum and ethanol buys its ethanol from Archer Daniel Midland (ADM) Company because it is the only large supplier of ethanol that has an ethanol manufacturing facility in Illinois and is able to meet the trucking company's delivery schedules. The selection of ADM to provide the ethanol was based on a(n):
     a. supplier value dimension.
     b. derived demand factor.
     c. evaluative criterion.
     d. performance measure.
     e. organizational buying criterion.

17. Many industrial buyers for manufacturing firms place great importance on delivery time because they often rely on a just-in-time inventory system. This system has increased the importance of which organizational buying criterion?
     a. low prices
     b. high quality
     c. on-time delivery
     d. customer service and follow-up
     e. cheap labor

18. Which of the following is an example of an evaluative criterion used in organizational buying?
     a. price
     b. warranties and claim policies
     c. technical capability
     d. ability to meet required delivery schedule
     e. all of the above

19. Which of the following statements about ISO 9000 certification is true?
    a. The ISO 9000 certification process was developed in the United States.
    b. ISO 9000 certification is the manufacturing equivalent of the Academy Award.
    c. Only U.S. companies recognize the significance of ISO 9000 certification.
    d. ISO 9000 certifies that a company operates at a specified level of quality management.
    e. None of the above correctly describes ISO 9000 certification.

20. _____ involves the deliberate effort by organizational buyers to build relationships that shape suppliers' products, services, and capabilities to fit the buyer's needs and those of its customers.
    a. Reverse marketing
    b. Demarketing
    c. Benchmarking
    d. Leapfrogging
    e. Reciprocity

21. The Danish Carsten Maersk is an ocean-going container ship that is longer and only a bit narrower than three football fields laid out end zone to end zone. If you were to set the ship's load of containers end to end, they would stretch 27 miles. To handle this ship and her sister ships, Los Angeles is building Maersk a completely new facility at a cost that could top $800 million. The terminal is rising in the middle of the harbor on dredged material and ten million tons of rock that will form a 685-acre island connected to the rest of California by rail line and highway. When the initial phase opened in 2002, Maersk, which has an exclusive 25-year lease, had room to dock three of these huge ships. Every city on the West Coast wanted to be selected by Maersk as a terminal city, but only the Port Authority of Los Angeles was able to build the relationships needed to convince Maersk it could handle the load. This is an example of:
    a. demarketing.
    b. inverse marketing.
    c. reverse marketing.
    d. inside-out marketing.
    e. upside-down marketing.

22. The U.S. Justice Department frowns on the practice of _____ because it restricts the normal operation of the free market.
    a. quantity discounting
    b. granting trade allowances
    c. reciprocity
    d. derived demand
    e. benchmarking

23. _____ is an industrial practice in which two organizations agree to purchase products and services from each other.
    a. Reverse marketing
    b. Demarketing
    c. Benchmarking
    d. Leapfrogging
    e. Reciprocity

24. Which of the following does NOT characterize organizational buyer-seller relationships?
    a. Purchases are often made after lengthy negotiations.
    b. Purchases are usually of large dollar values.
    c. Long-term relationships are often prevalent.
    d. Reciprocal arrangements can exist.
    e. Delivery schedules are largely irrelevant.

25. Which of the following statements about reciprocity is true?
    a. Reciprocity exists in certain types of counter-trade arrangements in international marketing.
    b. Reciprocity can restrict the normal operation of the free market.
    c. Reciprocity is occasionally addressed in a company's code of ethics.
    d. Views regarding reciprocal arrangements often vary across cultures.
    e. All of the above statements about reciprocity are true.

26. Which of the following statements accurately describes the people in the buying center of a medium-sized manufacturing plant?
    a. The composition of the buying center never changes.
    b. The buying center never contains cross-functional teams.
    c. The organizational buyer or purchasing agent is seldom a member of the buying center.
    d. The composition of the buying center depends on the specific item being purchased.
    e. None of the above statements accurately describes the people in the buying center of a medium-sized manufacturing plant.

27. The chief financial officer at the hospital is studying a request for a new piece of laser surgery equipment that will allow surgeons to perform less intrusive surgery and dramatically reduce postoperative problems. In terms of the buying center, the surgeons would be described as _____ even though they are not knowledgeable about engineering specifications of the laser equipment.
    a. gatekeepers
    b. owners
    c. influencers
    d. buyers
    e. deciders

28. The chief financial officer's secretary finds the salesperson for one particular company to be rude and pushy. As a result, she does not tell the salesperson about the potential sale. In terms of the buying center, the secretary is acting in the role of:
    a. gatekeeper.
    b. decider.
    c. buyer.
    d. influencer.
    e. user.

29. The chief financial officer has the formal authority and responsibility to select the supplier of laser surgery equipment and negotiate the terms of the contract. In terms of the buying center, his/her role is:
    a. gatekeeper.
    b. decider.
    c. buyer.
    d. influencer.
    e. user.

30. The publisher of the *Redwood Falls Gazette*, a weekly newspaper, decided the production department would be more efficient if a new computerized advertising layout system was purchased. In an effort to ensure a high quality, functional system was purchased, the publisher asked the newspaper's production manager for advice on specific features, components, and capabilities of the system. The production manager played the role of _____ in the newspaper's buying center.
     a. user
     b. gatekeeper
     c. influencer
     d. buyer
     e. decider

31. A talent promoter for the House of Blues wants to book one of the acts it represents into the Odeon Theater. The talent promoter offers to buy lunch for the receptionist of the manager of the Odeon. The talent promoter is probably trying to develop a friendly relationship with a(n):
     a. user.
     b. influencer.
     c. buyer.
     d. decider.
     e. gatekeeper.

32. When the fertilizer factory's safety manager went to check its supply of ammonia monitoring tags, she found she had none in stock. Since it is company policy to have at least five in stock at all times, she advised the purchasing agent to order Chem Express monitoring tags because she knew this supplier met the specifications required within her industry. The purchasing agent negotiated the terms of the purchase. In terms of the buying center, the safety manager had the role of:
     a. gatekeeper.
     b. decider.
     c. buyer.
     d. influencer.
     e. auctioneer.

33. _____ affect the buying decision by helping define the specifications for what is being purchased.
     a. Gatekeepers
     b. Users
     c. Influencers
     d. Buyers
     e. Deciders

34. Which of the following is most likely to be a straight rebuy buying situation for a municipality?
     a. a new patrol car for the police station
     b. a $13,000 computer program that allows consumers to pay fines online
     c. a central heating and air conditioning system for city hall
     d. a reorder of chemicals for the city's swimming pool
     e. a bronze memorial honoring its police and fire fighters

35. A straight rebuy is a(n) _____ while a modified rebuy is a(n) _____.
     a. exchange; resale
     b. reorder; exchange
     c. first-time order; reorder
     d. change; first-time order
     e. reorder; change

36. The maintenance crew chief told the head of the hotel housekeeping staff, "Call Ralph at Bright Ideas—we need another case of his light bulbs." This would be an example of a:
   a. new buy.
   b. straight rebuy.
   c. modified rebuy.
   d. make-buy.
   e. standard buy.

37. The Cleveland Cavaliers need new basketball uniforms for the upcoming NBA season. The team wants a new design and new colors for its road uniforms; many think the current design needs redefining. The purchase of new uniforms would be an example of a:
   a. modified rebuy.
   b. straight rebuy.
   c. new buy.
   d. standard buy.
   e. class buy.

38. Catfish growers in Mississippi are victimized by cormorants, birds that feed on catfish and catfish fingerlings. A typical grower can lose half of its stock annually to the hungry predator. After losing $60,000 to the birds last year, Quiver River Aquaculture, a catfish grower, is thinking about buying some kind of water scarecrow to protect its fish. Prices on such devices vary from $500 to $2,000. The purchase of such a device would be classified as a _____ buying situation.
   a. straight rebuy
   b. new buy
   c. service buy
   d. modified rebuy
   e. reverse buy

39. Which of the buying situations involves the highest level of risk?
   a. straight rebuy
   b. new buy
   c. service buy
   d. modified rebuy
   e. reverse buy

40. Which of the following statements about how the buying situation affects buying center behavior is true?
   a. Only a very few people are involved in a new buy buying situation.
   b. The problem is well-defined in a new buy buying situation.
   c. . If the purchase is a new buy for a manufacturer, the seller should be prepared to act as a consultant to the buyer.
   d. The decision time required for a straight rebuy is long.
   e. Technical and operating personnel have a great deal of influence in a straight rebuy buying situation.

41. Organizational buying behavior:
   a. is similar to consumer buying behavior.
   b. is the decision-making process organizations use to establish the need for products and identify, evaluate, and choose among alternative brands and suppliers.
   c. involves five different stages of activities.
   d. will require organizational members to formulate a make-buy decision.
   e. is accurately described by all of the above.

42. When the fertilizer factory's safety manager checked its supply of ammonia monitoring tags, she found that she had none in stock. Since it is company policy to have at least five in stock at all times, she asked the purchasing agent to order the monitoring tags. In terms of the buying decision process, her discovery is an example of:

      a. problem recognition.
      b. a value analysis.
      c. information search.
      d. evaluative opportunity.
      e. purchase opportunity.

43. A(n) _____ is an evaluation of whether a product or its parts will be purchased from outside suppliers or built by the firm.

      a. purchase evaluation
      b. evaluative opportunity
      c. value analysis
      d. make-buy decision
      e. evaluative buy

44. Soon after Shell Solar was formed to make solar power panels that convert sunlight into energy, its engineers had to decide whether to manufacture the batteries that would store the energy or to purchase them from a German company. This would be an example of a(n) _____ decision.

      a. marketing mix
      b. make-buy
      c. reciprocal
      d. reseller buying
      e. derived-demand

45. A _____ is a systematic appraisal of the design, quality, and performance of a product to reduce purchasing costs. It is conducted during the information search of the buying decision process.

      a. vendor analysis
      b. SWOT analysis
      c. business-level assessment
      d. value analysis
      e. cognitive assessment

46. During the third stage of the organizational purchase decision process, the organization engages in:

      a. information review.
      b. preemptive behavior.
      c. alternative evaluation.
      d. purchase financing.
      e. problem recognition.

47. Grainger, the largest U.S. distributor of maintenance, repair, and operations supplies to industrial customers, was one of the first retailers to transfer its paper catalog to its website. One of the reasons Grainger decided to sell online was because:

      a. everyone else was doing it.
      b. it substantially reduced buyer order-processing time.
      c. it increased form utility.
      d. it narrowed Grainger's potential customer base.
      e. it increased marketing costs.

48. Online buying in organizational markets is prominent because Internet/Web technology:
   a. increases marketing costs.
   b. reduces the need for timely information.
   c. substantially reduces buyer order processing costs.
   d. narrows the potential customer base for many products.
   e. is accurately described by all of the above.

49. In the construction industry, online trading communities, called _____, that bring together buyers and suppliers enable a general contractor to manage and coordinate the many suppliers, subcontractors, architects, and engineers necessary to complete a project.
   a. sell-side solutions
   b. indirect e-procurement sites
   c. demand-side exchanges
   d. e-marketplaces
   e. buy-side solutions

50. In a _____, a buyer communicates a need for a product or service and would-be suppliers are invited to bid in competition with each other.
   a. supply-side exchange
   b. demand-side exchange
   c. reverse auction
   d. conventional e-exchange
   e. traditional auction

ANSWER KEY

Answers to Questions & Problems

Organizational Buyers

1. Reseller markets
2. Government markets
3. Industrial markets
4. Reseller markets
5. Government markets
6. Industrial markets
7. Global market

Derived Demand Characteristics

Example: Intel Pentium Chip--Dell Computers demand increases significantly.

Characteristics of Organizational Buying Behavior--Buying Criteria

Suggested ranking:

	College Student	Small Business	General Motors
Price	1	1	6
Quality	3	4	2
Delivery	5	6	5
Technical capability	4	2	1
Warranties	2	3	4
Past performance	6	5	3
Production facilities	7	7	7

Roles in the Buying Center

Bob Miller—decider
Ms. Browne—gatekeeper
Rebecca Nelson—influencer, purchaser
Tom Watson—user

Stages in an Organizational Buying Decision

Example:

1. Breakdown
2. Brochures
3. References supplied by manufacturer
4. Less emotional
5. Formal evaluation

Buy Classes

1. Straight rebuy
2. New buy
3. Modified rebuy

Answers to Sample Multiple Choice Questions

1. c p. 148; LO 1	14. a p. 151; LO 2	27. c p. 157; LO 3	40. c p. 157; LO 3
2. e p. 148; LO 1	15. c p. 153; LO 2	28. a p. 157; LO 3	41. e p. 158-160; LO 2
3. c p. 148; LO 1	16. e p. 153; LO 2	29. c p. 157; LO 3	42. a p. 159-160; LO 2
4. d p. 149; LO 1	17. c p. 153; LO 2	30. c p. 157; LO 3	43. d p. 160; LO 2
5. e p. 148; LO 1	18. e p. 153-154; LO 2	31. e p. 157; LO 3	44. b p. 160; LO 2
6. a p. 149; LO 1	19. d p. 154; LO 2	32. b p. 157; LO 3	45. d p. 160; LO 2
7. b p. 149; LO 1	20. a p. 154; LO 2	33. c p. 157; LO 3	46. c p. 160; LO 2
8. d p. 149; LO 1	21. c p. 154; LO 2	34. d p. 157; LO 3	47. b p. 161; LO 4
9. c p. 150	22. c p. 155; LO 2	35. e p. 157; LO 3	48. c p. 161; LO 4
10. c p. 151	23. e p. 155; LO 2	36. b p. 157; LO 3	49. d p. 162; LO 4
11. e p. 152; LO 2	24. e p. 155; LO 2	37. a p. 157; LO 3	50. c p. 163; LO 4
12. b p. 151; LO 2	25. e p. 155; LO 2	38. b p. 157; LO 3	
13. e p. 151; LO 2	26. d p. 156; LO 3	39. b p. 157; LO 3	

Note: LO indicates learning objective.

CHAPTER 7

REACHING GLOBAL MARKETS

<u>Why is Chapter 7 important</u>? Marketing worldwide involves an environmental scanning to learn the culture, geography, and, perhaps more importantly, the history of a country. Adapting the marketing mix for the global market is the challenge of today's corporations.

Global Marketing Strategy: The practice of standardizing marketing activities when there are cultural similarities and adapting them when cultures differ.

CHAPTER OUTLINE

I. DYNAMICS OF WORLD TRADE

    A. World Trade Flows
        1. Global perspective
        2. United States perspective

    B. Competitive Advantage of Nations
        1. Factor conditions
        2. Demand conditions
        3. Related and supporting industries
        4. Company strategy, structure, and rivalry

II. MARKETING IN A BORDERLESS ECONOMIC WORLD

    A. Decline of Economic Protectionism
        1. Tariffs
        2. Quotas

    B. Rise of Economic Integration
        1. European Union
        2. North American Free Trade Agreement
        3. Asian free trade agreements

    C. Global Competition among Global Companies for Global Consumers
        1. Global competition
        2. Global companies
            a. International firms
            b. Multinational firms
            c. Transnational firms
        3. Global consumers

    D. Emergence of a Networked Global Marketplace

III. A GLOBAL ENVIRONMENTAL SCAN

    A. Cultural Diversity
        1. Values
        2. Customs
        3. Cultural symbols
        4. Language
        5. Cultural ethnocentricity

    B. Economic Considerations
        1. Stage of economical development
            a. Developed countries
            b. Developing countries
        2. Economic infrastructure
        3. Consumer income and purchasing power
        4. Currency exchange rates

    C. Political-Regulatory Climate
        1. Political stability
        2. Trade regulations

IV. GLOBAL MARKET-ENTRY STRATEGIES

    A. Exporting
        1. Indirect exporting
        2. Direct exporting

    B. Licensing
        1. Contract manufacturing
        2. Contract assembly
        3. Franchising

    C. Joint Ventures

    D. Direct Investment

V. CRAFTING A WORLDWIDE MARKETING PROGRAM

    A. Product and Promotion Strategies
        1. Product extension
        2. Product adaptation
        3. Product invention

    B. Distribution Strategy

    C. Pricing Strategy
        1. Dumping
        2. Gray market

You should be able to place these key terms in the outline and be able to discuss them.

back translation

balance of trade

consumer ethnocentrism countertrade

cross-cultural analysis cultural symbols

currency exchange rate customs

direct investment

dumping

Economic Espionage Act

exporting

Foreign Corrupt Practices Act

global brand

global competition

global consumers

global marketing strategy

gray market

gross domestic product

joint venture

multidomestic marketing strategy

protectionism

quota

semiotics

strategic alliances

tariffs

values

World Trade Organization

QUESTIONS & PROBLEMS

WORLD TRADE FLOWS

All nations and regions of the world do not participate equally in world trade.

Answer the following questions concerning world trade flows:

1. Who is the world's largest exporter and importer of goods and services?_____

2. What percentage of world trade involves countertrade?_____

3. Is the trade feedback effect an argument for or against free trade among nations? Why?_____
_____

4. Who is the world leader in terms of GDP?_____

5. Under which conditions does a country have a surplus in their balance of trade, and under which conditions does a country have a deficit in their balance of trade?_____

6. Who are the three largest exporters to the United States?_____

7. Who is Asia's largest export market?_____

COMPETITIVE ADVANTAGE OF NATIONS

Harvard Business School Professor Michael Porter suggests a "diamond" to explain a nation's competitive advantage and why some industries and firms become world leaders. He identified four key factors:

Factor conditions
Demand conditions
Related and supporting industries
Company strategy, structure, and rivalry

Match the correct factor with the examples listed below:

1. These factors include the conditions governing the way a nation's businesses are organized and managed, along with the intensity of domestic competition._____

2. Firms and industries seeking leadership in global markets need clusters of world-class suppliers that accelerate innovation._____

3. These include both the number and sophistication of domestic customers for an industry's product.
_____

4. These reflect a nation's ability to turn its natural resources, education, and infrastructure into a competitive advantage._____

5. The Dutch lead the world in cut flowers because of their research in cultivation, packaging, and shipping._____

6. The Italian shoe industry has become the world leader because of intense domestic competition that enhances quality and innovation._____

7. Japan's sophisticated consumers demand quality in their TVs and radios, thereby making Japan's producers the world leaders in the electronics industry._____

8. The German leadership in printing relates directly to the cluster of supporting German suppliers.

_____

EMERGENCE OF A BORDERLESS ECONOMIC WORLD

Answer the following questions:

1. What three challenges need response in the global marketplace?

_____
_____
_____

2. What is the difference between a tariff and a quota?_____

3. What does WTO stand for and why is it important?_____

_____

4. What does NAFTA stand for and why is it important?_____

_____

Two other important factors when doing a cross-culture analysis are semiotics (the correspondence between symbols and their role in the assignment of meaning for people) and back translation (where a word or phrase is retranslated into the original language by a different interpreter to catch errors). Very often companies don't even know that there are questions about symbols, customs, values, or language to be asked.

Two more factors to consider are cultural ethnocentricity (the belief that aspects of one's culture are superior to another's) and consumer ethnocentricity (the tendency to believe that it is inappropriate, indeed immoral, to purchase foreign-made products) greatly inhibit global marketing.

CULTURAL DIVERSITY

A thorough cross-cultural analysis involves an understanding of and appreciation for the values, customs, symbols, and language of other societies.

Values
Customs
Cultural symbols
Language

Match the correct term to the appropriate example below:

1. In Japan, women give men chocolates for Valentine's Day._____

2. A door-to-door salesman would have difficulty in Italy because it is improper for a man to call on a woman if she is home alone._____

3. Americans are superstitious about the number 13, therefore, many hotels don't have a thirteenth floor.
_____

4. The brand name "Vicks," an American vapor-rub, means "sexual intimacy" in German; the name was changed to "Wicks."_____

ECONOMIC CONSIDERATIONS

Economic considerations important to marketers include:

Stage of economic development
Economic infrastructure
Consumer income and purchasing power
Currency exchange rate

Identify which consideration would be most important for the following countries:

1. Russia_____
2. Bosnia_____
3. Haiti_____
4. Uganda_____

GLOBAL MARKET ENTRY STRATEGIES

Companies utilize four strategies to enter the international marketplace. They are:

Exporting
Licensing
Joint Ventures
Direct investment

Identify which strategy would be best to use in the following situations:

1. A company receives a request for its product from a foreign retailer._____

2. General Electric buys a Hungarian lighting company._____

3. Paul Mueller Company, a producer of stainless steel dairy and brewery equipment, opens up the Dutch market but finds it necessary to manufacture there._____

4. A software firm with cash flow problems receives a request from Bull, the French computer manufacturer, to utilize their new software package._____

CRAFTING A WORLDWIDE MARKETING EFFORT

Strategies for bringing products to the worldwide marketplace include:

Product extension
Product adaptation
Product invention

Which of the strategies would be best in the following situation?

1. McDonald's entering the Canadian market._____

2. Campbell Soups discovers that the English market has no knowledge of "condensed" soups.

_____

3. Saturn has to make right-hand drive cars for the Japanese market._____

CAN YOU PASS THE TEST?
Sample Multiple Choice Questions

1. Which of the following statements about the dynamics of world trade is true?
    a. The dollar value of world trade has more than doubled in the past decade.
    b. Manufactured goods account for 75 percent of world trade.
    c. One-fourth of world trade includes services such as telecommunications, transportation, insurance, education, etc.
    d. World trade will likely exceed $11.5 trillion by 2005.
    e. All of the above statements about the dynamics of world trade are true.

2. _____ is the practice of using barter rather than money for making global sales.
    a. Gray marketing
    b. Countertrade
    c. Dumping
    d. Black marketing
    e. Global swapping

3. _____ is the monetary value of all goods and services produced in a country in one year.
    a. Gross national product
    b. Disposable income
    c. Gross domestic product
    d. Gross domestic profit
    e. Net domestic profit

4. The balance of trade:
    a. refers to the economic need for a nation to export the same amount as it imports.
    b. refers to the need of a nation to break even.
    c. is the difference between the monetary value of a nation's imports and its domestic production.
    d. is overseen by the World Trade Organization (WTO).
    e. is the difference between the monetary value of a nation's exports and imports.

5. The trade feedback effect is one argument for:
    a. protectionism.
    b. increased tariffs and quotas.
    c. international trade associations.
    d. decreasing a nation's imports.
    e. free trade agreements.

6. Which of the following statements best describes the relationship between the imports into the U.S. and the exports from the U.S. during the last 30 years?
    a. No accurate data is available on trade imports and exports.
    b. The volume of imports and exports has consistently decreased.
    c. Imports into the U.S. and exports have been about equal, indicating balanced trade.
    d. Exports have exceeded imports, indicating a continuing trade surplus.
    e. Imports have exceeded exports, indicating a continuing trade deficit.

7. Which of the following is NOT one of the elements of Michael Porter's diamond of national competitive advantage?
   a. factor conditions
   b. demand conditions
   c. company strategy, structure, and rivalry
   d. cultural conditions
   e. related and supporting industries

8. A nation's ability to turn its natural resources, education, and infrastructure into a competitive advantage is reflected in:
   a. structural conditions.
   b. demand conditions.
   c. socio-cultural conditions.
   d. competitive conditions.
   e. factor conditions.

9. Which of the following is an example of a demand condition?
   a. natural resources
   b. existence of supplier clusters
   c. sophistication of consumers
   d. intensity of competition
   e. wage rates

10. Although there are many factors contributing to the success of major global marketers, a common theme seems to be that they:
   a. first became involved with a formalized trade organization (such as the EU, NAFTA, etc.).
   b. specialized in services rather than consumer goods.
   c. employed a multi-cultural or multi-national staff.
   d. first succeeded in intense domestic competition.
   e. were the largest company in their industry.

11. The practice of shielding one or more sectors of a country's economy from foreign competition through the use of tariffs or quotas is called:
   a. the rule of protective domain.
   b. ethnocentrism.
   c. domestic imperialism.
   d. protectionism.
   e. blocked currency.

12. Tariffs imposed on bananas by Western European countries cost consumers $2 billion a year. This is an example of:
   a. protectionism.
   b. domestication.
   c. polycentrism.
   d. semiotics.
   e. gray marketing.

13. _____ are restrictions placed on the amount of a product allowed to enter or leave a country.
    a. Tariffs
    b. Countertrade fees
    c. Ethnocentric restrictions
    d. Trade binding agreements
    e. Quotas

14. Tariffs serve primarily to:
    a. encourage foreign trade.
    b. equalize production capacity.
    c. raise prices on imports.
    d. limit the quantity of goods leaving the domestic market.
    e. provide consumers with the most competitively priced goods.

15. More than 100 U.S. sawmills from Washington to Arkansas have closed recently. As a result the U.S. timber industry is demanding quantity limits, or _____, on Canadian softwood lumber imports.
    a. quotas
    b. countertrade fees
    c. ethnocentric restrictions
    d. trade binding agreements
    e. tariffs

16. The restriction on the importing of garments made in Cambodia into the U.S. is lower for those manufacturers that allow their factories to be monitored by the International Labor Organization (ILO). These restrictions are examples of:
    a. GATT taxes.
    b. blocked currencies.
    c. tariffs.
    d. foreign excise taxes.
    e. quotas.

17. The World Trade Organization (WTO):
    a. was formed by the major industrialized nations of the world.
    b. is a permanent institution that sets rules governing trade between its members.
    c. uses panels of trade experts to settle disputes.
    d. has the authority to issue binding decisions.
    e. is accurately described by all of the above.

18. Negotiations are under way to create a 34-country Free Trade Area of the Americas. This regional agreement would be most like:
    a. the WTO.
    b. NAICS.
    c. the League of Nations.
    d. the UN.
    e. the EU.

19. The European Union (EU) has benefited its member nations by providing:
    a. the free flow of goods, services, capital, and labor across borders within the EU.
    b. abundant marketing opportunities because it is no longer necessary to market products and services on a nation-by-nation basis.
    c. European-wide distribution from fewer locations, given open borders.
    d. issuance of a common currency, the euro, replacing 12 national currencies.
    e. all of the above.

20. Covisint is a collaboration among automakers and technology partners to realize gains through increased efficiencies. This collaboration is an example of:
    a. ethnocentric competition.
    b. a strategic alliance.
    c. exporting.
    d. licensing.
    e. a free trade agreement.

21. Collaborative relationships are becoming a common way to meet the demands of global competition. Global _____ are agreements between two or more independent firms to cooperate for the purpose of achieving common goals such as a competitive advantage or customer value creation.
    a. monopolies
    b. oligopolies
    c. restraints of trade
    d. strategic alliances
    e. assertive interferences

22. A company that uses a multidomestic marketing strategy:
    a. standardizes all of its marketing activities.
    b. does not engage in marketing outside of its national borders.
    c. has as many different product variations, brand names, and advertising programs as countries in which it does business.
    d. has a transnational view of the world.
    e. is able to more efficiently achieve economies of scale than companies that use a global marketing strategy.

23. Transnational companies use a(n) _____ strategy.
    a. domestic-oriented
    b. transactional exchange
    c. multidomestic marketing
    d. ethnocentric marketing
    e. global marketing

24. Theodore Levitt wrote a book titled *The Marketing Imagination*. In the book, Levitt argues that consumers the world over are becoming very similar in their wants and behaviors. Levitt asserts marketers should standardize their marketing strategies and activities in order to benefit from economies of scale. Levitt is encouraging marketers to adopt a _____ marketing strategy.
    a. global
    b. multinational
    c. multidomestic
    d. customized
    e. reactive

25. A firm that views the world as consisting of unique parts and markets to each part differently is called a(n):
        a. economic intruder.
        b. foreign exploiter.
        c. international firm.
        d. multinational firm.
        e. transnational firm.

26. A cross-cultural analysis is part of a(n):
        a. global environmental scan.
        b. correlation analysis.
        c. economic audit.
        d. national feasibility study.
        e. transactional exchange study.

27. Cleanliness is a _____ that permeates Japan. Some banks advertise that they actually wash the money deposited in them before it is recirculated. Pentel makes a germ-free pen for the Japanese market with the slogan "The pen is mightier than the bacterium."
        a. value
        b. cultural ethnocentrism
        c. protectionist perspective
        d. consumerist perspective
        e. cognitive attitude

28. Fast food restaurants in Germany serve beer because that is the way people do things there. This is an example of:
        a. cultural learning.
        b. stereotypes.
        c. motivation.
        d. customs.
        e. self-concept.

29. General Mills designed a cake mix especially for preparation in the rice cookers used by Japanese consumers. The product failed because the Japanese take pride in the purity of their rice and did not want to contaminate their cookers with another food product. This product failed as the result of a(n) _____ that General Mills did not foresee.
        a. idiosyncrasy
        b. ethic
        c. demographic pattern
        d. custom
        e. belief

30. _____ is an area of study that examines the correspondence between symbols and their role in the assignment of meaning for people.
        a. Comparative psychology
        b. Cultural anthropology
        c. Field anthropology
        d. Semiotics
        e. Ethnocentric sociology

31. Rembrandt toothpaste emphasizes in its ads its ability to whiten teeth. This promotion would be unsuccessful in some Southeastern Asia countries where yellowed or blackened teeth are considered desirable status symbols. The fact that the product benefit is not a benefit worldwide is an example of differences in:
    a. cultural symbols.
    b. values.
    c. ethics.
    d. morals.
    e. religious belief.

32. Having developed a great slogan for your business, you want to see how the slogan works in Spanish. You ask a translator to convert it into Spanish and then ask a second translator to convert the phrase into English. This is:
    a. counter-language.
    b. ethnographic calibration.
    c. language mirroring.
    d. semiotic culture.
    e. back translation.

33. Even though there are hundreds of different languages and dialects, the three major languages used in global diplomacy and commerce are:
    a. English, Japanese, and German.
    b. English, French, and Spanish.
    c. Japanese, Spanish and French.
    d. Japanese, Spanish and English.
    e. Spanish, English, and German.

34. Concerned about the growing prevalence of English on the Web, a French state institution founded in the 17th century to maintain the purity of the language unveiled a dictionary of newly-coined French equivalents to English Internet terms in 2000. This is symptomatic of the difficulties in doing business in France because in many situations, the business must be conducted in French. The French could be described as having:
    a. cultural ethnocentrism.
    b. consumer polycentrism.
    c. cultural commitment.
    d. a cross-cultural bias.
    e. cultural imperialism.

35. Consumer ethnocentrism:
    a. defines the cumulative amount of time and effort a consumer is willing to spend when making a purchase decision.
    b. is the tendency to believe that it is inappropriate and even immoral to purchase foreign-made products.
    c. refers to consumer tendencies to create relationships with products they buy frequently.
    d. relates closely to consumer demand for free trade areas.
    e. is accurately described by none of the above.

36. An economic scan of a global marketplace should:
    a. examine the countries' currency exchange rate.
    b. compare the economic development in different countries.
    c. assess the economic infrastructure of these countries.
    d. measure consumer income in the countries.
    e. do all of the above.

37. The two major groupings of stages of economic development helpful to global marketers are:
     a. capitalistic and communist.
     b. developed and underdeveloped.
     c. developed and developing.
     d. capitalistic and developing.
     e. free enterprise and planned economy.

38. Concern about the availability of telephone lines within a country relates to:
     a. economic infrastructure.
     b. media.
     c. distribution capabilities.
     d. exchange rate.
     e. ability to encode and decode messages.

39. In Venezuela and Chile, a consumer can purchase wireless local, wireless long distance, and have access to a local Internet service provider in additional to his or her phone services. In Peru, a consumer can purchase wireless local services, but no Internet access is generally available. In Argentina, a consumer can buy wireless local service and Internet service, but not wireless long-distance service. These communication differences indicate the differences in these countries:
     a. capital infrastructure.
     b. political infrastructure.
     c. economic infrastructure.
     d. geopolitical network.
     e. ecosystem.

40. Political stability and trade regulations are included in an assessment of a country's _____.
     a. cultural diversity
     b. economic development
     c. political-regulatory climate
     d. technological leadership
     e. competitive climate

41. Indirect exporting occurs when a firm sells its domestically produced goods in a foreign country:
     a. in violation of a quota.
     b. without paying import duties.
     c. without paying export duties.
     d. through an intermediary.
     e. without billing in blocked currency.

42. Contract manufacturing is:
     a. offering the right to a trademark, patent, trade secret, or similarly valued items of intellectual property in return for a royalty or fee.
     b. contracting with a foreign firm to manufacture products according to stated specifications.
     c. contracting between a foreign country and a local firm to invest together to create a local business.
     d. having a company handle its own exports directly, without intermediaries.
     e. exporting through an intermediary, which often has the knowledge and means to succeed in selling a firm's product abroad.

43. Two variations of licensing are:
     a. direct and indirect.
     b. strategic alliance and joint venture.
     c. direct investment and joint venture.
     d. franchising and strategic alliance.
     e. contract manufacturing and contract assembly.

44. A joint venture is:
    a. offering the right to a trademark, patent, trade secret, or similarly valued items of intellectual property in return for a royalty or fee.
    b. contracting with a foreign firm to manufacture products according to certain specifications.
    c. when a foreign company and a local firm invest together to create a local business.
    d. having a company handle its own exports directly, without intermediaries.
    e. exporting through an intermediary, which often has the knowledge and means to succeed in selling a firm's product abroad.

45. Japanese automobile manufacturer Mazda began production of the Premacy SUV in 2001 at a plant it built in the Chinese province of Haiku. This plant is an example of:
    a. direct investment.
    b. foreign licensing.
    c. a joint venture.
    d. a strategic alliance.
    e. exporting.

46. A U.S. company that sold virtually the same product in its international markets that it sells in the United States is using a _____ strategy.
    a. product adaptation
    b. product extension
    c. transactional exchange
    d. market harvesting
    e. product invention

47. Fran Wilson Creative Cosmetics sells its Moodmatcher lipstick through Japanese distributors that reach Japan's beauty salons. This is an example of:
    a. indirect exporting.
    b. direct exporting.
    c. licensing.
    d. joint venture.
    e. direct investment.

48. The Canadian Magazine Publisher's Association (CMPA) recently predicted the demise of many Canadian magazines because the World Trade Organization (WTO) made it legal for U.S. publishers to introduce magazines into the Canadian market without incurring the start-up costs involved in launching a new magazine. By using split-run magazines (modifying the U.S. edition so they contain Canadian ads), U.S. magazine publishers could offer lower rates to advertiser and sell the magazines for less money than Canadian publishers could. According to the CMPA, the U.S. magazine publishers would be engaged in:
    a. gray marketing.
    b. a countertrade.
    c. dumping.
    d. black marketing.
    e. a parasitic relationship.

49. Product extension and product adaptation strategies use _____ around the world.
     a. identical products
     b. identical pricing
     c. promotional messages adapted to each country
     d. identical promotional messages
     e. a dual adaptation strategy

50. _____, also called parallel importing, is a situation where products are sold through unauthorized channels of distribution.
     a. countertrading.
     b. gray marketing.
     c. black marketing.
     d. dumping.
     e. ethnocentric relationships.

ANSWER KEY

Answers to Questions & Problems

World Trade Flows

1. The United States
2. 20%
3. Yes, exports create higher incomes that create more demand for imports
4. The United States
5. When the monetary value of exports exceeds the monetary value of imports. The reverse, an excess of monetary value of imports over exports, yields a deficit balance of trade.
6. Japan, Canada, and Mexico
7. The United States

Competitive Advantage of Nations

1. Factor conditions
2. Related and supporting industries
3. Demand conditions
4. Factor conditions
5. Related and supporting industries
6. Company strategy, structure, and rivalry
7. Demand conditions
8. Related and supporting industries

Emergence of a Borderless Economic World

1. Gradual decline of economic protectionism
   Formal economic integration and free trade among nations
   Global competition among global companies for global customers
2. Tariff—tax on imports
   Quota—restrictions on amounts of imports allowed
3. World Trade Organization—successor to the GATT agreements that focuses on settled trade disputes
4. North American Free Trade Agreement—it brings the US, Canada, and Mexico into a one market trade area

Cultural Diversity

1. Customs
2. Values
3. Cultural symbols
4. Language

Economic Considerations

1. Currency
2. Economic infrastructure
3. Consumer income and purchasing power
4. Stage of economic development

Global Market Entry Strategies

1. Exporting
2. Direct investment
3. Joint ventures
4. Licensing

Crafting a Worldwide Marketing Effort

1. Product extension
2. Product invention
3. Product adaptation

Answers to Sample Multiple Choice Questions

1. e p. 170 LO 1	14. c p. 174 LO 2	26. a p. 181 LO 3	38. a p. 186 LO 3
2. b p. 170 LO 1	15. a p. 175 LO 2	27. a p. 181 LO 3	39. c p. 186 LO 3
3. c p. 171 LO 1	16. e p. 175 LO 2	28. d p. 182 LO 3	40. c p. 188 LO 3
4. e p. 171 LO 1	17. e p. 175 LO 2	29. d p. 182 LO 3	41. d p. 190 LO 4
5. e p. 171 LO 1	18. e p. 177 LO 2	30. d p. 182-183 LO 3	42. b p. 191 LO 4
6. e p. 171 LO 1	19. e p. 176 LO 2	31. a p. 182 LO 3	43. e p. 191 LO 4
7. d p. 172 LO 1	20. b p. 177 LO 2	32. e p. 184 LO 3	44. c p. 191 LO 4
8. e p. 172 LO 1	21. d p. 177 LO 2	33. b p. 184 LO 3	45. a p. 192 LO 4
9. c p. 172 LO 1	22. c p. 178 LO 2	34. a p. 184 LO 3	46. b p. 193 LO 5
10. d p. 173 LO 1	23. e p. 178 LO 2	35. b p. 184 LO 3	47. a p. 190 LO 4
11. d p. 174 LO 2	24. a p. 178 LO 2	36. e p. 184-185 LO 3	48. c p. 195 LO 5
12. a p. 174 LO 2	25. d p. 178 LO 2	37. c p. 185 LO 3	49. d p. 194 LO 5
13. e p. 175 LO 2			50. b p. 196 LO 5

Note: LO indicates learning objective.

CHAPTER 8

MARKETING RESEARCH: FROM INFORMATION TO ACTION

<u>Why is Chapter 8 important</u>? Information is the lifeblood of any marketing program. This chapter illustrates how a company determines its information needs; the sources of that information and the best way to collect it; and finally, how to interpret and utilize that information. Information contributes the success of the promotion, pricing, distribution, and ultimately, the product itself.

Marketing Research: The process of defining a marketing problem and opportunity, systematically collecting and analyzing information, and recommending actions to improve an organization's marketing activities.

CHAPTER OUTLINE

I. STEPS IN MAKING EFFECTIVE DECISIONS

    A. Define the Problem
        1. Set the research objectives
            a. exploratory research
            b. descriptive research
            c. causal research
        2. Identify possible marketing actions
            a. measure of success
            b. possible marketing action

    B. Develop the Research Plan
        1. Specify constraints
        2. Identify data needed for marketing actions
        3. Determine how to collect data
            a. Concepts
            b. Methods
                i. sampling
                    - probability sampling
                    - non-probability sampling
                ii. statistical inference

    C. Collect Relevant Information
        1. Secondary data
            a. Internal
                i. financial statements
                ii. sales data
            b. External
                i. syndicated services
                ii. full-service research suppliers
                iii. limited-service research suppliers

           c. Advantages
               i. time
               ii. cost
           d. Disadvantages
               i. timeliness
               ii. fit to problem

****   4. Primary data
           a. Observational
           b. Questionnaire
               i. hypothesis generation
                   - individual interviews
                   - focus groups
               ii. hypothesis evaluation
                   - mail survey
                   - personal interviews
                   - telephone survey
           c. Panels and experiments
           d. Advantages
               i. timely (current)
               ii. specific
           e. Disadvantages
               i. costly
               ii. time consuming
      5. Using information technology to trigger marketing actions
           a. Sales "drivers"
           b. Key elements of an information system
           c. Data mining

    D. Develop Findings and Recommendations
        1. Analyze the data
        2. Presenting the findings

    E. Take Marketing Actions
        1. Make action recommendations
        2. Implement the action recomendations
        3. Evaluate the results
           a. Evaluating the decision itself
           b. Evaluating the decision process used

You should be able to place these key terms in the outline and be able to discuss them.

constraints	**observational data**
data	**primary data**
data mining	**probability sampling**
decision	**questionnaire data**
information technology	**sampling**
marketing research	**secondary data**
measures of success	**statistical inference**
nonprobability sampling	

QUESTIONS & PROBLEMS

MARKETING RESEARCH: FROM INFORMATION TO ACTION

STEP 1: DEFINE THE PROBLEM

Cadillac developed a profile of their typical customer and found that, among other things, his average age was over sixty. The primary product Cadillac offers is a large, luxury car with all the creature comforts. Cadillac Division and its dealers want to attract more young buyers to Cadillac. Cadillac Division wants to do this by advertising with younger role models and more emphasis on the Seville, its answer to the Lexus, Mercedes, and BMW. The dealer network wants a Cadillac version of the Chevrolet Suburban. All things considered, Cadillac is still the largest selling luxury car. What is the problem? Can market research help find a solution? Write out your statement of the problem._____

_____

_____

_____

STEP 2: DEVELOP THE RESEARCH PLAN

Decision factors are the different sets of variables—the alternatives and uncertainties—that combine to give the outcome of a decision. A thorough assessment of decision factors involves multiple alternatives. Very often these are generated by customers, employees, brainstorming sessions, and even by learning from competitors. These alternatives can be generated by phrases such as "what if..." or "in what ways..."

Assume you are trying to find a solution to major league baseball's attendance problems. List four alternatives that might help the situation:

1._____

2._____

3._____

4._____

Using your examples above, list four "uncertainties" that could adversely affect your outcome:

1._____

2._____

3._____

4._____

STEP 3: COLLECT RELEVANT INFORMATION

Defined broadly, three kinds of information used to solve marketing problems are concepts, methods, and data. There are two major types of concepts in marketing:

Hypothesis
New product concept

Using the information below, write an original hypothesis and use it to develop a new product concept:

Most college students will, at some point, take a course taught by a graduate student.
Most graduate students are not given any formal training in teaching methods.

Hypothesis:_____

New product concept:_____

METHODS

Marketing researchers often select a group of customers or prospects, ask them questions, and treat their answers as typical of all those in whom they are interested. Sampling has two variations:

Probability
Nonprobability

Decide whether the following statements are examples of probability or nonprobability sampling:

_____1. A junior high principal wants to study the use of alcohol by his students. He selects one hundred students by choosing every tenth name on his enrollment list.

_____2. A principal at the junior high across town wants to attempt the same study as the principal in the previous question, but he chooses the one hundred students with the lowest grade point average.

DATA

Secondary data are facts and figures that have already been recorded before the project at hand. Primary data are facts and figures that are newly collected for the project.

Determine which of the following is secondary or primary data:

_____1. A Ford Motor Company survey of new car owners.

_____2. An industry survey used by Coca-Cola to enter a new market.

_____3. The Census Data.

_____4. Internal sales data.

_____5. Results from a focus group on choices of airlines.

_____6. Nielsen ratings decide where to place advertising.

_____7. The J.D. Power report on new automobiles.

_____8. A company's financial statements.

_____9. Scanner data from the grocery store.

_____10. A telephone survey.

Questionnaire Data

What type of questionnaire data method should you use if you want to get as much information as possible? What if you need the information back as quickly as possible? What it you want opinion and need to ask more opened-ended questions?

Below are poorly constructed questions. Rewrite each question to obtain the most accurate data:

1. Do you exercise often?_____

2. Do you prefer the sadistic inhumane neutering of loving family pets or the benevolent construction of pet care shelters?_____

3. Whom do you live with? [] Parents [] Spouse_____

4. Do you read mysteries and science fiction? [] Yes, [] No_____

5. My weight is between: []100-120 lbs. []120-140 lbs. []140-160 lbs._____

6. How many students in your class ate breakfast last Monday?_____

EXPERIMENTS

Experiments involve obtaining data by manipulating factors under tightly controlled conditions to test cause and effect.

Identify the following variable(s) in the experiment given below:

independent variable
dependent variable
extraneous variable

A grocery manager set up a display of canned green beans at the end of an aisle with a large sign that said "Green Beans 3/$1.25." Down the aisle in their normal location, the identical green beans were being sold for $.40 per can. The store manager wanted to see if people tended to buy items in quantity (assuming that the price must be lower) rather than buy items priced individually.

1. Independent variable_____

2. Dependent variable_____

3. Extraneous variable_____

STEP 4: DEVELOP FINDINGS AND RECOMMENDATIONS

You are the marketing manager of a fast food hamburger franchise. You decide to open 100 of your stores for business at 7:00 a.m. in order to attract the breakfast market. There are a number of decisions that must be made.

1. If, during a one-week period, average breakfast sales are $610, what is your next course of action?
_____

You begin with the following quantifiable measures of success:

a. If during a trial-week period, breakfast sales are less than $500, discontinue project.

b. If during a trial-week period, breakfast sales are between $550 and $750, continue project temporarily, while exploring possible methods of increasing sales.

c. If sales exceed $750, open for breakfast on a permanent basis.

2. For the following situation, design an experiment that will help identify which three breakfast items should be served:

Based upon a four-state test, you decide there is a sufficient potential market for a breakfast operation. You must now decide what to serve. For maximum efficiency you want to serve only three main breakfast items. The following items can be prepared with little or no additional costs other than ingredients: omelets, egg sandwiches, pancakes, French toast, or fruit muffins._____
_____
_____
_____

3. For the following scenario, what questions should you ask, and what steps should you take to make the decision objectively?

On the basis of the experimental data you collected, you decide to serve omelets, pancakes, and egg sandwiches. After opening for business you still need to increase your sales in order to make the breakfast business permanent. A number of store managers comment that customers are asking for waffles for breakfast. You decide that it may be profitable to invest in the equipment to make waffles (something your competition has not done)._____
_____
_____
_____

4. You would like to design an experiment using two stores to determine if serving waffles is a viable alternative. List your specific measures of success:_____

5. Using the (hypothetical) information in the previous exercise, choose the best alternative and implement the chosen alternative:_____

STEP 5: TAKE MARKETING ACTIONS

When Coca-Cola studied the Pepsi taste tests and began conducting tests to find a formula people preferred to Pepsi, they found that the formula for "New Coke" was definitely preferred to Pepsi. They apparently thought that if "New Coke" is preferred over Pepsi and Pepsi is preferred over Coca-Cola then "New Coke" should be the preferred drink. The decision based on the results of the tests were not flawed, however, "New Coke" was a spectacular failure. What part did Coca-Cola fail to evaluate?_____

BASIC FORECASTING TERMS

Describe what is meant by:

1. Market or industry potential = _____

2. Sales or company forecast = _____

TWO BASIC APPROACHES TO FORECASTING

The two basic approaches to sales forecasting are (1) subdividing the total sales forecast (top-down forecast) or (2) building the total sales forecast by summing the components (buildup approach).

Use the Buying Power Index (BPI) to figure the sales percentage for the state of New Jersey using the following information:

BPI = (0.2 x percent of population) + (0.5 x percent of effective buying power) + (0.3 x percent of retail sales)

Percent of population	= 3.1778
Percent of effective buying power	= 3.7413
Percent of retail sales	= 3.4114

BPI = _____

If an automobile manufacturer estimates total market potential for sport utility vehicles in 2003 to be 200,000 units, what would the sales potential be for New Jersey (using the BPI alone)?_____

Use the buildup approach to forecast company sales based on the information given below:

	Units
East coast manager's regional forecast	28,000
Midwest manager's regional forecast	24,500
South manager's regional forecast	21,700
Southwest manager's regional forecast	19,700
West coast manager's regional forecast	29,900

Company forecast = _____units

SPECIFIC SALES FORECASTING TECHNIQUES

There are three specific sales forecasting techniques:

Judgments of decision maker
Surveys of knowledgeable groups
Statistical methods

Match the following methods to the correct sales forecasting technique:

1. Sales force survey forecast_____
2. Lost horse forecast_____
3. Linear trend extrapolation_____
4. Direct forecast_____
5. Trend extrapolation_____
6. Jury of executive opinion forecast_____

CAN YOU PASS THE TEST?
Sample Multiple Choice Questions

1. Sometimes studios get the good news in screen testings that a movie works with an audience, as did *Titanic.* Such screenings are _____ for the film industry.
    a. sales forecast
    b. marketing research
    c. strategic planning
    d. economic analysis
    e. brainstorming

2. Concept tests of plots using surveys, testing of marketing campaigns, sneak previews, and tracking studies are all examples of:
    a. marketing decision theory.
    b. SWOT analysis.
    c. marketing research techniques.
    d. target audience identification.
    e. survey of experts.

3. Marketing research:
    a. is a systematic process.
    b. a means to reduce risk and uncertainty.
    c. involves a series of steps.
    d. attempts to identify both marketing problems and opportunities.
    e. is accurately described by all of the above.

4. The first step in the marketing research approach involves:
    a. setting research objectives and identify possible marketing actions.
    b. specifying research constraints.
    c. determining primary and secondary data sources.
    d. determining how data are to be collected.
    e. developing the research plan.

5. The marketing vice-president for Game Boy noticed that some releases were selling more slowly than the rest and wants to investigate the situation. Which of the following describes appropriate research objectives for this project?
    a. to offer more quantity discounts
    b. to offer more trade deals
    c. to determine why some releases sell better than others
    d. to buy more print media advertising
    e. to offer special online deals

6. The second step in the marketing research approach involves:
    a. identifying action recommendations.
    b. collecting relevant information.
    c. developing findings.
    d. setting research objectives and identify possible marketing actions.
    e. developing the research plans.

7. Impiric is an integrated marketing solutions company. Whenever a client comes to it wondering why a product was not welcomed by its target audience or why customers have stopped buying another product, Impiric always suggests the marketing research process begins with:
     a. determining the target market.
     b. deciding how much time and money the client is willing to spend.
     c. defining the problem.
     d. defining the alternatives and uncertainties.
     e. developing and implementing the plan.

8. The memo written by the marketing manager to the vice-president of marketing research read, "Determine the highest price we can charge for this model without losing current customers." This was most likely an example of a(n)
     a. objective.
     b. constraint.
     c. assumption.
     d. measure of success.
     e. alternative.

9. Fisher-Price might set constraints on its decision to select either the old or the new version of the Chatter Telephone. Doing so is part of:
     a. defining the problem.
     b. collecting relevant information by specifying primary and secondary data.
     c. developing findings.
     d. developing the research plan.
     e. identifying possible marketing actions.

10. After developing the research plan, the next step in the marketing research process is to:
     a. specify the secondary and primary data to be used.
     b. evaluate the results.
     c. examine the alternatives.
     d. enumerate the uncertainties.
     e. experiment.

11. The owner of a retail mall is considering expanding its hours of operation. In a discussion with the marketing research firm, the research plan says, "To see which is more effective, staying open late at night or opening up earlier in the morning, let's distribute a questionnaire to all current customers, then hire someone to monitor sidewalk traffic at 7 AM and 6 PM, and see if there is any pertinent information in any of the recent trade journal." In which stage of the marketing research process would such a conversation occur?
     a. Define the problem.
     b. Develop the research plan.
     c. Collect relevant information.
     d. Develop findings and recommendations.
     e. Take marketing actions.

12. _____ sampling involves using precise rules to select the sample such that each element of the population has a specific known chance of being selected.
     a. Inferential
     b. Qualitative
     c. Probability
     d. Judgment
     e. Nonprobability

13. The approaches that can be used to solve part or all of a marketing research problem are called:
    a. market research proposals.
    b. marketing strategies.
    c. marketing tactics.
    d. SWOT analysis.
    e. methods.

14. "I want to question recent graduates about their transportation preferences. See if you can find some graduates still living in town." The marketing researcher is using:
    a. nonprobability sampling.
    b. probability sampling.
    c. extrapolation.
    d. statistical inference.
    e. criteria sampling.

15. Data, the facts and figures pertinent to the research problem, can be divided into two main types. They are _____ data.
    a. independent and dependent
    b. primary and secondary
    c. conceptual and factual
    d. extraneous and experimental
    e. measurable and nonmeasurable

16. The National Health Interview Survey is conducted annually by the Centers for Disease Control and Prevention. By examining information gathered from sampling it was able to announce that 14.1 percent of all Americans lacked healthcare insurance in 2005. A health care organization doing research on patient nonpayment would refer to this information as _____ data.
    a. proprietary
    b. primary
    c. secondary
    d. observational
    e. experimental

17. Assume that a representative sample of baseball fans in Greater Boston showed that they favored keeping the baseball stadium at Fenway Park rather than relocating it. The researchers who developed the survey would use _____ to determine that the rest of the community felt the same way.
    a. ethnographic research
    b. statistical inference
    c. data manipulation
    d. warehoused data
    e. internal secondary data

18. _____ are facts and figures that are newly collected for the project.
    a. primary data.
    b. internal secondary data.
    c. statistical inferences.
    d. external secondary data.
    e. experimental data.

19. A published survey reported on the usage of various types of advertising media for 2002. A television marketing manager that used information from this survey to create sales forecast for her cable station would be using _____ data.
        a. internal primary
        b. internal secondary
        c. external primary
        d. external secondary
        e. government census

20. Marketing Works, a market research firm located in Anchorage, Alaska, conducts survey research for retail stores around the world. It is an example of a firm that collects:
        a. primary data.
        b. informational data.
        c. technological data.
        d. secondary data.
        e. decision-based data.

21. A manufacturer of electronic toys is interested in consumers' attitudes toward its product line. All of the following can be a source for this type of marketing information EXCEPT:
        a. observation.
        b. mail questionnaire.
        c. in store-interview.
        d. telephone survey.
        e. focus group interview.

22. Which of the following statements describes a disadvantage associated with the gathering of observational data?
        a. Different observers typically draw the same conclusions from what they see.
        b. There is no training required for gatherers of observational data.
        c. Observational data is the least expensive form of primary data to gather.
        d. Observational data can readily be used to determine why consumers are acting in specific ways.
        e. It can be costly and unreliable when different observers report different conclusions in watching the same event.

23. Research and media firm Youth Culture published *Watch* magazine, a teen publication given out free to high school students, but the publication was unable to deliver response rates to coupons or sample offers that its advertisers expected. Youth Culture handed out surveys to learn how students felt about the publication. Feedback indicated teen boys and girls were demanding very different things from the publication. This feedback was the gleaned from _____ data.
        a. questionnaire
        b. internal secondary
        c. external secondary
        d. observational
        e. panel

24. A marketing research approach that uses a discussion leader to interview 6 to 10 past, present, or prospective customers is called:
        a. a depth (or individual) interview.
        b. an experiment.
        c. a focus group.
        d. small group dynamics.
        e. secondary data collection.

25. "Do you like pretzels and chips? __ Yes __ No," is a poorly worded question becauses:
    a. it is a leading question.
    b. it is actually two questions in one.
    c. it is a nonexhaustive question.
    d. it has no relevance.
    e. it asks for an opinion.

26. Which of the following is the best example of a dichotomous question?
    a. Why are you thinking about refinancing your home?
    b. Did you vote in the last presidential election?
    c. What kind of memories do you associate with the smell of freshly baked bread?
    d. What are your plans for this summer?
    e. How would you describe your favorite restaurant?

27. The question, "How many meals will you eat in restaurants in the next year?" is an example of a(n):
    a. leading question.
    b. two questions in one.
    c. question with non-exhaustive answers.
    d. unanswerable question.
    e. question with non-mutually exclusive answers.

28. Before opening six Torrid plus-size-only retail stores that cater to women aged 15-30, a great deal of information was gathered to determine what types of items should be carried, the image of the store, its advertising, etc. Which of the following is an example of a closed-ended question that might have been asked?
    a. Why would you want to shop at a store that carries plus-size clothing?
    b. In what ways might you be uncomfortable shopping at a plus-size-only retailer?
    c. Would you be interested in buying the Torrid merchandise on the Internet?
    d. What type of person would shop at Torrid?
    e. None of the above questions is an example of a closed-ended question.

29. Data obtained by manipulating factors under tightly controlled conditions to test cause and effect is an example of:
    a. questionnaire data.
    b. nonprobability sampling.
    c. an experiment.
    d. a panel.
    e. a model.

30. An experimenter served identical meals to people at six tables at an elegant restaurant. At each table there was a small lantern with a rheostat. Each table had a different brightness of lighting. There was a direct correlation between the time it took the people to finish their meals and the amount of artificial light from the lantern. The dependent variable in this experiment was:
    a. the degree of light.
    b. the personal eating habits of the subjects.
    c. experimenter bias in establishing guidelines.
    d. the length of time it took to finish the meal.
    e. the number of tables in the experiment.

31. According to marketing managers, which of the following is an example of a factor that influences sales?
   a. distribution
   b. the price
   c. advertising
   d. consumers
   e. all of the above

32. Marketers often use _____ to query their databases with "what if . . . ?" questions to determine how a hypothetical change in money spent on print media advertising would affect sales.
   a. sensitivity analysis
   b. statistical inferential analysis
   c. market potential predictors
   d. top-down forecasting
   e. situational analysis

33. An online retailer might use _____ to determine that customers who purchase flannel sheets also had a high probability of purchasing all-natural Christmas wreaths if the opportunity were made available.
   a. mutually exclusive research
   b. linear regression analysis
   c. data mining
   d. data warehousing
   e. hypothesis testing

34. The fourth step in the marketing research approach involves:
   a. determining how to collect and analyze data.
   b. collecting relevant information by specifying the use of primary or secondary data.
   c. identifying possible marketing objectives.
   d. analyzing data and presenting the findings.
   e. specifying constraints.

35. The essence of step five in the marketing research process is to:
   a. use both secondary and primary data.
   b. identify necessary marketing actions and then implement and monitor them.
   c. eliminate any ambiguity from the data collection.
   d. gather as much data as physically and financially possible.
   e. avoid the use of statistical inference.

36. Market researchers have delivered findings to Ocean Spray's product manager: (1) "cranberry" is not part of the language outside the U.S. and Canada and (2) the British like juice in boxes, not bottles. How can she use these facts to take marketing actions in an advertising campaign that will encourage consumers in the United Kingdom to try the new cranberry juice drink?
   a. Appeal to the British sense of humor while emphasizing the taste of cranberry juice by showing a small cranberry labeled "actual size" and a huge cranberry labeled "actual taste."
   b. Use a picture of the cranberry juice drink in a box so that consumers will know what to look for—and see that it's not in a bottle.
   c. Appeal to the British sense of adventure and travel by using a picture taken on Cape Cod, where Ocean Spray cranberries grow.
   d. Appeal to green and health-conscious consumers by providing information about vitamin content and the absence of any artificial colors, flavors, or preservatives.
   e. All of the above.

37. When a market researcher sets out to define a problem they:
    a. identify possible marketing actions.
    b. specify constraints.
    c. identify data needed for marketing actions.
    d. determine how to collect data.
    e. do all of the above.

38. Superba Cravats is a major marketer of men's bow ties. It estimates there are 20 million buyers of bow ties each year, that the average wearer of bow ties purchases 4 ties per year, and that the average price per bow tie is $10. Superba Cravats wants to increase its sales by raising the price. Which stage in the marketing research process is Superba Cravats in when it raises the average price to $12?
    s. define the problem
    b. develop the research plan
    c. collect relevant information
    d. develop findings
    e. take marketing actions

39. Superba Cravats is a major marketer of men's bow ties. It estimates there are 20 million buyers of bow ties each year, that the average wearer of bow ties purchases 4 ties per year, and that the average price per bow tie is $10. Superba Cravats is concerned that sales have not increased as expected. What stage in the marketing research process is Superba Cravats in?
    s. define the problem
    b. develop the research plan
    c. collect relevant information
    d. develop findings
    e. take marketing actions

40. There are three kinds of marketing research including exploratory, descriptive, and _____.
    a. top-down
    b. segregated
    c. causal
    d. bottom-up
    e. modular

41. _____ involves drawing conclusions about a population from a sample taken from that population.
    a. Sampling
    b. Probability sampling
    c. Nonprobability sampling
    d. Statistical inference
    e. Population inference

42. Which of the following are sources of collecting facts and figures pertinent to solving the marketing problem at hand?
    a. research reports
    b. customer letters
    c. sales call reports
    d. personal observational approaches
    e. all of the above

43. Which of the following is NOT an example of a "fuzzy front end" method of collecting data?
      a. having consumers take a photo of themselves when they snack
      b. having teenagers complete a drawing
      c. hiring "cool hunters"
      d. consulting Look-Look, for field correspondents
      e. all of the above ARE examples of a "fuzzy front end" method of collecting data.

44. What is the problem with the following question?
"Would you eat a healthy, low-carb snack?"
      a. leading question
      b. ambiguous question
      c. unanswerable question
      d. two questions in one
      e. nonmutually exclusive answers

45. What is the problem with the following question?
"Do you exercise regularly?"
      a. leading question
      b. ambiguous question
      c. unanswerable question
      d. two questions in one
      e. nonmutually exclusive answers

46. What is the problem with the following question?
"Would you snack on an apple with peanut butter and an orange?"
      a. leading question
      b. ambiguous question
      c. unanswerable question
      d. two questions in one
      e. nonmutually exclusive answers

47. Product and brand _____ are factors that influence sales.
      a. technologies
      b. solutions
      c. drivers
      d. forecasts
      e. extrapolations

48. Develop findings is the fourth step in the marketing research process. Which of the following are the two parts of this step?
      a. correlation analysis and data analysis
      b. hypothesis testing and data analysis
      c. the standard deviation method and presenting the findings
      d. extrapolate trends and test hypotheses
      e. analyze the data and present the findings

49. When marketing managers evaluate the results of the marketing research, they will evaluate:
    a. a technological forecast.
    b. the decision itself and the process used.
    c. the jury of expert opinion forecast and their decision.
    d. the Delphi forecast and the process used.
    e. a trend extrapolation and the resulting decision.

50. Which of the following are typical problems in wording questions?
    a. writing a leading question
    b. writing an ambiguous question
    c. writing an unanswerable question
    d. writing two questions in one
    e. all of the above are typical problems

ANSWER KEY

Answers to Questions & Problems

Define the Problem

Problem—How to reposition brand or redirect appeal? Yes, research can help.

Develop the Research Plan

Example: Autograph and photo parties with players before game

Uncertainties—another strike, rude players

Collect Relevant Information

Hypothesis—Since most graduate students have not had formal training, their teaching skills need to be improved.
New product concept—Design an instructional packet with guidelines for teaching techniques and classroom management.

Methods

1. Probability
2. Nonprobability

Data

1. Primary
2. Secondary
3. Secondary
4. Secondary
5. Primary
6. Secondary
7. Secondary
8. Secondary
9. Secondary
10. Primary

Questionnaire Data

Example: How often do you exercise? [] daily [] 3-5 times per week [] weekly [] seldom [] never

Experiments

1. Price/quantity
2. Green bean sales
3. Location

Develop Findings and Recommendations

Example:

1. Continue with promotion
2. Test omelets, pancakes, and fruit muffins at some locations and egg sandwiches, French toast, and fruit muffins at other locations. Vary according to sales.
3. How much demand will there be for waffles? Will the demand justify the added expense? Survey for interest and test for reception if interest is there.
4. Percent of breakfast items that are waffles. Compare revenue difference between those with waffles and those without.
5. Go with waffles.

Take Marketing Actions

What current Coke drinkers preferred.

Basic Forecasting Terms

1. Total forecast sales for the industry. Example: 16 million automobiles will be sold in the United States next year.
2. Estimate of sales for a particular company. With 1/3 of the market General Motors should sell 5.3 million cars next year.

Two Basic Approaches to Forecasting

BPI = 3.52963

New Jersey SUV demand = 7059

Company forecast = 123,800

Specific Sales Forecasting Techniques

1. Surveys of knowledgeable groups
2. Judgments of decision maker
3. Statistical methods
4. Judgments of decision maker
5. Statistical methods
6. Surveys of knowledgeable groups

Answers to Sample Multiple Choice Questions

1. b p. 205 LO 1	14. a p. 210 LO 1	26. b p. 218 LO 2	38. e p. 207 LO 1
2. c p. 204-205 LO 1	15. b p. 210 LO 2	27. d p. 217 LO 2	39. a p. 207 LO 1
3. e p. 204-205 LO 1	16. c p. 210 LO 2	28. c p. 218 LO 2	40. c p. 207-208 LO 1
4. a p. 207 LO 1	17. b p. 210 LO 1	29. c p. 220 LO 2	41. d p. 210 LO 1
5. c p. 207-208 LO 1	18. a p. 210 LO 2	30. d p. 220 LO 2	42. e p. 211 LO 2
6. e p. 207 LO 1	19. d p. 211 LO 2	31. e p. 221 LO 2	43. e p. 216 LO 2
7. c p. 207 LO 1	20. a p. 210 LO 2	32. a p. 222 LO 3	44. a p. 217 LO 2
8. a p. 207-208 LO 1	21. a p. 215 LO 2	33. c p. 223 LO 3	45. b p. 217 LO 2
9. d p. 209 LO 1	22. e p. 215 LO 2	34. d p. 223 LO 1	46. d p. 217 LO 2
10. a p. 207 LO 1	23. a p. 215 LO 2	35. b p. 225 LO 1	47. c p. 221 LO 3
11. c p. 207 LO 1	24. c p. 216 LO 2	36. e p. 225 LO 1	48. e p. 223 LO 1
12. c p. 210 LO 1	25. b p. 217 LO 2	37. a p. 207 LO 1	49. b p. 225-226 LO 1
13. e p. 209 LO 1			50. e p. 217 LO 1

Note: LO indicates learning objective.

CHAPTER 9

IDENTIFYING MARKET SEGMENTS AND TARGETS

<u>Why is Chapter 9 important</u>? This chapter shows how the tools of consumer behavior and environmental scanning can be used to classify and group consumers so that a company can more effectively reach them with the marketing mix. It also illustrates how to select which group or groups to pursue and how to appeal to each of them.

Market Segmentation: Aggregation of prospective buyers into groups that (1) have common needs and (2) will respond similarly to marketing actions.

CHAPTER OUTLINE

I. WHEN TO SEGMENT MARKETS

      A. One Product and Multiple Market Segments

      B. Multiple Products and Multiple Market Segments

      C. Segments of One: Mass Customization

II. STEPS IN SEGMENTING AND TARGETING MARKETS

      A. Group Potential Buyers into Segments
            1. Criteria
                  a. Potential for increased profit
                  b. Similarity of needs of potential buyers within a segment
                  c. Differences of needs of buyers among segments
                  d. Potential of a marketing action to reach a segment
                  e. Simplicity and cost of assigning potential buyers to segments
             2. Ways to segment consumer markets
                  a. Geographic
                  b. Demographic
                  c. Psychographic
                  d. Buying situation
                        i. benefits sought
                        ii. usage/patronage
             3. Ways to segment organizational markets
                  a. Geographic
                  b. Demographic: NAICS code
                  c. Demographic: Number of employees
                  d. Benefits sought

      B. Group Products to Be Sold into Categories

      C. Develop a Market-Product Grid and Estimate Size of Market(s)

D. Select Target Market(s)
    1. Criteria
        a. Market size
        b. Expected growth
        c. Competitive position
        d. Cost of reaching the segment
        e. Compatibility with the organization's objectives and resources
    2. Choose the segments

E. Take Marketing Actions to Reach Target Market(s)

III. POSITIONING THE PRODUCT

A. Approaches
    1. Head-to-head
    2. Differentiation

B. Product Positioning Using Perceptual Maps
    1. Identification of the important attributes for a product class
    2. Judgments of existing brands with respect to these important attributes
    3. Ratings of an "ideal" brand's attributes
C. Repositioning

IV. SALES FORECASTING TECHNIQUES

A. Forecasting Terms
    1. Market potential or industry potential
    2. Sales forecast or company forecast

B. Techniques
    1. Judgments of decision makers
        a. direct forecast
        b. "lost horse" forecast
    2. Survey of knowledgeable groups
        a. Survey of Buyers' Intentions
        b. salesforce survey
    3. Statistical methods
        a. trend extrapolation

You should be able to place these key terms in the outline and be able to discuss them.

company forecast	**product differentiation**
80/20 rule	**product positioning**
direct forecast	**product repositioning**
industry potential	**sales forecast**
linear trend extrapolation	**salesforce survey forecast**
lost-horse forecast	**survey of buyers' intentions forecast**
market potential	**synergy**
market-product grid	**trend extrapolation**
market segments	**usage rate**
perceptual map	

QUESTIONS & PROBLEMS

WHAT MARKET SEGMENTATION MEANS

Market segmentation involves aggregating prospective buyers into groups that (1) have common needs, and (2) will respond similarly to a marketing action. Market segments are a relatively homogeneous collection of prospective buyers.

Identify at least three distinct market segments for:

1. Shampoo

_____
_____
_____

2. Dry cleaners

_____
_____
_____

3. Book stores

_____
_____
_____

4. Personal computers

_____
_____
_____

Product differentiation involves a firm's using different marketing activities, such as product features and advertising, to help consumers perceive the product as different and better than competing ones.

Describe each firm's attempt at product differentiation:

Product	Product differentiation
Mountain Dew	_____
Dell computers	_____
Jeep	_____
Panasonic products	_____
Fox Network	_____

CRITERIA USED IN FORMING MARKET SEGMENTS

There are five principal criteria used when forming segments in a market:

       a. Potential for increased profit and return on investment
       b. Similarity of needs of potential buyers within a segment
       c. Difference of needs of buyers between segments
       d. Feasibility of a marketing action to reach a segment
       e. Simplicity and cost of assigning potential buyers to a segment

Using the Apple Computer example from your text, give a concrete illustration for each of the criteria listed above:

1._____

2._____

3._____

4._____

5._____

WAYS TO SEGMENT CONSUMER MARKETS

A. Variables that can be used to segment consumer markets can be divided into two main categories:

Customer characteristics
Buying situations

Which of the following statements below are examples of customer characteristics, and which are examples of buying situations?

1. Chrysler found that pickup trucks are widely used in the South and Southwest. Because many pickup truck drivers listen to country and western music, Chrysler advertises on C & W radio stations in this region.

_____

2. Del Monte now promotes a line of canned fruits and vegetables that have low salt and low sugar.

_____

3. Because well-known celebrities can't shop in peace due to "fan adoration," several mail order catalogues carry very exclusive, very expensive merchandise._____

4. A national beer company targets 60 percent of its advertising dollars to people who buy at least a case of beer per week._____

B. Common variables used to segment consumer markets include:

Region
Family size
Lifestyle
Benefits offered
Usage rate

Select a product and identify a specific market segment based on each of the following variables:

Variable	Product	Market Segment
1. Region (example)	Campbell's Nacho Cheese Sauce	Spicier in the West
2. Family size	_____	_____
3. Lifestyle	_____	_____
4. Benefits offered	_____	_____
5. Usage Rate	_____	_____

C. Market segmentation often identifies a segment of "nonusers." This category is also broken into two parts:

Prospects
Nonprospects.

What are the differences between a prospect and nonprospect? Identify a prospect and nonprospect for each of the following:

1. A CPA firm_____

2. An Internet site_____

3. Wendy's_____

4. Zales jewelers_____

5. Victoria's Secret_____

WAYS TO SEGMENT INDUSTRIAL MARKETS

Industrial markets are also categorized by customer characteristics and buying situations. There are four main dimensions when choosing variables to segment an industrial market:

Customer Characteristics:
      Geographic
      Demographic

Buying Situation:
      Nature of the good
      Buying condition

Using Figure (9-7) in the text as a guideline, select one variable from each main dimension and give a concrete example for it, then try to think of a product or service for which you might use this type of segmentation:

Main Dimension	Variable	Example	Product/Service
Geographic (example)	region	New England	Maple tree sap
Demographic	_____	_____	_____
Nature of good	_____	_____	_____
Buying Conditions	_____	_____	_____

SELECT TARGETS ON WHICH TO FOCUS EFFORTS

There are five different criteria for selecting target market segments:

Size
Expected growth
Competitive position
Cost of reaching the segment
Compatibility with the organization's objectives and resources

Using the example of Wendy's in Chapter 9, make statements (true or hypothetical to illustrate each of the five criteria above:

1._____

2._____

3._____

4._____

5._____

ANALYZING MARKET SEGMENTS USING CROSS TABULATION
Cross tabulation or cross-tabs, is a method of presenting and relating information having two or more variables. It is used to analyze and discover relationships in the data.

Movie Preference

Age	Comedy	Action	Romance
Ages 5-10	50	40	10
Ages 11-16	40	40	20
Ages 17-22	40	30	30

Answer the following questions using the (Age/Movie Preference) cross tabulation:

1. As a person grows older their preference for romantic movies:_____

2. The largest single segment for a movie that combined action and comedy:_____

3. The largest single segment for a movie that was a "romantic-comedy":_____

4. The segment that offers the greatest "growth" potential as a person gets older is:_____

PRODUCT POSITIONING

There are two major approaches to product positioning:

Head-to-Head
Product differentiation

Using television, radio, or print advertisements make a list of five current product campaigns using head-to-head positioning and five current product campaigns using product differentiation.

Head-to-head

1._____vs._____

2._____vs._____

3._____vs._____

4._____vs._____

5._____vs._____

Product Differentiation

1._____

2._____

3._____

4._____

5._____

CAN YOU PASS THE TEST?
Sample Multiple Choice Questions

1. _____ involves aggregating prospective buyers into groups that have common needs and will respond similarly to a marketing action.
     a. Product differentiation
     b. Market development
     c. Product positioning
     d. Market segmentation
     e. Needs differentiation

2. _____ involves aggregating prospective buyers into groups that (1) have common needs and (2) will respond similarly to a marketing action.
     a. Diversification
     b. Divestment
     c. Market segmentation
     d. Market augmentation
     e. Repositioning

3. KFC is a popular fast-food restaurant in the U.S. In opened its 500th restaurant in China in 2001 and is more popular than McDonald's in that country. One of the reasons is that when the company entered the Chinese market, it recruited its managers from Taiwan and the Chinese communities in the U.S. and Canada. This has been useful in coping with local Chinese governments and developing a distinctly different Chinese strategy, which includes Chicky, a friendly chicken character that has a strong appeal for children. To succeed in China, KFC used:
     a. product positioning.
     b. market sectioning.
     c. product differentiation.
     d. product segmentation.
     e. product base development.

4. Market segmentation is only a means to an end. In economist's terms, market segmentation relates supply (the organization's actions) to demand (_____).
     a. tactical goals
     b. government regulations
     c. customer needs
     d. strategic objectives
     e. product positions.

5. One advantage of a market-product grid is that it can be used to:
     a. make optimal decisions under conditions of uncertainty.
     b. screen many new product ideas in order to select the one with best long-run market potential.
     c. relate likely sales of products to prospective market segments.
     d. select representative samples of consumers for marketing research studies.
     e. relate the product life cycle to consumer demand.

6. *Seventh Heaven* is a television show that is designed to have a broad appeal to a wide number of groups. It is a show that is appropriate to watch with young children without having to worry about being embarrassed. It is a show that teaches the importance of moral values by showing teens on the show learning to cope with real-life problems without being too moralistic. It appeals to an older market because it is reminiscent of TV dramas of previous decades. This WB television show is an example of:
      a. one product with multiple market segments.
      b. multiple products with multiple market segments.
      c. synergy.
      d. mass customization.
      e. none of the above.

7. Paris Miki enables customers to help design their own eyeglasses, using a system that eliminates the need to try on countless pairs of eyeglasses to find the right one. This is an example of:
      a. mass customization.
      b. economies of scale.
      c. target marketing.
      d. how the 80/20 rule is implemented.
      e. repositioning.

8. Synergy is the increased customer value achieved through:
      a. performing organizational functions more efficiently.
      b. larger rebates at the point of sale.
      c. higher trade-in values for older model cars.
      d. the ability to be exposed to more informative advertising messages.
      e. more tax revenues for government.

9. When Mikki asked her father for his advice about marketing software for the disabled, he told her, "Reaching a segment requires a simple but effective marketing action. If no such action exists, don't segment." Mikki's father is expressing concern about the:
      a. feasibility of marketing actions to reach the segment.
      b. different needs of buyers among different segments.
      c. similarity of needs of potential buyers within a segment.
      d. simplicity and cost of assigning potential buyers to segments.
      e. potential for increased profit and ROI.

10. A different segment market usually requires a different marketing action that in turn means greater costs. If increased revenues don't offset extra costs, a marketer should _____ to reduce the number of marketing actions.
      a. increase the advertising budget
      b. try direct mail instead of broadcast advertising
      c. cancel current activities
      d. combine segments
      e. discontinue offering the good or service

11. Two general categories used to segment consumer markets are _____ and buying situations.
      a. demand frequency
      b. demand volume
      c. demand characteristics
      d. customer characteristics
      e. customer lifestyles

12. Which of the following criteria should a marketing manager use to develop segments for a market?
    a. differences of needs of buyers among segments
    b. potential for increased profit and ROI
    c. potential of a marketing action to reach a segment
    d. simplicity and cost of assigning potential buyers to segments
    e. all of the above

13. Which of the following statements demonstrates the formation of a segment based on region?
    a. In China KFC sells a much spicier chicken the farther away its restaurants are from the coastal areas.
    b. GE built a downsized microwave oven to hang under kitchen cabinets.
    c. Del Monte offers a line of canned fruit with no added sugar or artificial sweeteners.
    d. A fast food hamburger restaurant is open for breakfast on Sunday mornings but not on weekdays.
    e. A gourmet grocer advertises its services on a small-audience classical music station even though there is a much larger-audience rock station in the area.

14. Reaching a segment requires a simple but effective marketing action. If no such action exists, don't segment. This illustrates which of the criteria for forming market segments?
    a. differences of needs of buyers among segments
    b. potential for increased profit and ROI
    c. potential of a marketing action to reach a segment
    d. simplicity and cost of assigning potential buyers to segments
    e. similarity of needs of potential buyers within the segment

15. When the Benihana Frozen Foods Corporation began to offer its Famous Restaurant Classics meals in single serving packages, it was relying on a _____ segmentation variable to define a market based on serving size.
    a. regional
    b. demographic
    c. lifestyle
    d. geographic
    e. psychographic

16. Ford Motor Company uses the slogan "No Boundaries" for its ad campaigns for Ford SUVs. It invites people who want ultimate people-carrying and gear-storing capabilities "to be outfitted with the most far-reaching sports utility vehicle on earth." If the SUV campaign were simply geared to families with young children, it would be using _____ segmentation, but because the campaign is trying to appeal to people who don't like the restrictions of a sedan, who want to be able to pack up and leave at a moment's notice, and who enjoy freedom and independence, it is relying on _____ segmentation.
    a. socioeconomic; demographic
    b. psychographic; lifestyle
    c. geographic; usage rate
    d. demographic; usage rate
    e. demographic; psychographic

17. Which of the following statements demonstrates the formation of a segment based on household size?
    a. Campbell's makes spicier nacho cheese sauce for its distributors in Texas than it does in Maine.
    b. GE built a downsized microwave oven to hang under kitchen cabinets.
    c. Del Monte offers a line of canned fruit with no added sugar or artificial sweeteners.
    d. A fast food handburger restaurant is open for breakfast on Sunday mornings but not on weekdays.
    e. A gourmet grocer advertises its services on a small-audience classical music station even though there is a much larger-audience rock station in the area.

18. Hallmark stores contain many lines of greeting cards, all made by Hallmark to appeal to different target markets. The Shoebox line sells for $.99, which is a significantly lower price than some of the other Hallmark brands, in order to appeal to people on limited budgets. This is an example of _____ segmentation.
    a. psychographic
    b. behavior
    c. buying situation
    d. socioeconomic
    e. geographic

19. The headline of the ad for Sleep Number bed by Select Comfort read, "5 Reasons Why You'll Sleep Better on a Sleep Number Bed." From this information, you know that Select Comfort uses _____ segmentation.
    a. benefits sought
    b. psychographic
    c. demographic
    d. socioeconomic
    e. behavior

20. The publisher of *Generation Ñ* magazine defines its readers as first-generation Hispanics who were born and educated in the United States. This is an example of which type of segmentation variable?
    a. psychographic
    b. demographic
    c. geographic
    d. socioeconomic
    e. usage

21. A retirement plan designed specifically for farmers would rely on _____ consumer characteristics to segment its market.
    a. psychographic
    b. demographic
    c. geographic
    d. involvement
    e. usage

22. Publications designed for runners, stamp collectors, and gardeners would rely on _____ consumer characteristics to segment their market.
    a. psychographic
    b. demographic
    c. geographic
    d. socioeconomic
    e. usage

23. Miller beer once called itself "the champagne of bottled beer," and ads showed elegant women in long white dresses sipping beer from crystal goblets. Then the company discovered that most beer in the U.S. is consumed by men 18 to 30 years of age, and it changed the thrust of its marketing message to reflect the more productive target market. What segmentation variable has it focused on with the newer approach?
>   a. benefits sought
>   b. usage
>   c. product awareness
>   d. buyer intentions
>   e. buying condition

24. Golden Gallon convenience stores sell Golden Gallon brand milk. Every time a customer purchases a gallon of this brand and gives the clerk his or her Golden Gallon card, the card is punched. When the customer has accumulated enough marks, then he or she gets a free gallon milk. This is an example of segmentation by:
>   a. usage.
>   b. benefits offered.
>   c. demographics.
>   d. family size.
>   e. pyschographics.

25. Many larger hotel chains have rewards programs for their frequent guests. By participating in the programs, customers earn points for later free stays at these hotels. This is an example of the use of which type of segmentation variable?
>   a. psychographic
>   b. demographic
>   c. geographic
>   d. socioeconomic
>   e. usage rate

26. People who do NOT use a firm's product or service, and most likely never will, are called:
>   a. nonqualified prospects.
>   b. leads.
>   c. undefined prospects.
>   d. nonprospects.
>   e. disenfranchised prospects.

27. If the owners of a bakery want to increase sales of its baked goods by directing its marketing efforts towards the relatively small number of consumers who are responsible for purchasing the majority of the baked goods sold, it would be:
>   a. augmenting its market.
>   b. segmenting its market based on the 80/20 rule.
>   c. segmenting its market based on family size.
>   d. segmenting its market according to consumer interest.
>   e. segmenting its market according to consumer needs.

28. According to the 80/20 rule,:
>   a. 80 percent of a firm's sales come from 20 percent of its customers.
>   b. 80 percent of a firm's advertising budget goes to 20 percent of the available media.
>   c. 8- percent of a firm's product will fail, and only 20 percent are guaranteed to succeed.
>   d. 80 percent of a firm's organizational structure is involved in some facet of marketing, and 20 percent are in non-marketing positions.
>   e. 80 percent of a firm's customers typically only like 20 percent of the company's products.

29. Hallmark groups its products into four categories. They are flowers and gifts, cards and e-cards, Hallmark collectibles, and photo albums and scrapbooks. Why does Hallmark use product groupings?
    a. The groupings increase the number of market-product combinations on the market-product grid into a more manageable framework for subsequent analysis.
    b. Consumers buy more in illogically-organized environments.
    c. The products are grouped so people can relate to these product grouping in a more meaningful way.
    d. Product groupings can be generated quantitatively to show which adhere to the 80/20 rule.
    e. All of the above are reasons why Hallmark would use product groupings.

30. In developing a marketing strategy for your Wendy's restaurant, you determine that as many as 400 lunches per day are purchased by local college students who commute and eat at your restaurant. This is part of the process for:
    a. implementing the 80-20 rule.
    b. forming products to be sold into groups.
    c. developing a market-product grid and estimating size of markets.
    d. implementing a harvesting strategy.
    e. repositioning a product.

31. Which of the following is an example of a demographic organizational customer characteristic used for market segmentation?
    a. type of buy
    b. who buys
    c. region
    d. NAICS codes
    e. MSA, PMSA, and CMSA divisions

32. Harmony Products makes fertilizers used on golf courses. Which demographic market segmentation variable would provide the greatest benefit to the organization?
    a. NAICS codes
    b. annual sales
    c. buying condition
    d. nature of good
    e. number of locations

33. Which of the following is the example of criteria to be used in selecting a target market?
    a. competitive position
    b. market size
    c. expected growth
    d. compatibility with the organization's objectives and resources
    e. all of the above

34. Which of the following is a criterion for selecting a target market?
    a. similarity of needs of potential buyers within a segment
    b. difference of needs of sellers between segments
    c. feasibility of a marketing action to reach a segment
    d. simplicity and cost of assigning potential buyers to segments
    e. expected growth of segment

35. Which of the following is a criterion for selecting a target market?
    a. similarity of needs of potential buyers within a segment
    b. difference of needs of sellers between segments
    c. feasibility of a marketing action to reach a segment
    d. competitive position, or amount of competition in the segment
    e. simplicity and cost of assigning potential buyers to segments

36. Kellie Johnson makes jams and jellies that sell under the brand name of Victorian Kitchen. In developing a marketing strategy to sell her product line, she decides to buy an ad in the local shoppers' newspaper. Johnson has just:
    a. selected target market segments to reach.
    b. formed products to be sold into groups.
    c. developed a market-product grid and estimating size of markets.
    d. taken marketing actions to reach target markets.
    e. formed prospective buyers into segments.

37. In 1998 Apple re-focused on the consumer and education markets, introducing the iMac—the most innovative PC ever created according to many PC and business analysts. By the end of the year 800,000 units had been sold, making the iMac the greatest PC product launch ever. This strategy was successful primarily because it identified:
    a. innovative distributors.
    b. competitive advertising.
    c. important corporate computer needs.
    d. target market segments.
    e. usage rates among younger consumers.

38. The term market potential can be used interchangeably with the term:
    a. company forecast.
    b. sales potential.
    c. sales forecast.
    d. economic potential.
    e. industry potential.

39. A _____ is the least expensive type of forecast.
    a. direct
    b. lost-horse
    c. survey of buyers' intentions
    d. salesforce survey forecast
    e. trend extrapolation

40. When Harold Hansen was marketing manager at Creative Concepts Manufacturing Company, he estimated the company would sell a total of 500,000 of their new sandstone coasters decorated with Native American petroglyphs the first year on the market although the company had never before produced a product like that. What is this type of estimate called?
    a. a buildup
    b. a direct forecast
    c. a lost-horse farecast
    d. a Delphi forecast
    e. a salesforce forecast

41. What does the term product positioning refer to?
    a. a careful analysis of cross tabulations
    b. shelf locations in major chain, grocery, and department stores
    c. geographic segmentation, often within major metropolitan areas
    d. the place a product offering occupies in consumers' minds on important attributes
    e. an old and outdated concept no longer worthy of consideration in marketing planning

42. An ad campaign by the manufacturer of Progresso soup compares the richness of a bowl of Progresso chicken soup to that of Campbell's chicken and stars soup. This is an example of:
    a. differentiation positioning.
    b. nondescript segmentation.
    c. mutually exclusive segmentation.
    d. guerilla marketing.
    e. head-to-head positioning.

43. Children's Advil pain reliever positioned itself against Children's Tylenol pain reliever by running ads, which claimed that the Advil brand is superior because it works faster and longer than the Tylenol brand. This is an example of:
    a. head-to-head positioning.
    b. lateral positioning.
    c. differentiation.
    d. consumer positioning.
    e. cognitive positioning.

44. At a Hallmark store you can find several different product lines of greeting cards, including Fresh Ink, Nature's Sketchbook, Shoebox, Maxine, Mahogany, and Tree of Life cards. This is an example of:
    a. head-to-head positioning.
    b. lateral positioning.
    c. cognitive positioning.
    d. repositioning.
    e. differentiation positioning.

45. An approach to positioning a new product in the market is _____ positioning, which involves competing directly with competitors on similar product attributes in the same target market.
    a. perceptual
    b. psychological
    c. segmentation
    d. cross tabulated
    e. head-to-head

46. A graph displaying consumers' perceptions of product attributes across two or more dimensions is a:
    a. payoff table.
    b. growth matrix.
    c. market-product grid.
    d. perceptual map.
    e. consumer preference matrix.

47. Tate wants to create a graphic representation of how consumers feel about breakfast cereals based on sugar content and nutritional image. Which of the following tools should he use for this project?
    a. trend extrapolation graph
    b. market-product matrix
    c. market-customer attractiveness matrix
    d. cross-tabulation table
    e. perceptual map

48. _____ involves changing the place an offering occupies in a consumer's mind relative to competitive offerings.
   a. Reverse marketing
   b. Demarketing
   c. Repositioning
   d. Resegmenting
   e. Reverse targeting

49. SwissAir recently tried to expand, but because of a variety of reasons, it failed and had to declare bankruptcy. Prior to declaring bankruptcy, SwissAir engaged in several cost-cutting efforts, which alienated its customer base. After much effort, the company began operations again with the hope of attracting its previous customers back. Because it feared that a _____ strategy would not undo the damage to the brand name, the company opted for a totally new name and new look.
   a. segmentation
   b. differentiation
   c. repositioning
   d. probability
   e. inference

50. Post Grape-Nuts cereal has been marketed since early in the 20th century. Its market share has been steadily declining as consumers began associating it with something their grandfather ate. Post recently launched a campaign which invited consumers to try the crunchy cereal on top of their yogurt, their salad, or their bowl of soup as a delicious addition. This is an example of a _____ strategy.
a. perceptual mapping
b. product positioning
c. product differentiation
d. repositioning
e. psychographics

Answer Key

Answers to Questions & Problems

What Market Segmentation Means

Example:

1. Dry hair (need conditioners)
   Styled hair
   Dandruff suffers

Mountain Dew—flavor
Compaq computers—quality
Jeep—off-road vehicles
Panasonic products—technology
Fox Network—younger, more "hip"

Ways to segment Consumer Markets

1. Customer characteristics
2. Buying situations
3. Customer characteristics
4. Buying situation

Example:

CPA firm—prospect—company with bank credit needs; nonprospect—small business with in-house bookkeeper

Analyzing Market Segments Using Cross Tabulation

1. Increases
2. 5-10
3. 17-22
4. Romance

Product Positioning

Example:

Head-to-head—Tylenol, Advil

Product differentiation—Chrysler minivan, PT Cruiser, Mountain Dew

Answers to Sample Multiple Choice Questions

1. b p. 205 LO 1	14. a p. 210 LO 1	26. b p. 218 LO 2	38. e p. 207 LO 1
2. c p. 204-205 LO 1	15. b p. 210 LO 2	27. d p. 217 LO 2	39. a p. 207 LO 1
3. e p. 204-205 LO 1	16. c p. 210 LO 2	28. c p. 218 LO 2	40. c p. 207-208 LO 1
4. a p. 207 LO 1	17. b p. 210 LO 1	29. c p. 220 LO 2	41. d p. 210 LO 1
5. c p. 207-208 LO 1	18. a p. 210 LO 2	30. d p. 220 LO 2	42. e p. 211 LO 2
6. e p. 207 LO 1	19. d p. 211 LO 2	31. e p. 221 LO 2	43. e p. 216 LO 2
7. c p. 207 LO 1	20. a p. 210 LO 2	32. a p. 222 LO 3	44. a p. 217 LO 2
8. a p. 207-208 LO 1	21. a p. 215 LO 2	33. c p. 223 LO 3	45. b p. 217 LO 2
9. d p. 209 LO 1	22. e p. 215 LO 2	34. d p. 223 LO 1	46. d p. 217 LO 2
10. a p. 207 LO 1	23. a p. 215 LO 2	35. b p. 225 LO 1	47. c p. 221 LO 3
11. c p. 207 LO 1	24. c p. 216 LO 2	36. e p. 225 LO 1	48. e p. 223 LO 1
12. c p. 210 LO 1	25. b p. 217 LO 2	37. a p. 207 LO 1	49. b p. 225-226 LO 1
13. e p. 209 LO 1			50. e p. 217 LO 1

Note: LO indicates learning objective.

CHAPTER 10

DEVELOPING NEW PRODUCTS AND SERVICES

<u>Why is Chapter 10 important?</u> This chapter explains the first element of the marketing mix—the product and how products are classified. It illustrates the process of introducing a new product and how each step is vital to that product's success. It also shows some of the major reasons why a majority of all new products fail.

Product: A good, service, or idea consisting of a bundle of tangible and intangible attributes that satisfies consumers and is received in exchange for money or some other unit of value.

CHAPTER OUTLINE

I. VARIATIONS OF PRODUCTS

    A. Product Line
    B. Product Item
    C. Product Mix
    D. Classifying Products
        1. Type of user
            a. consumer good
            b. business good
        2. Tangibility
            a. nondurable good
            b. durable good

II. CLASSIFYING CONSUMER AND BUSINESS GOODS

    A. Consumer Goods
        1. Convenience goods
        2. Shopping goods
        3. Specialty goods
        4. Unsought goods

    B. Business Goods
        1. Production goods
            a. raw materials
            b. component parts
        2. Support goods
            a. installations
                i. buildings
                ii. fixed equipment
            b. accessory equipment
            c. supplies
            d. services

III. NEW PRODUCTS

    A. Newness
          1. Compared with existing products
          2. In legal terms
          3. From company's perspective
          4. From consumer's perspective
               a. continuous innovation
               b. dynamically continuous innovation
               c. discontinuous innovation

    B. Marketing Reasons for Failure
          1. Insignificant "point of difference"
          2. Incomplete market and product definition
          3. Too little market attractiveness
          4. Poor executive of the marketing mix
          5. Poor product quality or sensitivity to customer needs on critical factors
          6. Bad timing
          7. No economical access to buyers

    C. New Product Process
          1. Strategy development
                a. identify markets
               b. identify strategic roles
          2. Idea generation
                a. customer and supplier suggestions
               b. employee and co-worker suggestions
               c. research and development breakthroughs
               d. competitive products
          3. Screening and evaluation
                a. internal approach
               b. external approach
          4. Business analysis
          5. Development
          6. Market testing
                a. test marketing
               b. simulated test markets
          7. Commercialization

You should be able to place these key terms in the outline and be able to discuss them.

business analysis	**product line**
business goods	**product mix**
commercialization	**production goods**
consumer goods	**protocol**
convenience goods	**screening & evaluation**
failure fee	**shopping goods**
idea generation	**Six Sigma**
market testing	**slotting fee**
new-product process	**specialty goods**
new-product strategy development	**support goods**
product	**unsought goods**

QUESTIONS & PROBLEMS

CLASSIFYING PRODUCTS

Two major ways to classify products are by degree of tangibility and by the type of user.

Degree of tangibility

Classification by tangibility divides products into three groups:

Nondurable goods
Durable goods
Services

Classify the following products listed below by their degree of tangibility:

1. ketchup_____
2. paper plates_____
3. lawn care_____
4. day care_____
5. bath towels_____
6. carpeting_____

Many students mistake the term "durable good" for something that is physically strong. Whereas a fine delicate crystal vase is a durable good because it can be used again and again a fireplace log however, might be heavy and strong, but once it is burned it is gone! (The vase is durable, the log is nondurable)

Type of user

The second major type of product classification is based on the user.

Consumer goods
Business goods

Classify the following products according to user:

1. nails_____
2. cake mix_____
3. ball bearings_____
4. farm machinery_____
5. printing press_____
6. suitcase_____

CONSUMER GOODS CLASSIFICATION

Consumer goods can be further classified by considering three characteristics: (1) the effort the consumer spends on the decision, (2) the attributes used in purchase, and (3) the frequency of purchase.

Convenience goods
Shopping goods
Specialty goods
Unsought goods

Classify the following products by the type of consumer goods:

1. breath mints_____
2. personal computer_____
3. pianos_____
4. burial plots_____
5. life insurance_____

It is important to remember that there is no "master list" of what is a convenience good and what is a specialty good; the classification depends on the characteristics of the purchase decision in terms of time, importance, risk, etc. A pair of running shoes could be a shopping good to one person and a specialty good to another.

BUSINESS GOODS CLASSIFICATION

Business goods are classified not only on the attribute the consumer uses but also on how the item is to be used.

Production goods
Support goods

Classify the following business goods:

1. legal services for contracts_____
2. wood glue for fastening veneer_____
3. tomatoes for ketchup_____
4. coal for heating plant furnaces_____

There are four types of support goods. These include:

Installations
Accessory equipment
Supplies
Services

Match the correct industrial support goods classification with the examples listed below:

1. custodial work_____
2. stock warehouses_____
3. advertising agency_____
4. office chairs_____

Newness from the consumer's perspective

Newness from the consumer's perspective classifies new products according to the degree of learning required by the consumer.

Discontinuous innovation
Dynamically continuous innovation
Continuous innovation

Match the correct term to the statements or examples listed below:

1. Although this product can be somewhat disruptive, totally new behavior by the consumer is not required for its use._____

2. No new behaviors must be learned._____

3. Often a significant amount of time must be spent initially educating the consumer on how to use the product._____

4. An example of this type of product newness is the advent of automatic transmissions.
_____

5. An example of this type of product newness is the microwave oven._____

6. An example of this type of product newness is the disposable straight razor._____

NEW PRODUCTS AND WHY THEY FAIL

Proactive and reactive new product strategies:

There are two types of new product strategies:

Proactive strategy
Reactive strategy

Match the correct new product strategy to the statements below:

1. In response to IRI's videocart, Great Atlantic and Pacific Tea Company (A&P) started testing in-store electronic signs that showed ads and promotions._____

2. Spalding Sports Worldwide spent $1,000,000 developing a high-tech model tennis racket called the Pro Response Series._____

Having a real product advantage and a precise protocol are the greatest differences between those products that succeed and those that do not. This would be illustrated by a statement which identifies a well-defined target market before product development begins; specifies customers' needs, wants, and preferences; and carefully states what the product would be and do.

DEVELOPING NEW PRODUCTS

Idea Generation

What are the sources of ideas for new products? Which are likely to be most successful? (consider Crystal Pepsi and Netscape)_____

Screening and Evaluation

Who should participate in the screening of new product proposals? Why? (consider New Coke)_____
_____

Business Analysis

Check which of the following are performed at the business analysis stage of the new product process?

1. A determination is made as to whether the new product will help or hurt sales of existing products._____
_____

2. An assessment is made as to whether current distribution channels can be used or whether new channels will have to be developed._____

3. Costs for research and development are determined._____

4. Costs for production are determined._____

5. Forecasts are made for future sales._____

6. Forecasts are made for potential market share._____

7. A break-even analysis is performed._____

8. Estimates are made for return-on-investment to assess future profitability._____

Development

What problems are likely to arise during development? How can these effect the product and its marketing? (consider the Intel Pentium chip)_____
_____

Market Testing

The market testing stage of the new product process involves exposing actual products to perspective consumers under realistic purchase conditions to see if they will buy. Test marketing involves offering a product for sale on limited basis in a defined area. There are two commonly used market tests:

Standard markets
Selected controlled markets (forced distribution markets)

FILL IN THE BLANK WITH THE APPROPRIATE TERM:

1. Those test sites where companies sell a new product through normal distribution channels and monitor the results._____

2. Those test markets where the total test is conducted by an outside agency._____

Commercialization:

How do you determine when to commercialize the product? The video CD was introduced by RCA in the late 1970's and was a tremendous failure. They are successful now with very little change in technology. Why?_____
_____
_____

CAN YOU PASS THE TEST?
Sample Multiple Choice Questions

1. A product is a good, service, or idea consisting of a bundle of tangible and intangible attributes that satisfies consumers and is:
    a. received in exchange for money alone.
    b. received in exchange for money or other unit of value.
    c. always provides the selling company with profit.
    d. a tangible received in exchange for a person's time and effort.
    e. something people need as a result of a marketer-dominated source.

2. A _____ is a group of products that are closely related because they satisfy a class of needs, are used together, and sold to the same customer group, are distributed through the same type of outlets, and fall within a given price range.
    a. product mix
    b. market segment
    c. product segment
    d. product line
    e. marketing mix

3. A specific product as noted by a unique brand, size, or price is called a:
    a. product class.
    b. product type.
    c. product item.
    d. brand item.
    e. product line.

4. On the supermarket shelf, Veronica found Campbell Classics soups, Campbell Fun Favorites soups, Campbell Special Selection soups, and Campbell Healthy Request soups. This collection of products is called a:
    a. product mix.
    b. market segment.
    c. product segment.
    d. product line.
    e. marketing mix.

5. In addition to its canned soups, Campbell Soup Company manufactures Swanson Broth, Franco-American, Prego, Pepperidge Farm, and Pace brand products. This group of products is an example of a:
    a. product mix.
    b. market segment.
    c. product segment.
    d. product line.
    e. marketing mix.

6. Which of the following is NOT a synonym for business goods?
    a. B2B goods
    b. industrial goods
    c. consumer goods
    d. organizational goods
    e. All of the above are synonyms.

7. Which of the following is most clearly an example of a consumer good?
        a. Elmer's Glue-All for all porous materials
        b. GE light bulbs
        c. Hammermill printer paper
        d. FAO Schwartz teddy bears
        e. Dell computers

8. Which of the following is an example of a purchase of industrial goods?
        a. Ford buying paint for its automobiles
        b. a printing company buying paper
        c. an accounting firm buying a new computer system
        d. a construction company buying nails
        e. all of the above

9. The degree of _____ determines whether a product should be labeled as a durable or a nondurable good.
        a. homogeneity
        b. specialization
        c. tangibility
        d. market segmentation
        e. newness

10. Advertising is important for products such as Butterfinger candy bars and Dasani bottled water that are purchased frequently and at relatively low cost. Wide distribution in retail outlets is essential. Why?
        a. They are durable goods and cannot be sold without personal selling to answer consumers' questions.
        b. They are unsought goods so advertising targets consumers' impulsiveness.
        c. They are nondurable goods and easily substitutable so consumers need to be reminded of their existence.
        d. They are production goods and can easily go out of stock.
        e. They are semidurable goods, and advertising helps to maintain high inventories.

11. Which of the following is the best example of a convenience good?
        a. Sony CD player
        b. Lexus LS 400 luxury automobile
        c. flight on American Airlines
        d. *Roget's Thesaurus*
        e. bath soap

12. Which of the following statements about convenience goods is true?
        a. Convenience goods are infrequently purchased.
        b. Convenience goods have widespread availability.
        c. Consumers are very brand loyal when purchasing convenience goods.
        d. Convenience goods are typically relatively expensive.
        e. Consumers engage in some comparison shopping when buying convenience goods.

13. Which of the following is the best example of a shopping good?
        a. *People* magazine
        b. toothpaste
        c. Waterford crystal
        d. laptop computer
        e. chewing gum

14. You greatly admire a set of Ralph Lauren crystal goblets you see at a dinner party, and decide to buy four, despite the somewhat surprising price of $60 each. They are only available in your area in a Ralph Lauren Polo shop 40 miles from campus. Into which classification of consumer goods would the crystal goblets fall?
    a. convenience goods
    b. shopping goods
    c. specialty goods
    d. unsought goods
    e. derived goods

15. In terms of price, which of the following types of goods would most likely be relatively inexpensive?
    a. shopping goods
    b. convenience goods
    c. specialty goods
    d. unsought goods
    e. consumer goods

16. In terms of promotion, which of the following types of goods stress product differentiation from competitors?
    a. shopping goods
    b. convenience goods
    c. specialty goods
    d. unsought goods
    e. services

17. In terms of brand loyalty, consumers are very brand loyal and will not accept substitutes for which type of goods?
    a. shopping goods
    b. convenience goods
    c. specialty goods
    d. unsought goods
    e. services

18. The two broad classifications of business goods are:
    a. production or support.
    b. industrial or governmental goods.
    c. reseller or manufacturer goods.
    d. supplies or components
    e. tangibles and nontangibles.

19. Which of the following best illustrates the concept of derived demand?
    a. The number of retail stores in a downtown area decreases and demand for retail goods increases.
    b. An increase in the number of new single family homes results from a spurt in the gross national product.
    c. The heat wave results in an increased demand for air conditioners.
    d. Jet engine manufacturers experience increased sales because more tourists are taking international vacations.
    e. Honda's reducing its car prices causes GM to do the same.

20. Support goods are:
    a. products purchased by the ultimate consumer.
    b. products for which the consumer will compare several alternatives on several criteria.
    c. items used to assist in the production of other goods.
    d. items the consumer purchases frequently and with a minimum of shopping effort.
    e. products a consumer will make an effort to seek out and buy.

21. A small gas monitor that measures combustible gas, oxygen deficiency, carbon monoxide, and hydrogen sulfide levels simultaneously in a manufacturing environment is an example of what type of business product?
    a. production good
    b. accessory equipment
    c. installation
    d. supplies
    e. services

22. The 18-hole golf course that a subdivision developer had custom designed and built to attract more new home buyers to the subdivision would be an example of a(n):
    a. production good.
    b. accessory equipment.
    c. supply.
    d. installation.
    e. specialty good.

23. A product's newness can be defined in terms of:
    a. a legal perspective.
    b. how it compares with existing products.
    c. the company's perspective.
    d. the consumers' perspectives.
    e. all of the above.

24. Which of the following is NOT an attribute of a new product ?
    a. The product is less than 6 months old.
    b. The product requires a significant degree of "new" learning by consumers.
    c. The product is "new" in legal terms.
    d. The product is "new" from a competitor's perspective.
    e. The product is "new" from the organization's perspective.

25. A continuous innovation:
    a. disrupts consumer's normal routine but does not require totally new learning.
    b. establishes new consumption patterns among consumers.
    c. is promoted through product trials and personal selling.
    d. requires consumers to engage in no new learning.
    e. is promoted through an emphasis on its benefits and how they differentiate the product from the competition.

26. The addition of Sparkling Apple-Scented, Invigorating Breeze-Scented, and Summer Citrus-Scented versions of Mr. Clean antibacterial cleaning liquid is an example of:
    a. discontinuous innovation.
    b. phased innovation.
    c. continuous innovation.
    d. gradual innovation.
    e. dynamically continuous innovation.

27. Which of the following products at the time of its introduction was the best example of a discontinuous innovation?
        a. compact disc player
        b. disposable lighters
        c. automatic dishwashers
        d. liquid laundry detergent
        e. instant light charcoal

28. Built-in car seats for children require only minor bits of education and changes in behavior, so the marketing strategy is to educate prospective buyers on their benefits, advantages, and proper use. This is an example of:
        a. dynamically continuous innovation
        b. continuous innovation
        c. intermittent innovation
        d. discontinuous innovation
        e. dynamically discontinuous innovation

29. Which of the following is one of the reasons advanced for new-product failure?
        a. too great a level of market attractiveness
        b. superior execution of marketing mix
        c. complete product and market definition before product development starts
        d. significant point of difference between product and its competitors
        e. none of the above

30. Suppose you are a marketing consultant hired to analyze why a new reality television show failed to attract an audience in spite of the fact that there are at least a half a dozen successful reality shows on broadcast and cable television. Which of the following do you think could be a reason for the show's failure?
        a. poor product quality
        b. insignificant point of difference compared to shows already on the air
        c. bad timing
        d. poor execution of the marketing mix
        e. any of the above

31. The first stage in the new-product process is:
        a. the business analysis.
        b. the situational analysis.
        c. new-product strategy development.
        d. idea generation.
        e. none of the above.

32. The sequence of activities a firm uses to identify business opportunities and convert them into salable goods or services is called the:
        a. situation analysis.
        b. new-product process.
        c. strategic management process.
        d. industrial buying process.
        e. idea generation process.

33. Six Sigma is most closely related to:
    a. pricing strategies.
    b. quality management.
    c. organizational structure.
    d. operational planning.
    e. electronic commerce.

34. A small number of people from different departments in an organization who are mutually accountable to a common set of performance goals are called a(n):
    a. executive committee.
    b. corporate bureaucracy.
    c. cross functional team.
    d. interdepartmental autocracy.
    e. none of the above.

35. Sara Burns is the owner of a company called Spice and was looking for a new-product to go with her company's line of food condiments when a customer suggested combining spices with tea. This is an example of:
    a. accidental invention.
    b. bootlegging time.
    c. idea generation.
    d. management by walking around.
    e. serendipitous innovation.

36. _____ involves specifying the features of the product and marketing strategy needed to commercialize it and making necessary financial projections.
    a. SWOT analysis
    b. New-product assessment
    c. New-product extrapolation
    d. Business analysis
    e. Environmental audit

37. Which of the following statements about the screening and evaluation stage of the new-product process is true?
    a. The internal approach decides whether the new-product idea is technically feasible.
    b. Concept testing is part of the external approach.
    c. New-product ideas are eliminated during the screening and evaluation stage.
    d. Frito Lay's brand, Sun Chips, went through a concept test.
    e. All of the above statements about the screening and evaluation stage of the new-product process are true.

38. Product ideas that survive the business analysis stage of the new-product development process enter which stage next?
    a. development
    b. market testing
    c. concept testing
    d. commercialization
    e. none of the above

39. Sara Burns is the owner of a company called Spice and was looking for a new product to go with her company's line of food condiments when a customer suggested combining spices with tea. In the _____ stage of the new-product process, spices and tea were turned into a prototype.
    a. idea generation
    b. screening and evaluation
    c. business analysis
    d. development
    e. commercialization

40. Test marketing involves offering a product for sale on a limited basis:
    a. exclusively to company employees.
    b. to as broad a geographic region as possible.
    c. to a unidimensional target market.
    d. in a defined area.
    e. only on certain days of the week and hours of the day.

41. The market testing stage of the new-product process often involves test markets or simulated test markets in which the dependent variable is:
    a. consumer attitudes.
    b. price.
    c. advertising.
    d. brand awareness.
    e. sales.

42. Simulated test markets:
    a. can never be used as replacements for test marketing.
    b. are usually conducted at the manufacturing site.
    c. require the development of multiple focus groups who interview potential product users.
    d. cannot be used to make sales projections.
    e. are often used by consumer packaged goods manufacturers.

43. Test marketing is:
    a. almost always done, especially for consumer services.
    b. not usually done with services, expensive consumer products or costly industrial products.
    c. almost always done for new consumer products, including more expensive ones.
    d. not usually done with most products because of the time and expense involved.
    e. often not very helpful because the testing area is not representative of the entire sales area.

44. Which is the most expensive stage of the new-product development process?
    a. new-product strategy development
    b. business analysis
    c. market testing
    d. idea generation
    e. commercialization

45. For which of the following products is the manufacturer most likely to have to pay a slotting fee in order to gain a place on a retailer's shelves?
    a. disposable cameras
    b. CD-Rom games
    c. cake mix
    d. leather vests
    e. cotton towels

46. Slotting fees are paid by manufacturers to grocers in payment for space—or slots—in their warehouses and on their retail shelves. Such slotting fees significantly increase the cost of which stage of the new-product process for food manufacturers?
        a. business analysis
        b. new-product strategy development
        c. screening and evaluation
        d. commercialization
        e. idea generation

47. If a new grocery product does not achieve a predetermined sales target, some retailers require its manufacturer to pay a:
        a. trading allowance.
        b. failure fee.
        c. slotting fee.
        d. perquisite.
        e. promotional allowance.

48. Which of the following methods is commonly used in software development to speed up the development process?
        a. service rollout
        b. fast prototyping
        c. parallel development
        d. protocol enhancement
        e. market testing of the concept

49. Product prototypes are created during which stage of the new-product development process?
        a. development
        b. business analysis
        c. market testing
        d. idea generation
        e. commercialization

50. Kroger required that Birdseye pay $15,000 to get its new frozen stir-fry vegetable mix placed in the freezers of Kroger supermarkets. This payment is called a _____ by Kroger.
        a. retail goodwill fee
        b. bribe
        c. product support fee
        d. slotting fee
        e. product development fee

ANSWER KEY

Answers to Questions & Problems

Classifying Products

1. Nondurable
2. Nondurable
3. Services
4. Services
5. Durable
6. Durable

Type of User

1. Both
2. Consumer goods
3. Business goods
4. Business goods
5. Business goods
6. Consumer goods

Consumer Goods Classification

1. Convenience
2. Shopping
3. Specialty
4. Unsought
5. Unsought

Business Goods Classification

1. Support goods
2. Production goods
3. Production goods
4. Support goods

1. Services
2. Installations
3. Services
4. Accessory equipment

Newness from the Consumer's Perspective

1. Dynamically continuous innovation
2. Continuous innovation
3. Discontinuous innovation
4. Dynamically continuous innovation
5. Discontinuous innovation
6. Continuous innovation

New Products and Why They Fail

1. Reactive strategy
2. Proactive strategy

Developing New Products—Business Analysis

1. Yes
2. Yes
3. Yes
4. Yes
5. Yes
6. Yes
7. Yes
8. Yes

Market Testing

1. Standard markets
2. Selected controlled markets

Commercialization

Focus was on recording ability not picture quality. Most VCR and CD players were used with older TV's rendering the "quality of picture" argument moot.

Answers to Sample Multiple Choice Questions

1. b p. 262; LO 1	14. c p. 264; LO 2	26. c p. 268; LO 3	38. a p. 277; LO 5
2. d p. 262-263; LO 1	15. b p. 264; LO 2	27. c p. 268; LO 3	39. d p. 277-278; LO 5
3. c p. 263; LO 1	16. a p. 265; LO 2	28. a p. 268; LO 3	40. d p. 279; LO 5
4. d p. 263; LO 1	17. c p. 265; LO 2	29. e p. 269-271; LO 4	41. e p. 279; LO 5
5. a p. 263; LO 1	18. a p. 265; LO 2	30. e p. 269-271; LO 4	42. e p. 279; LO 5
6. c p. 263; LO 2	19. d p. 265; LO 2	31. c p. 272-273; LO 5	43. b p. 280; LO 5
7. d p. 263; LO 2	20. c p. 265; LO 2	32. b p. 272; LO 5	44. e p. 281; LO 5
8. e p. 263; LO 2	21. b p. 266; LO 2	33. b p. 273; LO 5	45. c p. 281; LO 5
9. c p. 264; LO 2	22. d p. 265; LO 2	34. c p. 273; LO 5	46. d p. 281; LO 5
10. c p. 264; LO 2	23. e p. 267-268; LO 3	35. c p. 273; LO 5	47. b p. 281; LO 5
11. e p. 264; LO 2	24. d p. 267-268; LO 3	36. d p. 277; LO 5	48. b p. 282; LO 5
12. b p. 264; LO 2	25. e p. 268; LO 3	37. e p. 276; LO 5	49. a p. 277; LO 5
13. d p. 264; LO 2			50. d p. 281; LO 5

Note: LO indicates learning objective.

CHAPTER 11

MANAGING PRODUCTS AND BRANDS

<u>Why is Chapter 11 important?</u> This chapter illustrates the importance of the marketing mix throughout the life of a product. It shows how utilizing different strategies with the mix elements can enhance each stage of a product's life cycle. In addition, it describes the importance of branding and choosing a good brand name.

Product Life Cycle: Concept describing the stages a new product goes through in the marketplace - introduction, growth, maturity, and decline.

CHAPTER OUTLINE

I. PRODUCT LIFE CYCLE

    A. Introduction Stage
        1. Promotion
            a. primary demand
            b. selective demand
        2. Price
            a. skimming
            b. penetration

    B. Growth Stage
        1. Competitor's appear
        2. Profit peaks
        3. Sales grow at increasing rate
        4. Product differentiation
        5. Expanded distribution

    C. Maturity Stage
        1. Leveling off of industry sales or product class revenue
        2. Marginal competitors leave
        3. Sales increase at decreasing rate
        4. Profit declines through price competition
        5. Marketing expenses directed at holding share

    D. Decline Stage
        1. Deletion
        2. Harvesting

    E. Dimensions
        1. Length of Product Life Cycle
        2. Shape of the Product Life Cycle
            a. generalized
            b. high learning
            c. low learning
            d. fashion
            e.   fad

3. Product level
   a. class
   b. form
4. Product Life Cycle and consumers
   a. diffusion of innovation
      i. innovators
      ii. early adopters
      iii. early majority
      iv. late majority
      v. laggards

II. MANAGING THE PRODUCT LIFE CYCLE

A. Product Modification
B. Market Modification
   1. Finding new users
   2. Increasing use
   3. Creating new use situations
C. Repositioning the Product
   1. Reacting to a competitor's position
   2. Reaching a new market
   3. Catching a rising trend
   4. Changing value offered
      a. trading up
      b. trading down

III. BRANDING AND BRAND MANAGEMENT

A. Brand Personality and Brand Equity

B. Licensing

C. Picking a Good Brand Name
   1. Suggests product benefits
   2. Memorable, distinctive, positive
   3. Fits company and product image
   4. No legal or regulatory restrictions
   5. Simple and emotional

D. Strategies
   1. Manufacturer branding
      a. multiproduct (blanket or family) branding
      b. co-branding
      c. multibranding
      d. eurobranding
   2. Private branding
   3. Mixed branding
   4. Generic branding

III. PACKAGING AND LABELING

   A. Creating Customer Value through Packaging and Labeling
   1. Communication benefits
   2. Functional benefits
   3. Perceptual benefits

   B. Global Trends in Packaging
   1. Environmental sensitivity
   2. Health and safety concerns

IV. PRODUCT WARRANTY

   A. Variations
   1. Express warranties
   2. Limited coverage warranties
   3. Full coverage warranties
   4. Implied warranties

   B. Importance
   1. Product liability
   2. Marketing advantage

You should be able to place these key terms in the outline and be able to discuss them.

brand equity	**multiproduct branding**	**warranty**
brand licensing	**packaging**	
brand name	**private branding**	
brand personality	**product class**	
branding	**product form**	
co-branding	**product life cycle**	
downsizing	**product modification**	
label	**trade name**	
market modification	**trademark**	
mixed branding	**trading down**	
multibranding	**trading up**	

QUESTIONS & PROBLEMS

PRODUCT LIFE CYCLE

There are four distinct stages in the product life cycle. Each stage suggests its own distinct marketing strategy.

Introduction stage
Growth stage
Maturity stage
Decline stage

INTRODUCTION STAGE

The Hewlett-Packard Color Laserjet at popular prices (around $3000) is considered in its introduction stage.

Describe the HP Color Laserjet in its introductory stage in terms of:

1. Marketing objective:_____

2. Competition:_____

3. Product:_____

4. Price:_____

5. Promotion:_____

6. Place:_____

Select the appropriate term for the statements below:

1. This pricing strategy is used to help recover research and development costs and to capitalize on price insensitivity of early buyers._____

2. This pricing strategy discourages competitors and helps build unit volume._____

GROWTH STAGE

Snapple flavored tea could be considered in its growth stage.

Describe Snapple in its growth stage in terms of:

1. Marketing objective:_____

2. Competition:_____

3. Product:_____

4. Price:_____

5. Promotion:_____

6. Place:_____

MATURITY STAGE

Hard Rock Cafe could be described as being in the mature stage of "theme" restaurants.

Describe Hard Rock Cafe in its maturity stage in terms of:

1. Marketing objective:_____

2. Competition:_____

3. Product:_____

4. Price:_____

5. Promotion:_____

6. Place:_____

DECLINE STAGE

Underwood Typewriter could be described as being in the decline stage of the Product Life Cycle.

Describe Underwood Typewriter in its decline stage in terms of:

1. Marketing objective:_____

2. Competition:_____

3. Product:_____

4. Price:_____

5. Promotion:_____

6. Place:_____

MODIFYING THE PRODUCT

Decide whether the following statements are examples of:

Increasing use
Creating new use situations
Finding new users

1. Tums antacid is now being advertised as an excellent calcium supplement._____

2. For years the makers of Dentyne chewing gum have advised people to chew Dentyne if they can't brush after every meal. Now they suggest chewing gum in those situations where you "can't smoke."_____
_____

3. Major American car makers are offering buying incentives to newly graduated college students who traditionally have had little or no credit history._____

PRODUCT REPOSITIONING

Product repositioning is changing the place a product occupies in a consumer's mind relative to competitive products. A firm can reposition a product by changing one or more of the four marketing mix elements. There are several reasons for repositioning a product:

Reacting to a competitor's position
Reaching a new market
Catching a rising trend
Changing the value offered

Match the reason for repositioning with the following examples:

1. Snickers candy bar was repositioned from a candy bar to a snack food, which has twice as large a market

_____

2. Mercedes traded down its line with the introduction of the Mercedes 190 sedan.

_____

3. Coke was repositioned as a slightly sweeter, less filling soft drink because Coca-Cola discovered that its 1984 market share in supermarkets was 2 percent behind Pepsi-Cola's.

_____

4. To reposition Marlboro cigarettes from female to male smokers, Philip Morris adopted a Western image for the cigarette and ran ads featuring a cowboy._____

BRANDING

Find an example of a brand name that best exemplifies each characteristic below:

1. The name should describe product benefits._____

2. The name should be memorable, positive, and distinctive._____

3. The name should fit the company or product image._____

4. The name should have no legal restrictions._____

5. The name should be simple and emotional._____

PACKAGING

The packaging component of a product refers to any container in which it is offered for sale and on which information is communicated. There are three main benefits of packaging:

Communication benefits
Functional benefits
Perceptual benefits

Two current trends in packaging deal with (1) environmental sensitivity (packaging materials, recycling, etc.), and (2) the health and safety aspects of the packages themselves (heat susceptor packaging).

Indicate the type of benefits or trend each package represents:

1. Cereal in resealable packages._____

2. Coca-Cola's new contoured bottle._____

3. Windex's refillable sprayer._____

4. Tylenol's sealed packages._____

5. Betty Crocker's brownie mix with Hershey's Chocolate pictured on the package._____

WARRANTIES

A warranty is a statement indicating the liability of the manufacturer for product deficiencies. There are four major types of warranties:

Express warranty
Limited-coverage warranty
Full warranty
Implied warranty

Match the type of warranty with the statement listed below:

1. Written statements of a manufacturer's liabilities for product deficiencies._____

2. Warranties assigning responsibility for product deficiencies to a manufacturer even though a retailer sold the item._____

3. A statement of liability by a manufacturer that has no limits of noncoverage._____

4. A manufacturer's statement indicating the bounds of coverage and noncoverage for any product deficiencies._____

CAN YOU PASS THE TEST?
Sample Multiple Choice Questions

1. A concept that describes the stages a new product goes through in the marketplace— introduction, growth, maturity, and decline is called:
   a. the retail life cycle.
   b. the product life cycle.
   c. the marketing mix.
   d. the product growth cycle.
   e. product commercialization.

2. The introduction stage of the product life cycle is characterized by:
   a. minimum profit.
   b. rapid sales growth.
   c. minimal advertising.
   d. a consistent low-price strategy.
   e. all of the above

3. The music industry has changed dramatically over the years. In the 1970s, consumers purchased 8-track tapes. In the 1980s, cassette tapes caused the decline of 8-track tapes. In fact, today consumers would experience difficulty in purchasing a new artist on 8-track tape. Now in the 2000s, compact discs have become very popular and are being purchased by music lovers of every age and background. As sales of compact discs continue to grow at an increasing rate, sales of cassette tapes are weakening, the profits are declining, and the product may face a fate similar to that of 8-track tapes. Based upon this information, you can correctly conclude cassette tapes are in the _____ stage, and compact discs are in the _____ stage of the product life cycle:
   a. decline; growth
   b. decline; introduction
   c. maturity; growth
   d. decline; maturity
   e. maturity; introduction

4. Scientists have discovered a new medical treatment but before they can market it, physicians and patients must be aware of its existence. In other words, its manufacturer must create _____ demand.
   a. selective
   b. primary
   c. derived
   d. generic
   e. secondary

5. Sales on flat-screen televisions are slow and profits are minimal despite the use of a skimming strategy. Heavy advertising has done little to move the innovation from the _____ stage of the product life cycle into the next.
   a. maturity
   b. growth
   c. introduction
   d. decline
   e. harvesting

6. Which of the following statements about the introduction stage of the product life cycle is true?
   a. During the introduction stage, efforts are made to increase primary demand.
   b. During the introduction stage, firms may choose a skimming pricing strategy.
   c. During the introduction stage, firms may choose a penetration pricing strategy.
   d. Because of large initial investment costs, industry profits often must go from negative to positive.
   e. All of the above statements about the introduction stage of the product life cycle are true.

7. A technology company has just begun to make a profit on its DVD-R discs (DVD discs in a recordable format). Its promotional expenditures are aimed at trying to persuade potential customers of the merits of its DVD-R discs. Even more money is being spent to develop the firm's distribution system for its DVD-R discs. Since Apple's iMac now comes with a DVD recorder as a standard part, a few other companies have started producing DVD-R discs for the market. What stage of the product life cycle is the DVD-R in?
   a. commercialization stage
   b. maturity stage
   c. growth stage
   d. decline stage
   e. introduction stage

8. Which of the following statements about the maturity stage of the product life cycle is true?
   a. Market attention during the maturity stage is often directed toward holding market share through further market differentiation.
   b. During the maturity stage, there is a slowing of total industry sales.
   c. Profit declines during the maturity stage because there is fierce price competition among many sellers.
   d. Fewer new buyers enter the market during the maturity stage.
   e. All of the above statements about the maturity stage of the product life cycle are true.

9. Hershey's chocolate bars have been marketed in the United States for more than 100 years, and are still a tremendous success, with a loyal following of consumers. The company began advertising several years ago to hold its market share, and it has introduced several distinctive new products. What stage of the product life cycle are Hershey's chocolate bars competing in?
   a. development
   b. introduction
   c. growth
   d. maturity
   e. decline

10. When a product is in the decline stage of its product life, there are typically two types of strategies used. They are:
   a. depletion and abandonment.
   b. harvesting and deletion.
   c. divestment and deletion.
   d. market development and product development.
   e. harvesting and skimming.

11. During the 1990s, there was a backlash against artificial colors in food and other consumer products. As a result, a lot of companies issued products that were clear. One example was Crystal Pepsi. The product never really found a market and was _____, or dropped from the Pepsi product line soon after its introduction.
    a. diversified
    b. aggregated
    c. segmented
    d. deleted
    e. harvested

12. Which of the following statements about the length of the product life cycle is true?
    a. The product life cycle is about the same length for most products.
    b. The amount of time it takes for a product to move through its product life is standardized.
    c. The availability of mass communications vehicles has lengthened product life cycles.
    d. As a rule, consumer products have shorter life cycles than industrial ones.
    e. All of the above statements about the length of the product life cycle are true.

13. Which of the following is a NOT a type of product life cycle?
    a. revolutionary
    b. low learning
    c. fashion
    d. high learning
    e. fad

14. Which of the following products is most likely to be classified as a low learning product?
    a. TiVo, which allows consumers to pause and fast-forward television shows while watching them
    b. Beyblades, a new toy idea from Japan similar to Pokemon
    c. Reddi-Whip chocolate topping in the aerosol can
    d. palm-size computers
    e. assemble-it-yourself furniture

15. AOLTV, Microsoft's UltimateTV, Warner Cable's Qube System, Time Warner's Full Serve Netowrk, ABC's Enhanced TV, TiVo, and ReplayTV are all examples of interactive television. They would collectively be referred to as a:
    a. marketing mix.
    b. product line.
    c. product mix.
    d. marketing class.
    e. product class.

16. Which type of product has equally rapid introduction and decline stages of the product life cycle?
    a. high learning products
    b. low learning products
    c. fashion products
    d. fad products
    e. abnormal products

17. Automobiles are an example of a _____, and SUVs are an example of a _____.
    a. product line; product class
    b. product family; product line
    c. product brand;product line
    d. product form; product class
    e. product class; product form

18. The concept of _____ explains how a new product spreads through the population.
    a. diffusion of innovation
    b. market aggregation
    c. consumer acceptance
    d. brand diffusion
    e. customer relationship management

19. As product adopters, members of the early majority typically:
    a. fear debt and use neighbors and friends as information sources.
    b. are skeptical and have below average social status.
    c. act with deliberation and use many informal social contacts.
    d. are leaders in social standing and have slightly above average education when compared to the other adopter classes.
    e. are venturesome, better educated than other product adopters, and use multiple sources of information.

20. Product managers are responsible for:
    a. managing existing products through the stages of the life cycle.
    b. developing and executing a marketing program for the product line described in the annual marketing program.
    c. approving ad copy, media selection, and package design for products.
    d. developing new products.
    e. doing all of the above.

21. Another name for product manager is:
    a. product supervisor.
    b. brand manager.
    c. marketing manager.
    d. advertising and promotion manager.
    e. sales manager.

22. Both Pepsi and Coke have introduced colas with an added squeeze of lemon flavor, hoping that this _____ will increase sales.
    a. trading down
    b. product modification
    c. product diffusion
    d. market diffusion
    e. trading up

23. Coca-Cola once launched an advertising campaign to encourage people to consider Coke for breakfast instead of their usual cup of coffee. This campaign was an example of a _____ strategy.
    a. trading down
    b. product modification
    c. market differentiation
    d. market modification
    e. trading up

24. With _____ strategies, a company tries to find new customers, increase a product's use among existing customers, or create new use situations.
    a. market differentiation
    b. trading down
    c. market modification
    d. reverse marketing
    e. product repositioning

25. Finding new uses for an existing product has been a major strategy in extending the life of Arm & Hammer Baking Soda. The product (unchanged from its original formula) is now being promoted as a dentifrice; a deodorizer for cat litter, carpeting, and refrigerators; and a fire extinguisher. Arm & Hammer is:
    a. finding new users through a product modification strategy.
    b. creating new use situations through a market modification strategy.
    c. increasing use by existing customers through a product modification strategy.
    d. modifying the product characteristics.
    e. demarketing the product.

26. _____ involves adding value to a product (or product line) by adding features or using higher-quality materials.
    a. Repositioning
    b. Market modification
    c. Trading up
    d. Product aggregation
    e. Trading down

27. Harry & David is a catalog retailer. At its inception, the company sold fruit baskets and popularized the "Fruit of the Month" concept. Since then the company has abandoned this restrictive definition of itself, expanded its product mix, and used its promotion to explain that it is the source of the perfect gift for every occasion. Harry & David used a _____ strategy.
    a. reinvention
    b. restoration
    c. reconfiguration
    d. realignment
    e. repositioning

28. A trade name is:
    a. any word, device (design, sound, shape or color), or combination of these used to distinguish a seller's goods or services.
    b. the part of a brand that can be spoken.
    c. the part of a brand that is a symbol or design and cannot be spoken.
    d. the commercial, legal name under which a company does business.
    e. the identification that a firm has legally registered its brand name so the firm has exclusive use of it.

29. The dynamic ribbon on the side of Coca-Cola products, and Target's red bull's-eye are all examples of:
    a. brand names.
    b. attention getters.
    c. servicemarks.
    d. copyrights.
    e. product marks.

30. The strategy of trading down involves:
    a. adding product features and using lower quality product materials.
    b. adding product features and using higher quality product materials.
    c. reducing product features and using lower quality product materials.
    d. reducing the number of features, quality, or price of a product.
    e. seeking a less price sensitive target market.

31. The ad campaign used for Menthos candy encourages the development of a _____ that is youth-oriented, unconventional, and fun.
   a. brand personality
   b. trademark character
   c. brand device
   d. character-based communication
   e. brand model

32. The primary benefit of branding for consumers is branding makes:
   a. products higher in quality.
   b. products lower in price.
   c. consumers more efficient shoppers.
   d. products higher in value.
   e. advertising unnecessary.

33. Which of the following statements about licensing is true?
   a. Only the licensor makes a profit in a licensing agreement.
   b. Licensing assists companies in entering foreign markets with minimal risk.
   c. The success of a licensing strategy is unrelated to the licensor's brand equity.
   d. Only the licensee makes a profit in a licensing agreement.
   e. Licensing agreements are not legally binding across national borders.

34. When selecting a good brand, a marketer should choose a name that:
   a. is complex to allow for a variety of connotations.
   b. does not suggest any particular benefits.
   c. is not be memorable because the product itself is what should be memorable.
   d. is ethnocentric in character.
   e. is described by none of the above.

35. Companies can employ several different branding strategies, including _____, multibranding, private branding, or mixed branding.
   a. retailer branding
   b. intermediary
   c. licensing
   d. multiproduct
   e. co-branding

36. Christopher Brosius, the maker of Demeter fragrances, knew that fragrance manufacturers combined several scents to create a perfume. He realized these fragrances smell wonderful on their own. He has bottled more than 150 different individual scents such as Woodsmoke, Lobster, and Chocolate. Each fragrance is sold using the Demeter brand name. Brosius uses _____ to market Demeter fragrances.
   a. multibranding
   b. family branding
   c. co-branding
   d. dual branding
   e. agent licensing

37. Multiproduct branding is often referred to as:
   a. umbrella branding.
   b. co-branding.
   c. family branding.
   d. subbranding.
   e. branding duality.

38. Gerber had tremendous brand equity with its baby food. The use of a _____ strategy to use the Gerber name on a bibs, plastic baby bottles, and pacifiers seemed logical.
    a. brand extension
    b. family branding
    c. co-branding
    d. blanket branding
    e. mixed branding

39. The Clorox Company manufactures several different brands of cat litter. Jonny Cat is an inexpensive clay mixture for multiple cats. Scoop-Away is for the fastidious cat owner who wants to be able to dispose of wastes immediately. Fresh Step is for cat owners who are concerned about litterbox odors. This is an example of a _____ strategy.
    a. family branding
    b. blanket branding
    c. co-branding
    d. multiproduct branding
    e. multibranding

40. Black & Decker uses a _____ strategy to reach the do-it-yourselfer market with the Black & Decker name and the construction professional market with the DeWalt name.
    a.   multibranding
    b.   generic branding
    c.   multiproduct branding
    d.   trademarked branding
    e.   private branding

41. _____ is the pairing of two brand names of two manufacturers on a single product.
    a. Multibranding
    b. Subbranding
    c. Multiproduct branding
    d. Co-branding
    e. Family branding

42. A branding strategy in which the company may market some products under its own name and other under that of a reseller is called:
    a. multibranding.
    b. generic branding.
    c. private branding.
    d. mixed branding.
    e. multiproduct branding.

43. Private branding is also called:
    a. reseller branding.
    b. franchising.
    c. manufacturer licensing.
    d. umbrella branding.
    e. merchandising.

44. Cherokee is a brand of clothing products found only at Target. Cherokee is an example of a(n):
    a. private brand.
    b. co-brand.
    c. manufacturer's brand.
    d. umbrella brand.
    e. blanket brand.

45. Which of the following statements does NOT describe a benefit associated with packaging?
    a. Packaging provides consumers with valuable and necessary information about directions regarding product usage and its composition.
    b. Packaging extends a product's shelf life.
    c. Packaging is an inexpensive product strategy to implement.
    d. Packaging potentially increases product sales.
    e. Packaging allows a company to differentiate its product from products of the competition.

46. A package can connote:
    a. country of origin or manufacture perceptions.
    b. economy, barter price, and distribution strategy.
    c. all of the elements of the marketing mix.
    d. product quality, company aize, and industry growth rate.
    e. consumerism, environmentalism, and industry ethical standards.

47. Packaging can provide a product with _____ benefits.
    a. brand equity
    b. communication
    c. functional
    d. perceptual
    e. all of the above

48. Warranties which specifically state the bounds of coverage, and more important, areas of noncoverage are called _____ warranties.
    a. limited-coverage
    b. functional
    c. implied
    d. strict-liability
    e. inferred

49. Merle purchased a blender and the blade came off the first time he tried to use it to blend a milkshake. Since he has no written guarantee, he must rely on a(n) _____ warranty to see that he at least gets a free replacement blender.
    a. implied
    b. express
    c. limited-coverage
    d. full-coverage
    e. functional

50. Which of the following statements about product warranties is true?
    a. There is no federal law governing the content of product warranties.
    b. Implied warranties are written statements of liabilities.
    c. Warranties create significant market advantages for the producer who uses them.
    d. Express warranties come in two formats—reseller and manufacturer.
    e. All of the above statements about product warranties are true.

ANSWER KEY

Answers to Questions & Problems

Product Life Cycle

Introduction Stage

Example:

1. Make HP Colorjet printers as popular as the Laserjet
2. Inkjet color printers
3. High quality color laserjet printer
4. About $3000, significantly lower (about 1/3 the price) of other color laser printers
5. Advertising, direct mail
6. Retail computer outlets

1. Skimming
2. Market penetration

Growth Stage

Example:

1. Become #1 alternative to colas.
2. All soft drinks
3. Flavored iced teas
4. Premium
5. Advertising
6. All retail outlets plus vending machines

Maturity Stage

Example:

1. Maintain #1 position
2. Planet Hollywood, All Star Cafe
3. Theme restaurants
4. Medium to high
5. Logo apparel, word-of-mouth
6. Major cities and tourist destinations

Decline Stage

Example:

1. Survival
2. Word processors, computers
3. Manual and electric typewriters
4. Low, under $100
5. None
6. Some office supply companies, small retailers

Modifying the Product

1. Finding new users
2. Increasing use
3. Creating new use situations

Product Repositioning

1. Catching a rising trend
2. Changing value offered
3. Reacting to a competitor's position
4. Reaching a new market

Branding

Example:

1. Easy-Off Oven Cleaner
2. Netscape
3. PowerMac
4. Exxon
5. Slice

Packaging

1. Functional benefits
2. Perceptual benefits
3. Functional benefits
4. Commutative benefits
5. Commutative benefits

Warranties

1. Express warranty
2. Implied warranty
3. Full warranty
4. Limited-coverage warranty

Answers to Sample Multiple Choice Questions

1. b p. 288; LO 1	14. c p. 293-294; LO 1	26. c p. 299; LO 2	38. a p. 304; LO 3
2. a p. 288-291; LO 1	15. e p. 294; LO 1	27. e p. 298; LO 2	39. e p. 305; LO 3
3. a p. 289; LO 1	16. d p. 294; LO 1	28. d p. 299; LO 3	40. a p. 305; LO 3
4. b p. 289; LO 1	17. e p. 294; LO 1	29. a p. 299; LO 3	41. d p. 305; LO 3
5. c p. 289; LO 1	18. a p. 294; LO 1	30. d p. 299; LO 2	42. d p. 306; LO 3
6. e p. 288-290; LO 1	19. c p. 295; LO 1	31. a p. 300; LO 3	43. a p. 306; LO 3
7. c p. 290-291; LO 1	20. e p. 297; LO 2	32. c p. 300; LO 3	44. a p. 306; LO 3
8. e p. 292; LO 1	21. b p. 297; LO 2	33. b p. 302; LO 3	45. c p. 307-309; LO 4
9. d p. 292; LO 1	22. b p. 297; LO 2	34. e p. 303; LO 3	46. a p. 308-309; LO 4
10. b p. 292; LO 1	23. d p. 297; LO 2	35. d p. 304; LO 3	47. e p. 307-309; LO 4
11. d p. 292; LO 1	24. c p. 297; LO 2	36. b p. 304; LO 3	48. a p. 309; LO 4
12. d p. 293; LO 1	25. b p. 297; LO 2	37. c p. 304; LO 3	49. a p. 310; LO 4
13. a p. 293-294; LO 1			50. c p. 310; LO 4

Note: LO indicates learning objective.

CHAPTER 12

MANAGING SERVICES

<u>Why is Chapter12 important</u>? Services marketing is the fastest growing area of marketing. Within this chapter you will see the differences in product management for services versus tangible products. The chapter illustrates the successful use of the marketing mix for a company offering a service product.

Services: Intangible items such as airline trips, financial advice, or automobile repair that an organization provides to consumers.

CHAPTER OUTLINE

I. UNIQUENESS OF SERVICES

    A. Four I's of Services
          1. Intangibility
          2. Inconsistency
          3. Inseparability
          4. Inventory

    B. Service Continuum

    C. Classifying Services
          1. Delivery by people or equipment
          2. Profit or non-profit organizations
          3. Government sponsored or not

II. HOW CONSUMERS PURCHASE SERVICES

    A. Purchase Process
          1. Search properties
          2. Experience properties
          3. Credence properties

    B. Assessing Service Quality

    C. Customer Contact and Relationship Marketing

III. MANAGING THE MARKETING OF SERVICES

    A. Internal Marketing

    B. Marketing Mix
          1. Product
              a. exclusivity
              b. branding
              c. capacity management

    2. Pricing

        a. to affect consumer perceptions

        b. to be used in capacity management

    3. Place

    4. Promotion

You should be able to place these key terms in the outline and be able to discuss them.

capacity management	**gap analysis**	**internal marketing**	**service continuum**
customer contact audit	**idle production capacity**	**off-peak pricing**	**services**
four I's of services			

QUESTIONS & PROBLEMS

THE FOUR I's OF SERVICES

There are four unique elements to services: intangibility, inconsistency, inseparability, and inventory. These four elements are referred to as the four I's of services.

Intangibility
Inconsistency
Inseparability
Inventory

Assume you own a car detailing service or a housesitting service, give at least one example of how you would compensate for each "I" of service:

1. intangibility_____
2. inconsistency_____
3. inseparability_____
4. inventory_____

THE SERVICE CONTINUUM

As companies look at what they bring to the market, there is a range from tangible to intangible, or product-dominant to service-dominant organizations, referred to as the service continuum.

Arrange the following in order from (1) most product-dominant to (13) most service-dominant entities:

	Rank
Purina Puppy Chow	_____
Levi's Jeans	_____
Raisin Bran	_____
Maupintour Travel	_____
Junior college professor	_____
Licensed practical nurse	_____
TCI Cablevision	_____
Burger King	_____
Broadway theater	_____
Graphic's Advertising	_____
Custom bootmaker	_____
Condominium	_____
Toyota Dealer	_____

CLASSIFYING SERVICES

Services can be classified in three different ways:

Delivered by people or equipment
Profit or nonprofit organization
Government-sponsored or not

Classify the services listed below into the most logical category:

1. Computer Dating Service_____

2. Food Safety and Inspection Service_____

3. MADD (Mothers Against Drunk Drivers)_____

4. Eat-In/Out Dinner Delivery_____

5. Internal Revenue Service_____

6. March of Dimes_____

7. Environmental Protection Agency_____

8. General Contractors_____

9. Pest Control Service_____

HOW CONSUMERS PURCHASE SERVICES

There are three important factors to be considered during the purchase process:

Search qualities
Experience qualities
Credence qualities

Match the correct quality to the statement or definition below:

1. Qualities which can only be discerned after purchase or during consumption._____

2. These qualities are common to medical diagnoses and legal services._____

3. Dualities that can be determined before purchase._____

4. Services such as restaurants and childcare have these qualities._____

5. Qualities or characteristics that the consumer may find impossible to evaluate even after purchase and consumption._____

6. Tangible goods such as jewelry, clothing, and furniture._____

SERVICE QUALILTY

Differences between the consumer's expectations and experiences are identified through gap analysis .

Describe a situation where your expectations far exceeded the actual outcome. Explain which element of the marketing mix was poorly executed, or which "I" of service was not addressed:

_____
_____
_____

CUSTOMER CONTACT AUDIT

A customer contact audit is the flow chart of the points of interaction between a consumer and a service provider.

Trace the points of customer contact when using the drive-in window of a fast food restaurant:

MANAGING THE MARKETING OF SERVICES

There are three areas of importance which should be considered in the product/service element of the marketing mix:

Exclusivity
Branding
Capacity management

Describe how each of these service issues differs from production goods:

1. Exclusivity_____
_____

2. Branding_____
_____

3. Capacity management_____
_____

PRICING

Pricing services plays two roles: (1) to affect consumer perceptions and (2) to be used in capacity management .

What are the two most common methods of pricing service?

1._____

2._____

What type of business would be hurt by "low" prices in terms of consumer perceptions:_____

List four types of services that use off-peak pricing.

1._____

2._____

3._____

4._____

DISTRIBUTION

Distribution is a major factor in developing a service marketing strategy because of the inseparability of services from the provider.

Charles Schwab now lets his customers make stock trades at home on their personal computer. Many banks have adopted not only ATM's (automatic teller machines), but also in-home banking by personal computer. How has this distribution philosophy helped to make them more competitive? Can you think of any other examples?_____

PROMOTION

In the past, advertising has been viewed negatively by many nonprofit and professional service organizations. Although opposition to advertising remains strong in some professional groups, the barriers to promotion are being broken down. In service marketing, publicity can play a major role in promotional strategy.

Explain what promotional tools you would use for each of the following and why:

1. Major League Baseball_____

2. A law firm_____

3. A new physician_____

4. Your college or university_____

5. A CPA firm_____

CAN YOU PASS THE TEST?
Sample Multiple Choice Questions

1. Hard Rock Café's Web page can be used as an entertainment portal to listen to and purchase music, buy memorabilia, and subscribe to digital music programming. These e-commerce elements add to the unique and distinctive _____ Hard Rock Café wants to create for its customers.
   - a. credence
   - b. tangibility
   - c. search
   - d. experience
   - e. evidence

2. Which of the following is a service provider?
   - a. a beauty salon
   - b. a veterinarian
   - c. a travel agency
   - d. a bank
   - e. all of the above

3. Which of the following statements about services is true?
   - a. The U.S. does not export services.
   - b. The marketing of services is the same as the marketing of goods.
   - c. Services are both tangible and intangible items.
   - d. Ten percent of new jobs created each year are in the services sector.
   - e. None of the above statements about services is true.

4. The four I's of service are:
   - a. intangibility, inseparability, inconsistency, and inventory.
   - b. interaction, innovation, intangibility, and independence.
   - c. independence, inconsistency, innovation, and inventory.
   - d. intangibility, independence, inelasticity, and information.
   - e. innovation, information, inventory, and inelasticity.

5. Because services are _____, they cannot be held, touched or seen before the purchase decision.
   - a. inconsistent
   - b. inseparable
   - c. independent
   - d. intangible
   - e. inelastic

6. Ads for security systems showing the system scaring away burglars when no one is home is one way service companies try to show service benefits and make the product seem less:
   - a. inconsistent.
   - b. inseparable.
   - c. independent.
   - d. intangible.
   - e. inelastic.

7. Consumers have more difficulty evaluating services than they do products; the difficulty results from the:
       a. intangibility of services.
       b. incongruity of services.
       c. inseparability of services from consumers.
       d. inflexibility of services.
       e. insignificance of services.

8. The fact that Mariah really liked the haircut she received two months ago and hated the one she was given yesterday at the same hair salon reflects the _____ nature of services.
       a. inconsistent
       b. inseparable
       c. independent
       d. intangible
       e. inelastic

9. A service provider uses _____ to reduce the inconsistency of its service offering.
       a. frequency discounts
       b. standardization and training
       c. capacity planning
       d. technology-based service
       e. people-based service

10. Organizations attempt to reduce the inconsistency of the delivery of services through:
       a. higher incentives to employees for satisfactory performance.
       b. automation.
       c. the reduction of customer contact points in the service delivery process.
       d. standardization and training.
       e. all of the above.

11. Don is graduating and takes his relative to dinner after the ceremony. At the restaurant, the waitperson never fills up their water glasses, ignores their requests and seems to "forget" about their table. Don notes that the last time he was at this same restaurant the experience was completely different (and MUCH better). This scenario illustrates the _____ of services.
       a. perishability
       b. intangibility
       c. inconsistency
       d. inseparability
       e. uniqueness of the service

12. Because services are _____, customers have a difficult time distinguishing the service itself from the service provider.
       a. inconsistent
       b. inseparable
       c. independent
       d. intangible
       e. inelastic

13. Canceling a flight because a pilot is not available illustrates the _____ nature of services.
       a. inconsistent
       b. inseparable
       c. independent
       d. intangible
       e. inelastic

14. The degree that inseparability is an issue for a service provider is determined by:
   a. the length of time the consumer takes with his or her purchase decision.
   b. how much training has been given the service provider's employees.
   c. the amount of excess capacity the service provider has.
   d. how standardized the services are that are being provided.
   e. how much interaction there is between the consumer and the service provider.

15. The _____ of service is the cost of paying the person used to provide the service along with any needed equipment.
   a. intangibility
   b. inconsistency
   c. inseparability
   d. inventory cost
   e. hidden cost

16. Inventory carrying costs for services is most closely related to:
   a. the 80/20 principle.
   b. the halo effect.
   c. idle production capacity.
   d. JIT management.
   e. none of the above

17. Andrea Arena is the owner of 2 Places at 1 Time, a concierge company. She and her staff of 60 perform everyday services such as walking the dog, picking up cleaning, waiting for the repairman, and going to the post office for people who are too busy to perform these simple acts themselves. She has often been hired by major corporations to perform services for their harried executives. In 1999, she had 108 employees, but economic momentum has slowed, and many of her major clients have sliced their budgets and eliminated perks like her service. At the point in time when Arena had more employees than she had need of, 2 Places at 1 Time was experiencing:
   a. off-peak pricing.
   b. idle production capacity.
   c. static demand.
   d. capacity management.
   e. capacity inventory.

18. For which of the following service providers would inventory carrying costs be greatest?
   a. Amtrak, the national railroad service
   b. House of Beauty, a hair salon
   c. Rover's, a kennel for boarding dogs
   d. H&R Block tax preparation office
   e. Worldwide Travel Agency

19. Which of the following companies has the most service-dominated offering?
   a. a fast-food restaurant
   b. a tailor
   c. a university
   d. an appliance repair center
   e. a landscaping company

20. A range of offerings from the tangible to the intangible or good-dominant to the service-dominant is called the:
   a. product continuum.
   b. tangibility line.
   c. inseparability span.
   d. customer contact audit.
   e. service continuum.

21. Service providers are typically classified according to:
   a. whether they offer intangible services.
   b. whether they are traded on the stock market or are privately held.
   c. how much idle production time they have.
   d. whether they use equipment or people to deliver the service.
   e. all of the above methods.

22. Which of the following is the BEST example of a people-based service?
   a. Cingular cell phone service
   b. a management consulting team
   c. an auto mechanic
   d. a cable television station
   e. an amusement park

23. Which of the following is the best example of an equipment-based service?
   a. lawn care
   b. taxis
   c. doctors
   d. lawyers
   e. janitorial services

24. The Girl Guides, a Canadian institution for more than 90 years, offers girls the chance to develop leadership skills. The Girl Guides is an example of a:
   a. service.
   b. for-profit organization.
   c. a tangible product provider.
   d. a vending machine operator.
   e. a professional service.

25. A nonprofit organization may pay taxes if:
   a. excess revenues exceed 18 percent of the budget.
   b. the organization is not considered to be religious institution.
   c. revenue is received from overseas subsidiaries.
   d. revenue-generating holdings are not directly related to the organization's core mission.
   e. money is to be spent on research and development, but it is taxed at a significantly lower rate.

26. Which of the following products is most likely to have experience properties?
   a. a designer dress
   b. legal advice
   c. an amusement park ride
   d. gall bladder surgery
   e. cancer chemotherapy

27. Sarah has a backache due to overexertion. She believes a massage would loosen her back muscles and make her feel better. She is concerned because a massage unlike a pair of shoes cannot be felt before she buys it. Sarah wishes that the massage had _____ properties.
   a. search
   b. form
   c. experience
   d. credence
   e. performance

28. When Theresa Martinez relocated from the East to the Midwest, she needed to find a bank with offices in her new state. Several banks offered the banking products (checking and savings accounts, loans, certificates of deposit) and financial products (mutual funds, insurance) available from her former bank, and she selected Wells Fargo. Later Theresa was impressed by the availability and willingness of people (tellers, personal bankers) to help her when she had questions. In this case, Wells Fargo affected Theresa's evaluation of the purchase through its:
   a. credibility properties.
   b. characteristic properties.
   c. experience properties.
   d. gap analysis.
   e. customer contact audit.

29. Many restaurants now ask consumers to evaluate their experience on a short questionnaire when they pay their bill. This assessment of consumer expectations and the actual experience is called a _____.
   a. gap analysis
   b. service survey
   c. customer profile analysis
   d. customer contact audit
   e. survey audit

30. _____ is used to identify the differences between the consumer's expectations and experience.
   a. Experiential measurement
   b. Correlation analysis
   c. A service audit
   d. Trend extrapolation
   e. Gap analysis

31. Which of the following is NOT an example of a dimension of service quality?
   a. reliability
   b. tangibles
   c. assurance
   d. synergy
   e. responsiveness

32. When selecting a place to eat, Andy always looks at the rating the restaurant received in the local restaurant guide. Since the guide is able to evaluate parts of the restaurant Andy cannot see, he believes this is a good way to predict the quality of the service he will receive. Andy bases his opinion of restaurants on the basis of which service quality dimension?
   a. assurance
   b. tangibles
   c. reliability
   d. responsiveness
   e. empathy

33. The customer at an amusement park is expressing concern about _____ when she wonders how frequently the rides are serviced and checked for flaws.
>   a. reliability
>   b. tangibles
>   c. assurance
>   d. empathy
>   e. responsiveness

34. The customer at an amusement park is expressing concern about _____ when she wonders why so many of the light bulbs need replacing in the signs and on the rides.
>   a. reliability
>   b. tangibles
>   c. assurance
>   d. empathy
>   e. responsiveness

35. The dimension of service quality called _____ is the ability to perform the promised service dependably and accurately.
>   a. assurance
>   b. accuracy
>   c. reliability
>   d. responsiveness
>   e. empathy

36. The dimension of service quality called _____ is knowledge and courtesy of employees and their ability to convey trust and confidence.
>   a. sympathy
>   b. empathy
>   c. assurance
>   d. responsiveness
>   e. reliability

37. A(n) _____ is a flowchart of the points of interaction between consumer and service provider.
>   a. service map
>   b. service gap analysis
>   c. customer contact audit
>   d. service audit
>   e. contact continuum

38. The customer contact audit would be most important in which of the following service industries?
>   a. shoe repair
>   b. cable television
>   c. plumbing
>   d. rental cars
>   e. package delivery service

39. A service encounter occurs when:
>   a. a customer places an order at burger king.
>   b. a hotel guest asks for extra towels.
>   c. a customer reserves a rental car.
>   d. a restaurant patron asks for his or her check
>   e. any of the above occur.

40. Which of the following (is) are benefit(s) of relationship marketing efforts directed at service customers?
        a. the continuity of a single provider
        b. customized service delivery
        c. reduced stress due to a repetitive purchase process
        d. an absence of switching costs
        e. all of the above

41. _____ is based on the concept that a service organization must focus on its employees before successful programs can be directed to its customers.
        a. Internal marketing
        b. Marketing to stakeholders
        c. Functional training
        d. Benefit implementation
        e. Benefit planning

42. A patent gives a manufacturer of goods exclusive rights for 17 years. A major difference between goods and services is that:
        a. services can be patented for the life of the creator.
        b. services can be patented for 21 years.
        c. services can be patented only for 10 years.
        d. services cannot be patented.
        e. there is no need to patent services.

43. Andrea Arena is the owner of 2 Places at 1 Time, a concierge company. She and her staff of 60 perform everyday services such as walking the dog, picking up cleaning, waiting for the repairman, and going to the post office for people who are too busy to perform these simple acts themselves. This is a strong service brand name because it suggests:
        a. the company has international experience.
        b. the benefits provided by the service.
        c. the company is employee-owned.
        d. the company is a nonprofit organization.
        e. the service concept is patented.

44. An airport limousine service will meet people at their homes and deliver them to or bring them home from their local airport. Because demand is much higher before 9 a.m. and after 5 p.m. during weekdays, it must be concerned with:
        a. exclusivity.
        b. image management.
        c. branding.
        d. inconsistency.
        e. capacity management.

45. A Broadway theater that charges a different price for evening and matinee shows is:
        a. offering it customers a trade promotion.
        b. using discount pricing.
        c. unconcerned about idle capacity.
        d. trying to extend the service encounter.
        e. using off-peak pricing.

46. The headline in a newspaper advertisement for American Airlines proclaimed, "Florida: $199 Round Trip!" A closer examination of the advertisement revealed the special low price airfare applied only to specific travel dates. That is, the $199 price applied to tickets to Florida during the months of July and August. If a consumer wished to travel to Florida during the peak travel times of October through May, the price of the ticket was $499. The airline was engaging in _____ by offering lower prices for tickets during less desirable travel times.
   - a. price gouging
   - b. price differentiation
   - c. off-peak pricing
   - d. bait-and-switch pricing
   - e. package pricing

47. Which of the following should be communicated to consumers when promoting services?
   - a. courteous service
   - b. availability
   - c. location
   - d. quality
   - e. all of the above

48. Nonprofit services cannot control who sees a public service announcement or when the message is given because:
   - a. PSAs tie up too large a percentage of the service's advertising budget.
   - b. PSAs are traditionally boring and not well designed.
   - c. timing and location of the PSA are under the control of the medium, not the organization.
   - d. PSAs have a very limited reach or scope.
   - e. PSAs are a form of two-way communication.

49. Changes in the services industry in the future will primarily be driven by two factors. They are expanding scope in the global economy and:
   - a. reverse marketing.
   - b. third-world development.
   - c. technological development.
   - d. global synergy.
   - e. the elimination of ethnocentricity.

50. The value of promotion for many services is to show the _____ of purchasing the service.
   - a. cost
   - b. benefits
   - c. price
   - d. location
   - e. all of the above

ANSWER KEY

Answers to Questions & Problems

The Four I's of Services

Example:

1. Name or servicemark
2. Training
3. Staffing
4. Scheduling

The Service Continuum

Suggested ranking:

	Rank
Purina Puppy Chow	2
Levi's Jeans	3
Raisin Bran	1
Maupintour Travel	9
Junior college professor	13
Licensed practical nurse	12
TCI Cablevision	8
Burger King	7
Broadway theater	11
Graphic's Advertising	10
Custom bootmaker	6
Condominium	4
Toyota Dealer	5

Classifying Services

1. Delivered by people or equipment
2. Government sponsored
3. Non-profit
4. Delivered by people or equipment
5. Non-profit
6. Government sponsored
7. Delivered by people or equipment
8. Delivered by people or equipment

How Consumers Purchase Services

1. Experience qualities
2. Credence qualities
3. Search qualities
4. Experience qualities
5. Credence qualities
6. Search qualities

Customer Contact Audit

Example:

Greeting—timeliness, friendliness
Order taking—correctness of order and price
Order delivery—speed, correctness

Managing the Marketing of Services

Example:

1. Custom service—individualized
2. Gives tangibility
3. Load factors and timing

Pricing

1. Cost plus percentage of cost
2. Target return on investment

Example: Downtown hotels would be hurt by low prices.

1. Airlines
2. Movie theaters
3. Theme parks
4. Hotels

Distribution

Example:

On-line accounting systems

Promotion

Example:

1. Autograph signings, picture opportunities, family nights with group pricing.

Answers to Sample Multiple Choice Questions

1. d p. 316; LO 1	14. e p. 318-319; LO 1	26. c p. 323; LO 3	38. d p. 325-326; LO 4
2. e p. 316; LO 1	15. d p. 319; LO 1	27. a p. 323; LO 3	39. e p. 325; LO 4
3. e p. 316-317; LO 1	16. c p. 319; LO 1	28. c p. 323; LO 3	40. e p. 326; LO 4
4. a p. 317-318; LO 1	17. b p. 319; LO 1	29. a p. 324; LO 3	41. a p. 327; LO 5
5. d p. 317; LO 1	18. a p. 319; LO 1	30. e p. 324; LO 3	42. d p. 327; LO 6
6. d p. 317; LO 1	19. c p. 320; LO 2	31. d p. 324; LO 3	43. b p. 327; LO 6
7. a p. 317-318; LO 1	20. e p. 319; LO 2	32. b p. 324; LO 3	44. e p. 327-328; LO 6
8. a p. 318; LO 1	21. d p. 321-322; LO 2	33. a p. 324; LO 3	45. e p. 328; LO 6
9. b p. 318; LO 1	22. b p. 320-321; LO 2	34. b p. 324; LO 3	46. c p. 328; LO 6
10. d p. 318; LO 1	23. b p. 320-321; LO 2	35. c p. 324; LO 3	47. e p. 329; LO 6
11. c p. 318; LO 1	24. a p. 322; LO 2	36. c p. 324; LO 3	48. c p. 329; LO 6
12. b p. 318-319; LO 1	25. d p. 322; LO 2	37. c p. 325; LO 4	49. c p. 329
13. b p. 318-319; LO 1			50. b p. 329; LO 6

Note: LO indicates learning objective.

CHAPTER 13

BUILDING THE PRICE FOUNDATION

<u>Why is Chapter 13 important?</u> This chapter begins the process of pricing a product. The following are shown within this chapter: the pricing constraints, both interneal and external, and the pricing objectives that motivate a compnany's pricing policy. In addition, there is a thorough discussion of the revenues and costs and their relationship to pricing policy and the market environment.

Price: The money or other considerations (including other goods and services) exchanged for the ownership or use of a good or service.

CHAPTER OUTLINE

I. NATURE AND IMPORTANCE OF PRICE

    A. Price as an Indicator of Value
    B. Price in the Marketing Mix

II. STEPS IN SETTING PRICE

    A. Identify Pricing Constraints and Objectives
        1. Identifying pricing constraints
            a. demand for product class, product, and brand
            b. newness of product: stage of Product Life Cycle
            c. single product versus product line
            d. cost of producing and marketing product
            e. cost of changing price and time period they apply
            f. type of competitive market
                i. pure monopoly
                ii. oligopoly
                iii. monopolistic competition
                iv. pure competition
            g. competitor's prices
        2. Identifying pricing objectives
            a. profit
            b. sales
            c. market share
            d. unit volume
            e. survival
            f. social responsibility

B. Estimate Demand and Revenue
    1. Fundamentals of estimating demand
        a. demand curve
        b. demand factors
            i. consumer tastes
            ii. price and availability of other products
            iii. consumer income
    2. Fundamentals of estimating revenue
        a. total revenue
        b. average revenue
        c. marginal revenue
        d. price elasticity of demand

C. Determine Cost, Volume, and Profit Relationships
    1. Cost
        a. total cost
        b. fixed cost
        c. variable cost
        d. marginal cost
    2. Marginal analysis and profit maximization
    3. Break-even analysis

You should be able to place these key terms in the outline and be able to discuss them.

average revenue(AR)	marginal analysis	total cost(TC)
barter	marginal cost(MC)	total revenue(TR)
break-even analysis	marginal revenue(MR)	unit variable
break-even chart	price(P)	cost(UVC)value
break-even point(BEP)	price elasticity of demand	value-pricing
demand curve	pricing constraintspricing	variable cost(VC)
demand factors	objectives	
fixed cost(FC)	profit equation	

QUESTIONS & PROBLEMS

PRICE

The basic profit equation is: Profit = Total revenue - Total cost. Sometimes we become so concerned with memorizing formulas that we forget to use common sense to figure out how those formulas were devised in the first place. Many other formulas in this chapter are simply expansions or variations of this basic price equation formula. **THINK**, don't just memorize.

For example:

Profit = (Total revenue)-(Total cost)

=[unit price x quantity sold]-[fixed cost + (unit variable cost x quantity sold)]

COMMON MARKETING ABBREVIATIONS

TR = TOTAL REVENUE
MR = MARGINAL REVENUE
AR = AVERAGE REVENUE
TC = TOTAL COST
FC = FIXED COST
VC = VARIABLE COST
MC = MARGINAL COST
Q = QUANTITY
P = PRICE
BEP = BREAK-EVEN POINT
UVC = UNIT VARIABLE COST
PLC = PRODUCT LIFE CYCLE
E = ELASTICITY

IDENTIFYING PRICING CONSTRAINTS

There are seven primary pricing constraints:

Demand for product class, product and brand
Newness of product (stage of Product Life Cycle)
Single product versus product line
Cost of producing and marketing product
Cost of changing price and time period they apply
Type of competitive market
Competitor's prices

Decide which constraint(s) affects the following products:

1. local telephone service_____

2. an electric car_____

3. typewriters_____

4. a word processing program_____

5. credit cards with "smart card" technology_____

IDENTIFYING PRICING OBJECTIVES

Expectations that specify the role of price in an organization's marketing and strategic plans are pricing objectives. There are six main pricing objectives:

profit
sales
market share
unit volume
survival
social responsibility

Match the correct pricing objectives to the examples below:

1. An airline in bankruptcy cuts its fares._____

2. BIC prices its pens at 1/3 the cost of its leading competitor._____

3. Ford gives yearend incentives on Taurus to make sure it beats the Honda Accord for the number one car in the US._____

4. Coca-Cola begins to use returnable bottles and charge a deposit on them._____

5. America On-Line gives its software away and lowers connect prices for new customers._____

6. Rolls Royce continues to price its cars at a substantial premium over the rest of the industry._____

DEMAND CURVES

A demand curve shows a maximum number of products consumers will buy at a given price. Below is a demand schedule showing the relationship between unit price and demand.

	UNIT PRICE (in dollars)	DEMAND (in units)
A.	250	200
B.	200	400
C.	150	600
D.	100	800
E.	50	1000

Plot a demand curve using the information listed above:

Determine total revenue at each point:

      1. A = _____

      2. B = _____

      3. C = _____

      4. D = _____

      5. E = _____

Using the information in example "A", plot a total revenue curve:

Assuming a selling price of $50 per unit, fixed costs of $20,000, and a unit variable cost of $30, calculate the break-even point in dollars and units.

      1. BEP (Dollars)_____

      2. BEP (Units)_____

PRICE ELASTICITY

Price elasticity of demand (E) is defined as the percentage change in quantity demanded relative to a percentage change in price.

Elasticity(E)= $[(Q_1-Q_0)$ (divided by) $Q_0]$ (divided by) $[(P_1-P_0)$ (divided by) P_0

where
      Q_0 = Initial quantity demanded
      Q_1 = New quantity demanded
      P_0 = Initial price
      P_1 = New price

Price elasticity of demand is not the same over all possible prices of the product.
Price elasticity may be expressed three ways:

1. If elasticity is greater than one, total revenue will be higher after a price decrease. The product demand is called "price elastic."

2. If elasticity is less than one, total revenue will be lower after a price decrease. The product demand is called "price inelastic."

3. If elasticity is equal to one, total revenue is the same as before, and the product demand is called "unitary elastic."

Using the information below, (1) calculate elasticity, and (2) determine whether the type of product demand is:

        Elastic
        Inelastic
        Unitary Elasticity

1. Elasticity = _____
   Type_____

Initial Quantity	10,000
New Quantity	12,000
Initial Price	$2,000
New Price	$1,000

2. Elasticity = _____
   Type_____

Initial Quantity	10,000
New Quantity	15,000
Initial Price	$2,000
New Price	$1,000

3. Elasticity = _____
   Type_____

Initial Quantity	10,000
New Quantity	30,000
Initial Price	$2,000
New Price	$1,000

COST CONCEPTS

Students almost always have problems deciding which items are fixed costs and which items are variable costs; there is no "master" list. Variable cost are always related directly to the amount of product produced or sold. Test yourself, if you have to incur any expense for the production of a single new unit, then the expense is a variable cost. If you sell hot dogs, hot dog buns will be a variable cost even though you have to buy them all the time. If you sell one more hot dog, you will have to buy one more hot dog bun, if you sell three hot dogs, you will have to incur the expense of three more buns. The cost incurred varies directly with the quantity produced or sold.

Many students don't think of utility bills as being fixed costs since they vary from month to month. This is not so! Regardless of the varying amounts, you will always have a utility bill and there is not a direct relationship to the quantity of product produced or sold. If you have a hot dog stand, you have to pay for the bun warmer electricity whether there are eight hot dog buns inside or 28. There is no direct correlation between the cost of electricity and whether you have sold one more hot dog or not. Therefore, the electricity is a fixed cost.

MARGINAL ANALYSIS AND PROFIT MAXIMIZATION

Marginal analysis means that as long as revenue received from the sale of an additional product (marginal revenue) is greater than the additional cost of producing and selling it (marginal cost), a firm will expand its output of that product.

Answer the following questions:

1. Marginal revenue follows a_____slope.

2. The essence of marginal revenue is to operate up to the output quantity at which:_____

BREAK-EVEN ANALYSIS

Use the following information to determine the break-even point in dollars and in units:

Fixed costs:	$12,000
Variable costs:	$8
Unit variable price:	$14

BEP dollars = _____

BEP units = _____

Determine how many units need to be produced in order to obtain a profit of $75,000:

profit = (P x Q) - [FC + (UVC x Q)]

P = $25
UVC = $5
FC = $25,000

Units produced = _____

A common mistake in using the profit formula is failing to "change the sign" when removing the brackets from the second part of the equation. The " + " sign becomes a "-" sign between the FC and the (UVC x Q).

FORMULA REVIEW

Write out the formulas, definitions, or equations for the following:

1. Price = _____

2. Profit = _____

3. Total Revenue = _____

4. Average Revenue = _____

5. Marginal Revenue = _____

6. Elasticity = _____

7. Total cost = _____

8. Fixed cost = _____

9. Variable cost = _____

10. Marginal cost = _____

11. BEP = _____

CAN YOU PASS THE TEST?
Sample Multiple Choice Questions

1. Which of the following is a particular type of price?
     a. rent
     b. retainer
     c. fee
     d. interest
     e. all of the above

2. Which of the following is a particular type of price?
     a. operating costs
     b. liquidity
     c. equitable medium
     d. college tuition
     e. stockholders' equity

3. Which of the following is NOT part of the price equation for a bank loan obtained by a small business?
     a. allowance for collateral
     b. rebate
     c. cash discount
     d. special activity fees
     e. list price

4. When Al. Johnson traded his 1968 Ford Mustang for a new roof on his two-story house, it was an example of a:
     a. negotiated fee.
     b. contractual due.
     c. barter.
     d. collateral agreement.
     e. trade allowance

5. A company that manages apartments decides to buy 17 new dishwashers at a list price of $750 each as replacements for old dishwashers in a small apartment complex it owns. Because the company is buying more than 10 dishwashers, it is eligible for a $150 per unit quantity discount. Financing charges total $20 per unit. The company gets $10 per dishwasher for the 17 dishwashers traded in. What is the actual price the company will pay for each dishwasher?
     a. $590
     b. $600
     c. $610
     d. $730
     e. $760

6. Value can be defined as:
     a. price minus costs.
     b. the ratio of perceived benefits to price.
     c. the percentage of price that is not directly related to costs.
     d. the ratio of price to perceived benefits.
     e. the ratio of total costs to price.

7. Katherine was shopping for a new pair of sunglasses. While in the Marshall Field's department store in the shopping center, Katherine visited the optical department. Here she found a pair of Oakley brand sunglasses that she considered very attractive. However, the price of $225 was more than she expected to pay for sunglasses and asked the salesperson why the glasses carried such a high price tag. The salesperson informed Katherine that the $225 ensured her of the finest quality glasses featuring ultra-strong titanium frames and specially formulated lenses, which would protect Katherine from all harmful UV and blue light. Finally, the lenses would offer optimum optical clarity, and the glasses would "look great" on Katherine. The salesperson was attempting to help Katherine realize the value offered by the Oakley glasses by:

    a. comparing the features of the glasses to those of other glasses.
    b. comparing the ratio of perceived benefits to the price of the glasses.
    c. creating a value analysis for katherine.
    d. creating a price/cost/benefit equation.
    e. comparing the technology of the glasses to the price of the glasses.

8. The first step in setting a selling price is to:

    a. select an approximate price level.
    b. estimate cost, volume, and profit relationships.
    c. estimate demand and revenue.
    d. identify pricing constraints and objectives.
    e. evaluate consumer perception of product through the use of perceptual maps.

9. Ships Ahoy is a small company that makes model sailboat kits priced at $120 each. (There is no quantity discount.) The costs of the materials that go into each kit are $45. It costs $5 in labor to assemble a kit. The company has monthly expenses of $1,000 for rent and insurance, $200 for heat and electricity, $500 for advertising in sailing and hobby magazines, and $3,500 for the monthly salary of its owner. If Ships Ahoy sells 150 kits in a given month, its monthly profit will be:

    a. $5,300.
    b. $10,500.
    c. $12,700.
    d. $12,800.
    e. $15,700.

10. Which term describes factors that affect price and include: newness of the product, whether it is part of a product line, and cost of changing a price?

    a. price fixings
    b. pricing constraints
    c. price elasticities
    d. pricing demands
    e. pricing margins

11. Which of the following is an example of a pricing constraint?

    a. demand for the product
    b. stage in the product life cycle
    c. production costs
    d. type of competitive market
    e. all of the above

12. Which of the following statements about price constraints is true?
   a. The number of potential buyers is not a price constraint.
   b. As a result of price constraints, a product in the introduction stage is more likely to be priced lower than a product in the maturity stage of its life cycle.
   c. A company can charge more for a product competing against similar products in its market then it can for a totally new product to the market.
   d. Price changes are less costly for an e-commerce retailer than for a bricks-and-mortar retailer.
   e. All of the above statements about price constraints are true.

13. Pharmacist and new father Kenneth Kramm wanted his son to take his medicine, but it was a battle. As a result Kramm developed FLAVORx, a liquid medicine-flavoring system that can mask the taste or smell of medicine. FLAVORx tastes of strawberry or grape and has no effect on the medicinal value of the drug to which it is added. It is the first product of its kind. Because Flavorx is in the _____ stage of the product life cycle, the price of the medicine-flavoring system should be _____ than the price that would usually be charged.
   a. introductory; lower
   b. growth; lower
   c. introductory; higher
   d. growth; higher
   e. maturity; lower

14. The former Soviet republic Turkmenistan is in Central Asia and is one of the last countries on the planet to gain Internet access. The only Internet service provider for the entire country is Turkmen Telecom. There is no need for price competition, promotion competition, or product differentiation because Turkmen Telecom is a(n):
   a. free enterprise.
   b. pure monopoly.
   c. oligopoly.
   d. monopolistic competitor.
   e. pure competitor.

15. Which of the following statements about pricing in various types of competitive markets is true?
   a. Price competition is commonplace in monopolies.
   b. Product differentiation is not used in oligopolies.
   c. Product differentiation is not used in monopolies.
   d. There is less advertising used with monopolistic competition than with any other competitive market type.
   e. Product differentiation is not used in monopolistic competition.

16. Within a pure competition,:
   a. seller sets the price.
   b. product differentiation is commonplace.
   c. advertising is used extensively.
   d. price competition is prevalent.
   e. none of the above is true.

17. The competitive market situation in which many sellers compete on nonprice factors is called:
   a. a pure monopoly.
   b. an oligopoly.
   c. monopolistic competition.
   d. pure competition.
   e. monopolistic oligopoly.

18. The marketplace sets the price for soybeans, so farmers who are trying to sell their soybean crops don't have to create a pricing strategy. The soybeans are sold in a(n) _____ market.
    a. oligopoly
    b. pure monopoly
    c. pure competition
    d. monopolistic competition
    e. monopolistic oligopoly

19. A target return objective is an example of a _____ objective.
    a. profit
    b. market share
    c. sales
    d. survival
    e. socially responsible

20. Which of the following is NOT one of the six major pricing objectives discussed in the text?
    a. profit
    b. unit volume
    c. break even
    d. survival
    e. market share

21. Companies often pursue a market share objective when:
    a. implementing a harvesting strategy.
    b. industry sales are relatively flat or declining.
    c. product sales are seasonal.
    d. industry sales are annually increasing.
    e. a graph of annual industry sales no longer looks like a normal curve.

22. Pharmaceutical companies that manufacture drugs for AIDS patients have been asked to provide free drugs to Africa where the disease is of epidemic proportions. So far, most of the companies have continued to charge for the medication. People who believe the pharmaceutical companies should provide free AIDS medication and recognize their obligation to act altruistically want the companies to have a _____ pricing objective.
    a. target return
    b. marginal profit
    c. unit volume
    d. survival
    e. social responsibility

23. For the Christmas seasons in 2000 and 2001, Service Merchandise, a discount retailer that specialized in jewelry, stated that in order to continue operation it would need to have a profitable season. In 2000, it achieved this _____ objective, but it was unsuccessful in 2001.
    a. profit
    b. market share
    c. sales
    d. survival
    e. socially responsible

24. Which of the following is LEAST important for estimating product demand?
    a. the content and context of its advertising
    b. consumer tastes
    c. price
    d. availability of substitute products
    e. consumer income

25. Which of the following statements about the factors that influence demand is true?
    a. As the availability of close substitutes increases, the demand for a product increases.
    b. As real consumer income increases, demand for a product increases.
    c. As the price of close substitutes increases, demand for a product declines.
    d. Changing consumer tastes have little impact on demand for a product.
    e. All of the above statements about the factors that influence demand are true.

26. Consumer tastes, price, substitute availability, and consumer income are collectively referred to as:
    a. supply shifters.
    b. macromarketing factors.
    c. demand factors.
    d. supply determinants.
    e. revenue factors.

27. Which of the following statements about demand curves is true?
    a. Most demand curves slope up and to the right.
    b. A demand curve can be calculated by multiplying price times quantity.
    c. Most demand curves slope down and to the right.
    d. Marketers typically determine price by extending the demand curve beyond the range of prices to which it supplies.
    e. Changes in the demand curve have a direct relationship to changes in fixed costs.

28. According to the equation, _____ equals unit price of the product times quantity of the product sold.
    a. average revenue
    b. total revenue
    c. price elasticity
    d. marginal revenue
    e. revenue elasticity

29. Ships Ahoy is a small company that makes model sailboat kits priced at $120 each. (There is no quantity discount.) The costs of the materials that go into each kit are $45. It costs $5 in labor to assemble a kit. The company has monthly expenses of $1,000 for rent and insurance, $200 for heat and electricity, $500 for advertising, and $3,500 for the monthly salary of its owner. Last month the company sold 150 kits. Ships Ahoy's total revenue for the month was:
    a. $3,500.
    b. $6,750.
    c. $7,500.
    d. $10,500.
    e. $18,000.

30. Marginal revenue is:
    a. monies made after all fixed costs are covered.
    b. monies made after fixed and variable costs are covered.
    c. the amount by which marginal costs exceed fixed costs.
    d. the profit made on an additional unit of product sold.
    e. none of the above.

31. Price elasticity of demand is defined as:
     a. total revenue divided by quantity.
     b. the slope of the total revenue curve.
     c. total revenue divided by quantity times price.
     d. the percentage of change in total revenue.
     e. the percentage change in quantity demanded relative to a percentage change in price.

32. Which of the following statements about price elasticity of demand is true?
     a. Price elasticity with unitary demand is less than 1.
     b. The more substitutes a product has, the less likely it is to be price elastic.
     c. With inelastic demand, a reduction in price increases total revenue.
     d. With inelastic demand, price elasticity is less than 1.
     e. None of the above statements about price elasticity of demand is true.

33. Elastic demand exists when a(n):
     a. a small percentage decrease in price produces a smaller percentage increase in quantity demanded and total revenue falls.
     b. a small percentage decrease in price produces a larger percentage increase in quantity demanded and total revenue increases.
     c. an increase in price causes a larger increase in quantity demanded and total revenue increases.
     d. the quantity demanded remains the same regardless of level of price and total revenue is unchanged.
     e. a small percentage decrease in price produces a smaller percentage decrease in quantity demanded and total revenue increases.

34. Which of the following is most likely to be price inelastic?
     a. Rolling Stones concert tickets
     b. a cruise around the world
     c. designer eyeglasses
     d. salt
     e. expensive cell phones

35. _____ exists when the percentage change in price is identical to the percentage change in quantity demanded.
     a. Product substitution
     b. Quantity inelasticity
     c. A price margin
     d. Unitary demand
     e. Price inelasticity

36. Market analysts for a large cereal company estimated that price elasticity of demand for presweetened cereal is 1.97, but that the entire market for ready-to-eat cereals exhibits price elasticity of demand of 0.36. Most likely, this information will be collected by managers in which step of the price-setting process?
a. identifying pricing constraints and objectives
b. estimating the break-even point
c. estimating demand and revenue
d. selecting an appropriate (approximate) price level
e. making special adjustments to list or quoted price

37. _____ tells a firm that it should expand product output as long as revenue received from the sale of an additional product is greater than the additional cost of production and selling it.
    a. Environmental audit
    b. Internal audit
    c. Profit-expense assessment
    d. Marginal analysis
    e. Break-even analysis

38. Fixed cost refers to:
    a. the sum of the expenses that vary directly with the quantity of the product produced and sold.
    b. the total expense incurred by a firm in producing and marketing a product or service.
    c. expenses that are stable and do not change with the quantity of the product that is produced and sold.
    d. the consideration exchanged for the ownership or use of a good or service.
    e. total expenses incurred in producing or selling one additional unit of product.

39. Which of the following is the best example of a fixed cost for a manufacturer of seating for arenas, stadiums, and theaters?
    a. the tubular steel used in the arms and legs
    b. molded plastic seats
    c. salary of CEO
    d. labor overtime wages
    e. non-union hourly wages

40. Which of the following is the best example of a variable cost for a book publishing company?
    a. paper
    b. salary of CEO
    c. rent on office space
    d. interest on bank loan
    e. insurance on warehouse where it stores its completed books

41. Ships Ahoy is a small company that makes model sailboat kits priced at $120. The costs of the materials that go into each kit are $45. It costs $5 in labor to assemble a kit. The company has monthly expenses of $1,000 for rent and insurance, $200 for heat and electricity, $500 for advertising, and $3,500 for the monthly salary of its owner. Ships Ahoy's unit variable cost for its kits is:
    a. $45.
    b. $50.
    c. $120.
    d. $170.
    e. cannot be determined from the information provided.

42. Which of the following would be an example of a variable cost for a publication like *SHAPE* magazine that is targeted to young women seeking a healthier lifestyle?
    a. increase in women in targeted demographics
    b. salary of publisher
    c. rent for parking deck used by employees
    d. paper and ink
    e. advertising purchased by new accounts

43. When a U-shaped marginal cost curve, total cost increases at the slowest rate when:
    a. marginal cost equals fixed cost.
    b. marginal cost is equal to marginal revenue.
    c. marginal cost is at a minimum.
    d. marginal costs are greater than total costs.
    e. marginal revenue is at its greatest.

44. The fixed cost for manufacturing Grandma's plum jam is $10,500, and the variable costs for manufacturing one jar of the jam is $1.50. The jam sells for $5 a jar. Calculate the break-even point quantity.
    a. 1,200 jars
    b. 1,385 jars
    c. 1,800 jars
    d. 3,000 jars
    e. 6,000 jars

45. A 13-ounce bottle of Prairie Herb vinegar sells for $13.25. Variable costs include $1.20 for ingredients, $.75 for the bottle, and $.60 miscellaneous costs. Fixed costs for the company is $21,400. Calculate the break-even point quantity.
    a. 1,355 bottles
    b. 1,894 bottles
    c. 1,615 bottles
    d. 2,000 bottles
    e. 8,236 bottles

46. The owner of a small restaurant that sells take-out fried chicken and biscuits pays $2,500 in rent each month, $500 in utilities, $750 interest on his loan, insurance premium of $200, and advertising on local buses $250 a month. A bucket of take-out chicken, the only menu item, is priced at $9.50. Unit variable costs for the bucket of chicken are $5.50. At what level of sales of dollars of revenue will the restaurant break-even?
    a. $9,386.00
    b. $9,500.00
    c. $9,975.00
    d. $29,925.00
    e. $39,900.00

47. You have been asked to calculate the break-even point for a new line of shirts. The selling price will be $35 per shirt. The labor costs will be $5 per shirt. Theadministrative costs of operating the company are estimated to be $60,000 annually and the sales and marketing expenses are $20,000 a year. Additionally, the cost of materials will be $10 per shirt. What is the break-even quantity?
    a. 1,175 shirts
    b. 2,286 shirts
    c. 3,000 shirts
    d. 4,000 shirts
    e. 16,000 shirts

48. Ace Shoe Company sells heel replacement kits for men's shoes. It has fixed costs of $6 million and unit variable costs of $5 per pair. If the company charges $15 per pair, how many pairs must it sell to break even?
    a. 300,000 kits
    b. 400,000 kits
    c. 600,000 kits
    d. 1,200,000 kits
    e. 2,000,000 kits

49. Ace Shoe Company sells heel replacement kits for men's shoes. It has fixed costs of $6 million and unit variable costs of $5 per pair. Ace is considering a switch from manual labor to an automated process. New equipment would cost an additional $4 million per year while lowering variable costs by $3 per shoe repair kit. How many kits would Ace have to sell at $15 per pair to make $2 million in profits in the next year with the automated process?

    a. 169,231 kits
    b. 666,667 kits
    c. 705,883 kits
    d. 800,000 kits
    e. 923,077 kits

50. A _____ is most often used in marketing to study the impact on profits of changes in price, fixed costs, and variable costs.

    a. Gantt chart
    b. break-even chart
    c. ROI analysis
    d. cross-tabulation
    e. demand curve

ANSWER KEY

Answers to Questions & Problems

Identifying Pricing Constraints

1. Type of competitive market
2. Cost of production and marketing product
3. Demand for product, class, or brand
4. Competitors' prices
5. Newness of product

Identifying Pricing Objectives

1. Survival
2. Sales
3. Unit volume
4. Social responsibility
5. Market share
6. Profit

Demand Curves

1. A = 50,000
2. B = 80,000
3. C = 90,000
4. D = 80,000
5. E = 50,000

1. BEP $ = 50,000
2. BEP units = 1000

Price Elasticity

1. Elasticity = .4—inelastic

2. Elasticity = 1—unitary elasticity

3. Elasticity = 4—elastic

Marginal Analysis and Profit Maximization

1. Declining
2. MR = MC

Break-Even Analysis

$ = 28,000
Units = 2000

Units produced = 5000

Formula Review

1. Price = list price - discount allowances + extra fees

2. Profit = (P x Q) - [FC + (UVC x Q)]

3. Total Revenue = P x Q

4. Average Revenue = TR/Q

5. Marginal Revenue = change in TR \ change in Q

6. Elasticity = % change in Q / % change in P

7. Total Cost = TVC + FC

8. Fixed Cost = the sum of all stable company expenses which do not vary directly with quantity produced and sold.

9. Variable Cost = the sum of the company expenses that vary directly with quantity produced and sold.

10. Marginal Cost = the change in TC / the change in Q

11. BEP = FC/(P - UVC)

Answers to Sample Multiple Choice Questions

1. e p. 336; LO 1	14. b p. 343; LO 2	26. c p. 345; LO 3	38. c p. 350; LO 5
2. d p. 336; LO 1	15. c p. 343; LO 2	27. c p. 345; LO 3	39. c p. 350; LO 5
3. a p. 337; LO 1	16. e p. 343; LO 2	28. b p. 346; LO 3	40. a p. 350; LO 5
4. c p. 337; LO 1	17. c p. 343; LO 2	29. e p. 346; LO 3	41. b p. 350; LO 5
5. c p. 337-338; LO 1	18. c p. 343; LO 2	30. e p. 346-347; LO 3	42. d p. 350; LO 5
6. b p. 338; LO 1	19. a p. 340; LO 2	31. e p. 348; LO 4	43. b p. 351; LO 5
7. b p. 338; LO 1	20. c p. 340-341; LO 2	32. d p. 348-349; LO 4	44. d p. 352; LO 6
8. d p. 340; LO 2	21. b p. 340-341; LO 2	33. b p. 348-349; LO 4	45. d p. 352; LO 6
9. a p. 339; LO 1	22. e p. 341; LO 2	34. a p. 348-349; LO 4	46. c p. 352; LO 6
10. b p. 341-342; LO 2	23. d p. 341; LO 2	35. d p. 348-349; LO 4	47. d p. 352; LO 6
11. e p. 341-342; LO 2	24. a p. 345; LO 3	36. c p. 348-349; LO 4	48. c p. 352; LO 6
12. d p. 341-342; LO 2	25. b p. 345; LO 3	37. d p. 351; LO 5	49. e p. 352; LO 6
13. c p. 342; LO 2			50. b p. 354; LO 6

Note: LO indicates learning objective.

CHAPTER 14

ARRIVING AT THE FINAL PRICE

<u>Why is Chapter 14 important?</u> This chapter continues the pricing process examining the selection of the appropriate price for a product. It discusses the strategy for pricing products and the types of pricing incentives that are utilized in both consumer and business-to-business marketing.

Price: The money or other considerations (including other goods and services) exchanged for the ownership or use of a good or service.

CHAPTER OUTLINE

I. SELECT AN APPROXIMATE PRICE LEVEL

A. Demand-Oriented
  1. Skimming
     a. enough perspective customers are willing to buy the product immediately at the high initial price to make these sales profitable
     b. the high initial price will not attract competition
     c. lowering the price has only a minor affect on increasing the sales volume and reducing the unit costs
     d. customers interpret the high price as signifying high quality
  2. Penetration pricing
     a. many segments of the market are price sensitive
     b. a low initial price discourages competitors from entering the market
     c. unit production and marketing costs fall dramatically as production volumes increase
  3. Prestige pricing
  4. Price lining
  5. Odd-even pricing
  6. Target pricing
  7. Bundle pricing
  8. Yield management pricing

B. Cost-Oriented Approaches
  1. Standard markup pricing
  2. Cost-plus pricing
     a. cost-plus percentage-of-cost pricing
     b. cost-plus fixed-fee pricing
  3. Experience curve pricing

C. Profit-Oriented Approaches
  1. Target profit pricing
  2. Target return-on-sales pricing
  3. Target return-on-investment pricing

D. Competition-Oriented Approaches
    1. customary pricing
    2. above-, at-, or below-market pricing
    3. loss-leader pricing

II. SET THE LIST OR QUOTED PRICE

A. One-Price Policy

B. Flexible-Price Policy

C. Company, Customer, and Competitive Effects
    1. Company effects
    2. Customer effects
    3. Competitive effects

D. Balancing Incremental Costs and Revenues

III. MAKE SPECIAL ADJUSTMENTS TO THE LIST OR QUOTED PRICE

A. Discounts
    1. Quantity discounts
        a. noncumulative
        b. cumulative
    2. Seasonal discounts
    3. Trade (functional) discounts
    4. Cash discounts

B. Allowances
    1. Trade-in allowances
    2. Promotional allowances

C. Geographic Adjustments
    1. FOB origin pricing
    2. Uniform delivered pricing
        a. single-zone pricing
        b. multiple-zone pricing
        c. FOB with freight allowed pricing
        d. basing point pricing

D. Legal and Regulatory Aspects of Pricing
    1. Price fixing
        a. horizontal
        b. vertical
    2. Price discrimination
    3. Deceptive pricing
    4. Geographical pricing
    5. Predatory pricing

You should be able to place these key terms in the outline and be able to discuss them.

above-, at-, or below-market pricing

basing-point pricing

bundle pricing

cost-plus pricing

customary pricing

everyday low pricing

experience curve policy

flexible-price policy

FOB origin pricing

loss-leader pricing

odd-even pricing

one-price policy

penetration pricing

predatory pricing

prestige pricing

price discrimination

price fixing

price lining

price war

product-line pricing

promotional allowances

quantity discounts

skimming pricing

standard markup pricing

target pricing

target profit pricing

target return-on- investment pricing

target return-on-sales

uniform delivered pricing

yield management pricing

QUESTIONS & PROBLEMS

DEMAND-ORIENTED PRICING

1. RC has been testing Royal Crown Premium Draft Cola, targeting the high end of the market. This new soft drink is priced significantly higher than regular RC, Coca-Cola, and Pepsi. What type of pricing does this represent? Is this the type of product that can utilize this type of pricing?_____

2. General Motors original strategy was to have a starter car, the Chevrolet, for the new car owner at an entry level price; then the consumer would be "moved up" to the Pontiac at a slightly higher price, then on to the Oldsmobile and Buick, and finally to the Cadillac. Each line of cars had it own identity (in fact, the Buick was once known as the doctor's car) and appealed to a certain market in their price range. The ultimate, the Cadillac was almost three times the cost of the Chevrolet. What type of pricing does this represent? Do you think it would work today?

3. The Saturn introduced its new "entry level" car priced at $10,495. What type of pricing does this represent? What is wrong with this price?_____

4. The new "all-in-one " account at the local bank includes no-service charge checking, free checks, a safe deposit box, free travelers checks, and a reduced rate on a Visa card. What type of pricing is this? Why do companies use this type of pricing?_____

5. When the original BIC pen was introduced, it was priced at 19 cents. The most popular pen at the time cost 99 cents. What two types of pricing are represented here? What is the goal of each?_____

COST-ORIENTED PRICING

1. What type of product would indicate the use of a cost-plus percentage-of-cost pricing policy?_____

2. Under what conditions would you choose a cost plus fixed fee over a cost-plus percentage-of-cost pricing strategy?_____

PROFIT-ORIENTED APPROACHES

Assume you wish to establish a price for custom-made computer covers using target profit pricing:

Variable cost is constant at $25 per unit
Fixed cost is constant at $1,200.
Demand is insensitive up to $45 per unit
A target profit of $2,500 is sought at an annual volume of 500 units.

Suggested Price:_____

Using the information above, but seeking a 20 percent return on sales, determine your price using target return on sales pricing.

Suggested Price:_____

COMPETITION-ORIENTED APPROACHES

1. List at least three specific products or product types that use customary pricing (other than those cited in the text):

_____
_____
_____

2. On many weekends you will find Coca-Cola priced at $1.99 per six-pack, while 7UP is priced at $3.29 per six-pack and Pepsi and Slice are priced at $2.29 per six-pack. Identify each as an example of the levels of the above, at-, or below market pricing strategy._____
_____

3. Wal-Mart runs a sale on Randy Travis CD's for $3.99. What type of pricing does this represent?_____
_____

SPECIAL ADJUSTMENTS TO LIST OR QUOTED PRICE

There are three special adjustments to the list or quoted price:

Discounts
Allowances
Geographical adjustments

Match the correct term to the statements below:

_____1. A bathing suit manufacturer offered a 20 percent reduction in price to retailers placing their orders by December 4th.

_____2. A pizza parlor issued special lunch cards. Every time a patron had lunch at the parlor, his card was stamped. Whenever a card had twelve stamps, the patron received a free pizza for lunch.

_____3. A manufacturer of garden tools using wholesalers and retailers quoted his price as list price less /30/15/net.

_____4. A supermarket manager agrees to promote a new line of sugarfree gum by sponsoring a "bubble-blowing contest." In appreciation, the manufacturer sends one free case of gum for every three purchases.

_____5. A gas station chain offers its customers a lower price on gas if they pay cash instead of using credit cards.

6. A supermarket offered a special price on new brooms to customers who brought their old brooms to the store. The old brooms were displayed by the door next to a barrel of new brooms.

_____7. A telephone company offered a special rate of $10 an hour for phone calls anywhere in the continental United States.

_____8. A company that sells materials for "build-it-yourself" homes charges a different fee depending upon how far you live from their warehouses.

LEGAL AND REGULATORY ASPECTS OF PRICING

1. A local store advertises a VCR at $89.95, but only has one of that model in the store. When customers come in and inquire the sales personnel guide the customer to a model priced at $159.95. If asked about the advertised model the store simply says they are "all out" of those. Is this a type of illegal pricing? Why?___

_____
_____
_____

2. Wal-Mart has been accused of pricing prescriptions below cost in order to drive local pharmacies out of business. What type of pricing is this? What law would this come under?_____

_____

3. Giant Corporation sells office supplies to local office supply stores. For companies who have been long time customers, Giant discounts on all orders. For new customers, no discounts are given even though quantities and locations are virtually the same. Is this a violation under the Robinson-Patman Act? Why?

_____
_____

CAN YOU PASS THE TEST?
Sample Multiple Choice Questions

1. Which of the following is an example of types of approaches used to select approximate price levels to use to set prices?
> a. demand-based approaches
> b. cost-based approaches
> c. competition-based approaches
> d. profit-based approaches
> e. all of the above

2. In which step of the price setting process would a new-product manager be deciding whether to adopt a penetration or a skimming pricing strategy for a new product she is about to introduce to the market?
> a. Make special adjustments to the list or quoted price.
> b. Select an approximate price level.
> c. Estimate demand and revenue.
> d. Identify price constraints and objectives.
> e. Set list or quoted price.

3. When microwave ovens were in the introduction stage of the product life cycle, some consumers were willing to pay exorbitant prices for the innovative ovens. Taking advantage of this strong consumer desire, marketers set the price for microwave ovens at the highest initial price customers with a very strong desire for the product were willing to pay. Marketers of microwave ovens were using a _____ pricing strategy.
> a. skimming
> b. penetration
> c. prestige
> d. price lining
> e. bundle

4. Demand-oriented approaches to selecting approximate price levels to use to set prices place most emphasis on:
> a. competitors' products.
> b. profit.
> c. expected customer tastes and preferences.
> d. cost
> e. competitors' prices.

5. Which of the following statements about penetration pricing is true?
> a. Penetration pricing is the exact opposite of prestige pricing.
> b. In some situations, penetration pricing may follow skimming pricing.
> c. A firm introducing a new , patented product is most likely to use penetration pricing.
> d. Penetration pricing is an effective strategy when enough prospective customers are willing to buy the product immediately at the high initial price.
> e. Penetration pricing works most effectively when customers equate high price and high quality.

6. When Hallmark cards introduced a line of $.99 cards (about half the price of the previously least expensive cards sold by Hallmark), the greeting card company was trying to appeal to a mass market that was price sensitive. Hallmark was using a _____ pricing strategy.
   a. prestige
   b. skimming
   c. penetration
   d. return-on-investment
   e. experience-curve

7. Manufacturers will sometimes estimate the price that the ultimate consumer would be willing to pay for a product. They then work backward though markups taken by retailers and wholesalers to determine what price they can charge wholesalers for the product. This practice is called:
   a. skimming pricing.
   b. price lining.
   c. cost-plus pricing.
   d. target pricing.
   e. return-on-investment pricing.

8. The demand curve for which type of pricing method slopes downward and to the right, then turns back to the left?
   a. skimming pricing
   b. penetration pricing
   c. price lining
   d. demand-backward pricing
   e. prestige pricing

9. _____ is a method of setting price by estimating the price consumers would be willing to pay for the item and then working backward to assure necessary margins for the retailers and wholesalers.
   a. Penetration pricing
   b. Price lining
   c. Cost plus percentage-of-cost pricing
   d. Cost plus fixed fee pricing
   e. Target pricing

10. If you were to buy five tulip bulbs from the Breck's Holland Bulb catalog in five separate orders, you will pay $29.99, but if you order its assortment (1 each of five different tulip bulbs), you pay $19.99. Breck's uses:
   a. standard markup pricing.
   b. bundle pricing.
   c. prestige pricing.
   d. price lining.
   e. demand-backward pricing.

11. Which of the following retailers would likely use standard markup pricing?
   a. Store selling Swiss watches
   b. Jaguar dealer
   c. Camera store selling Canon and other name brands
   d. Escada boutique
   e. Safeway

12. _____ pricing is the most commonly used method to set prices for industrial products.
   a. Cost-plus
   b. Target
   c. Standard markup
   d. Experience curve
   e. Target return-on-sales

13. The two versions of cost-plus pricing are:
   a. static cost-plus pricing and dynamic cost-plus pricing.
   b. standard-markup cost-plus pricing and accelerated-markup cost-plus pricing.
   c. cost-plus fixed-fee pricing and cost-plus percentage-of-cost pricing.
   d. skimming pricing and penetration pricing.
   e. cost-oriented pricing and profit-oriented pricing.

14. Which cost-based pricing method entails adding a fixed percentage to the cost of all items in a specific product class?
   a. experience curve pricing
   b. cost plus fixed-fee pricing
   c. demand backward pricing
   d. standard markup pricing
   e. target profit pricing

15. For which of the following products would you be most likely to find prestige pricing used?
   a. soda
   b. newspaper
   c. perfume
   d. cd
   e. television set

16. When a firm is hired to construct a world-class golf course, it is a one-of–a-kind project and often requires unforeseen expenses. Companies that contract to build golf courses typically add a fixed percentage to the total unit cost to take care of these unplanned costs. This pricing method is called:
   a. competition-oriented pricing.
   b. target return-on-investment pricing.
   c. target return-on-sales pricing.
   d. cost-plus-fixed-fee pricing.
   e. cost-plus-percentage-of-cost pricing.

17. Sears offers a Craftsman radial saw for $499.99, a MACH 3 razor set is $6.99, and a bottle of Windex glass cleaner is on sale for 99 cents. These firms are using:
   a. price lining.
   b. skimming pricing.
   c. a one-price policy.
   d. target return pricing.
   e. odd-even pricing.

18. Target profit pricing is:
   a. adjusting the price of a product so it is "in line" with that of its largest competitor.
   b. setting the price of a line of products at a number of different price points.
   c. adding a fixed percentage to the cost of all items in a specific product class.
   d. setting prices to achieve a profit that is a specified percentage of the sales volume.
   e. setting a price based on a specific annual dollar target volume of profit.

19. Lewis Edibles, Inc. is a small manufacturer of barbecue sauce. Variable cost for a pint of the barbecue sauce is $1.21. Fixed cost for the operation is $12,500. Demand is insensitive to price up to $8.25 per pint jar. If a target profit of $4,000 is sought on an annual volume of 3,000 jars, what is the per pint jar price (rounded to the nearest quarter)?
>   a. $8.25
>   b. $7.50
>   c. $6.00
>   d. $6.75
>   e. $4.25

20. Which of the following companies would be most likely to use target return-on-investment pricing?
>   a. a public utility
>   b. a florist shop
>   c. a book publisher
>   d. a veterinarian
>   e. a farmer

21. For which of the following products are you most likely to see the manufacturer using customary pricing?
>   a. bedroom furniture
>   b. laptop computers
>   c. fresh produce
>   d. sodas
>   e. laundry detergent

22. An ad campaign by Suave shampoo asked television viewers to identify the hair that was shampooed and conditioned with Suave products and the hair on which expensive salon hair-care products were used. The idea of the ad was that a person could not tell by looking that a woman was using the much cheaper Suave brand. By making price its selling point, Suave is most likely using:
>   a. demand backward pricing.
>   b. below-market pricing.
>   c. loss-leader pricing.
>   d. prestige pricing.
>   e. skimming pricing.

23. Another name for flexible-price policy is:
>   a. price lining.
>   b. dynamic pricing.
>   c. holistic pricing.
>   d. price synergy.
>   e. parasitic pricing.

24. When you buy a Wilson Sting tennis racket from a discount store, you are offered the product at a single price. You can buy it or not, but there is no variation in price under the seller's:
>   a. penetration strategy.
>   b. odd-even pricing.
>   c. one-price policy.
>   d. bundle-pricing policy.
>   e. flexible-price policy.

25. Different brands within a company's product line generally have different profit margins; higher price lines have higher profit margins. For example, Nike Variety tennis shoes have variable costs of $6 and sell for $24; whereas, Nike Wimbleton tennis shoes have variable costs of $10 and sell for $48. It must be true that:
    a. demand is unrelated to price.
    b. Nike is using a cost-plus percentage-of-cost pricing strategy.
    c. Nike is using a product-line pricing strategy.
    d. demand is unrelated to product quality.
    e. consumers do not use price as an indication of quality.

26. Lab Safety sells a line of general-duty gloves made out of nitrile rather than latex. The cheapest model it sells costs $1.49 per pair. Its top of the line runs $5.60 a pair, and it offers two other variations priced in between. Lab Safety uses _____ pricing.
    a. target
    b. experience curve
    c. product-line
    d. dynamic
    e. prestige

27. Marketers are advised to consider cost cutting only when:
    a. selective demand for the product will grow if prices are raised.
    b. primary demand for a product class will grow if prices are lowered.
    c. when they are able to reduce all prices as well.
    d. the company has no technological advantage over its competitors.
    e. there is no primary demand for the product.

28. A small gasoline station manager observes that while gasoline sales have been steady, the service side of her business has fallen off and mechanics are often idle. She decides to offer a promotion—an oil change for $10 with a coupon mailed to 800 households in a 2-mile radius from her station. The $10 will just cover the costs of the oil change, and the cost of printing and mailing is $1000. She hopes the promotion will increase regular maintenance service calls, whose average price is $40 (Average materials and labor costs per job is $30.) How many additional maintenance service jobs must result for the promotion to break even? (Disregard opportunity costs, goodwill effects, and any additional revenues.)
    a. 70 maintenance jobs
    b. 80 maintenance jobs
    c. 100 maintenance jobs
    d. 300 maintenance jobs
    e. 400 maintenance jobs

29. At the photocopy shop, one copy is 10 cents, but 50 copies are 5 cents each. This is an example of:
    a. slotting allowance.
    b. functional discount.
    c. quantity discount.
    d. cash discount.
    e. geographical adjustment.

30. Toro offers _____ to encourage wholesalers and retailers to stock up on lawn mowers in January and February and snow throwers in July and August.
    a. seasonal discounts
    b. cash discounts
    c. functional discounts
    d. promotional allowances
    e. trade discounts

31. The other name for trade discount is a:
    a. slotting allowance.
    b. cash discount.
    c. promotional discount.
    d. functional discount.
    e. markdown discount.

32. When Marcia buys gas at her local station, she pays $.03 a gallon less if she pays cash instead of charging the gas purchase on her credit card. This is an example of a:
    a. slotting allowance.
    b. cash discount.
    c. promotional discount.
    d. functional discount.
    e. markdown discount.

33. A manufacturer does marketing research and estimates consumers will accept a price of $250 for a jacket. If the manufacturer expects to offer trade discounts of 40/10/5 to retailers, wholesalers, and agents, what price will the manufacturer receive for the jacket?
    a. $75
    b. $89.25
    c. $95.75
    d. $99.75
    e. $128.25

34. Rick's Bike Shop allows customers to use a credit card for purchases. The shop pays 3 percent of the sale to the credit card company. To promote more business, Rick decides to offer a lower price to customers paying cash—that price being 3 percent less than the standard list price. Rick is giving his customers a(n):
    a. functional discount.
    b. trade-in allowance.
    c. promotional allowance.
    d. cash discount.
    e. everyday low price.

35. Which of the following statements about geographical adjustments to price is correct?
    a. In FOB origin pricing, the seller selects the mode of transportation.
    b. In FOB with freight allowed pricing, the seller adds the transportation costs to the list price.
    c. Multiple-zone pricing is sometimes referred to as "postage-stamp" pricing.
    d. Basing point pricing seems to have been used in industries where freight expenses are a significant part of the total cost to the buyer.
    e. All of the above statements about geographical adjustments to price are correct.

36. Which of the following is NOT a type of delivered pricing method?
    a. FOB with freight-allowed pricing
    b. FOB origin pricing
    c. freight absorption pricing
    d. multiple-zone pricing
    e. single-zone pricing

37. Uniform delivered pricing means:
    a. title of goods remains with the manufacturer until sold to the ultimate consumer.
    b. pricing and title of goods passes to the buyer upon arrival at final destination.
    c. title of the goods passes to the buyer at the point of shipment.
    d. price the seller sets includes all transportation costs.
    e. title of goods passes to the buyer when the state boundary is crossed.

38. Many cruise lines pay the customer's airfare to the point of cruise departure. What type of price adjustment are the cruise lines using?
    a. skimming pricing
    b. promotional pricing
    c. quantity discount pricing
    d. uniform delivered pricing
    e. prestige pricing

39. Postage stamp pricing is another name for _____ pricing.
    a. FOB with freight-allowed
    b. FOB origin
    c. basing-point
    d. multiple-zone
    e. single-zone

40. What geographical pricing method is used by the United States Postal Service for a first-class letter?
    a. FOB with freight-allowed
    b. FOB origin
    c. basing-point
    d. multiple-zone
    e. single-zone

41. For which of the following products is its manufacturer or producer most likely to use basing-point pricing?
    a. laptop computers
    b. furniture
    c. pottery
    d. bicycles
    e. coal

42. Which of the following statements about price fixing is true?
    a. Price fixing is illegal under the Clayton Act.
    b. The Robinson-Patman Act makes price fixing illegal.
    c. Vertical price fixing is also called resale price maintenance.
    d. Horizontal price fixing involves controlling agreements between independent buyers and sellers whereby sellers are required to not sell products below a minimum retail price.
    e. No companies have ever been convicted of vertical price fixing.

43. Mark Johnson, the manager of a discount consumer electronics store, has been approached by the manufacturer of a popular and profitable line of compact disk storage racks regarding the retail price charged for the racks at Johnson's store. The manufacturer's representative has implied that if Johnson doesn't raise the retail prices for the storage racks to those charged by the manufacturer's non-discount customers, Johnson's supply of racks may be severely curtailed. The manufacturer is guilty of attempting:
    a. horizontal price-fixing.
    b. resale price maintenance.
    c. price discrimination.
    d. predatory pricing.
    e. bait and switch pricing.

44. What do bait-and-switch, bargains conditional on other purchases, and comparisons with suggested price have in common?
        a. They are all examples of deceptive pricing practices.
        b. They are all ways that retailers use to calculate selling price.
        c. They are all ways manufacturers use to determine trade discounts.
        d. They are three different ways of taking a cash discount.
        e. They are three forms of predatory pricing.

45. _____ is the practice of charging a very low price for a product with the intent of driving competitors out of business.
        a. Price lining
        b. Experience curve pricing
        c. Predatory pricing
        d. Bait-and-switch pricing\
        e. Prestige pricing

46. Which of the following statements about geographical pricing is true?
        a. Geographical pricing is one type of pricing that has never fallen under the scrutiny of the U.S. legal system.
        b. FOB origin pricing is legal.
        c. Geographical pricing has come under more government scrutiny than any other pricing policy.
        d. FOB freight-allowed pricing practices are illegal.
        e. Basing-point pricing is the only form of geographical pricing that is not under some type of legal restriction.

47. In which step of the price setting process would a new product manager be deciding whether to offer the product for one price or a flexible price?
        a. identify pricing objectives and constraints
        b. determine cost, volume, and profit relationships
        c. select an approximate price level
        d. set list or quoted price
        e. make special adjustments to list or quoted price

48. Which of the following are part of step five of the price setting process, set list or quoted price?
        a. consider company, customer, and competitive effects
        b. make adjustments to list or quoted price
        c. decide whether to use skimming or penetration pricing
        d. decide on geographical adjustments
        e. decide whether to package two products together for the price of one

49. The Consumer Goods Pricing Act affects which of the following pricing practices?
        a. horizontal price fixing
        b. vertical price fixing
        c. predatory pricing
        d. deceptive pricing
        e. price discrimination

50. The Robinson-Patman Act governs which of the following?
        a. horizontal price fixing
        b. vertical price fixing
        c. predatory pricing
        d. deceptive pricing
        e. geographical pricing

ANSWER KEY

Answers to Questions & Problems

Demand-Oriented Pricing

1. Prestige, no, it is a convenience good
2. Price lining
3. Odd-even pricing, about $500 too high
4. Bundle pricing, to sell slow moving goods sometimes.
5. Market penetration and skimming. market share and profits

Cost-Oriented Pricing

1. One-of-a-kind or few-of-a-kind
2. Buying highly technical, few-of-a-kind products

Profit-Oriented Pricing

1. $32.40
2. $34.25

Competition-Oriented Approaches

2. Coke—below; 7UP—above; Pepsi and Slice—at

3. Loss leader

Special Adjustments to List or Quoted Price

1. Discounts
2. Discounts
3. Discounts
4. Allowances
5. Discounts
6. Allowances
7. Geographic adjustments
8. Geographic adjustments

Legal and Regulatory Aspects of Pricing

1. Yes, bait and switch
2. Predatory pricing
3. Yes, price discrimination

Answers to Sample Multiple Choice Questions

1. e p. 362; LO 1	14. d p. 366; LO 1	26. c p. 372; LO 2	38. d p. 378-379; LO 3
2. b p. 362; LO 1	15. c p. 366; LO 1	27. b p. 373; LO 2	39. e p. 379; LO 3
3. a p. 362; LO 1	16. e p. 366; LO 1	28. c p. 374; LO 2	40. e p. 379; LO 3
4. c p. 362; LO 1	17. e p. 364; LO 1	29. c p. 379375; LO 3	41. e p. 379; LO 3
5. b p. 363; LO 1	18. e p. 367; LO 1	30. a p. 375; LO 3	42. c p. 380; LO 4
6. c p. 363; LO 1	19. e p. 367-368; LO 1	31. d p. 376; LO 3	43. b p. 380; LO 4
7. d p. 364; LO 1	20. a p. 368; LO 1	32. b p. 376-373; LO 3	44. a p. 381; LO 4
8. e p. 363-364; LO 1	21. d p. 370; LO 1	33. e p. 376-377; LO 3	45. c p. 381-382; LO 4
9. e p. 364; LO 1	22. b p. 370; LO 1	34. d p. 376-377; LO 3	46. b p. 381; LO 4
10. b p. 364; LO 1	23. b p. 371; LO 2	35. d p. 378; LO 3	47. d p. 362; LO 1
11. e p. 366; LO 1	24. c p. 371; LO 2	36. b p. 378; LO 3	48. a p. 362; LO 1
12. a p. 366; LO 1	25. c p. 372; LO 2	37. d p. 378-379; LO 3	49. b p. 379; LO 4
13. c p. 366; LO 1			50. e p. 279; LO 4

Note: LO indicates learning objective.

CHAPTER 15

MANAGING MARKETING CHANNELS AND WHOLESALING

<u>Why is Chapter 15 important?</u> This chapter illustrates the types of middlemen utilized in getting a product to the ultimate customer and importance of selecting the proper channels to use. It discusses the various types of distribution strategies available and how, once selected, to avoid conflict within those channels.

Marketing Channels: A system of distribution which consists of individuals and firms involved in the process of making a product or service available for use or consumption by consumers or individuals users.

CHAPTER OUTLINE

I. NATURE AND IMPORTANCE OF MARKETING CHANNELS

    A. Marketing Channels of Distribution
        1. Middleman
        2. Agent or broker
        3. Wholesaler
        4. Retailer
        5. Distributor
        6. Dealer

    B. Value Created by Intermediaries
        1. Functions performed by intermediaries
            a. Transactional function
            b. Logistical function
            c. Facilitating function
        2. Consumer benefits from intermediaries
            a. Time utility
            b. Place utility
            c. Form utility
            d. Possession utility

II. CHANNEL STRUCTURE AND ORGANIZATION

    A. Consumer Goods and Services
        1. Direct
        2. Indirect

    B. Industrial Goods and Services
        1. Direct
        2. Indirect

    C. Electronic Marketing Channels

    D. Direct Marketing Channels

E. Multiple Channels and Strategic Alliances

F. Channel Intermediaries
    1. Merchant wholesalers
        a. general merchandise wholesalers
        b. specialty merchandise wholesalers
        c. rack jobbers
        d. cash-and-carry wholesalers
        e. drop shippers (desk jobbers)
        f. truck jobbers
    2. Agents and brokers
        a. manufacturer's agents
        b. selling agents
        c. brokers
    3. Manufacturer's branches and offices

G. Vertical Marketing Systems and Channel Partnerships
    1. Corporate systems
        a. forward integration
        b. backward integration
    2. Contractual systems
        a. wholesaler-sponsored voluntary chains
        b. retailer-sponsored cooperatives
        c. franchising
    3. Administered systems
    4. Channel partnerships

IV. CHANNEL CHOICE AND MANAGEMENT

A. Factors Affecting Channel Choice and Management
    1. Environmental factors
    2. Consumer factors
    3. Product factors
    4. Company factors

B. Channel Design Considerations
    1. Target market coverage
        a. extensive distribution
        b. exclusive distribution
        c. selective distribution
    2. Satisfying buyer requirements
        a. information
        b. convenience
        c. variety
        d. attendant services
    3. Profitability

C. Global Dimensions

D. Channel Relationships: Conflict, Cooperation, and Law
      1. Conflict
          a. vertical
          b. horizontal
      2. Cooperation
      3. Legal considerations
          a. dual distribution
          b. vertical integration
          c. exclusive dealing
          d. tying arrangements
          e. refusal to deal
          f. resale restrictions

You should be able to place these key terms in the outline and be able to discuss them.

brokers	**dual distribution**	**manufacturer's agents**
channel captain	**electronic marketing channel**	**marketing channel**
channel conflict	**exclusive distribution**	**merchant wholesalers**
channel partnership	**franchising**	**selective distribution**
direct channel	**indirect channels**	**selling agents**
direct marketing channels	**industrial distributor**	**strategic channels alliance**
disintermediation	**intensive distribution**	**vertical marketing systems**

QUESTIONS & PROBLEMS

RATIONALE FOR INTERMEDIARIES

Intermediaries make possible the flow of products from producers to buyers by performing three basic functions. They are:

Transactional functions
Logistical functions
Facilitating functions

Decide whether the following functions are transactional, logistical, or facilitating functions:

1. marketing information and research_____

2. sorting_____

3. risk taking_____

4. buying_____

5. storing_____

6. financing_____

7. grading_____

8. transporting_____

9. assorting_____

10. selling_____

DIRECT MARKETING

Direct marketing includes mail-order selling, direct-mail sales, catalog sales, telemarketing, video-text, and televised home shopping.

Tell how each of the following products uses direct marketing:

1. Music CD's and tapes_____

2. Clothing manufacturers_____

3. Book publishers_____

4. America On-Line_____

5. Sears_____

6. MCI_____

MERCHANT WHOLESALERS

There are two main types of merchant wholesalers: full-service wholesalers and limited-service wholesalers
.

Indicate whether the following wholesalers are full-service wholesalers or limited-service wholesalers:

1. drop shipper_____

2. rack jobber_____

3. general merchandise wholesaler_____

4. cash and carry wholesaler_____

5. truck jobbers_____

6. specialty merchandise wholesaler_____

VERTICAL MARKETING SYSTEMS (VMS)

A corporate vertical marketing system is a combination of successive stages of production and distribution under a single ownership. A corporate vertical marketing system may use either forward or backward integration.

Match the correct term with the examples or statements listed below:

> Forward integration
> Backward integration

1. Sears owns a substantial share of Whirlpool, on whom it depends for its Kenmore appliances._____

2. Sherwin Williams distributes its paint through a system of company-owned retail outlets._____

3. Zales Corporation, the largest jewelry retailer, owns its diamond cutting and polishing facility, as well as its own jewelry manufacturing plant._____

4. Hart, Shaffner, and Marx, which manufactures men's clothing, also owns over 200 retail outlets nationwide._____

Under a contractual vertical marketing system, independent production and distribution firms integrate their efforts on a contractual basis to obtain greater functional economies and marketing impact than they could achieve alone. Three variations of contractual marketing systems exist:

Wholesaler-sponsored voluntary chains
Retailer-sponsored cooperatives
Franchising

Match the correct form of contractual marketing system with the statements below:

1. Ford Motor Corporation licenses dealers to sell its cars subject to various sales and service conditions.
_____

2. The Associated Grocers is a group of small independent retailers, which formed an organization that operates a wholesale facility cooperatively. They concentrate their buying power through the wholesaler and plan collaborative promotional and pricing activities._____

3. Wholesalers who contract with smaller, independent retailers to standardize and coordinate buying practices, merchandising programs, and inventory management. I.G.A. and Western Auto are examples.
_____

4. H & R Block licenses individuals or firms to provide tax preparation services to the public._____
_____

CHANNEL DESIGN CONSIDERATIONS

There are three types of distribution density:

Intensive distribution
Selective distribution
Exclusive distribution

Match the type of distribution density to the statements below:

1. Only one retail outlet in a specified geographic area carries the firm's products._____

2. A firm tries to place its products or services in as many outlets as possible._____

3. A firm selects only a few retail outlets in a specific area to carry its products._____

4. BMW uses this approach in order to maintain product image and also to have more control over the selling effort of its dealers._____

5. Hallmark Cards is able to maintain good dealer relationships because it limits the number and maintains the quality of outlets it sells through._____

6. Convenience goods are typically distributed in this manner._____

There are three main considerations affecting channel design:

Target market coverage
Satisfying buyer requirements
Profitability

Match the consideration affecting channel design with the statements or examples listed below:

1. Major universities have begun to offer their "executive" programs off-campus at an industry site in order to reach the growing corporate market._____

2. Companies must decide the best way to satisfy needs for information, convenience, variety, and attendant services._____

3. A new company has to decide which marketing channel to use. They have to take into consideration costs of distribution, advertising, and selling expenses, relative to revenues generated._____

CHANNEL RELATIONSHIPS

Decide whether the following statements are examples of vertical conflict or horizontal conflict:

1. H.J. Heinz Company is embroiled in a conflict with its supermarkets in Great Britain because the supermarkets are promoting and displaying private brands at the expense of Helm brands._____

2. The owner of a downtown McDonald's complained vehemently to the franchiser when he learned that plans for the new enclosed mall included another McDonald's Restaurant._____

3. Friction emerged between Chrysler and its dealers when the company expected dealers to shoulder the burden of its $500 rebate program._____

4. K-Mart store managers complained to Kenner that Venture stores were getting faster delivery during the holiday rush period._____

CAN YOU PASS THE TEST?
Sample Multiple Choice Questions

1. Marketing channels can most readily be compared with a(n):
    a. atlas.
    b. pipeline.
    c. dramatic play.
    d. database.
    e. cloverleaf.

2. Individuals and firms involved in the process of making a good or service available for use or consumption by consumers or industrial users are considered members of a:
    a. distribution line.
    b. marketing channel.
    c. consortium.
    d. cartel.
    e. distribution mix.

3. Which of the following statements correctly defines one of the terms used for intermediaries?
    a. An agent or broker is an intermediary who simply sells to consumers.
    b. A dealer is a more precise term for an intermediary than distributor.
    c. A wholesaler is an intermediary that sells to other intermediaries.
    d. A middleman is any intermediary who only sells to consumer markets.
    e. A middleman is an intermediary who had legal authority to act on behalf of the buyer.

4. Which of the following statements about the terms used for marketing intermediaries is true?
    a. The most precise terms used to describe marketing intermediaries are dealer and distributor.
    b. A retailer sells to business markets.
    c. An agent has no legal authority to act on behalf of a manufacturer.
    d. A middleman is any intermediary between manufacturer and end-user markets.
    e. A broker is a synonym for a dealer.

5. In terms of distribution, when marketing channel members are engaged in gathering, storing, and dispersing of products, they are performing _____ functions.
    a. logistical
    b. transformational
    c. facilitating
    d. implementing
    e. transactional

6. Which of the following is an example of a logistical function that is commonly performed by an intermediary?
    a. financing
    b. buying
    c. grading
    d. providing marketing information
    e. transporting

7. When the grocery store offers cartons of eggs in five sizes, it has performed which intermediary function?
   a. grading
   b. assorting
   c. storing
   d. sorting
   e. merchandising

8. A snack vending machine located in a motel at which you arrive at 2 A.M., and you are hungry creates _____ utility.
   a. time and creation
   b. place and time
   c. form and place
   d. possession and form
   e. application and time

9. World Book Educational Products selling its encyclopedias door to door is an example of which type of marketing channel?
   a. direct channel
   b. indirect channel
   c. strategic channel alliances
   d. marketing channel
   e. dual distributive channel

10. The most indirect channel for consumer goods incorporates agents, wholesalers, and retailers and is most commonly used when:
   a. there are only a few large manufacturers but many small retailers.
   b. there are low-cost, low unit volume goods.
   c. there are many small manufacturers and many small retailers.
   d. there is too large an inventory to be carried by wholesalers.
   e. there are many manufacturers with a limited inventory competing for a small group of retailers.

11. When Joann buys a Pez candy dispenser on eBay her dispenser will be mailed by the person who sold it. This is an example of:
   a. an indirect channel.
   b. a producer channel.
   c. a static channel.
   d. a direct channel
   e. none of the above.

12. In many ways, _____ in business markets are like wholesalers in consumer channels.
   a. food brokers
   b. real estate agents
   c. industrial users
   d. industrial distributors
   e. ultimate consumers

13. _____ employ the Internet to make goods and services available for consumption or use by consumers or industrial buyers.
   a. Internet distribution channels
   b. Electronic marketing channels
   c. Virtual marketing channels
   d. Consumer-responsive channels
   e. Product-driven marketing channels

14. Which of the following is an example of a direct marketing channel?
   a. catalog sales
   b. televised home shopping
   c. telemarketing
   d. interactive media
   e. all of the above

15. Mikasa dishes are sold at upscale department stores and at outlet malls. This is an example of:
   a. bimodal positioning.
   b. dual distribution.
   c. indirect placement.
   d. dual-level placement.
   e. dual targeting.

16. A recent innovation in marketing channels whereby one firm's marketing channel is used to sell another firm's products is called a(n):
   a. dual distribution.
   b. a strategic channel alliance.
   c. cooperative distribution.
   d. a integrated channel alliance.
   e. a multi-channel venture.

17. Merchant wholesalers:
   a. are independently owned.
   b. take title to the merchandise they handle.
   c. are classified as either full-line or limited-line wholesalers.
   d. are also called industrial distributors.
   e. are accurately described by all of the above.

18. Which type of wholesaler offers a relatively narrow range of products but has an extensive assortment within the product lines carried?
   a. general merchandise wholesaler
   b. limited-service wholesaler
   c. specialty merchandise wholesaler
   d. cash and carry wholesaler
   e. drop shipper

19. Which of the following is an example of a limited-service wholesaler?
   a. broker
   b. manufacturers' agent
   c. drop shipper
   d. full-line wholesaler
   e. selling agent

20. Rack jobbers are wholesalers who:
  a. furnish the shelves that display merchandise in retail stores, perform all channel functions, and sell on consignment to retailers.
  b. take title to merchandise but sell only to buyers who call on them, pay cash for merchandise, and furnish their own transportation for merchandise.
  c. own the merchandise they sell but do not physically handle, stock, or deliver it.
  d. have a small warehouse from which they stock their trucks for distribution to retailers.
  e. work for several producers and carry noncompetitive, complementary merchandise in an exclusive territory.

21. Truck jobbers are wholesalers who:
  a. furnish the racks or shelves that display merchandise in retail stores, perform all channel functions, and sell on consignment to retailers.
  b. take title to merchandise but sell only to buyers who call on them, pay cash for merchandise, and furnish their own transportation for merchandise.
  c. own the merchandise they sell but do not physically handle, stock, or deliver it.
  d. have a small warehouse from which they stock their trucks for distribution to retailers.
  e. work for several producers and carry noncompetitive, complementary merchandise in an exclusive territory.

22. Brokers would most likely be found selling:
  a. apples, cherries, and plums.
  b. furniture.
  c. electronic equipment.
  d. office supplies.
  e. insurance.

23. BizBuyer.com, ITRadar.com.and Onvia.com are all Internet companies that are called "go-betweens." If a business needs bids on installing a waste water treatment center, it can visit one of these sites, list its requirements, and ask for bids. Since the purpose of these websites it to put buyer and sellers together so that a sale can be made, these three websites can be categorized as:
  a. brokers.
  b. selling agents.
  c. manufacturer's representatives.
  d. manufacturers' agents.
  e. administrators.

24. A(n) _____ does not carry inventory, typically performs only a sales function, and serves as an alternative to agents and brokers.
  a. industrial distributor
  b. intermediary
  c. drop shipper
  d. manufacturer's sales office
  e. manufacturer's branch office

25. The purpose of a vertical marketing system is to:
  a. dissuade retailers from dealing with other manufacturers or wholesalers.
  b. limit the number of retail outlets served, or maintain a limited service region.
  c. achieve channel economies and maximum marketing impact.
  d. eliminate competition by narrowing the channel from supplier to consumer.
  e. maximize the number of wholesalers a supplier can deal through.

26. The three major types of vertical marketing systems are:
    a. profit-based, stakeholder-based, and international-based.
    b. corporate, contractual, and administered.
    c. forward-based, backward-based, and horizontal.
    d. strategic, tactical, and operational.
    e. marketing-derived, management-derived, and finance-derived.

27. If Black & Decker, a manufacturer of hand tools and small appliances, opens a retail store in an outlet mall, it is an example of:
    a. backward integration.
    b. product diversification.
    c. horizontal integration.
    d. horizontal diversification.
    e. forward integration.

28. Sears operates a network of warehouses as part of its distribution system. Sears also obtains over 50 percent of its goods from companies that it partly or wholly owns. Sears is engaged in:
    a. dual distribution.
    b. forward integration.
    c. backward integration.
    d. horizontal integration.
    e. strategic alliance.

29. Which type of contractual vertical marketing system involves a contractual relationship between a wholesaler and small independent retailers to standardize and coordinate buying practices, merchandising programs, and inventory management efforts?
    a. service-sponsored retail franchise system
    b. retailer-sponsored cooperative
    c. administered vertical marketing system
    d. manufacturer-sponsored retail franchise system
    e. wholesaler-sponsored voluntary chain

30. The most visible form of _____ vertical marketing systems is franchising.
    a. contractual
    b. strategic
    c. administered
    d. international-based
    e. corporate

31. A contractual arrangement between a parent company and an individual or firm that allows the individual or firm to operate a certain type of business under an established name and according to specific rules is called:
    a. a corporate vertical marketing system.
    b. a wholesaler sponsored voluntary chain.
    c. a retailer sponsored cooperative.
    d. franchising.
    e. an administered vertical marketing system.

32. Because Procter and Gamble has a broad product assortment and is able to obtain excellent cooperation from supermarkets in displaying, promoting, and pricing its products, Procter and Gamble represents which type of vertical marketing system?
- a. corporate vertical marketing system
- b. integrated vertical marketing system
- c. contractual vertical marketing system
- d. administered vertical marketing system
- e. interactive vertical marketing system

33. Bombardier makes corporate jets. The aircraft company relies on outside suppliers for design support and to share development costs and market risks. For its newest plane, the Continental, Bombardier has about 30 prime suppliers – about ten of those have been involved since the initial design phase. Bombardier and its suppliers have entered into a:
- a. franchise.
- b. channel partnership.
- c. selling agency.
- d. limited-service marketing system.
- e. corporate vertical marketing system.

34. _____ are commonly used in the automobile industry. With this system, a manufacturer licenses dealers to sell its cars subject to various sales and service conditions.
- a. Service-sponsored producer franchise systems
- b. Service-sponsored retail franchise systems
- c. Manufacturer-sponsored wholesale systems
- d. Manufacturer-sponsored retail franchise systems
- e. Administered vertical marketing systems

35. Which of the following is an example of factors that directly affects channel choice and management?
- a. product factors
- b. company factors
- c. consumer factors
- d. environmental factors
- e. all of the above

36. _____ mean(s) that a firm tries to place its products and services in as many outlets as possible.
- a. Selective distribution
- b. A direct channel of distribution
- c. Seasonal discounts
- d. Intensive distribution
- e. Wholesaling

37. When Kraft Foods introduced Planters Trail Mix snack food, it was a low-involvement convenience product. Which type of distribution should Kraft have used with this new product?
- a. exclusive distribution
- b. direct distribution
- c. intensive distribution
- d. dual distribution
- e. selective distribution

38. Which type of distribution should Gucci use for its Yves Saint Laurent brand?
    a. primary
    b. selective
    c. targeted
    d. exclusive
    e. focused

39. The target market coverage and distribution intensity associated with shopping goods such as overcoats, work boots, and dining room furniture is called:
    a. intensive distribution.
    b. exclusive distribution.
    c. selective distribution.
    d. primary distribution.
    e. secondary distribution.

40. When Apple Computer opened the Apple stores to allow customers to create a less stressful and more supportive environment for shopping for a new PC, Apple used:
    a. dual distribution.
    b. forward integration.
    c. backward integration.
    d. horizontal integration.
    e. strategic alliance.

41. One channel design issue is to gain access to channels and intermediaries that satisfy at least some of the interests buyers might want fulfilled when they purchase a firm's products. One of those interests is attendant services. Which of the following is an example of an attendant service?
    a. point-of-purchase displays that explain a sales contest.
    b. warranty agreements
    c. the ability to repair damaged merchandise
    d. close location
    e. all of the above

42. Kiertsu is:
    a. the severing of channel relationships.
    b. Japanese channel relationships.
    c. a Japanese beer.
    d. a full-line wholesaler in Korea.
    e. the channel captain.

43. _____ arises when one channel member believes another channel member is engaged in behavior that prevents it from achieving its goals.
    a. Channel conflict
    b. Distribution discord
    c. Channel disruption
    d. Goal barrier
    e. Distributive dissent

44. When a channel member bypasses another member and sells or buys product direct, this is termed:
    a. disintermediation.
    b. unethical.
    c. vertical conflict.
    d. horizontal conflict.
    e. resale restrictions.

45. Waldenbooks and Barnes & Noble book sellers would be likely to engage in _____ conflict if both wanted to have exclusive rights to the newest Harry Potter book.
    a. vertical
    b. disintermediated
    c. target marking
    d. horizontal
    e. administered

46. Which of the following is the source of power determining which channel member will be the channel captain?
    a. economic power
    b. expertise
    c. identification with a particular channel member
    d. legitimate rights through contracts
    e. any of the above

47. Which of the following statements about channel captains is true?
    a. Retailers can never assume the role of channel captain.
    b. A firm becomes a channel captain after an election.
    c. The use of a channel captain is one of the primary sources of horizontal conflict.
    d. Only wholesalers can be channel captains.
    e. None of the above statements about channel captains is true.

48. Which of the following statements about the legal considerations associated with channel conflict are true?
    a. Dual distribution is never illegal.
    b. Vertical integration can be illegal if it has the potential to lessen competition.
    c. Full-line forcing is a special kind of vertical integration.
    d. Exclusive dealing is legal as long as consumers are aware that the practice is being used.
    e. Under the Clayton Act, tying arrangements are always legal.

49. Questions of legality regarding tying arrangements and exclusive dealing would most likely occur in:
a. corporate systems.
b. administered systems.
c. franchises.
d. manufacturing.
e. retail-sponsored cooperatives.

50. A(n) _____ is a supplier's attempt to stipulate to whom distributors may resell the supplier's products and in what specific geographical areas or territories they may sell.
a. resale restriction
b. oligopolistic practice
c. monopolistic practice
d. refusal to deal
e. tying arrangement

ANSWER KEY

Answers To Questions & Problems

Rationale for Intermediaries

1. Facilitating functions
2. Logistical functions
3. Transactional functions
4. Transactional functions
5. Logistical functions
6. Facilitating functions
7. Facilitating functions
8. Logistical functions
9. Logistical functions
10. Transactional functions

Direct Marketing

1. Direct mail, mail order
2. Direct mail, catalog, TV home shopping
3. Direct mail, mail order
4. Direct mail, catalog
5. Catalog, TV home shopping
6. Telemarketing, direct mail

Merchant Wholesalers

1. Limited-service wholesalers
2. Limited-service wholesalers
3. Full-service wholesalers
4. Limited-service wholesalers
5. Limited-service wholesalers
6. Full-service wholesalers

Vertical Marketing Systems

1. Backward integration
2. Forward integration
3. Backward integration
4. Forward integration

1. Franchising
2. Retailer-sponsored cooperatives
3. Wholesaler sponsored voluntary chains
4. Franchising

Channel Design Considerations

1. Exclusive distribution
2. Intensive distribution
3. Selective distribution
4. Exclusive distribution
5. Selective distribution
6. Intensive distribution

1. Target market coverage
2. Satisfying buyer requirements
3. Profitability

Channel Relationships

1. Vertical conflict
2. Horizontal conflict
3. Vertical conflict
4. Horizontal conflict

Answers to Sample Multiple Choice Questions

1. b p. 396; LO 1	14. e p. 401; LO 2	26. b p. 405; LO 2	38. d p. 409; LO 3
2. b p. 396; LO 1	15. b p. 402; LO 2	27. e p. 405; LO 2	39. c p. 410; LO 3
3. c p. 396; LO 1	16. b p. 402; LO 2	28. c p. 405; LO 2	40. b p. 405; LO 2
4. d p. 396; LO 1	17. e p. 403; LO 2	29. e p. 406; LO 2	41. c p. 411; LO 3
5. a p. 398; LO 1	18. c p. 403; LO 2	30. a p. 406; LO 2	42. b p. 412; LO 3
6. e p. 398; LO 1	19. c p. 403; LO 2	31. d p. 406; LO 2	43. a p. 412; LO 4
7. a p. 398; LO 1	20. a p. 404; LO 2	32. d p. 407; LO 2	44. a p. 412; LO 4
8. b p. 398; LO 1	21. d p. 404; LO 2	33. e p. 405; LO 2	45. d p. 412; LO 4
9. a p. 399; LO 2	22. a p. 404; LO 2	34. d p. 406; LO 2	46. e p. 413; LO 4
10. c p. 399; LO 2	23. a p. 404; LO 2	35. e p. 407-408; LO 3	47. e p. 413; LO 4
11. d p. 399; LO 2	24. d p. 405; LO 2	36. d p. 409; LO 3	48. b p. 413; LO 4
12. d p. 399; LO 2	25. c p. 405; LO 2	37. c p. 409; LO 3	49. c p. 414; LO 4
13. b p. 400; LO 2			50. a p. 414; LO 4

Note: LO indicates learning objective.

CHAPTER 16

INTEGRATING SUPPLY CHAIN AND LOGISTICS MANAGEMENT

<u>Why is Chapter 16 important?</u> This chapter examines the flow of products to the ultimate consumer and how to make that as efficient as possible. It shows how the proper selection of transportation, storage, and timing can reduce costs and lead to greater customer satisfaction.

Logistics Management: Organizing the cost-effective flow of raw materials, in-process inventory, finished goods, and related information from point-of-origin to point-of-consumption to satisfy customer requirements.

CHAPTER OUTLINE

I. SIGNIFICANCE OF SUPPLY CHAIN AND LOGISTICS MANAGEMENT

    A. Relating Marketing Channels, Logistics, and Supply Chain Management
        1. Logistics Management
            a. elements
                i. flow
                ii. cost-effective
                iii. customer service
            b. important factors
                i. number, weight, volume, and perishability
                ii. number of material supply points
                iii. number of material processing points
                iv. number of product consumption points
        2. Supply Chain Management

    B. Supply Chain Management and Marketing Strategy
        1. Understand the customer
        2. Understand the supply chain
        3. Harmonize the supply chain with the marketing strategy

II. INFORMATION AND LOGISTICS MANAGEMENT OBJECTIVE IN A SUPPLY CHAIN

    A. Information's Role in Supply Chain—Responsiveness and Efficiency

    B. Total Logistics Cost Concept

    C. Customer Service Concept
        1. Time
        2. Dependability
        3. Communication
        4. Convenience

III. KEY LOGISTICS FUNCTIONS IN A SUPPLY CHAIN

A. Transportation
 1. Criteria
   a. cost
   b. time
   c. capability
   d. dependability
   e. accessibility
   f. frequency
 2. Railroads
 3. Motor carriers
 4. Air carriers and express companies
 5. Freight forwarders

B. Warehousing and Materials Handling
 1. Storage warehouses
 2. Distribution centers
 3. Materials handling

C. Order Processing

D. Inventory Management
 1. Reasons for inventory
   a. to offer buffer against variations in supply and demand
   b. to provide better service
   c. to promote production efficiencies
   d. to provide a hedge against price increases
   e. to promote purchasing and transportation discounts
   f. to protect the firm from contingencies
 2. Inventory costs
   a. capital costs
   b. inventory service costs
   c. storage costs
   d. risk costs
 3. Supply chain strategies
   a. just-in-time (JIT) concept
   b. Vendor-managed inventory

IV. REVERSE LOGISTICS

You should be able to place these key terms in the outline and be able to discuss them.

customer service
efficient consumer response
electronic data interchange (EDI)
just-in-time (JIT) concept
lead time
logistics
logistics management
materials handling

quick response
reverse logistics
supply chain
supply chain management
third-party logistics providers
total logistics cost
vendor-managed inventory

QUESTIONS & PROBLEMS

INTEGRATING SUPPLY CHAIN AND LOGISTICS MANAGEMENT

Supply chain management is organizing the movement and storage of a finished product to the customer. Logistics management is organizing the cost-effective flow of raw materials, in-process inventory, finished goods, and related information from point-of-origin to point-of-consumption to satisfy customer requirements.

1. What factors account for the trend of increased emphasis on logistics systems?_____
_____

2. List four different factors that determine the relative importance of a firm's logistics system:

1. _____

2._____

3._____

4._____

LOGISTICS SYSTEMS

Federal Express developed its own tracking systems and inventory control system and now works with company's needing a complete logistics system, especially those looking for just-in-time inventory. Many of the companies contracting with Federal Express are high tech firms. Answer the following questions:

1. What is the key objective of the logistics system?_____
_____

2. What is the primary advantage of strategic alliances?_____
_____

3. What is the purpose of an electronic data interchange and what can it do?_____
_____

TOTAL LOGISTICS COST CONCEPT

List the key elements in total logistics cost:

1._____

2._____

3._____

4._____

5._____

6._____

7._____

8._____

9._____

CUSTOMER SERVICE CONCEPT

Customer service is the ability of a logistics system to satisfy users in terms of time, dependability, communications, and convenience. How would each of these facets of customer service be important to the following businesses?

1. Pizza Hut_____

2. Quick Lube_____

3. A 7-11 convenience store_____

4. CompUSA_____

5. A local florist_____

MAJOR LOGISTICAL FUNCTIONS

Transportation

There are five basic modes of transportation: railroads, motor carriers, air carriers, pipelines, and water carriers. All can be evaluated on six basic service dimensions: cost, time, capability, dependability, accessibility, and frequency.

List the relative advantages and disadvantages for the modes of transportation listed below:

	<u>Advantages</u>	<u>Disadvantages</u>
Rail	_____	_____
Truck	_____	_____
Air	_____	_____
Pipeline	_____	_____
Water	_____	_____

To capitalize on the advantages and avoid the disadvantages, many firms use intermodal transportation. Make sure you know the meanings of the terms: TOFC, and piggyback transportation. Many times, smaller companies can't afford major transportation costs. These companies are able to make use of freight forwarders. Freight forwarders are firms that accumulate small shipments into larger lots and then hire a carrier to move them, usually at reduced rates. Air freight forwarders, or express companies, are firms that market air express services to the general public.

WAREHOUSING AND MATERIALS HANDLING

Warehouses may be classified in one of two ways: (1) storage warehouses and (2) distribution centers.

Answer the following questions:

What is the significant difference between storage warehouses and distribution centers?

_____

What are two major difficulties with materials handling?

1._____

2._____

INVENTORY MANAGEMENT

The major problem in managing inventory is maintaining the delicate balance between too little and too much of it.

List the six traditional reasons for carrying inventory:

1._____

2._____

3._____

4._____

5._____

6._____

Part of Wal-Mart's success has come from outstanding physical distribution and logistics management systems. They have made a science of cost control. Discuss how each of the six traditional reasons for carrying would affect a firm like Wal-Mart._____
_____
_____

INVENTORY STRATEGIES

The just-in-time (JIT) inventory supply system operates with very lean inventories to hold down costs and requires fast, on-time delivery.

List at least three relative advantages and disadvantages of the "JIT" inventory strategy for a company like Dell Computer:

Advantages	Disadvantages
_____	_____
_____	_____
_____	_____

CAN YOU PASS THE TEST?
Sample Multiple Choice Questions

1. _____ involves those activities that focus on getting the right amount of the right products to the right place at the right time at the lowest possible cost.
    a. Inventory management
    b. Warehousing
    c. Materials handling
    d. Logistics
    e. Information management

2. A _____ is a sequence of firms that perform activities required to create and deliver a good or service to consumers or industrial users.
    a. supply chain
    b. logistical management
    c. inventory handling technique
    d. quick response system
    e. disintermediation

3. UPS Logistics earned more than $1 billion in revenue in a recent year and is one of the fastest growing divisions of UPS. UPS Logistics designs and manages entire transportation and customer service networks for global clients that include Ford Motor Co. and National Semiconductor. UPS Logistics:
    a. creates utility for these companies' customers.
    b. assumes the role of freight forwarder.
    c. increases the number of steps in the value proposition.
    d. assumes the role of drop shipper.
    e. does not influence their clients' supply chain.

4. Supply chain is a sequence of firms that perform activities required to _____ to consumers or industrial users.
    a. create and deliver a good or service
    b. decrease the length of the value chain
    c. increase the amount of inventory sent
    d. disintermediate
    e. increase the number of steps in the value proposition

5. All of the following are reasons for the increased emphasis on logistics systems EXCEPT:
    a. logistics focuses on flow of product.
    b. logistics is cost-effective.
    c. re-regulation of the trucking and railroad industries to insure that price-gouging tactics will no longer be practiced.
    d. large growth in the differentiation of products to respond to changes in consumer demand.
    e. logistics provides expected customer service levels.

6. Logistics management is organizing the cost-effective flow of raw materials, in-process inventory, finished goods, and related information from point-of-origin to point-of-consumption to:
    a. satisfy customer requirements.
    b. create maximum profit.
    c. maintain organizational culture.
    d. eliminate all competition.
    e. do none of the above.

7. In a recent year, customers could link to Cisco's website to configure, price, and order $1 billion a month of its networking equipment. Cisco then sent orders back out across the Internet to board producers and assemblers including Celestica, Flextronics, Jabil, and Solectron. Products were built and tested to Cisco standards, sometimes with procedures run remotely by Cisco. Most were then drop-shipped to buyers, untouched by human hands on Cisco's payroll. This is a description of Cisco's:
        a. just-in-time inventory system.
        b. electronic data interchange (edi).
        c. strategic information alliance.
        d. supply chain.
        e. product-specific delivery system.

8. Customers currently link to Cisco's website to configure, price, and order its networking equipment. Cisco then sends orders back out across the Internet to board producers and assemblers including Celestica, Flextronics, Jabil, and Solectron. Products are built and tested to Cisco standards, sometimes with procedures run remotely by Cisco. Most are then drop-shipped to buyers, untouched by human hands on Cisco's payroll. The individuals who monitor these transactions and make sure each is performed in a cost-effective and timely fashion are engaged in:
        a. supply chain management.
        b. total distribution cost management.
        c. point-to-point management.
        d. just-in-time management.
        e. materials handling.

9. The first step in selecting a supply chain is to:
        a. understand the customer.
        b. develop a product.
        c. locate potential bottlenecks.
        d. elect a channel captain.
        e. evaluate potential modes of transportation.

10. Supply chain management impacts all of the following aspects of the marketing mix strategy EXCEPT:
        a. the target market selection decision.
        b. product mix decisions.
        c. pricing decisions.
        d. promotion decisions.
        e. distribution decisions.

11. Which of the following statements about supply chains is true?
        a. Managers must never make trade-offs between efficiency and responsiveness—both are equally important.
        b. Cross-docking is the most efficient supply chain for all retailers.
        c. Supply chains should not be designed on the basis of customer needs.
        d. The most efficient supply chain is a responsive supply chain.
        e. None of the above statements about supply chains is true.

12. Cross-docking is most closely related to:
        a. efficient supply chain activities.
        b. intermodal transportation.
        c. increasing lead time.
        d. reverse logistics.
        e. drop shipping.

13. The objective of information and logistics management in a supply chain is to:
    a. create a supply chain with effective bottlenecks.
    b. balance total logistical cost factors with customer service factors so that customers are adequately satisfied.
    c. maximize profit.
    d. ensure that the company acts socially responsible.
    e. minimize logistics costs while delivering maximum customer service.

14. Information on customer demand patterns received through _____ allows Eli Lilly to produce and stock drugs in anticipation of customer needs.
    a. form utility
    b. electronic data interchange
    c. an administered vertical system
    d. a horizontally integrated distribution system
    e. intermodal transportation

15. Schneider National is a logistics firm that places on-board computers in each of its trucks. By using communication satellites, the Schneider's customer service representatives located in Green Bay, Wisconsin, can tap into a truck's on-board computer to find out exactly when a customer's order will arrive and the specific items included in the order. Schneider National is using _____ to provide more meaningful information to its customers.
    a. electronic data manipulation
    b. just-in-time inventory systems
    c. product-specific delivery system
    d. electronic data interchange
    e. creative computer imagery

16. An Extranet:
    a. is a more expensive form of electronic data interchange.
    b. has replaced manual order processes for most large companies.
    c. is a form of third-party logistics service provider.
    d. provide buffers between customers and manufacturers.
    e. permits business-to-business communications between a manufacturer, its suppliers and distributors.

17. Devlin Applied Design, a Canadian company, developed a(n) _____ for BASF to allow North American body shops to purchase materials such as paint and sandpaper directly via the Web. Since body shop professionals are typically not web savvy, Devlin designed a simple, user friendly, visual interface that allows users intuitively to order products via computer.
    a. personalized internet
    b. internet-free system
    c. e-commerce developed interface (edi)
    d. customized search engine
    e. Extranet

18. Which of the following is an element of total logistics cost?
    a. new product development
    b. advertising
    c. inventories
    d. personal selling
    e. all of the above

19. Total logistics cost for a company that sells wastewater treatment and disposal systems would include:
    a. a lost sale due to a stockout of a particular system.
    b. the costs of processing an order received from a hospital laundry.
    c. the costs of shipping the system from the manufacturer to the buyer.
    d. the costs of processing a system that was returned because of a faulty gauge.
    e. all of the above.

20. For a supply chain manager, one of the customer service factors that must be balanced against total logistics cost factors is:
    a. compatibility.
    b. context.
    c. customer interface.
    d. dependability.
    e. customization.

21. Saks Fifth Avenue employs a quick response system to order fast-moving fashion items. Saks' point-of-sales scanner records each sale. When stock falls below a minimum level, the system automatically sends an electronic order to the vendor (e.g., Donna Karan), which processes the order within 48 hours. This system has effectively reduced the _____.
    a. customer response cycle.
    b. product flow.
    c. lead time.
    d. supply lag.
    e. logistical lag.

22. Another name for lead time is:
    a. break-even time.
    b. point of economic order.
    c. rebuy time.
    d. replenishment time.
    e. point of reorder.

23. Which of the following customer-service components is likely to be most critical for Ford when it purchases original-issue automobile tires (tires put on new Ford cars)?
    a. lead time
    b. dependability and on-time delivery
    c. communication
    d. convenience
    e. none of the above

24. Quick response and efficient consumer response delivery systems are most closely related to:
    a. intermodal transportation.
    b. piggybacking.
    c. freight forwarding.
    d. just-in-time inventory strategies.
    e. reverse logistics.

25. Celarix.com is a member of the supply chain for many e-commerce businesses. It provides them with distribution software that manages tariffs and exchange rates for companies that ship internationally. Celarix.com is an example of a(n):
    a. channel captain.
    b. third-party logistics provider.
    c. administered supply chain member.
    d. contractual supply chain member.
    e. corporate supply chain member.

26. The four key logistical functions in a supply chain include warehousing and materials handling, order processing, inventory management, and:
   a. communication between buyer and seller.
   b. effective handling of problems.
   c. order cycle time.
   d. transportation.
   e. on-time delivery of product.

27. Coldwater Creek is a retailer and mail-order company. Because of its proficiency at filling orders, it has contracts to fill orders received by several e-commerce companies. Coldwater Creek is an example of a:
   a. freight jobber.
   b. freight forwarder.
   c. rack jobber.
   d. third-party logistics provider.
   e. wholesaler.

28. Which of the following is NOT one of the basic service criteria that distribution managers typically use to evaluate modes of transportation?
   a. accessibility
   b. cost
   c. assurance
   d. time
   e. frequency

29. A unit train is:
   a. a train with one locomotive.
   b. one that does not keep to a specific schedule because it is used only for special purpose hauling.
   c. used as a warehouse facility to accumulate small shipments into larger ones until it becomes financially feasible to transport the entire load.
   d. dedicated to one commodity using permanently coupled cars that run a continuous loop from a single origin to a single destination and back.
   e. combines trucking with the railroad to provide dual distribution for high-valued freight.

30. The Montana Coal Company needs to move its coal to intermediaries on the Atlantic coast who in turn will sell it to end users. The best means of transportation for the company to employ under normal conditions is:
   a. air carriers.
   b. motor carriers.
   c. water carriers.
   d. railroads.
   e. pipelines.

31. Which of the following statements about the modes of transportation is true?
   a. One of the disadvantages of water transportation when compared to the other modes is small capacities.
   b. When compared to other modes of transportation, air is the least expensive.
   c. The fastest mode of transportation is pipelines.
   d. When compared to the other modes of transportation, water and pipelines are slow.
   e. Water and rail are relatively expensive.

32. Which mode of transportation would be fast, expensive, and safest for easily damaged merchandise?
      a. water
      b. pipelines
      c. air
      d. railroad
      e. truck

33. When John Mellencamp went on his Rural Electrification Tour he did fifteen concerts in less than six weeks. Using what you have learned about modes of transporation, which mode would have been the best for carrying the lighting, stages, and other concert requirements from Fargo, North Dakota, to Evansville, Indiana?
      a. air
      b. railroad
      c. water
      d. pipeline
      e. truck

34. When used in discussing transportation, the acronym TOFC means:
      a. trailer on flatcar.
      b. transport on fixed carriage.
      c. truck or flat cartage.
      d. trade-off for cost.
      e. transport of flexible conveyance.

35. Piggyback is another name for:
      a. Extranet ordering.
      b. an efficient materials handling system.
      c. cross-docking.
      d. information management using EDI.
      e. trailer on flatcar.

36. All intermodal approaches have one thing in common, which is:
      a. they are all less expensive than single mode transportation.
      b. they provide protection against weather sensitivity.
      c. they are more costly than single mode transportation.
      d. they combine different transportation modes to get the best features of each.
      e. they use some form of container moved by railroad for part of the distance.

37. Vancouver-based TransLink, the Regional Transportation Network, is responsible for collecting and consolidating smaller shipments into larger ones and then transporting them throughout British Columbia. TransLink is an example of:
      a. a freight forwarder.
      b. a disintermediary.
      c. a channel captain.
      d. a cross-docker.
      e. intermodal transportation.

38. When a firm accumulates small shipments into larger lots and has Delta Air Lines handle the shipments on its regularly scheduled passenger flights, the firm is assuming the role of:
      a. gatekeeper.
      b. freight forwarder.
      c. freight jobber.
      d. chartered logistics provider.
      e. in-house logistics provider.

39. The two types of warehouses are:
    a. storing warehouses and activity warehouses.
    b. full-service warehouses and limited-service warehouses.
    c. cooperative warehouses and independent warehouses.
    d. multi-use warehouses and specialized warehouses.
    e. distribution centers and storage warehouses.

40. _____ involves moving goods over short distances into, within, and out of warehouses and manufacturing plants.
    a. Electronic data interchange
    b. Cross-docking
    c. Materials handling
    d. Efficient consumer response delivery system
    e. Vertical integration

41. One of the problems associated with materials handling is:
    a. finding the right transportation modes.
    b. meeting government regulations.
    c. a high rate of loss and damage.
    d. locating the facility in which to perform the activity.
    e. convincing buyers that it is an important activity.

42. _____ are the opportunity costs that result from tying up funds in inventory instead of using them in more profitable investments.
    a. Capital costs
    b. Inventory service costs
    c. Warehousing costs
    d. Order-processing costs
    e. Risk costs

43. Which of the following types of product is most likely to have the highest risk costs?
    a. coal
    b. bricks
    c. sugar
    d. apples
    e. office supplies

44. Which of the following is an example of a storage cost that would be considered a part of inventory costs?
    a. warehousing space and materials handling costs
    b. costs due to possible loss, damage, pilferage, or obsolescence
    c. opportunity costs resulting from tying up funds in inventory instead of using them in other, more profitable investments
    d. costs of the finished goods inventory itself
    e. costs such as insurance and taxes that are present in many states

45. Alberto-Culver Canada is the number three provider of hair care products in Canada. It first set up operation in downtown Etobicoke, Ontario in 1961. By 1966, it had to move its facility to the edge of town so that it was closer to its raw suppliers and, thus, would be able to operate with very low inventories and require suppliers to make fast on-time deliveries. So in 1966, Alberto-Culver Canada implemented what today is called a(n):
   a. disintermediation
   b. intermodal transportation
   c. just-in-time (jit) concept
   d. reverse logistics
   e. demarketing

46. The just-in-time concept requires very low inventories but fast, on-time delivery. When must parts needed for production arrive from suppliers?
   a. neither before nor after they are needed
   b. at least the day before they are needed
   c. three to four days before they are needed
   d. one week before they are needed
   e. as far in advance as possible

47. Vendor-managed inventory (VMI) is an inventory-management system whereby the:
   a. manufacturer's agent uses third-part logistical service providers.
   b. supplier determines the product amount and assortment a customer needs and automatically delivers the appropriate items.
   c. retailer creates a distribution trade-off between efficiency and cost.
   d. cross-docking specialist manages inventory for more than one retailer.
   e. manufacturer becomes the channel captain as a result of its distribution differentiation strategy.

48. Pharmaceutical companies such as Eli Lilly and SmithKline Beecham use _____ to make sure retailers carrying their products maintain predetermined inventory levels in stock. The pharmaceutical companies due this by a daily monitoring of sales at individual stores.
   a. supplier-managed inventory
   b. supply chain inventory
   c. logistics-managed inventory
   d. just-in-time system
   e. vendor-managed inventory

49. Reverse logistics is most closely related to:
   a. consumerism.
   b. cause-related marketing.
   c. a diversification growth strategy.
   d. vertical integration.
   e. green marketing.

50. Hi-Tech Recycling Canada, a computer and electronics recycling firm based in Toronto, is a lucrative business that focuses on the disposal of obsolete computer systems. Every monitor has four to six pounds of lead, which is mixed with phosphorous to protect users from radiation. The problem is that if the computers are thrown away in landfills, the lead and the phosphorous can get into the water supply, which is why many landfills won't accept computers. Hi-Tech Recycling Canada is divided into different divisions for taking care of computer board and memory recovery (which can often be recycled). The monitors it disposes of in accordance with legal regulations. Hi-Tech Recycling Canada has made a business out of:
   a. the green movement.
   b. the millennium waste-reduction initiative.
   c. reverse materials handling.
   d. reverse logistics.
   e. reduced landfill waste initiative.

ANSWER KEY

Answers to Questions & Problems

Relating Physical Supply, Physical Distribution, and Logistics

1. A large growth in the differentiation of products in order to respond to consumer demands and federal deregulation of transportation industries.

2. Number, weight, volume, and perishability of raw materials and final products
   Number of material supply points
   Number of material processing points
   Number of product consumption points

Logistics Systems

1. Minimize relevant logistics costs while delivering maximum customer service.

2. Better service through better information.

3. Links computers between manufacturer and transportation company to transmit all necessary documents for better service.

Total Logistics Cost Concept

1. Traffic and transportation
2. Warehousing and storage
3. Packaging
4. Materials handling
5. Inventory control
6. Order processing
7. Customer service level
8. Plant and warehouse site location
9. Return goods handling

Customer Service Concept

Example:

Pizza Hut—quick service, dependability of product (consistent), communications of offer, and convenient

Major Logistical Functions

Example:

Rail—advantages—large loads, inexpensive; disadvantages—time, dependability, accessibility, and frequency

Warehousing and Materials Handling

Goods are intended to "rest" for some time in storage warehouses; distribution centers are designed for facilitating timely movement of goods.

1. High labor costs
2. High rates of loss and damage

Inventory Management

1. To offer a buffer against variations in supply and demand

2. To provide better service for those who wish to be served on demand

3. To promote production efficiencies

4. To provide a hedge against price increases by suppliers

5. To promote purchasing and transportation discounts

6. To protect the firm from contingencies such as strikes and shortages

Inventory Strategies

Example: Advantages—keeps inventory costs down
Disadvantages—unanticipated large orders

Answers to Sample Multiple Choice Questions

1. d p. 422; LO 1	14. b p. 428; LO 3	26. d p. 432; LO 4	38. b p. 434; LO 4
2. a p. 422; LO 1	15. d p. 428; LO 3	27. d p. 432; LO 4	39. e p. 434; LO 4
3. a p. 422; LO 1	16. e p. 428; LO 3	28. c p. 432; LO 4	40. d p. 435; LO 4
4. a p. 422; LO 1	17. e p. 428; LO 3	29. d p. 433; LO 4	41. c p. 435; LO 4
5. c p. 422; LO 1	18. c p. 428; LO 3	30. d p. 433; LO 4	42. a p. 436; LO 4
6. a p. 422; LO 1	19. e p. 428; LO 3	31. d p. 433; LO 4	43. d p. 437; LO 4
7. d p. 422; LO 1	20. d p. 429; LO 3	32. c p. 433; LO 4	44. a p. 437; LO 4
8. a p. 422; LO 1	21. c p. 430; LO 3	33. e p. 433; LO 4	45. c p. 437; LO 4
9. a p. 424; LO 2	22. d p. 430; LO 3	34. a p. 433; LO 4	46. a p. 437; LO 4
10. a p. 423-424; LO 1	23. b p. 430; LO 3	35. e p. 433; LO 4	47. b p. 437; LO 4
11. e p. 424-425; LO 2	24. d p. 430; LO 3	36. d p. 433; LO 4	48. e p. 437; LO 4
12. a p. 426; LO 2	25. b p. 432; LO 4	37. a p. 434; LO 4	49. e p. 438; LO 4
13. e p. 427; LO 3			50. d p. 438; LO 4

Note: LO indicates learning objective.

CHAPTER 17

RETAILING

Why is Chapter 17 important? Retailing is the channel of distribution with which we are most familiar. This chpater illustrates the services a retailer providers a company and the typers of reetailers that are available in the marketplace. It shows how retailers are classified and how the selection of the retail outlet is keyed to the type of product offered.

Retailing: All activities involved in selling, renting, and providing goods and services to ultimate consumers for personal, family, or household use.

CHAPTER OUTLINE

I. VALUE OF RETAILING

    A. Consumer Utilities Offered by Retailing
        1. Time
        2. Place
        3. Possession
        4. Form

    B. Economic Value
        1. Employment
        2. Sales

II. CLASSIFYING RETAIL OUTLETS

    A. Form of Ownership
        1. Independent Retailer
        2. Corporate Chain
        3. Contractual System

    B. Level of Service
        1. Self Service
        2. Limited Service
        3. Full Service

    C. Merchandise Line
        1. Depth of Line
            a. Specialty outlets
                1. limited line
                2. single line
            b. Category "killers"
        2. Breadth of Line
            a. General merchandise store
            b. "Scrambled" merchandising
                1. hypermarkets
                2. supercenters

D. Non-Store Retailing
    1. Automatic Vending
    2. Direct Marketing
        a. Direct mail and catalogs
        b. Television home shopping
        c. On-line retailing
        d. Telemarketing
    3. Direct Selling

III. RETAILING STRATEGY

    A. Positioning
        1. Retail Positioning Matrix
            a. Breadth of product line
            b. Value added
        2. Keys to Positioning
            a. Identity with advantage
            b. Recognition of identity by customers

    B. Retailing Mix
        1. Goods and Services
            a. Retail pricing
                i. markup
                ii. markdown
                    a. everyday low pricing
                    b. everyday fair pricing
                iii. timing
                iv. off-price
                    a. warehouse club
                    b. factory outlet
                    c. single-price or extreme value
        2. Physical Distribution (Store Location)
            a. Central business district
            b. Regional shopping center
            c. Community shopping center
            d. Strip shopping center
            e. "Power" shopping center
        3. Retail image and atmosphere
            a. functional qualities
            b. psychological attributes

IV. CHANGING NATURE OF RETAILING

    A. Wheel of Retailing

    B. Retail Life Cycle

V. FUTURE CHANGES IN RETAILING

    A. Multichannel Retailing

    B. Impact of Technology

    C. Changing Shopping Behavior

You should be able to place these key terms in the outline and be able to discuss them.

breadth of product line
category management
central business district
community shopping center
depth of product line
form of ownership
hypermarket
intertype competition

level of service
merchandise line
multichannel retailers
off-price retailing
power center
regional shopping centers
retail life cycle
retail positioning matrix

retailing
retailing mix
scrambled merchandising
shrinkage
strip location
telemarketing
wheel of retailing

QUESTIONS & PROBLEMS

VALUE OF RETAILING

Retailing is an important marketing activity. Not only do producers and consumers meet through retailing actions, but retailing also creates customer value and has a significant impact on the economy. To consumers, the value of retailing is in the form of utilities provided. Retailing's economic value is represented by the people employed in retailing, as well as by the total amount of money exchanged in retail sales.

Wal-Mart's innovation was to bring discount stores to small town America; Dell Computer found that PC's had become "generic" and people wanted complete systems; PC Flowers knew that some consumers put off every until the last minute and yet still needed to buy gifts and remembrances; and Walt Disney company saw the need to make it easier for consumers to buy Disney "paraphernalia" leading to the Disney Stores and Catalogs. Discuss the utilities of each of these strategies.

CLASSIFYING RETAIL OUTLETS

Retail outlets can be classified by 1) Form of ownership; 2) Level of service; and 3) Merchandise line. These in turn can be classified as store or non-store retailing. There are several types of non-store retailing: Direct Marketing, including direct mail, in-home shopping, computer-assisted (videotex), and teleshopping; Direct Selling; and Automatic Vending." The form of ownership can be that of an independent retailer; a corporate chain; or a contractual system. Level of service ranges from self-service to limited service to full service; while the merchandise line is referred to by the breadth or the depth of the line carried.

Over the last decade, companies have expanded into non-store retailing. Sears has dropped their "Big Book," the full-line catalog and issued a series of smaller directed catalogs. It has also entered into agreement with QVC Shopping Channel to sell Craftsmen Tools and other Sears products on cable and joint-ventured Prodigy, an on-line computer service, with IBM which allows on-line computer shopping. IBM and Compaq, given the challenge of direct marketers such as Dell and Gateway, have started operations such as IBM Direct, to sell directly to consumers. Other companies, such as Sharper Image and Victoria's Secret, have gone the other direction from direct mail catalogs into retail outlets. A company in Vancouver, British Columbia, now offers a vending machine which accepts and processes credit cards. It has recently used this technology to sell both disposable cameras for Kodak and long distance phone cards for MCI. Discuss how each type of retailing can affect each classification category.

Retailing Classification

Retailing Type	Form of Ownership	Level of Service	Merchandise Line
Retail Store	_____	_____	_____
Non-Store:	_____	_____	_____
Direct Mail	_____	_____	_____
In-Home Shopping	_____	_____	_____
Teleshopping	_____	_____	_____
Computer-assisted	_____	_____	_____
Automatic Vending	_____	_____	_____

RETAILING STRATEGY

Using the 4 P's, product, price, promotion, and place, a retail store develops a strategy that will best position itself for the customers it seeks to attract. They develop a retailing mix utilizing such tools as the Retail Positioning Matrix. The Wheel of Retailing and the Retail Life Cycle help provide guidance for the retailer over the long run of the business.

The hardware industry has progressed from the general store, which carried everything for small communities; to the specialized hardware store, which was really a building and home supply store with tools and supplies; to hardware stores which sell everything from bicycles to hammers to gas fireplaces; to hardware departments of discount stores and major retailers like Sears; to large "category killers," like Builder's Square and Home Depot, which are the old specialized hardware stores carried out to a mega-size. In addition, you have catalog companies like Brookstone, which specialize in "hard to find tools," that have opened retail stores in large malls; not a normal place for hardware.

Discuss how each type of hardware outlet fits into the following concepts:

RETAIL POSITIONING MATRIX

The retail positioning matrix is a matrix developed by the MAC Group, Inc., a management consulting firm. This matrix positions retail outlets on two dimensions: breadth of product line and value added.

Using the Retail Positioning Matrix shown in Figure 18-7 on page xxx of your test, position each type of hardware outlet on a retail matrix of two dimensions: Breadth of Product Line and Value Added.

	Breadth of Product Line	Value Added
General Store	_____	_____
Specialized Hardware	_____	_____
Household and Hardware	_____	_____
Hardware Departments	_____	_____
Hardware Mega-stores	_____	_____
Hardware Specialty Catalogs	_____	_____

RETAILING MIX

In developing retail strategy, managers work with the retailing mix which includes: (1) goods and services, (2) physical distribution, and (3) communications tactics. Decisions relating to the mix focus on the consumer. There are three basic areas of importance: pricing, store location, image and atmosphere.

Identify each type of hardware outlet in relation to the focus of their retailing mix.

	Pricing	Store Location	Image & Atmosphere
General Store	_____	_____	_____
Specialized Hardware	_____	_____	_____
Household and Hardware	_____	_____	_____
Hardware Departments	_____	_____	_____
Hardware Mega-stores	_____	_____	_____
Hardware Specialty Catalogs	_____	_____	_____

RETAIL PRICING

A retailer purchased an order of brass candlesticks. The price paid was $30 per pair. The candlesticks were first offered for sale to customers at $60 per pair. Although before the holidays the candlesticks sold well, by February they were hardly selling at all. The price was then reduced to $45.

Using the information above, determine:

1. Original markup_____
2. Markdown_____
3. Maintained markup_____
4. Another name for maintained mark-up is:_____

Answer the following questions:

1. What is the difference between discount retailers and off-price retailers?

_____
_____
_____

2. What are two common types of off-price retailing?

_____
_____
_____

WHEEL OF RETAILING

The Wheel of Retailing describes how new forms of retail outlets enter the market. Entering the market as low-status, low-margin stores, they gradually add services, fixtures and other amenities that increase their status. Eventually, they attract new competition in the low-status, low-margin area and the cycle begins again.

Using the Wheel of Retailing shown in Figure 18-10 on page xxx of your test, discuss the evolution of the retail hardware industry using the Wheel of Retailing concept.

RETAIL LIFE CYCLE

The Retail Life Cycle describes the growth and decline of retail outlets. There are four stages in the retail life cycle: 1) Early Growth; 2) Accelerated Development; 3) Maturity Phase; & 4) Decline Stage.

Identify on the table below at what stage are each of the types of hardware retailing today.

	Early Growth	Accelerated Development	Maturity Phase	Decline Stage
General Store	_____	_____	_____	_____
Specialized Hardware	_____	_____	_____	_____
Household and Hardware	_____	_____	_____	_____
Hardware Departments	_____	_____	_____	_____
Hardware Mega-stores	_____	_____	_____	_____
Hardware Specialty Catalogs	_____	_____	_____	_____

FUTURE CHANGES IN RETAILING

Two exciting trends in retailing—the increasing impact of technology and the changing shopping behavior of consumers—are likely to lead to many changes for retailers and consumers in the future. Technology has already had a tremendous affect on retailing, ranging from payment systems, the ordering process, promotional outlets, to distribution methods. Pick two retail products such as computers, pre-recorded music, or clothing, and describe how each has been affected by technology. Next pick a product where consumer shopping behavior has been altered affecting the traditional retail market.

CAN YOU PASS THE TEST?
Sample Multiple Choice Questions

1. _____ includes all activities involved in selling, renting, and providing goods and services to ultimate customers for personal, family, or household use.
       a. Distribution
       b. Direct marketing
       c. Direct selling
       d. Retailing
       e. Marketing

2. Which of the following utilities do retailers provide consumers?
       a. form
       b. time
       c. possession
       d. place
       e. all of the above

3. CoCroft Music Shop is advertised as "the piano store that offers ten free lessons with the purchase of a new piano." If the free lessons are seen as charngin or enhancing the product (the piano), what type of consumer utility does the shop provide?
       a. time
       b. place
       c. possession
       d. form
       e. product

4. During the days after Halloween, Hickory Farms sets up kiosks in many shopping centers for customers who might not be able to travel to a center that contains a full-sized store. By creating these seasonal stores in a variety of locations, Hickory Farms is creating _____ utility.
       a. time
       b. place
       c. possession
       d. form
       e. performance

5. In terms of sales in dollars, which retailer is the largest?
       a. apparel and accessory stores
       b. drug stores
       c. automotive dealers
       d. eating and drinking establishments
       e. building material and hardware stores

6. Level of service refers to:
       a. breadth and depth of goods provided.
       b. degree of product liability held by the manufacturer.
       c. degree of service provided to the customer.
       d. relationship between the manufacturer, the retailer, and the consumer.
       e. manner in which services are provided.

7. In which form of retail outlet could you most likely be your own boss and provide your customers with a high degree of personal service?
        a. corporate chain
        b. administered system
        c. contractual system
        d. independent retailer
        e. sole incorporation

8. IGA is a group of neighborhood grocers that have banded together to create a _____ in which they can achieve economies of scale in promotion and purchasing.
        a. administered horizontal marketing system
        b. retailer-sponsored cooperative
        c. franchise system
        d. wholesaler-sponsored voluntary chain
        e. corporate chain

9. Franchising is a type of:
        a. administered system.
        b. contractual system.
        c. vertically integrated chain.
        d. retail-sponsored cooperative.
        e. corporate system.

10. At which level of service would the retail customer perform the greatest number of functions?
        a. exclusive service
        b. selective service
        c. self-service
        d. limited service
        e. full-service

11. Urban Fare is a Canadian supermarket that caters to customers who want to cook at home. It offers free cooking classes, has frequent demonstrations by cookbook authors, and has employees who are knowledgeable about food preparation. Customers do make their own selections once they have decided what to prepare. Urban Fare offers its customers:
        a. exclusive service.
        b. economies-of-scale service.
        c. self-service.
        d. limited service.
        e. full-service.

12. Lands' End carries men's, women's, and children's clothing plus towels, sheets, blankets, and decorative household items. In addition, it carries luggage of various kinds as well as all types of accessories. The variety of products that Lands' End carries is collectively referred to as its:
        a. breadth of product line.
        b. marketing mix.
        c. promotable mix.
        d. points of service encounter.
        e. customer service mix.

13. The assortment of each item a store carries is referred to as its:
        a. retailing mix.
        b. depth of product line.
        c. breadth of product line.
        d. level of service.
        e. method of operation.

14. An independent hardware store that stocks and sells children's toys, cell telephones, fishing rods, and commonly used pots and pans is using:
        a. a harvesting strategy.
        b. scrambled merchandising.
        c. disintermediation.
        d. reverse marketing.
        e. hypermarketing.

15. Which of the following statements about hypermarkets is true?
        a. Hypermarkets have a very deep product line that is not very broad.
        b. Hypermarkets are more popular in the United States than in Europe.
        c. Hypermarkets are a form of scrambled merchandising.
        d. Merchandise in hypermarkets are typically priced 10 to 20 percent higher than it would be if it were being sold in discount stores.
        e. Hypermarkets do not sell food products.

16. Which type of store gives shoppers the greatest variety of merchandise?
        a. a specialty clothing store
        b. a limited line gift store
        c. a hypermarket
        d. a clothing outlet
        e. a discount store

17. A type of retail outlet that focuses on one type of product at very competitive prices and often dominates the market is called a:
        a. general merchandise store.
        b. specialty outlet.
        c. hypermarket.
        d. category killer.
        e. regional dominator.

18. A supercenter:
        a. is an auto service center that sells and leases cars as well as repairs them.
        b. is a type of specialty outlet.
        c. combines a typical merchandise store with a full-size grocery.
        d. is a mall with more than 100 stores and several important anchor stores.
        e. is another name for a hypermarket.

19. When a local bakery competes with a discount store, it is an example of:
        a. scrambled merchandising.
        b. vertical conflict.
        c. contractual conflict.
        d. intratype competition.
        e. intertype competition.

20. Which of the following is an example of nonstore retailing?
        a. online retailing
        b. direct selling
        c. automatic vending
        d. telemarketing
        e. all of the above

21. Travelers are often in need of small convenience products and food items such as soft drinks. Airports, train and bus stations, and commuter stops do not have stores or stores that are open 24 hours each day; they are good locations for which type of nonstore retailing?

  a. catalog and direct mail
  b. online retailing
  c. telemarketing
  d. automatic vending
  e. all of the above

22. Which of the following statements explains why Bill received the Lands' End catalog (for big and large men) after he purchased three XXL t-shirts from Lands' End catalog?

  a. The catalog merchant wanted to increase the number of catalogs its customers were receiving.
  b. His receipt of that particular catalog was most likely coincidental.
  c. Lands' End was responding to the increased usage of catalogs by traditional retailers.
  d. Lands' End sent him a specialty catalog because Bill was identified in their database as a market niche.
  e. None of the above statements explains why Bill received the Lands' End catalog.

23. Direct mail and catalog retailing are examples of:

  a. hypermarkets.
  b. vending machines.
  c. scrambled merchandising.
  d. online retailing.
  e. nonstore retailing.

24. To plan her wedding, Virginia went to www.theknot.com where she purchased her dress and veil, ordered bridesmaid dresses, linked to a local printer and ordered invitations, and rented a chapel. Virginia used _____ retailing.

  a. bricks-and-mortar
  b. catalog
  c. general merchandise
  d. online
  e. flex-response

25. Which of the following statements about telemarketing is true?

  a. Shopping bots are computers that place automated telemarketing calls.
  b. Direct mail is typically viewed as more efficient than telemarketing.
  c. Telemarketing has declined in popularity as companies have searched for ways to decrease costs.
  d. As the use of telemarketing grows, consumer privacy has become a greater concern.
  e. All of the above statements about telemarketing are true.

26. Direct selling is sometimes called:

  a. telemarketing.
  b. personal selling.
  c. door-to-door retailing.
  d. direct marketing.
  e. integrated sales.

27. The retail positioning matrix positions retail stores on two dimensions. They are: breadth of product line and:

  a. value added.
  b. depth of product line.
  c. organizational structure.
  d. market share.
  e. market attractiveness.

28. Dillard's and Parisian's are two department store chains that have high value added and broad product lines. They pay close attention to store design and product lines. Merchandise in these stores often has a high margin of profit and is of high quality. Such stores typically provide:
     a. direct ordering from television infomercials.
     b. prompt mail-order delivery.
     c. low levels of service.
     d. moderate levels of service.
     e. high levels of service.

29. The retail pricing, store location, retail communication and merchandise chosen by a store are known collectively as the:
     a. wheel of retailing.
     b. distribution mix.
     c. consumer-retailer matrix.
     d. retailing mix.
     e. retailing triad.

30. Someone examining a store's retailing mix would most likely look at:
     a. its product variety and assortment.
     b. its advertising.
     c. its location.
     d. its pricing.
     e. all of the above.

31. Markup is:
     a. the difference between the final selling price and how the customer values the product.
     b. selling brand name merchandise at lower than regular prices.
     c. the amount added to the cost the retailer paid for a product to reach the final selling price.
     d. the amount added by the manufacturer to achieve the desired retail price.
     e. the reduction in retail price, usually expressed as a percentage equal to the amount reduced, divided by the original price, and multiplied by 100.

32. Another term for gross margin is:
     a. original markup.
     b. maintained markup.
     c. markdown.
     d. off-price.
     e. discount price.

33. Wal-Mart and Home Depot have eliminated the need for most markdowns by adopting which of the following pricing strategies?
     a. everyday low pricing
     b. high-low pricing
     c. targeted rate of return pricing
     d. slotting allowances
     e. experience curve pricing

34. When Josh visited his local department store, he saw three clocks with bent hands that would not longer work, a planter with a chipped corner, and an opened package of cotton balls. Retailers refer to what Josh saw as:
     a. pilferage.
     b. shrinkage.
     c. opportunity costs.
     d. depreciation.
     e. product obsolescence.

35. Off-price retailing is the:
    a. difference between the final selling price and the retailer's cost.
    b. sale of brand name merchandise at lower than regular prices.
    c. sales of merchandise at maintained markups.
    d. the amount added by the manufacturer to achieve the desired retail price.
    e. reduction in retail price and is usually expressed as gross margin retailing.

36. Which of the following statements about off-price retailing is true?
    a. Wal-Mart and Kmart are both examples of off-price retailers.
    b. Target is an example of an off-price retailer.
    c. Selection at off-price retailers is unpredictable.
    d. Off-price retailers use the same marketing channels as discount stores to buy merchandise.
    e. Home Depot and Office Depot are examples of off-price retailers.

37. A regional shopping center:
    a. consists of 50 to 150 stores.
    b. typically attracts customers who live or work within a 5- to 10-mile radius.
    c. contain two or three anchor stores.
    d. is larger than a community shopping center.
    e. is accurately described by all of the above.

38. Which of the following retail operations would most likely be viewed as an anchor store in a regional shopping center?
    a. Foot Locker shop
    b. a locally owned bookstore
    c. Longhorn Steakhouse
    d. Macy's department store
    e. Radio Shack shop

39. Value-retail centers:
    a. are also called power centers.
    b. are outlet stores for mail-order retailers.
    c. require an annual membership fee (usually $25) for the privilege of shopping there.
    d. have clusters of stores to serve people who are within a 5- to 10-minute drive and live in a population base under 30,000.
    e. combine outlet stores, off-price retailers, and department store clearance centers.

40. Regional shopping centers often contain two or three anchor stores. An anchor store is:
    a. any store that has been operating in the community for at least ten years.
    b. any store that has a total annual revenue equal to or above $5 million per year.
    c. any store carrying full depth of line.
    d. any store (usually over 50,000 square feet) which practices scrambled merchandising.
    e. a well-known national or regional store.

41. Tudor Laundry is a new dry cleaning and laundry company. The owner wants to attract people who will be within a 5 to 10 minute drive of the business. The best location for this new dry-cleaning and laundry service would be:
    a. the central business district.
    b. a regional shopping center.
    c. a community shopping center.
    d. a strip location.
    e. a power center.

42. Music, floor covering, soft lighting, and store layout all work together to create a retail store's:
    a. atmosphere.
    b. format.
    c. success convergence.
    d. depth of product line.
    e. marketing mix.

43. The largest inventory of wedding dresses in the Southeast can be found at Low's Bridal and Formal in Brinkley, Arkansas. The store is located in an old railroad hotel. It has high ceilings, dark woodwork, heavy chandeliers, and a lobby where customers can find refreshments and sometimes be surrounded by music that might be played at weddings. This description refers to the store's:
    a. atmosphere.
    b. image.
    c. psychological attributes.
    d. antecedent attributes.
    e. synergistic format.

44. _____ describes how new forms of retail outlets enter the market.
    a. The theory of retailing
    b. The wheel of retailing
    c. The retail continuum
    d. The theory of time and place utility
    e. Maslow's hierarchy

45. Which of the following is NOT one of the stages in the retail life cycle?
    a. accelerated development
    b. early growth
    c. initiation
    d. decline
    e. maturity

46. The key goal for retailers in the accelerated development phase of the retail life cycle is to:
    a. establish a dominant position in the fight for market share.
    b. delay entering the decline stage of the life cycle.
    c. find ways of discouraging their customers from moving to low-margin, mass-volume outlets.
    d. establish a retail concept which is a sharp departure from existing competition.
    e. cover start-up costs.

47. Accelerated development in the retail life cycle is similar to which stage in the product life cycle?
    a. introduction phase
    b. growth
    c. maturity
    d. decline
    e. harvest

48. Retailers like Eddie Bauer and The Disney Store that sell at retail stores, through their catalogs, and at their online websites are examples of _____ retailers.
    a. intratype
    b. multichannel
    c. vertically integrated
    d. multimediary
    e. facilitating

49. Multichannel retailers:
    a. mainly have their retail outlets in the central business district.
    b. recongnize that the Internet is an effective relationship-building medium.
    c. benefit from the synergy of sharing information among their different channel operations.
    d. typically reduce the size of their target markets.
    e. all of the above.

50. Credit cards may well be replaced by smart cards, which store information on computer chips instead of magnetic strips. More than 33 million smart cards are in use in Europe and Asia, where consumers value the faster service (no waiting for approval of credit card or check) and stored information (such as airline seat preference). What is the benefit to merchants?
    a. consumers will spend more
    b. merchants will be able to ignore small purchases
    c. government regulation will increase usage
    d. merchants will save 5-7%
    e. all of the above

ANSWER KEY

Answers to Questions & Problems

Value of Retailing

All of these strategies target the place utility

Classifying Retail Outlets

Example:

General Store   single owner   personal service   broad line of merchandise

Retailing Positioning Mix

Example:

General Store   broad line of merchandise   personal service value added

Retailing Mix

Example:

General Store   full retail price   single location (town center)   homey, cluttered

Retail Pricing

1. $30
2. $15
3. $15
4. gross margin

1. The off-price retailer buys excess inventory from the manufacturer at less than wholesale, while the discounter takes less of a markup on regular wholesale price.

2. Warehouse club and factory outlet store

Retail Life Cycle

Example:

General Store—decline
Specialized Hardware—decline
Household and hardware—maturity
Hardware departments—maturity
Hardware mega-stores—accelerated growth
Hardware specialty catalogs—early growth

Answers to Sample Multiple Choice Questions

1. d p. 422; LO 1	14. b p. 428; LO 3	26. d p. 432; LO 4	38. b p. 434; LO 4
2. a p. 422; LO 1	15. d p. 428; LO 3	27. d p. 432; LO 4	39. e p. 434; LO 4
3. a p. 422; LO 1	16. e p. 428; LO 3	28. c p. 432; LO 4	40. d p. 435; LO 4
4. a p. 422; LO 1	17. e p. 428; LO 3	29. d p. 433; LO 4	41. c p. 435; LO 4
5. c p. 422; LO 1	18. c p. 428; LO 3	30. d p. 433; LO 4	42. a p. 436; LO 4
6. a p. 422; LO 1	19. e p. 428; LO 3	31. d p. 433; LO 4	43. d p. 437; LO 4
7. d p. 422; LO 1	20. d p. 429; LO 3	32. c p. 433; LO 4	44. a p. 437; LO 4
8. a p. 422; LO 1	21. c p. 430; LO 3	33. e p. 433; LO 4	45. c p. 437; LO 4
9. a p. 424; LO 2	22. d p. 430; LO 3	34. a p. 433; LO 4	46. a p. 437; LO 4
10. a p. 423-424; LO 1	23. b p. 430; LO 3	35. e p. 433; LO 4	47. b p. 437; LO 4
11. e p. 424-425; LO 2	24. d p. 430; LO 3	36. d p. 433; LO 4	48. e p. 437; LO 4
12. a p. 426; LO 2	25. b p. 432; LO 4	37. a p. 434; LO 4	49. e p. 438; LO 4
13. e p. 427; LO 3			50. d p. 438; LO 4

Note: LO indicates learning objective.

CHAPTER 18

INTEGRATED MARKETING COMMUNICATIONS AND DIRECT MARKETING

<u>Why is Chapter 18 important</u>? This chapter outlines the tools of communications used by a business to tell their markets about their products. It illustrates how the different elements of the promotional are used for different types of products, customers, and buying situations. It then outlines the designing of a successful promotional campaign.

Communication: The process of conveying a message to others, requiring six elements: a source, a message, a channel of communication, a receiver, and the processes of encoding and decoding.

CHAPTER OUTLINE

I. THE COMMUNICATION PROCESS

      A. Encoding and Decoding

      B. Feedback

      C. Noise

II. THE PROMOTION ELEMENTS

      A. Advertising

      B. Personal Selling

      C. Public Relations

      D. Sales Promotion

      E. Direct Marketing

III. INTEGRATED MARKETING COMMUNICATION--DEVELOPING THE PROMOTIONAL MIX

      A. Target Audience

      B. Product Life Cycle
          1. Introduction stage
               a. inform
          2. Growth stage
               a. persuade
          3. Maturity stage
               a. maintain
               b. remind
          4. Decline stage

C. Product Characteristics
    1. Complexity
    2. Risk
    3. Ancillary services

D. Stages of the Buying Decision
    1. Prepurchase stage
    2. Purchase stage
    3. Postpurchase stage

E. Channel Strategies
    1. Push strategy
    2. Pull strategy

F. Integrated Marketing Communication

IV. DEVELOPING THE PROMOTIONAL PROGRAM

A. Identifying the Target Audience

B. Specifying Promotional Objectives
    1. Hierarchy of effects
        a. awareness
        b. interest
        c. evaluation
        d. trial
        e. adoption
    2. Qualities
        a. designed for a well-defined target audience
        b. be measurable
        c. cover a specified time period

C. Setting the Promotional Budget
    1. Percentage of sales
    2. Competitive parity
    3. All-you-can-afford
    4. Objective and task
        a. determine promotional objectives
        b. outline tasks to accomplish objective
        c. determine promotional costs of performing these tasks

D. Selecting the Right Promotional Tools

E. Designing the Promotion

F. Scheduling the Promotion

G. Executing and Evaluating the Promotional Program

V. DIRECT MARKETING

A. Growth of Direct Marketing

B. Value of Direct Marketing
1. Direct ordering
2. Lead generation
3. Traffic generation

C. Direct Marketing Issues
1. Technological
2. Global
3. Ethical

You should be able to place these key terms in the outline and be able to discuss them.

advertising	**field of experience**	**public relations**
all-you-can-afford budgeting	**hierarchy of effects**	**publicity**
channel of communication	**integrated marketing communications**	**pull strategy**
communication	**lead generation**	**push strategy**
competitive parity budgeting	**message**	**receivers**
decoding	**noise**	**response**
direct marketing	**objective and task budgeting**	**sales promotion**
direct orders	**percentage of sales budgeting**	**source**
encoding	**personal selling**	**traffic generation**
feedback	**promotion mix**	

QUESTIONS & PROBLEMS

THE COMMUNICATION PROCESS

List the five elements required for communication to occur:

1._____

2._____

3._____

4._____

5._____

Encoding and Decoding are essential to communication. Encoding is the process of having the sender transform an abstract idea into a set of symbols. Decoding is the reverse, or the process of having the receiver take a set of symbols, the message, and transform them back to an abstract idea. For the message to be communicated effectively, the sender and receiver must have a mutually shared field of experience—similar understanding and knowledge. Feedback is the communication flow from receiver back to sender and indicates whether the message was decoded and understood as intended. Noise can adversely affect how the receiver decodes a message. Noise can include such things as printing mistakes, visual clutter, busy-looking photos, etc.

PROMOTIONAL MIX

A company can communicate with consumers by using one or more of five promotional alternatives:

Advertising
Personal selling
Publicity
Sales promotion
Direct marketing

Identify which method of promotion is being used:

1. Ebert and Roeper critique current motion pictures. Their evaluation of a movie can have a significant effect on box office sales._____

2. Tupperware dealers do product demonstrations in homes. They sell new products, replace broken products, and give personal advice on kitchen organization. Consumer feedback through dealers has resulted in many new and innovative product ideas._____

3. Toyota Motor Sales purchased a full-page color advertisement in Business Week Magazine to promote its 1985 Family Camry._____

4. Colgate Palmolive mailed samples of its Ajar Dishwashing Liquid along with a $0.25 store coupon.

_____

5. To supplement their retail stores, Shaper Image maintains a Web page and sends out millions of catalogs on a regular basis. _____

List advantages and disadvantages for each of the four promotional elements:

	Advantages	**Disadvantages**
1. Advertising	_____	_____
2. Personal selling	_____	_____
3. Publicity	_____	_____
4. Sales promotion	_____	_____
5. Direct Marketing	_____	_____

PRODUCT LIFE CYCLE

The composition of the promotional mix changes over the four product life cycle stages.

Match the product life-cycle stage to the objectives below:

Introduction stage
Growth stage
Maturity stage
Decline stage

1. Gain brand preference and solidify distribution._____

2. Increase the level of consumer awareness._____

3. Maintain existing buyers, encourage brand loyalty._____

4. Few promotional objectives; little money is spent on the promotional mix._____

During which stage in the product life cycle would you expect the relative emphasis of the promotional mix elements to be as follows?

1. Sales promotion is less, publicity is not a factor, the major promotional element is advertising, which stresses brand differences, and personal selling is used to solidify the channel of distribution._____

2. Usually a period of phaseout and little money is spent on any element of the promotional mix._____

3. Advertising's role is reduced to reminding buyers of the product's existence. Sales promotion in the form of discounts and coupons are offered to both ultimate consumers and intermediaries. Sales force maintains satisfaction of intermediaries._____

4. All promotional elements are stressed, trial samples may be sent, and sales force approaches new intermediaries._____

PRODUCT CHARACTERISTICS

State whether the promotional emphasis would be towards (1) personal selling, or (2) advertising:

1. A relatively complex product like a VAX minicomputer._____

2. A product with little social, physical, or monetary risk, such as Bayer aspirin._____

3. A statistical software program featuring sales, technical, and service support._____

In designing the proper blend of elements in the promotional mix, companies consider three product characteristics: complexity, degree of risk, and ancillary service. Complexity, refers to the technical sophistication of the product; risk, refers to the risk to the consumer in terms of financial, social, and physical factors; and ancillary services refers to the degree of service or support required after the sale.

CUSTOMER'S STAGE OF DECISION MAKING

Knowing the customer's stage in decision making can also affect the promotional mix. There are three stages in a consumer's purchase decision:

Prepurchase stage
Purchase stage
Postpurchase stage

At which stage in the consumer purchase decision would the following statements hold true?

1. The importance of personal selling is highest and the impact of advertising is lowest; sales promotion in the form of price discounts can be very helpful._____

2. Advertising and personal selling help reduce the buyer's feelings of anxiety; sales promotion in the form of coupons can help encourage repeat purchases._____

3. Advertising is more helpful than personal selling; sales promotion in the form of free samples encourages low-risk trial._____

HIERARCHY OF EFFECTS

After the target audience is identified a decision must be reached on what the advertising campaign is to accomplish. Consumers can be said to respond in terms of a hierarchy of effects.

Awareness
Interest
Evaluation
Trial
Adoption

Match the correct stage to the statements below:

1. Through a favorable experience on the first trial, the consumer's repeated purchase and use of the product or brand._____

2. Consumers' appraisal of how they feel about the product or brand._____

3. The consumer's actual first purchase and use of the product or brand._____

4. The consumer's ability to recognize and remember the product or brand name.

_____

5. An increase in the knowledge of the product or brand until he knows and likes some of its features.

_____

6. Within 30 days after our ad in Sunday magazine we have 10,000 customers call our toll-free number requesting life insurance information._____

7. Within three months 75 percent of all restaurants in town know about our line of cleaning services.

_____

8. During the month of January fifty women participate in a free workout at our spa.

_____

9. Have 15 percent of consumers rate this news program as the most informative by 1997.

_____

10. After two weeks of heavy advertising and five free newspapers to all non-subscribers on each route each news carrier gains an average of five new subscribers.

_____

CHANNEL STRATEGIES

Find a current example of a push strategy and a pull strategy:

1. Push:_____

2. Pull:_____

SELECTING PROMOTIONAL TOOLS

In which of the following situations would you emphasize advertising and in which of these situations would you emphasize personal selling?

1. Pull channel strategy_____

2. Great geographic dispersion of customers_____

3. High level of ancillary services_____

4. Purchase stage of purchase decision_____

5. Product simple to understand_____

6. Small DMU (Decision-Making Unit)_____

7. Push channel strategy_____

8. Complex product_____

9. Large DMU (Decision-Making Unit)_____

10. Ultimate consumer is target market_____

11. Low risk purchase_____

12. Geographic concentration of customers_____

13. Target market of resellers and industrial buyers_____

14. High risk purchase_____

15. Prepurchase stage of purchase decision_____

16. Low level of ancillary services_____

SETTING THE ADVERTISING BUDGET

After setting the advertising objectives a company must decide on how much to spend.
There are several methods used to set the advertising budget:

Percentage-of-sales budgeting
Competitive parity budgeting
All-you-can-afford budgeting
Objective-and-task budgeting

Match the method of advertising budget to the statements below:

1. Our chief competitor is placing three full-page color ads in Good Housekeeping magazine. We must direct enough funds through advertising to cover at least three full-page color ads, if not more.

_____

2. Our gross sales last year were $300,000 and our anticipated sales for next year are $400,000. Let's budget our advertising based on five percent of the average of last year's sales and this year's anticipated sales, or $17,500._____

3. "How much money can we possibly allocate for advertising?" "Fine, then, that's what we need."

_____

4. We have to reach at least 75 percent of the commuters in a 50-mile radius. In order for us to do that we'll have to advertise on local radio between 6-8 a.m. and 4-6 p.m. This will cost us $3,700. If we can't afford full coverage we can cut the evening ads to one hour.

_____

DIRECT MARKETING

There are three types of response goals that make direct marketing valuable and have contributed to its level of growth as a marketing communications tool. They are:

Direct orders
Lead generation
Traffic generation

For the statements below, please indicate the response goal sought in each promotion.

1. IBM places advertising in The Wall Street Journal introducing a new laptop computer giving a toll-free number and web address to get more information. _____

2. Donny Osmond appears on a late night cable television commercial to sell an album of his greatest hits. He accepts credit cards through his toll-free number and the album is not available in stores. _____

3. A vacation community sends out letters to families within a 200-mile radius offering a new color television to any family who comes out and receives a guided tour of their facilities. _____

CAN YOU PASS THE TEST?
Sample Multiple Choice Questions

1. The promotional mix includes advertising, personal selling, sales promotion, public relations and
_____.
  - a. promotion channel
  - b. communication chain
  - c. marketing matrix
  - d. direct marketing
  - e. media mix

2. The Hot Springs Visitors Bureau created and paid for an ad describing the attractions of the area. In terms of the communication process, the bureau is a:
  - a. receiver.
  - b. source.
  - c. decoder.
  - d. message
  - e. channel.

3. An ad for Mercedes Benz ran in *Road and Track* magazine. In terms of the communication process, the magazine is a:
  - a. channel.
  - b. source.
  - c. message.
  - d. decoder.
  - e. encoder

4. L'Oréal created an advertisement for its Visible Lift makeup. In terms of the communication process, the _____ in the ad for Visible Lift makeup informed prospective customers that the makeup reduced fine facial lines after 30 days of use and evened out skin tones.
  - a. channel
  - b. message
  - c. decoder
  - d. source
  - e. feedback

5. In a brainstorming session for a new drug to lower cholesterol, the members of the marketing department agreed the benefits of the new drug could best be promoted by comparing the drug to those currently on the market. In terms of the communication process, the encoding of the message would most likely be undertaken by its:
  - a. communication channel.
  - b. medium.
  - c. decoder.
  - d. source.
  - e. feedback recipient.

6. For a message to be communicated effectively, the sender and receiver must have a mutually shared
_____, a similar understanding and knowledge.
     a. cognitive dissonance
     b. behavioral experience
     c. reference group
     d. field of experience
     e. state of motivation

7. Communication problems, which are the result of misinterpretation, can be attributed to:
     a. incorrect grammatical usage.
     b. poor photographic reproduction.
     c. different fields of experience.
     d. the use of a medium with too much noise.
     e. all of the above.

8. Most Monday nights Jay Leno devotes part of his show to reading headlines, ads, etc. that don't say what
the person who wrote them intended for them to say. Often the headlines have misprints. According to the
text, these misprints are an example of:
     a. channel misdirection.
     b. parallel transmission.
     c. encoding errors.
     d. noise.
     e. reception barriers.

9. Dwayne saw an ad promoting Texas as a tourist destination. The ad contained a postage-paid reply card
which could be used to request more information. In terms of the communication process, the mailing in of
the postcard with a request for further information is an example of:
     a. encoding.
     b. a receiver response.
     c. feedback.
     d. an exchange cycle.
     e. a message loop.

10. The marketing professor wanted to do everything possible to ensure her students understood her
lectures. Accordingly, she used examples of marketing activities with which most students had recent
experience. For example, the professor discussed the marketing exchanges between students and grocers,
college bookstores, convenience stores and clothiers. The examples used by the professor were her attempt
to _____ her message so as to encourage understanding on the part of her students.
     a. effectively initiate
     b. effectively encode
     c. effectively decode
     d. eliminate noise in
     e. pre-communicate

11. Which of the following statements about advertising is true?
     a. Advertising is any directly paid form of nonpersonal communication.
     b. Advertising has no disadvantages.
     c. Advertising is any paid form of communication.
     d. Advertising uses customized interaction.
     e. Advertising is any paid form of personal communication.

12. Mass selling occurs with:
    a. personal selling, advertising, and public relations.
    b. direct marketing and personal selling.
    c. public relations, advertising, personal selling, sales promotions, and direct marketing.
    d. personal selling and advertising.
    e. advertising, sales promotions, and public relations.

13. Which element of the promotional mix has the inherent weakness of high absolute costs, and difficulty in receiving good feedback?
    a. advertising
    b. personal selling
    c. sales promotion
    d. publicity
    e. direct marketing

14. Customized interaction occurs with:
    a. personal selling, advertising, and public relations.
    b. public relations, advertising, personal selling, sales promotions, and direct marketing.
    c. personal selling and direct marketing.
    d. advertising, sales promotions, and public relations.
    e. direct marketing and advertising.

15. Which of the following statements about personal selling is true?
    a. Personal selling is a one-way flow of communication.
    b. The flexibility of personal selling is always viewed as one of its primary advantages.
    c. Personal selling tends to increase wasted coverage.
    d. On a cost-per-contact basis, personal selling is the least expensive of all the five promotional elements.
    e. None of the above statements about personal selling is true.

16. Wasted coverage can most easily be reduced by which of the methods of promotion?
    a. sales promotion
    b. public relations
    c. advertising
    d. public service announcements
    e. personal selling

17. Which of these promotional elements has the inherent weakness of extremely high expenses per exposure?
    a. advertising
    b. personal selling
    c. sales promotion
    d. publicity
    e. direct marketing

18. Publicity:
    a. is nonpersonal.
    b. is an indirectly paid presentation of an organization, good, or service.
    c. is seen by consumers as having a high degree of credibility.
    d. is often the most important role of public relations.
    e. is accurately described by all of the above.

19. Every issue of *Taste of Home* magazine features two or three entrepreneurs who have turned some skill or other resource into a successful small business. Since these featured businesses do not pay for this exposure, they are benefiting from:
     a. publicity.
     b. advertising.
     c. direct marketing.
     d. personal selling.
     e. a public service announcement.

20. _____ is a short-term inducement of value offered to arouse interest in buying a good or service.
     a. A public service announcement
     b. Publicity
     c. Advertising
     d. Sales promotion
     e. Personal selling

21. _____ uses direct communication with consumers to generate a response in the form of an order, a request for further information, or a visit to a retail outlet.
     a. Advertising
     b. Personal selling
     c. Sales promotion
     d. Publicity
     e. Direct marketing

22. A firm produces the tools for replacing the rivets used in assembling airplanes, heavy-equipment, and specialized rail cars. The key to making a sale is communicating the application information to the line engineers who oversee repairs and the cost savings information to the accountants in charge of service maintenance budgets. Which promotional element would be most appropriate?
     a. advertising
     b. personal selling
     c. sales promotion
     d. public relations
     e. all of the above equally

23. A firm's _____ is the combination of one or more of the promotional elements it chooses to use.
     a. marketing mix
     b. product mix
     c. product line
     d. promotional mix
     e. product assortment

24. Which promotional element is particularly important to business buyers?
     a. advertising
     b. personal selling
     c. publicity
     d. sales promotion
     e. rebates

25. Which of the following statements about the growth stage of the product life cycle is true?
    a. The primary promotional activity during the growth stage is to inform consumers about the product.
    b. The primary promotional element used during the growth stage is advertising.
    c. The primary promotional element used during the growth stage is sales promotions.
    d. Price cuts and discounts are most commonly offered during the growth stage.
    e. The primary promotional activity during the growth stage is to remind consumers about the product.

26. At which stage in the product life cycle are discounts and coupons offered to both consumers and intermediaries to maintain loyal buyers?
    a. introduction
    b. growth
    c. maturity
    d. incubation
    e. decline

27. The _____ stage in the product life cycle is usually a period of phaseout for the product, and little money is spent in the promotional mix.
    a. decline
    b. maturity
    c. divestment
    d. harvesting
    e. diversity

28. The proper blend of elements in the promotional mix also depends on the type of product. Three specific characteristics should be considered. They are:
    a. price, quality, and utility.
    b. quality, complexity, and consumer involvement.
    c. complexity, degree of risk, and ancillary services.
    d. warranties, after-sale service, and quality.
    e. tangibility, perishability, and homogeneity.

29. Albert Corporate Searchware is a type of search engine companies use at their websites to handle customer questions. When promoting the product, Albert must be aware of how _____ affect(s) which promotional elements should be used.
    a. the complexity of the product
    b. the ancillary services needed to use the product
    c. the financial risks associated with making such a major purchase
    d. the risk of making a company more vulnerable to hackers
    e. all of the above

30. The proper blend of elements in the promotional mix depends on the type of product. Three specific characteristics should be considered: complexity, _____, and ancillary services.
A. lifestyle
B. flexibility
C. message
D. risk
E. channel

31. When a manufacturer directs the promotional mix to channel members to gain their cooperation in ordering and stocking the product, it is using a(n) _____ strategy.
     a. push
     b. pull
     c. inertia
     d. exclusivity
     e. logistics

32. Which promotional elements typically play the greatest roles in a push strategy?
     a. personal selling and sales promotions
     b. advertising and direct marketing
     c. direct marketing and public relations
     d. public relations and advertising
     e. advertising, personal selling, and public relations

33. An ad in a consumer magazine for Nexium, a newly introduced prescription-only drug that relieves heartburn, exemplifies the use of:
     a. a pull strategy.
     b. a decoding device.
     c. a noise reduction system.
     d. a push strategy.
     e. advertising for a product in the maturity stage of its product life cycle.

34. An advertisement for Stanley brand hammers features a headline, which proclaims, "In a durability test, the competitor's hammer lasted 60 seconds. If you happen to need one for longer than that, buy a Stanley hammer." The advertisement is an element of the promotional mix which is directed towards the ultimate consumer, not towards retailers or wholesalers. This is an example of a(n) _____ strategy.
     a. push
     b. promotional integration
     c. pull
     d. promotional aggregation
     e. sales promotion

35. The acronym IMC stands for:
     a. internal marketing communications.
     b. individualized marketing classifications.
     c. integrated marketing communications.
     d. integrated media customization.
     e. individualized marketing customization.

36. All of the following steps are part of the process used to develop an organization's promotion program EXCEPT:
     a. identify the target audience.
     b. specify the advertising objectives.
     c. write the advertising copy.
     d. pretest the advertising.
     e. schedule the advertising program.

37. Which of the following is a stage in the development of a promotion program?
     a. scheduling the promotion
     b. selecting the right promotional tools
     c. setting the promotional budgets
     d. identification of the target audience
     e. all of the above

38. In the hierarchy of effects, interest is defined as:
   a. the consumer's ability to recognize and remember the product or brand name.
   b. the consumer's appraisal of the product or brand on important attributes.
   c. an increase in the consumer's desire to learn about some of the features of the product or brand.
   d. a favorable experience on the first trial, resulting in the consumer's repeated purchase and use of the product or brand.
   e. the consumer's first actual purchase and use of the product or brand.

39. Someone in the evaluation stage of the hierarchy of effects for Jamba Juice smoothies would:
   a. be unaware of the product.
   b. not be interested in learning anything about the smoothies.
   c. be eager to appraise Jamba Juice's smoothies on important attributes.
   d. try the smoothies.
   e. return to Jamba Juice regularly to try new flavors.

40. No matter what the specific objective might be, from building awareness to increasing repeat purchases, promotion objectives should possess three important qualities. They should cover a specified time period, be measurable and:
   a. rely on fear.
   b. be designed for a well-defined target audience.
   c. be humorous.
   d. appeal to intermediaries.
   e. be designed to win creative awards.

41. When sales go down, many firms try to correct the problem by increasing promotion. However, the use of _____ budgeting would instead cause its user to decrease promotion budgets after a downturn in sales.
   a. percentage of sales
   b. competitive parity
   c. all-you-can-afford
   d. objective and task
   e. relative scale

42. All-you-can-afford budgeting is a budgeting method:
   a. that allocates funds to promotion as a percentage of past or anticipated sales, in terms of either dollars or units sold.
   b. that matches the competitor's absolute level of spending or the proportion per point of market share.
   c. that allocates funds to promotion only after all other budget items are covered.
   d. whereby the company determines its promotion objectives, outlines the tasks necessary to accomplish these objectives, and determines the promotion cost of performing these tasks.
   e. that allocates funds to promotion based on the greatest percentage of possible available revenue.

43. A local florist who sets her promotional budget at $3,000 because that is the amount set by her nearest competitors is using which budgeting method?
   a. all-you-can-afford budgeting
   b. objective and task budgeting
   c. percentage of sales budgeting
   d. comparative budgeting
   e. competitive parity budgeting

44. Objective and task budgeting is a budgeting method:
   a. which allocates funds to promotion as a percentage of past or anticipated sales, in terms of either dollars or units sold.
   b. which matches the competitor's absolute level of spending or the proportion per point of market share.
   c. which allocates funds to promotion only after all other budget items are covered.
   d. whereby the company determines its promotion objectives, outlines the tasks to accomplish these objectives, and determines the promotion cost of performing these tasks.
   e. which allocates funds to promotion based on the greatest percentage of possible available revenue.

45. The best approach to setting the promotional budget is _____ budgeting.
   a. all-you-can-afford
   b. objective and task
   c. percentage of sales
   d. percentage of profit

46. Which of the following statements about direct marketing is true?
   a. The Internet is a direct marketing channel.
   b. Most people who are employed in direct marketing are employed in advertising.
   c. Most direct marketing expenditures are spent on television.
   d. Most direct marketing sales are made through direct mail and catalogs.
   e. All of the above statements about direct marketing are true.

47. Direct marketing uses direct communication to generate a response in the form of a(n):
   a. direct order
   b. lead generation bottleneck
   c. traffic generation issue
   d. indirect order
   e. first mover advantage

48. During a recent Super Bowl, various commercials talked about mlife and invited viewers to visit mlife.com. These ads were designed to:
   a. act as a marketing segmentation tool.
   b. determine the target market for the new service.
   c. speed up movement through the hierarchy of effects.
   d. generate a request for further information.
   e. be an inquiry test.

49. _____ is designed to motivate people to request additional information.
   a. Direct marketing
   b. Traffic generation
   c. Prospect management
   d. Inquiry testing
   e. Lead generation

50. Which of the following could be an ethical issue for direct marketers?
   a. use of customer databases
   b. concerns about privacy
   c. a proliferation of e-mail advertising
   d. inappropriately timed telephone solicitations
   e. none of the above

ANSWER KEY

Answers to Questions & Problems

The Communications Process

1. Source
2. Message
3. Channel of communication
4. Receiver
5. The processes of encoding and decoding

Promotional Mix

1. Publicity
2. Personal selling
3. Advertising
4. Sales promotion

Example: Advertising, advantage—reaches broad audience; disadvantage—expensive

Product Life Cycle

1. Growth
2. Introduction
3. Maturity
4. Decline

1. Growth
2. Decline
3. Maturity
4. Introduction

Product Characteristics

1. Personal selling
2. Advertising
3. Advertising

Customer's Stage of Decision Making

1. Purchase stage
2. Postpurchase stage
3. Prepurchase stage

Hierarchy of Effects

1. Adoption
2. Evaluation
3. Trial
4. Awareness
5. Interest

6. Interest
7. Awareness
8. Trial
9. Evaluation
10. Adoption

Selecting Promotional Tools

1. Advertising
2. Personal selling
3. Personal selling
4. Personal selling
5. Advertising
6. Personal selling
7. Personal selling
8. Personal selling
9. Advertising
10. Advertising
11. Advertising
12. Advertising
13. Personal selling
14. Personal selling
15. Advertising
16. Advertising

Setting the Advertising Budget

1. Competitive parity
2. Percentage of sales
3. All-you-can-afford
4. Objective and task

Direct Marketing

1. Lead generation
2. Direct orders
3. Traffic generation

Answers to Sample Multiple Choice Questions

1. d p. 470; LO 1	14. c p. 473; LO 2	26. c p. 477; LO 3	38. c p. 482; LO 5
2. b p. 470; LO 1	15. e p. 474; LO 2	27. a p. 477; LO 3	39. c p. 482; LO 5
3. a p. 471; LO 1	16. e p. 474; LO 2	28. c p. 478; LO 3	40. b p. 482; LO 5
4. b p. 470; LO 1	17. b p. 474; LO 2	29. e p. 478; LO 3	41. a p. 483; LO 5
5. d p. 470; LO 1	18. e p. 474; LO 2	30. d p. 478; LO 3	42. c p. 484; LO 5
6. d p. 472; LO 1	19. a p. 474; LO 2	31. a p. 480; LO 4	43. e p. 483; LO 5
7. e p. 472; LO 1	20. d p. 475; LO 2	32. a p. 480; LO 4	44. d p. 484; LO 5
8. d p. 472; LO 1	21. e p. 475; LO 2	33. a p. 481; LO 4	45. b p. 484; LO 5
9. c p. 472; LO 1	22. b p. 474; LO 2	34. c p. 481; LO 4	46. a p. 475; LO 2
10. b p. 472; LO 1	23. d p. 476; LO 2	35. c p. 470; LO 1	47. a p. 475; LO 2
11. a p. 473; LO 2	24. b p. 476; LO 2	36. d p. 482; LO 5	48. d p. 475; LO 2
12. e p. 472-473; LO 2	25. b p. 476-477; LO 3	37. e p. 482; LO 5	49. e p. 475; LO 2
13. a p. 473; LO 2			50. e p. 475; LO 2

Note: LO indicates learning objective.

CHAPTER 19

ADVERTISING, SALES PROMOTION, AND PUBLIC RELATIONS

<u>Why is Chapter 19 important?</u> This chapter illustrates the types of advertising and sales promotional tools and how they can be used effectively. It goes through the steps to plan and execute a successful advertising program and looks at the effective use of public relations and publicity. In addition, it studies the different types of media and when they are best utilized.

Advertising: Any paid form of non-personal communication about an organization, good, service, or idea by an identified sponsor.

CHAPTER OUTLINE

I. TYPES OF ADVERTISEMENTS

    A. Product
           1. Pioneering (informational)
           2. Competitive (persuasive)
           3. Reminder

    B. Institutional
           1. Advocacy
           2. Pioneering
           3. Competitive
           4. Reminder

II. DEVELOPING THE ADVERTISING PROGRAM

    A. Identifying the Target Audience

    B. Specifying Advertising Objectives

    C. Setting the Advertising Budget

    D. Designing the Advertisement
           1. Message content
                a. fear appeal
                b. sex appeal
                c. humorous appeal
           2. Creating the actual message

E. Selecting the Right Media
    1. Media selection decision
        a. target audience
        b. type of product
        c. nature of message
        d. campaign objectives
        e. available budget
        f. costs of alternative media

    2. Goals
        a. maximizing exposure
        b. minimizing costs
    3. Basic terms
        a. reach
        b. rating
        c. frequency
        d. gross rating points (GRP)
        e. cost per thousand (CPM)

F. Different Media Alternatives
    1. Television
    2. Radio
    3. Magazines
    4. Newspapers
    5. Yellow pages
    6. Internet
    7. Outdoor
    8. Other media
    9. Selection criteria

G. Scheduling the Advertising
    1. Factors
        a. buyer turnover
        b. purchase frequency
        c. forgetting rate
    2. Approaches
        a. continuous
        b. flighting
        c. pulse

III. EXECUTING THE ADVERTISING PROGRAM

A. Pretesting
    1. Portfolio tests
    2. Jury tests
    3. Theater tests

B. Carrying Out the Advertising Program
    1. Full-service agencies
    2. Limited-service agencies
    3. In-house agencies

IV. Evaluating the Advertising Program

    A. Posttesting
        1. Aided recall
        2. Unaided recall
        3. Attitude tests
        4. Inquiry test
        5. Sales tests
    B. Making Needed Changes

V. SALES PROMOTION

    A. Importance

    B. Consumer-oriented Sales Promotions
        1. Coupons
        2. Deals
        3. Premiums
        4. Contests
        5. Sweepstakes
        6. Samples
        7. Loyalty programs
        8. Point-of-purchase displays
        9. Rebates
       10. Product placement

    C. Trade-Oriented Sales Promotions
        1. Allowances and discounts
        2. Cooperative advertising
        3. Training of distributors' sales force

VI. PUBLIC RELATIONS

    A. Publicity Tools
        1. News release
        2. News conference
        3. Public service announcements (PSAs)
        4. High-visibility individuals

VII. Increasing the Value of Promotion
    A. Building long-term relationships
    B. Self-regulation

You should be able to place these key terms in the outline and be able to discuss them.

advertising
consumer-oriented sales promotions
cooperative advertising
cost per thousand
frequency
full-service agencies
gross rating points
infomercials
in-house agencies
institutional advertisements

limited-service agencies
posttests
pretests
product advertisements
product placement
publicity tools
rating
reach
trade-oriented sales promotions

QUESTIONS & PROBLEMS

PRODUCT ADVERTISING

Product advertising focuses on selling a product or service and can take three forms:

Pioneering
Competitive
Reminder

Match the correct form of product advertising with the definitions or statements below:

1. Advertising that promotes a specific brand's features and benefits. One form shows one brand's strengths relative to another's._____

2. Advertising that tells what a product is, what it can do, and where it can be found. The key objective is to inform the target market._____

3. This form of advertisement is used to reinforce previous knowledge of a product or a service. A variation of this form of advertisement, reinforcement advertising, is used to reassure current users they made the right choice._____

INSTITUTIONAL ADVERTISING

There are four alternative forms of institutional advertising:

Advocacy advertisements
Pioneering institutional advertisements
Competitive institutional advertisements
Reminder institutional advertisements

Match the correct form of institutional advertising to the definitions or statements below:

1. These advertisements are used for a new announcement, such as, what a company is, what it can do, or where it is located._____

2. These advertisements promote the advantages of one product class over another.

_____

3. These advertisements state the position of a company on a given issue.

_____

4. These advertisements bring the name of the company to the attention of their target market.

_____

DEVELOPING THE ADVERTISING PROGRAM

What are the six steps used in developing the advertising program?

1._____

2._____

3._____

4._____

5._____

6._____

SALES PROMOTION

There are numerous sales promotion alternatives:

Coupons
Deals
Premiums
Contests
Sweepstakes
Samples
Continuity programs
Point-of-purchase displays
Rebates

List an example of each of the sales promotion alternatives below:

1. Coupons_____

2. Deals_____

3. Premiums_____

4. Contests_____

5. Sweepstakes_____

6. Samples_____

7. Continuity programs_____

8. Point-of-purchase displays_____

9. Rebates_____

TRADE-ORIENTED SALES PROMOTIONS

There are three major approaches to trade-oriented sales promotions:

Allowances and discounts (merchandise, case, and finance allowances)
Cooperative advertising
Training of distributors' sales force

Match the type of trade-oriented sales promotion with the examples or statements below (be specific):

1. This reimburses a retailer for extra in-store support or special featuring of the brand._____

2. Manufacturers allow discounts on each case ordered during a specific time period._____

3. This may involve the production of educational pamphlets or manufacturer sponsored national sales meetings._____

4. Retailers are paid for financing costs or financial losses associated with consumer sales promotions.____
_____

5. Usually the manufacturer pays a percentage, often 50% of the cost of advertising, up to a certain dollar limit, which is based on the amount of the purchases the retailer makes of the manufacturer's products._____
_____

PUBLICITY

Three publicity tools that are available to the public relations director are news releases, news conferences, and public service announcements (PSAs).

Find an example of each of the three types of publicity tools:

News releases_____

News conferences_____

PSAs_____

MESSAGE CONTENT

Information and persuasive content can be combined in the form of an appeal to provide a basic reason for the consumer to act. There are three commonly used methods of appeal:

Fear appeal
Sex appeal
Humorous appeal

Find the best current example (in your opinion) of advertisements that incorporate each of the forms of appeal listed above:

Advertisement	Type of Appeal	Media
1._____	_____	_____
2._____	_____	_____
3._____	_____	_____

BASIC MEDIA TERMS

Media buyers speak a language of their own, so every advertiser involved in selecting the right media for their campaigns must be familiar with some common terms used in the advertising industry.

Define the following advertising terms:

1. Reach_____

2. Rating_____

3. Frequency_____

4. Gross rating points_____

5. Cost per thousand_____

6. Splitting 30s_____

7. Wasted coverage_____

DIFFERENT MEDIA ALTERNATIVES

List the advantages and disadvantages of the media alternatives:

	<u>Advantages</u>	<u>Disadvantages</u>
1. Television	_____	_____
2. Radio	_____	_____
3. Magazines	_____	_____
4. Newspapers	_____	_____
5. Direct mail	_____	_____
6. Outdoor	_____	_____

SCHEDULING THE ADVERTISING

There is no correct schedule to advertise a product, but three factors must be considered. These factors include:

Buyer turnover
Purchase frequency
Forgetting rate

Match the correct term to the statements listed below:

1. The speed with which buyers forget the brand if advertising is not seen._____

2. How often new buyers enter the market to buy the product._____

3. The more frequently the product is purchased the less repetition is required._____

TIMING

Setting schedules requires an understanding of how the market behaves. Most companies tend to follow one of these basic approaches.

Steady "drip" schedule
Flighting "intermittent" schedule
Pulse "burst" schedule

Match the correct scheduling approach to the statements below:

1. Periods of advertising are scheduled between periods of no advertising to reflect seasonal demand.
_____

2. A flighting schedule is combined with a steady schedule because of increases in demand, heavy periods of promotions, or introduction of a new product.
_____

3. When seasonal factors are unimportant, advertising is run at a steady or regular schedule throughout the year._____

PRETESTING ADVERTISING

Pretesting is done to determine whether the advertisement communicates the intended message, or to select the best alternative version of an advertisement. There are three common forms of pretesting:

Portfolio tests
Jury tests
Theater tests

Match the correct form of pretesting with the statements below:

1. This is used to test copy alternatives. The test ad is placed in a booklet with several other ads and stories. Subjects are asked to read through and give their impressions of the ad on several evaluative scales.
_____

2. The ad is shown to a panel of consumers: the panel rates how much they liked the ad, how much it drew their attention, how attractive it was, etc._____

3. This is the most sophisticated form of pretesting. Consumers are invited to view a new movie or television show. During the show, commercials are shown. Viewers register their feeling about the advertisements either on hand held electronic recording devices used during the viewing or on questionnaires afterwards._____

CARRYING OUT THE ADVERTISING PROGRAM

The responsibility for actually carrying out the advertising program can be handled in one of three ways:

Full-service agency
Limited-service agency
In-house agency

Match the correct term to the statements below:

1. The firm's own advertising staff may provide full services or a limited range of services.
_____

2. Specializes in one aspect of the advertising process such as providing creative services to develop the advertising copy or buying previously unpurchased media space.
_____

3. Provides the most complete range of services, including market research, media selection, copy development, art work, and production._____

POSTTESTING METHODS

There are several posttesting methods:

Aided recall
Unaided recall
Attitude tests
Inquiry tests
Sales tests

Match the correct posttesting method to the statements below:

1. This technique questions respondents without any prompting to determine whether they saw or heard advertising messages._____

2. This technique offers additional product information, samples, or premiums in response to consumer requests. Ads generating the most inquiries are presumed to be the most effective.

_____

3. After being shown an ad, respondents are asked whether their previous exposure to it was through reading, viewing, or listening._____

4. This technique involves studies such as controlled media comparison experiments and consumer purchase tests._____

5. Respondents are asked questions to measure changes in their dispositions towards a particular product following an advertising campaign._____

CAN YOU PASS THE TEST?
Sample Multiple Choice Questions

1. _____ is any paid form of non-personal communication about an organization, good, service, or idea by an identified sponsor.
   - a. Publicity
   - b. Sales promotion
   - c. Advertising
   - d. Personal selling
   - e. Direct marketing

2. The three types of product adverting are:
   - a. consumer, business, and governmental.
   - b. pioneering, competitive, and reminder.
   - c. service, business good, and consumer good.
   - d. individual, household, and business.
   - e. motivational, socio-cultural, and informational.

3. Another name for pioneering advertising is _____ advertising.
   - a. informational
   - b. motivational
   - c. primary
   - d. persuasive
   - e. first-mover-advantage

4. Yamaha Corp. has developed a device that reduces the volume of trumpets by more than 30 decibels—to the level of a whisper. A microphone picks up the sound, feeds it to an amplifier, and then to headphones that allow the musician to hear the music at a normal volume. What form of product advertising is the company likely to use?
   - a. reminder
   - b. competitive
   - c. pioneering
   - d. institutional
   - e. objective

5. Competitive product and brand advertising is typically used to:
   - a. inform the target market.
   - b. identify the target market.
   - c. persuade the target market.
   - d. reinforce previous knowledge.
   - e. state the position of the advertiser on an issue.

6. An ad for California Almonds Association describes the nuts as low in saturated fat, high in vitamin E, cholesterol free, and delicious. This ad is most likely an example of _____ advertising.
   - a. pioneering institutional
   - b. motivational
   - c. primary
   - d. persuasive
   - e. competitive institutional

7. When Godiva chocolates runs a magazine ad with the headline "Spend Your Birthday With The Ones You Love," it has created _____ advertising.
      a. parity
      b. direct sales
      c. pioneering
      d. comparative
      e. reminder

8. At the beginning of the school year in September, Pfizer Pharmaceutical ran an ad in several women's magazines in which it suggested that the timing may be right for vaccination. Pfizer was using _____ advertising.
      a. pioneering
      b. competitive
      c. advocacy
      d. reminder
      e. comparative

9. The California Pistachio Growers Association has an ongoing ad campaign in which it encourages people to think of pistachios when they think of good times and good friends. The goal of the ad is to increase consumption of pistachio nuts. The ads are examples of _____ ads.
      a. competitive institutional
      b. competitive product
      c. advocacy
      d. pioneering product
      e. pioneering institutional

10. The first step in developing the advertising program is:
      a. budgeting.
      b. making media selections.
      c. identifying the target audience.
      d. setting advertising quotas.
      e. specifying advertising objectives.

11. All of the following steps are part of the planning process used to develop an organization's advertising program EXCEPT:
      a. identify the target audience.
      b. specify the advertising objectives.
      c. write the advertising copy.
      d. pretest the advertising.
      e. schedule the advertising program.

12. An ad for a drug that reduces an individual's cholesterol count is headlined, "Will a heart attack make your life run out before your grandson tastes his first ice cream?" This headline uses a(n) _____ appeal.
      a. fear
      b. informational
      c. motivational
      d. humor
      e. behavioral

13. Which of the following statements describes a problem with using sex appeals in advertising?
      a. what men find sexy, women don't.
      b. what women find sexy, men don't.
      c. sex appeal typically fails to gain audience attention.
      d. the sex appeal of the ad can distract the audience from the product.
      e. sex appeals have no effect on senior citizens.

14. Advertisers who use a celebrity spokesperson believe that the ads are more likely to influence sales. This is probably due to the influence of:
      a. opinion leaders.
      b. dissociative reference groups.
      c. cultural icons.
      d. social classes.
      e. personal influences.

15. The use of Michael Jordan in Hanes underwear commercials rather than an unknown model is an example of a very popular form of advertising today—the use of:
      a. a fear appeal.
      b. a snob appeal.
      c. an appeal to pride.
      d. a sex appeal.
      e. a celebrity spokesperson.

16. _____ is defined as the percentage of households in a market that are tuned to a particular television show or radio station.
      a. gross rating points
      b. reception rate
      c. target audience reach
      d. rating
      e. share

17. The vice-president of marketing of Fabric Gallery has been told to invest the company's advertising dollars wisely. Which of the following measures could be used to compare the financial effectiveness of its advertising expenditures for different media?
      a. reach
      b. rating
      c. GRPs
      d. CPM
      e. frequency

18. Which of the following is the most widely used advertising medium in terms of dollars spent?
      a. magazines
      b. internet
      c. direct mail
      d. television
      e. newspapers

19. Gross rating points:
      a. are also call cpm.
      b. equal reach multiplied by frequency.
      c. reach times cpm.
      d. frequency times cpm.
      e. reach divided by frequency.

20. _____ occurs when people outside the target market for the product see a firm's advertisement.
   a. Media divergence
   b. Dual exposure
   c. Over-coverage
   d. Wasted coverage
   e. Extended advertising

21. One of the disadvantages associated with advertising on television is:
   a. its ability to target specific audiences.
   b. high cost.
   c. uncertain effectiveness.
   d. the ease with which recognition tests can be used to measure ad results.
   e. its interactivity.

22. One reason for using radio as an advertising medium is:
   a. its high cost.
   b. its long lead time required for the placement of an ad.
   c. its inability to use humor.
   d. its multi-sensory appeal.
   e. none of the above.

23. Which of the following is an example of a trend that is having a major impact on newspapers today?
   a. decreasing cost of production and distribution
   b. the appearance of free newspaper advertising to increase readership
   c. the growth of online newspapers
   d. the decrease of local advertising
   e. all of the above

24. Which of the following statements about the Internet as an advertising medium is true?
   a. The Internet provides audio and video capabilities.
   b. Ads are black and white.
   c. Internet ads are similar to print ads in that they offer only a visual message.
   d. Internet advertising is the most effective form of advertising.
   e. All of the above statements about the internet as an advertising medium are true.

25. The most common format for an Internet ad is the:
   a. banner ad.
   b. interstitials.
   c. pop-ups.
   d. mini-sites.
   e. skyscrapers.

26. A retail store marketing vice president is developing an advertising budget using the objective and task method. She has the objective of clearing slow-moving merchandise from her shelves and is trying to choose between radio and newspaper ads. Which of the following is an advantage of radio relative to newspaper as a means of achieving the objective?
   a. better reach
   b. more effective visuals
   c. ads can be saved by consumers
   d. better segmentation capability
   e. more effective in conveying complex information

27. Which of the following statements about how advertising is scheduled is true?
    a. The lower the buyer turnover, the greater the amount of advertising is required.
    b. The less frequently the product is purchased, the less repetition of the ad is required.
    c. The forgetting rate is not important for consumer products.
    d. The higher the buyer turnover, the greater the amount of advertising is required.
    e. None of the above statements about how advertising is scheduled are true.

28. A basic approach to scheduling, in which periods of advertising are scheduled between periods of no advertising to reflect seasonal demand is called:
    a. sustaining.
    b. dripping.
    c. flighting.
    d. pulsing.
    e. bursting.

29. Portfolio tests are:
    a. used in pretesting.
    b. classified as aided recall and unaided recall.
    c. commonly used in posttesting.
    d. used to determine whether an advertisement is achieving its objectives.
    e. primarily used by specialty agencies to prove their effectiveness.

30. Jury tests:
    a. present a panel of consumers with an ad and ask for their reactions concerning the ad's effectiveness, appeal, etc.
    b. present a panel of consumers with an ad for a limited period of time. the ad is then removed, and the respondents are asked to recall as much pertinent information as possible.
    c. present consumers with a sample of a product and several different advertisements for the product. they are asked to select the one they think is most effective and explain why.
    d. present consumers with a hidden ad, which they are asked to recall.
    e. use electronic devices during or questionnaires after consumers view an advertisement to measure viewer response or feelings.

31. When a company uses a(n) _____, it is using its own advertising staff to provides the advertising services needed by the company.
    a. intrafirm agency
    b. promotional department
    c. full-service agency
    d. in-house agency
    e. limited-service agency

32. Which of the following is an example of a posttest?
    a. an attitude test
    b. a theater test
    c. a portfolio test
    d. a jury test
    e. all of the above

33. As a subscriber to *Real Simple* magazine, Kelly was asked by a researcher, which ads she remembered seeing in the most recent issue of the magazine. Then she was asked questions about the content and appearance of the ads she remembered. The researcher was using _____ to test the effectiveness of ads in the magazine.
        a. inquiry testing
        b. concept testing
        c. unaided recall
        d. portfolio testing
        e. aided recall

34. When preparing his grocery shopping list, Winston actively scans the supermarket ads in the local newspaper for coupons, rebates, and sale items. While in the store, Winston also looks for free samples of new products and products he hasn't purchased previously. The coupons, rebates, sale items, and free samples are all examples of:
        a. advertising.
        b. publicity.
        c. personal selling.
        d. sales promotion.
        e. direct marketing.

35. For marketers, the primary objective of a deal is to:
        a. extend a product's life cycle.
        b. increase trial among potential customers as a retaliation against competitors' actions.
        c. encourage present customers to buy more, which should minimize brand switching behavior.
        d. encourage new product trial.
        e. encourage repeat purchases.

36. The term "self-liquidating" is most closely associated with which type of consumer-oriented sales promotions?
        a. coupons
        b. product placement
        c. premiums
        d. point-of-purchase displays
        e. contests and sweepstakes

37. The ad advised readers to "try your skill at using our cream cheese to create an exciting new recipe and you may be the winner of a trip for two to Hawaii." This ad was promoting a:
        a. premium.
        b. sweepstakes.
        c. deal.
        d. contest.
        e. end-run sample.

38. Which of the following statements about contests and sweepstakes is true?
        a. The contest is where the consumers apply their skill or analytical or creative thinking to try to win a prize.
        b. The sweepstakes is purely a game of chance.
        c. The Federal Trade Commission has issued laws governing both sweepstakes and contests.
        d. Sales tend to drop at the conclusion of the sweepstakes.
        e. All of the above statements about contests and sweepstakes are true.

39. When Allyn went to get his newspaper, he found the paper in a plastic bag along with a box containing one dose of Alka-Seltzer Heartburn Relief medication. Which type of sales promotion is Alka-Seltzer using?
      a. a sample
      b. a deal
      c. a premium
      d. a point-of-purchase display
      e. a introductory offer

40. Marriott offers a credit card with which users can earn points, which can be redeemed for stays in Marriott hotels and resorts. This is an example of a(n):
      a. rebate program.
      b. loyalty program.
      c. amenity sampler.
      d. self-liquidating premium.
      e. trade allowance.

41. A brochure in the literature sent to retailers began with the following statement: "Retailers, these new sunglasses come with their own attractive free-standing carousel that fits perfectly next to your cash register." Which sales promotion does this exemplify?
      a. a sample
      b. a free standing insert
      c. a premium
      d. a point-of-purchase display
      e. a deal

42. The frequent appearance of Snapple drink on UPN's *Roswell* TV show is an example of:
      a. product placement.
      b. intangible sampling.
      c. opinion leader sampling.
      d. a referential promotion.
      e. self-liquidating promotion.

43. Freight allowances and floor stock protection programs are both examples of:
      a. functional tools.
      b. merchandise allowances.
      c. finance allowances.
      d. consumer promotions.
      e. case allowances.

44. A _____ is a discount on each case of goods ordered during a specific period of time
      a. functional allowance
      b. merchandise allowance
      c. case allowance
      d. finance allowance
      e. manufacturer's allowance

45. The most frequently used public relations tool is:
      a. product placement.
      b. product sampling.
      c. sales training courses.
      d. publicity.
      e. loyalty programs.

46. A news conference is a(n):
    a. announcement regarding changes in the company or product line.
    b. free space or time in a newspaper or on a broadcast medium.
    c. publicity tool which utilizes high-visibility individuals in lobbying activities.
    d. meeting of top news executives to decide advertising policy.
    e. an informational meeting to which representatives of the media are invited.

47. The acronym PSA stands for:
    a. promotional service agency.
    b. public service announcement.
    c. publicity-service arrangement.
    d. promotional sales agreements.
    e. personal selling advice.

48. The appearance of the participants in the *Survivors: Marquesas* series on the *Early Show* prior to the first episode of the series was an example of:
    a. product placement.
    b. publicity.
    c. a trade allowance.
    d. a sales promotion.
    e. a continuity program.

49. Why are advertising agencies integrating public relations, direct marketing, advertising, and sales promotions into highly integrated programs and starting to refer to themselves as communications consulting firms?
    a. to avoid self-regulation
    b. to take advantage of publicity opportunities
    c. to allow multimedia approaches that engage consumers
    d. to respond to newly enacted federal trade commission regulations
    e. to do all of the above

50. Which of the following statements about self-regulation in the advertising industry is true?
    a. Other than self-regulation, there is no regulation of the advertising industry.
    b. Advertising agencies are strongly opposed to self-regulation efforts.
    c. Self-regulation will require advertising agencies to reflect the values of society in their promotional activities.
    d. Because consumers have complete confidence in advertising and the agencies that create it, self-regulation is unnecessary.
    e. None of the above statements about self-regulation in the advertising industry is true.

ANSWER KEY

Answers to Questions & Problems

Product Advertising

1. Competitive
2. Pioneering
3. Reminder

Institutional Advertising

1. Pioneering
2. Competitive
3. Advocacy
4. Reminder

Developing the Advertising Program

1. Identifying the target audience
2. Specifying advertising objectives
3. Setting the advertising budget
4. Designing the advertisement
5. Selecting the right media
6. Scheduling the advertising

Basic Media Terms

1. Reach_____

2. Rating_____

3. Frequency_____

4. Gross rating points_____

5. Cost per thousand_____

6. Splitting 30s_____

7. Wasted coverage_____

Different Media Alternatives

Example: Television—advantages—reach; disadvantages—cost

Scheduling the Advertising

1. Forgetting rate
2. Buyer turnover
3. Purchase frequency

Timing

1. Intermittent
2. Burst
3. Drip

Pretesting Advertising

1. Portfolio test
2. Jury test
3. Theater test

Carrying Out the Advertising Program

1. In-house
2. Limited-service
3. Full-service

Posttesting Methods

1. Unaided recall
2. Inquiry test
3. Aided recall
4. Sales test
5. Attitude test

Answers to Sample Multiple Choice Questions

1. d p. 470; LO 1	14. c p. 473; LO 2	26. c p. 477; LO 3	38. c p. 482; LO 5
2. b p. 470; LO 1	15. e p. 474; LO 2	27. a p. 477; LO 3	39. c p. 482; LO 5
3. a p. 471; LO 1	16. e p. 474; LO 2	28. c p. 478; LO 3	40. b p. 482; LO 5
4. b p. 470; LO 1	17. b p. 474; LO 2	29. e p. 478; LO 3	41. a p. 483; LO 5
5. d p. 470; LO 1	18. e p. 474; LO 2	30. d p. 478; LO 3	42. c p. 484; LO 5
6. d p. 472; LO 1	19. a p. 474; LO 2	31. a p. 480; LO 4	43. e p. 483; LO 5
7. e p. 472; LO 1	20. d p. 475; LO 2	32. a p. 480; LO 4	44. d p. 484; LO 5
8. d p. 472; LO 1	21. e p. 475; LO 2	33. a p. 481; LO 4	45. b p. 484; LO 5
9. c p. 472; LO 1	22. b p. 474; LO 2	34. c p. 481; LO 4	46. a p. 475; LO 2
10. b p. 472; LO 1	23. d p. 476; LO 2	35. c p. 470; LO 1	47. a p. 475; LO 2
11. a p. 473; LO 2	24. b p. 476; LO 2	36. d p. 482; LO 5	48. d p. 475; LO 2
12. e p. 472-473; LO 2	25. b p. 476-477; LO 3	37. e p. 482; LO 5	49. e p. 475; LO 2
13. a p. 473; LO 2			50. e p. 475; LO 2

Note: LO indicates learning objective.

Chapter 20 – Personal Selling and Sales Management

CHAPTER 20

PERSONAL SELLING AND SALES MANAGEMENT

<u>Why is Chapter 20 important</u>? Personal selling is the lifeblood of much of the marketing function, especially the business-to-business segment. This chapter illustrates the participants in the personal selling process and their selection and management. It also outlines the personal selling process showing how to make it more effective.

Personal Selling: The two-way flow of communication between a buyer and seller, often in a face-to-face encounter, designed to influence a person's or group's purchase decision.

CHAPTER OUTLINE

I. SCOPE AND SIGNIFICANCE OF PERSONAL SELLING AND SALES MANAGEMENT

    A. Nature of Personal Selling and Sales Management

    B. Pervasiveness of Selling

    C. Personal Selling in Marketing

    D. Creating Customer Value through Salespeople: Relationship and Partnership Selling

II. FORMS OF PERSONAL SELLING

    A. Order Taking
        1. Outside order takers
        2. Inside order takers

    B. Order Getting

    C. Sales Support Personal
        1. Missionary salespeople
        2. Sales engineer
        3. Team selling
            a. conference selling
            b. seminar selling

III. PERSONAL SELLING PROCESS: BUILDING RELATIONSHIPS

    A. Prospecting
        1. Lead
        2. Prospect
        3. Qualified prospect

    B. Preapproach

    C. Approach

337

D. Presentation
   1. Stimulus-response format
   2. Formula selling format
   3. Need-satisfaction format
      a. adaptive selling
      b. consultative selling
   4. Handling objections
      a. acknowledge and convert the objection
      b. postpone
      c. agree and neutralize
      d. accept the objection
      e. denial
      f. ignore the objection

E. Close
   1. Trial close
   2. Assumptive close
   3. Urgency close

F. Followup

IV. SALES MANAGEMENT PROCESS

A. Sales Plan Formulation
   1. Setting objectives
      a. output related
      b. input related
      c. behaviorally related
   2. Organizing the salesforce
      a. types of sales personnel
         i. own salesforce
         ii. independents agents
      b. structure
         i. geography
         ii. customer type
         iii. product or service
         iv. major account management
      c. salesforce size
         i. number of accounts
         ii. frequency of calls
         iii. length of calls
         iv. time devoted to selling
   3. Developing account management policies

B. Sales Plan Implementation
   1. Salesforce recruitment and selection
      a. job analysis
      b. job description
         i. to whom the salesperson reports
         ii. how a salesperson interacts with other company personnel
         iii. the customers to be called on
         iv. the specific activities to be carried out
         v. physical and mental demands of the job
         vi. types of products and services to be sold
      c. job qualifications
         i. imagination and problem-solving ability
         ii. honesty
         iii. intimate product knowledge
         iv. attentiveness reflected in responsiveness to buyer needs and customer loyalty and follow-up
   2. Salesforce training
   3. Salesforce motivation and compensation
      a. clear job description
      b. effective sales management practices
      c. a sense of achievement
      d. proper compensation, incentives, or rewards
         i. straight salary
         ii. straight commission
         iii. combination
   4. Salesforce evaluation and control
      a. quantitative assessments
      b. behavioral evaluation
   5. Salesforce automation
      a. computerization
      b. communication

You should be able to place these key terms in the outline and be able to discuss them.

account management policies	**need-satisfaction presentation**	**sales engineer**
adaptive selling	**order getter**	**salesforce automation**
consultative selling	**order taker**	**sales management**
emotional intelligence	**partnership selling**	**sales plan**
formula selling presentation	**personal selling**	**sales quota**
major account management	**personal selling process**	**stimulus-response presentation**
missionary salespeople	**relationship selling**	**team selling**
		workload method

QUESTIONS & PROBLEMS

PERSONAL SELLING IN MARKETING

What three major roles does personal selling play in a firm's overall marketing efforts?

1._____

2._____

3._____

The practice of building ties based on a salesperson's attention and commitment to customer needs over time is called relationship selling. This involves mutual respect and trust among buyers and sellers.

THE MANY FORMS OF PERSONAL SELLING

Which of the following activities are performed by order takers and which are performed by order getters?

1. Handles routine product orders and/or reorders._____

2. Generates new sales volume._____

3. Identifies new customers and sales opportunities._____

4. Maintains sales volume._____

5. Focuses on straight rebuy purchase situations._____

6. Requires significant clerical training._____

7. Performs order processing functions._____

8. Acts as a creative problem solver._____

9. Focuses on new buy and modified rebuy purchase situations._____

10. Represents complex products with many options._____

SALES SUPPORT PERSONNEL

Sales support personnel augment the selling effort of order getters by performing a variety of services.

Missionary salespeople
Sales engineer
Team selling

Match the correct type of sales support personnel to the examples below:

1. Ms. Pedrotti prepares promotions and information packets for hospitals. She promotes the purchase of new pharmaceutical products although she does not directly solicit orders._____

2. A computer firm sends out three people on sales calls: one to explain the product's technical capabilities, one to explain the software, and a third to arrange logistics such as price, delivery, and installation._____

3. Mr. Green, an electrical engineer works in the sales department. He does not solicit sales but provides any and all information concerning the electrical function of the product his company manufactures and sells._____

THE PERSONAL SELLING PROCESS

Prospecting

Personal selling begins with prospecting, the search for and qualification of potential customers. There are three types of prospects:

Lead
Prospect
Qualified prospect

Match the type of prospect to the definition below:

1. A customer who wants and needs a product._____

2. The name of a person who may be a possible customer._____

3. A person who wants a product, can afford the product, and has the decision power to buy the product.
_____

List at least five ways to generate leads and prospects (use creativity):

1._____

2._____

3._____

4._____

5._____

PREAPPROACH AND APPROACH STAGE

One of the major competitive advantages IBM had over its mainframe computer competitor's was its sales personnel. When IBM came in to make a presentation, they were prepared. They knew the prospect's business and how a computer, an IBM computer, would benefit that business. Consider the following situation. A company, which prepared specialized reports for the financial services industry, was in the market to upgrade their computer system. IBM and Unisys were the two companies making presentations. Both companies had made cold calls and supplied the company officers with literature and specifications. At the presentation, Unisys presented a prepackaged system directed toward someone in the "publishing" industry complete with canned programs for data entry on the computer. IBM, by doing the necessary preapproach preparation, knew the company wrote its own software and really needed high-speed computing and high-speed, quality printers. Their presentation was geared to the company's needs. It doesn't take much imagination to guess who got the sale.

You are a salesperson for a major office furniture and equipment manufacturer. You have been invited in to present your products to several new tenants of the Trump Tower in New York. What type of preapproach questions and preparations do you need? If these tenants are a law firm, advertising agency and real estate firm, what will you approach be?

The approach stage is very important in international settings. In many societies outside the United States, considerable time is devoted to non-business talk designed to establish a rapport between buyers and sellers.

PRESENTATION

The presentation is at the core of the order getting selling process, and its objective is to convert a prospect into a consumer by creating a desire for the product or service.

There are three types of presentation format:

Stimulus-response format
Formula selling format
Need-satisfaction format

Match the type of selling presentation with the examples or statements below:

1. A popular version of this format is the canned sales presentation._____

2. After you select a new Polo dress shirt, the salesperson suggests a matching club tie._____

3. This format emphasizes probing and listening by the salesperson to identify needs and interests of prospective buyers._____

4. The salesperson tries many appeals, hoping to "hit the right button."_____

5. This approach is most consistent with the marketing concept._____

6. This format is commonly used in telephone and door-to-door selling and treats every prospect the same regardless of differences in needs or preferences._____

Answer the following questions:

1. Assume you are a salesperson at an upscale women's clothing store. Demonstrate how you would use suggestive selling:_____

_____

_____

2. Design a canned sales presentation for someone selling burial plots over the telephone (keep it to one paragraph)._____

_____

_____

_____

_____

3. What is adaptive selling?_____

4. What is consultative selling?_____

CLOSE

The closing stage in the selling process involves obtaining a purchase commitment from the prospect. There are three common closing methods:

Trial close
Assumptive close
Urgency close

Match the correct type of close to the statements below:

1. This technique involves asking the prospect to make a decision on some aspect of the purchase.

_____

2. This technique is used to commit the prospect quickly by making reference to the timeliness of the purchase._____

3. This technique entails asking the prospect to make choices concerning delivery, warranty, or financing terms._____

FOLLOW-UP

The selling process does not end with the closing of a sale.

List two reasons why follow-up is such an important policy (in your opinion):

1._____

2._____

THE SALES MANAGEMENT PROCESS

List the three interrelated functions of sales management:

1._____

2._____

3._____

What are the three tasks in sales plan formulation?

1._____

2._____

3._____

ORGANIZATIONAL STRUCTURE

If a company elects to employ its own salespeople, then it must choose an organizational structure based on (1) geography, (2) customer, or (3) product/service.

Which type of organizational structure is best described by the statements below:

1. This structure minimizes travel time, expenses, and duplication of selling effort._____

2. When specialized knowledge is required to sell certain types of products, this structure is suggested.
_____

3. When different buyers have different needs, this structure is suggested._____

4. This structure often leads to higher administrative costs since two or more separate sales forces represent the same products._____

5. Reporting to the General Sales Manager are the Eastern and Western Regional Sales Managers.
_____

6. At Magic Micros, John sells the company's line of six microcomputers to existing customers and prospects in his territory. About once a week John will meet his friend Jane (who also works for Magic) in a customer's waiting room. Jane sells the company's line of specialized software and consulting services.
_____

The "workload method" is the most commonly used determinate of salesforce size.

$$NS = (NC \times CF \times CL)/ AST$$

where,

NS = Number of salespeople
NC = Number of customers
CF = Call frequency
CL = Average call length
AST = Average selling time available per sales person per year

Apple Computer has 15,000 retail outlets and company policy mandates at least one call per month per store. An average sales call takes three hours. Each Apple salesperson spends 50% of each 2,000-hour work-year selling.

Use the workload method to determine the number of salespeople Apple needs to service these accounts:

NS = _____

SALES PLAN IMPLEMENTATION

The sales plan is a statement describing what is to be achieved and where and how the selling effort of salespeople is to be deployed. Formulating the sales plan is the most basic of the three sales management functions.

What are the three tasks in sales plan implementation?

1._____

2._____

3._____

Salespeople are paid by using one of three plans. Each method has special uses, advantages, and disadvantages.

      Straight salary compensation plan
      Straight commission compensation plan
      Combination compensation plan

Which methods of compensation are being described by the examples or statements below:

1. Provides little incentive, necessitates close supervision of salespersons_____

2. Especially useful when highly aggressive selling is required_____

3. Provides a certain amount of financial security while still providing some financial incentive_____
_____

SALES FORCE EVALUATION AND CONTROL

What are the two tasks in evaluation and control?

1._____

2._____

Sales force evaluation uses both quantitative and behavioral objectives. Quantitative evaluations can be either input- or output-related.

Identify whether the basis of sales force evaluation is quantitative or behavioral:

1. Account management policies_____

2. Number of sales calls_____

3. Product knowledge_____

4. Communication skills_____

5. Appearance_____

6. Number of new accounts_____

7. Number of reports submitted to superiors_____

8. Accounts generated_____

SALESFORCE AUTOMATION

Discuss how automation has enhanced the sales forces' ability to use the marketing mix, i.e., 4 P's of marketing.

CHAPTER 20

CAN YOU PASS THE TEST?
Sample Multiple Choice Questions

1. Personal selling:
   a. involves the two-way flow of communication.
   b. is designed to influence a person or group's purchase decision.
   c. has changed as a result of advances in telecommunications.
   d. is not always done face-to-face.
   e. is accurately described by all of the above

2. Personal selling:
   a. occurs when Keith sees an advertisement in *Sports Illustrated.*
   b. is a one-way flow of communication between buyer and seller.
   c. occurs when Becca sees a character on *Friends* eating a Snickers bar.
   d. occurs when Girl Scouts ask you to buy a box of cookies.
   e. is not part of the promotion mix.

3. _____ involves planning the selling program and implementing and controlling the personal selling effort of the firm.
   a. Relationship marketing
   b. Team selling
   c. Personal selling
   d. Sales management
   e. Sales engineering

4. Bombardier makes corporate jets and its strategy involves streamlining production activities, maintaining its reputation for quality, and reducing its costs. It has developed the Continental, an airplane assembled from just a dozen large component parts. All parts are supplied by carefully chosen independent companies that share the development costs and market risk with Bombardier as part of being its suppliers. To sell subassemblies to Bombardier, the salespeople for its supplier companies used:
   a. order processing.
   b. order taking.
   c. customer value creation.
   d. relationship selling.
   e. transactional selling.

5. Partnership selling is sometimes called:
   a. relationship marketing.
   b. transactional marketing.
   c. transformational selling.
   d. enterprise selling.
   e. strategic allying.

6. An order taker is a:
   a. salesperson who specializes in identifying, analyzing, and solving customer problems, but who does not actually sell products and services.
   b. salesperson who processes routine orders or reorders for products that were already sold by the company.
   c. salesperson who identifies prospective customers, provides customers with information, persuades customers to buy, closes sales, and follows up on a customer's use of a product or service.
   d. person on the selling team who are responsible for obtaining qualified leads.
   e. member of the sales support team who does not directly solicit orders but rather concentrates on performing promotional activities and introducing new products.

7. When Monica phoned the toll-free number she found in her American Girl catalog to order a costume for her granddaughter's doll, she talked to a(n) _____ with whom she placed her order.
   a. order taker
   b. order getter
   c. missionary salesperson
   d. sales engineer
   e. fulfillment shipper

8. Inside order takers are also called:
   a. managers.
   b. directors.
   c. missionaries.
   d. salesclerks.
   e. go-getters.

9. Which of the following statements about order getting is true?
   a. A salesperson who is an order getter works 40 hours a week.
   b. Order getting requires a high degree of creativity and customer empathy.
   c. Order getters are sometimes called order clerks.
   d. Order getters never work by telephone.
   e. All of the above statements about order getting are true.

10. _____ is the practice of using the telephone rather than personal visits to contact customers.
   a. Cross-docking
   b. Cold canvassing
   c. Buttonholing
   d. Outbound telemarketing
   e. Lobbying

11. Safety expert Larry Shipiner works for TransWave International, a company that markets patented electronic sensors as an early warning device for locating potential problems with buried pipelines. Shipiner discusses pipeline safety issues with gas, oil, and water companies and explains new federal regulations on pipeline maintenance. He determines what potential safety problems exist, but he does not solicit orders—that is done by a sales team that designs a warning system to meet the specifications of the buyer. Shipiner is an example of a(n):
   a. sales support tech.
   b. inside order taker.
   c. sales manager.
   d. outside order taker.
   e. sales engineer.

12. Conference selling and seminar selling are:
    a. other names for outbound telemarketing.
    b. two types of team selling.
    c. most commonly used in transactional exchanges.
    d. sales training methods in which a new salesperson learns how to sell by observing his or her sales manager sell.
    e. two methods of selling that do not require the salesperson to use a close.

13. The increasing importance of nurturing long-term and widespread relationships with customers has led many firms to adopt a selling approach that uses several professionals to make a sale and win a contract. This approach is called:
    a. cooperative selling.
    b. team selling.
    c. missionary selling.
    d. account management.
    e. the augmented salesforce approach.

14. The first step in the personal selling process is the:
    a. closing.
    b. follow-up.
    c. prospecting.
    d. preapproach.
    e. approach.

15. At which stage in the personal selling process does a salesperson gain the prospect's attention?
    a. prospecting
    b. preapproach
    c. introduction
    d. initial canvassing
    e. approach

16. During the prospecting stage of the personal selling process, the salesperson will typically locate three types of prospects. They are:
    a. innovators, adopters, and laggards.
    b. innovators, users, and nonusers.
    c. major, minor, and potentially major prospects.
    d. leads, prospects, and qualified prospects.
    e. new-buy, modified new-buy, and straight rebuy.

17. Roman, Inc. is a company that makes gifts and collectibles. When its southeastern sales rep is driving through a community on her way to make a sales call, she looks for small independent florists and gift shops. When she finds a retailer she knows is not carrying Roman products, she stops and makes a sales call. The company's sales rep uses _____ to find prospects.
    a. stimulus response selling
    b. the preapproach
    c. cold canvassing
    d. cross-docking
    e. traffic generation

18. During the _____ stage of the personal selling process, the salesperson may try to learn what kind of personality the prospect has, whether the prospect favors a particular sports team, or has no interests outside the company.
    a. closing
    b. follow-up
    c. prospecting
    d. preapproach
    e. approach

19. At the _____ stage in the personal selling process, a salesperson gains a prospect's attention, stimulates interest, and builds the foundation for the sales presentation itself.
    a. prospecting
    b. preapproach
    c. approach
    d. qualifying
    e. trial close

20. Suggestive selling is an example of:
    a. an unethical mode of selling.
    b. stimulus-response selling.
    c. a perfect application of formula selling.
    d. enterprise selling.
    e. a need-satisfaction sales presentation.

21. A waitress at a Cracker Barrel restaurant is using _____ when she asks a family if they have left any room for dessert.
    a. stimulus-response selling
    b. formula-selling
    c. need-satisfaction
    d. consultative selling
    e. a transactional sales presentation

22. Jason is a new salesperson who sells refurbished amusement park rides that are found in malls and shopping centers. As he was in the middle of his sales presentation, the mall owner's secretary interrupted with an important message. When the owner told Jason to continue, Jason had to start over at the very beginning of his sales presentation because he was using a _____ sales presentation.
    a. formula selling
    b. leading question
    c. need-satisfaction
    d. suggestive selling
    e. stimulus-response

23. Which of the following is NOT an example of a typical method a salesperson could use to handle an objection?
    a. postpone the objection
    b. stimulate further objections
    c. deny the objection
    d. accept the objection
    e. agree with the objection and neutralize it

24. As a salesperson asks questions about a prospect's office operations, the prospect asks, "What I really want is quality bond paper at the lowest price I can get." The salesperson stops asking questions and pulls out a comparative price list that shows the company's paper is the lowest priced on the market. The salesperson has engaged in:
        a. adaptive selling.
        b. suggestive selling.
        c. formula selling.
        d. consultative selling.
        e. relationship selling.

25. The _____ is a selling format that emphasizes probing and listening by salespeople to identify what prospective buyers are interested in , want, and need.
        a. formula selling presentation
        b. stimulus-response presentation
        c. need-satisfaction presentation
        d. modified rebuy presentation
        e. straight rebuy presentation

26. Which of the following statements should the salesperson use to agree with and neutralize an objection?
        a. "I think I might be able to explain that better to you after showing you this diagram."
        b. "Yes, you're right, it is lighter, but that is done intentionally to make your work easier."
        c. "That's true. It does have a shorter shelf life, but that hasn't really been a problem. It is so popular it never gets to stay on the shelf that long anyway."
        d. "Where did you hear that? Your source must have erroneous information."
        e. "As I was saying, . . . "

27. When marketing to Asian countries, global marketers must be aware that a "yes" may have multiple meanings in these countries. A "yes" used by a prospect from an Asian culture can:
        a. convey that a presentation is understood and agreed to.
        b. convey that a presentation is understood but not agreed to.
        c. simply an acknowledgment that the other person is talking but the listener does not understand the communication.
        d. convey that a presentation is understood but other people must be consulted before any commitment is possible.
        e. mean any or all of the above.

28. Haas and Wilkerson is the largest independently-owned provider of entertainment insurance in the U.S. The company's salesperson has just finished presenting her sales presentation to a rodeo promoter and has asked, "Do you want coverage to start on the day of setup or the day the events are actually held?" The Hass and Wilkerson salesperson has just engaged in which step of the personal selling process?
        a. closing
        b. follow-up
        c. prospecting
        d. preapproach
        e. approach

29. Haas and Wilkerson is the largest independently-owned provider of entertainment insurance in the U.S. The company's salesperson has just about finished presenting her sales presentation to a rodeo promoter and has asked, "Do you want coverage to start on the day of setup or the day the events are actually held?" The Hass and Wilkerson salesperson has used a(n) _____ close.
        a. urgency
        b. empathetic
        c. trial
        d. amenable
        e. acquiescent

30. SRC Refrigeration markets refrigerated display cases for flowers. At the end of her sales presentation, the SRC salesperson asks, "Will you be wanting to make monthly payments of $75 with a 10 percent down payment or will you be writing a check for the full amount today?" She has just executed a(n):
        a. assumptive close.
        b. consultative close.
        c. proactive close.
        d. urgency close.
        e. adaptitve.

31. The _____ is a statement describing what is to be achieved and where and how the selling effort of salespeople is to be deployed.
        a. job description
        b. job specification
        c. sales task assignment
        d. marketing plan
        e. sales plan

32. Formulating the sales plan involves three tasks. The first step is _____. It is following by organizing the sales force and developing account management policies.
        a. hiring sales reps
        b. developing the marketing plan
        c. establishing the budget
        d. setting objectives
        e. strategic planning

33. The sales manager instructed the salesperson to "make five hundred customer contacts between January 1st and July 1st." The sales manager used a(n) _____ sales objective.
        a. output-related
        b. input-related
        c. behavior-related
        d. canvassing
        e. market-related

34. Which of the following statements describes an advantage achieved when replacing independent sales agents with an internal sales force?
        a. With independent agents, the selling company has greater flexibility in scheduling and transferring salespeople.
        b. Independent agents are more motivated to work on nonselling duties.
        c. The use of an internal sales forces is usually less costly with a lower sales volume
        d. With an internal sales force, there are additional types of rewards available for salespeople beyond just money, such as health and retirement benefits.
        e. All of the above statements describe advantages achieved when replacing independent sales agents with an internal sales force.

35. Which salesforce organizational structure minimizes travel time, expenses, and duplication of effort?
   a. management
   b. customer
   c. product
   d. geographical
   e. market

36. ABB is a Swiss-based manufacturer of industrial equipment with annual sales of $30 billion. At one time, ABB had a sales force that sold only generators, one that only sold boilers, another that only sold transformers, and so forth. Each of its salespeople was an expert on the items he or she sold. Its sales force was organized by:
   a. workload.
   b. customer type.
   c. geography.
   d. product.
   e. customer size.

37. _____ is a variation of the customer organization structure.
   a. Sales management
   b. Formula selling
   c. Adaptive selling
   d. Consultative selling
   e. Major account management

38. The workload method is:
   a. a common approach to setting sales quotas.
   b. a common approach for determining the size of the salesforce.
   c. similar to the break-even method of forecasting.
   d. is a fairly inflexible method of determining sales routes.
   e. none of the above.

39. _____ policies specify whom salespeople should contact, what kinds of selling and customer service activities should be engaged in, and how these activities should be carried out.
   a. Sales-response
   b. Territorial management
   c. Account management
   d. Customer contact
   e. Relationship upgrade

40. An account management policy would specify:
   a. what kind of selling activities should be used when a particular account.
   b. how the salesforce is to be recruited.
   c. how many salespeople should be recruited to meet organizational goals.
   d. how the salesforce will be compensated.
   e. what training methods will be used for the individual salespeople.

41. Emotional intelligence has five dimensions. They are self-motivation, self-awareness, the ability to manage one's emotions and impulses, empathy, and:
   a. social skills.
   b. the ability to psychoanalyze others.
   c. personal hygiene.
   d. personal habits.
   e. a desire for power.

42. Applied to recruiting and selecting salespeople, a _____ is a written document that describes job relationships and requirements that characterize each sales position.
   a. job description.
   b. sales plan
   c. job analysis
   d. performance contract
   e. personal performance plan

43. A straight salary compensation plan is a compensation plan:
   a. that assigns the same percentage of commission regardless of a product's size or value, frequency of sale, or difficulty level of sales effort.
   b. in which a salesperson is paid a specified salary plus a commission and/or bonus on sales or profits he or she generates.
   c. for determining a fair and equitable compensation plan that includes a weighted system for different types of items or different-sized territories.
   d. in which the salesperson is paid a fixed fee per week, month, or year.
   e. in which a salesperson's earnings are directly tied to the sales or profits he or she generates.

44. Which form of compensation provides salespeople with the greatest incentive to make sales?
   a. straight salary compensation plan
   b. straight commission compensation plan
   c. combination compensation plan
   d. weighted compensation plan
   e. delayed compensation plan

45. A combination compensation plan is a compensation plan:
   a. that assigns the same percentage of commission regardless of a product's size or value, frequency of sale, or difficulty level of sales effort.
   b. in which a salesperson is paid a specified salary plus a commission on sales or profits he or she generates.
   c. for determining fair and equitable compensation that includes a weighted system for different types of items or different sized territories.
   d. in which the salesperson is paid a fixed amount per week, month, or year.
   e. is accurately described by none of the above.

46. Which of the following is an example of a nonmonetary reward that might be used to motivate a salesperson to higher achievement?
   a. a bonus
   b. recognition at the annual sales meeting
   c. an expense account
   d. a cash payment for finding the most leads
   e. reimbursement for gas mileage

47. Which of the following is an example of a quantitative assessment that might be used to evaluate a salesperson's activities?
   a. the manager's feelings about the salesperson
   b. the salesperson's willingness to engage in nonselling activities
   c. the salesperson's code of ethics
   d. the number of sales closed successfully
   e. the salesperson's years of experience

48. Which of the following is an example of a subjective assessment that might be used to evaluate a salesperson's activities?
  a. the salesperson's product knowledge
  b. the number of accounts the salesperson calls on weekly
  c. the dollar value of the sales the salesperson has negotiated
  d. the number of cold calls the salesperson makes weekly
  e. the expenses incurred by the salesperson related to his or her sales

49. _____ is the use of technology designed to make the sales function more effective and efficient.
  a. Decentralization
  b. Field computerization
  c. Salesforce automation
  d. Commercial hacking
  e. Media convergence

50. Computer hardware and software for sales account analysis, time management, order processing, and follow-up are all examples of:
  a. e-management.
  b. resource requirements planning (rrp).
  c. enterprise resource planning (erp).
  d. partnering technology
  e. salesforce automation (sfa).

ANSWER KEY

Answers to Questions & Problems

Personal Selling in Marketing

1. Salespeople are critical links between the firm and its customers.

2. Salespeople are the company in the customer's eye.

3. It may play a dominant role in the firm's marketing program typically when a firm uses a push marketing strategy.

The Many Forms of Personal Selling

1. Order taker
2. Order getter
3. Order getter
4. Order taker
5. Order taker
6. Order taker
7. Order taker
8. Order getter
9. Order getter
10. Order getter

Sales Support Personnel

1. Missionary salespeople
2. Team selling
3. Sales engineer

The Personal Selling Process

1. Prospect
2. Lead
3. Qualified prospect

Example: D&B reports on new businesses

Preapproach and Approach Stage

Example: type of firm, workplace only or customer contact

Presentation

1. Formula selling
2. Stimulus-response
3. Need-satisfaction
4. Stimulus-response
5. Need-satisfaction
6. Formula selling

1. (individual work)

2. (individual work)

3. A need-satisfaction sales presentation involving adjusting the sales presentation to fit the selling situations.

4. A need-satisfaction sales presentation where the salesperson focuses on problem definition and serves as an expert on problem recognition and resolution.

Close

1. Trial close
2. Urgency close
3. Assumptive close

Follow-Up

Example: to make further sales in the future.

The Sales Management Process

1. Sales plan formulation
2. Sales plan implementation
3. Evaluation and control of salesforce

1. Setting objectives
2. Organizing the salesforce
3. Developing account management policies

Organizational Structure

1. Geography
2. Product/service
3. Customer
4. Customer
5. Geography
6. Product/service

$NS = (15000 \times 12 \times 3) / 1000 = 540$

Sales Plan Implementation

1. Salesforce recruitment and selection
2. Salesforce training
3. Salesforce motivation

1. Straight salary
2. Straight commission
3. Combination

Sales Force Evaluation and Control

1. Quantitative assessments
2. Behavioral evaluation

1. Quantitative
2. Quantitative
3. Behavioral
4. Behavioral
5. Behavioral
6. Quantitative
7. Quantitative
8. Quantitative

Salesforce Automation

Example:

Product—better product knowledge

Price—up-to-the-minute quotes

Promotion—better and more current presentations

Place—in touch with headquarters for tracking orders

Answers to Sample Multiple Choice Questions

1. e p. 528; LO 1	14. c p. 534; LO 3	26. c p. 537; LO 3	38. b p. 543; LO 4
2. d p. 528; LO 1	15. e p. 534; LO 3	27. e p. 538; LO 3	39. c p. 544; LO 4
3. d p. 528; LO 1	16. d p. 534; LO 3	28. a p. 538-539; LO 3	40. a p. 544; LO 4
4. d p. 530; LO 1	17. c p. 534-535; LO 3	29. c p. 538; LO 3	41. a p. 545; LO 4
5. d p. 530; LO 1	18. d p. 534; LO 3	30. a p. 539; LO 3	42. a p. 545; LO 4
6. b p. 531; LO 2	19. c p. 534; LO 3	31. e p. 540; LO 4	43. d p. 546; LO 4
7. a p. 531; LO 2	20. b p. 536; LO 3	32. d p. 540; LO 4	44. b p. 546; LO 4
8. d p. 531; LO 2	21. a p. 536; LO 3	33. b p. 540; LO 4	45. b p. 546; LO 4
9. b p. 531-532; LO 2	22. a p. 536-537; LO 3	34. d p. 541; LO 4	46. b p. 547; LO 4
10. d p. 532; LO 2	23. b p. 537-538; LO 3	35. d p. 541; LO 4	47. d p. 547; LO 4
11. e p. 532; LO 2	24. a p. 537; LO 3	36. d p. 543; LO 4	48. a p. 547; LO 4
12. b p. 532-533; LO 2	25. c p. 537; LO 3	37. e p. 543; LO 4	49. c p. 548; LO 4
13. b p. 533; LO 2			50. e p. 548; LO 4

Note: LO indicates learning objective.

CHAPTER 21

IMPLEMENTING INTERACTIVE AND MULTICHANNEL MARKETING

<u>Why is chapter 21 important</u>? With the phenomenal growth of Internet commerce comes the need to understand how to utilize all forms of electronic marketing. This chapter illustrates who is using the Internet and how to identify them. In addition, it shows how to recognize those products that are most likely to be successfully marketed on the Internet and how to utilize multichannel marketing to reach online consumers.

Interactive Marketing: Involves buyer-seller electronic communications in a computer-mediated environment in which the buyer controls the kind and amount of information received from the seller.

CHAPTER OUTLINE

I. CREATING CUSTOMER VALUE, RELATIONSHIPS, AND EXPERIENCES IN THE MARKETSPACE

    A. Customer Value Creation in Marketspace

    B. Interactivity, Individuality, and Customer Relationships in Marketspace
          1. Choiceboards
             a. choiceboard
             b. collaborative filtering
          2. Personalization
             a. permission marketing
    C. Creating an Online Customer Experience
          1. Context
          2. Content
          3. Customization
          4. Connection
          5. Communication
          6. Community
          7. Commerce

II. ONLINE CONSUMER BEHAVIOR AND MARKETING PRACTICE IN MARKETSPACE
    A. The Online Consumer
          1. Profiling the online consumer
          2. Online consumer lifestyle segmentation
             a. click-and-mortar
             b. hunter-gatherers
             c. brand loyalists
             d. time-sensitive materialists
             e. hooked, online, and single
             f. ebivalent newbies

B. Online Consumer Purchasing Behavior
    1. What online consumers buy
    2. Why consumers shop and buy online: The six C's
        a. convenient
           i. bots
           ii. eight-second rule
        b. choice
        c. customization
           i. customerization
        d. communication
           i. marketer-to-consumer email notification
           ii. consumer-to-marketer buying and service requests
           iii. consumer-to-consumer chat rooms and instant messaging
           iv. web communities
           v. blogs
           vi. spam
           vii. viral marketing
        e. cost
           i. dynamic pricing
        f. control
           i. portals
           ii. cookies
    3. When and where online consumers shop and buy

III. MULTICHANNEL MARKETING TO THE ONLINE CONSUMER

A. Integrating and Leveraging Multiple Channels with Multichannel Marketing

B. Implementing Multichannel Marketing
    1. transactional websites
    2. promotional websites

You should be able to place these key terms in the outline and be able to discuss them.

blogs	customerization	permission marketing
bots	dynamic pricing	personalization
choiceboard	eight-second rule	portals
collaborative filtering	interactive marketing	spam
cookies	multichannel marketing	viral marketing
customer experience	online consumers	Web communities

360

QUESTIONS & PROBLEMS

Interactivity, Individuality, and Customer Relationships in Marketspace

Choiceboards and collaborative filtering are tools of interactive marketing.

Identify the type of interactive marketing tool represented in the examples below:

1. Dell Computer Corporation sells PCs and servers from its Web site to companies nationwide. The site is arranged so buyers can select from computer systems designed for home, home office, small business, corporations, government, and education. _____

2. Amazon.com regularly sends emails to current customers suggesting titles that may be of interest to that person based on past purchases. _____

3. Ford allows a customer to "build" their car online and receive MSRP quotes based on what they build. _____

Creating an Online Customer Experience

The customer experience online is created by the seven web site design elements:

Context
Content
Customization
Connection
Communication
Community
Commerce

While each of these is present in most web sites, certain elements are emphasized based on the objectives of the company for its web site. Pick a web site and analyze each of the elements present. Which element is most important or most prominent in the site you chose?

Online Consumer Lifestyle Segmentation

Online consumers are segmented by six different lifestyles:

Click-and-mortar
Hunter-gathers
Brand loyalists
Time-sensitive materialists
Hooked, online, and single
Ambivalent newbies

Match the situations below with the online lifestyle described.

1. Now that her first child has left for college, Kim goes online to see where she can find the best deal on wallpaper and window dressings to redecorate the now empty bedroom. _____

2. John has just heard music from a new CD and decides he needs it immediately. He goes online to check the inventory of the local Best Buy location. Discovering it is in stock, he immediately goes to the store to purchase the CD. _____

3. Dorothy just remembered her mother's birthday and immediately goes online to order a present to be sent out for overnight delivery. _____

4. Bill spends much of his free time playing games, bidding on eBay items, and in general doing everything he can online. _____

5. Irene regularly shops at Clearwater Creek and Land's End through their online stores. She feels they have the highest quality at the lowest prices. _____

6. Mary just started using the Internet and loves to look up various ailments for which she may have symptoms. _____

What and Why Consumers Buy Online

Consumers prefer to buy online for six reasons. These are identified as the "Six Cs" and they are:

Convenience
Choice
Cost
Customization
Communication
Control

Identify the reason behind each of the following consumer actions:

1. Amazon.com gives consumers the availability of millions of book titles, including textbooks.

_____

2. The Chicago Cubs Web site offers fans the ability to ask questions of players and management and talk baseball with other Cub fans. _____

3. Dell Computer Corporation will let you "build your own computer" at their Web site.

_____

4. Southwest Airlines offers bonus miles and special ticket prices for booking flights online.

_____

5. Expedia.com allows consumers to compare fares, flights, and availability of all airlines.

_____

6. Banks offering Internet banking allow customers to manage their bank accounts 24 hours a day, 365 days a year. _____

CAN YOU PASS THE TEST?
Sample Multiple Choice Questions

1. When buyers and sellers engage in exchange relationships in a tangible environment inhabited by people, facilities (stores and offices), and physical objects, they are in:
> a. the traditional marketplace.
> b. the marketspace.
> c. a e-commerce storefront.
> d. a virtual shopping mall.
> e. an exchange portal.

2. Which of the following statements about marketspace is true?
> a. In terms of economic significance, marketspace is more important than traditional marketplaces.
> b. Marketspace retailers are unable to create time and place utility like traditional marketplaces.
> c. The greatest marketspace opportunity for marketers lies in its potential to create form utility.
> d. Marketspace has eliminated the need for comparison shopping.
> e. Marketspace has eliminated the need for market customization.

3. The greatest marketspace opportunity for marketers lies in its:
> a. potential to create form utility.
> b. ability to make time and place utility seem irrelevant.
> c. quick fulfillment potential.
> d. economic strength.
> e. location in the retail life cycle.

4. Although the economic significance of electronic commerce is small compared to the traditional marketplace, it has captured the eye and imagination of marketers because the marketspace:
> a. will totally replace the traditional marketplace in the near future.
> b. is less competitive than the traditional marketplace.
> c. offers unique possibilities for customer value creation that exceed those of the traditional marketplace.
> d. mainly attracts male customers.
> e. all the above.

5. Which of the following examples shows how electronic commerce creates customer value through form utility?
> a. Recreational Equipment, an outdoor gear marketer, receives 35 percent of its orders on its website between 10:00 p.m. and 7:00 a.m. when its retail stores are closed.
> b. Twenty percent of book sales at Amazon.com are from buyers who live outside the U.S.
> c. Travelocity.com provides almost immediate access to and confirmation of travel arrangements and accommodations.
> d. Bluefly.com, an apparel company, encourages customers to develop their own catalog free of unwanted items.
> e. All of the above.

6. Individuality and interactivity are important capabilities that marketers derive from Internet/Web technology. Both capabilities are important building blocks for buyer-seller relationships. For these relationships to develop, companies must:
> a. make customers understand they have a say in the kind of goods and services they buy.
> b. listen to customers and respond to their needs.
> c. empower customers to take charge of the timing and extent of the interaction.
> d. treat their customers as individuals.
> e. do all of the above.

7. _____ involves two-way buyer-seller electronic communication in a computer-mediated environment in which the buyer controls the kind and amount of information received from the seller.
    a. Integrated marketing communication
    b. Direct selling
    c. The e-communication channel
    d. Interactive marketing
    e. Telemarketing

8. Educational publisher Irwin/McGraw-Hill allows instructors to visit is Primus site and publish customized books comprised of content from its published books. An instructor can select the information he or she wants included in a text. Irwin/McGraw-Hill will deliver the hardcopy of the text for the instructor's students in about four weeks. The selection of text material is made possible through the use of a:
    a. seller menu.
    b. seller cookie.
    c. content screen.
    d. choiceboard.
    e. bot.

9. Collaborative filtering is a(n):
    a. form of mass marketing.
    b. example of a cause-related marketing activity.
    c. electronic buying center.
    d. electronic gatekeeper.
    e. process that automatically groups people with similar buying intentions, preferences, and behaviors.

10. After visiting Mystery Guild's website a few times, users notice that the books featured are the kind of mysteries they have bought or looked at before. This is the result of:
    a. personalization.
    b. content analysis.
    c. mass marketing.
    d. multichannel websites.
    e. market aggregation.

11. Educational publisher Irwin/McGraw-Hill allows instructors to visit is Primus site and publish customized books comprised of content from its published books. An instructor can select the information he or she wants included in a text. Irwin/McGraw-Hill will deliver the hardcopy of the text for the instructor's students in about four weeks. This is an example of a high degree of:
    a. choiceboards.
    b. personalization.
    c. collaborative filtering.
    d. hierarchical individualization.
    e. media convergence.

12. _____ is the solicitation of a consumer's consent to receive e-mail and advertising based on personal data supplied by the consumer.
    a. Opt-out marketing
    b. Seller personalization
    c. E-mail intermediation
    d. E-mail facilitation
    e. Permission marketing

13. When Beth visited the AmericanGirl website to buy a doll for her daughter, she was asked if she wanted to receive e-mail that would notify her of new product offerings. By asking if it could send her e-mails, AmericanGirl.com was using:
     a. direct selling.
     b. connectivity.
     c. context communication.
     d. empathetic communication.
     e. permission marketing.

14. From an interactive marketing perspective, _____ is defined as the sum total of the interactions a customer has with a company's website from the initial look at a home page through the entire purchase decision process.
     a. consumer digitalization
     b. website encounter
     c. customer experience
     d. the connectivity of a site
     e. interactive marketing

15. Which of the following is NOT an example of a major design element used when creating a website?
     a. connection
     b. consensus
     c. customization
     d. community
     e. commerce

16. In terms of the customer experience, content is defined as the:
     a. text, pictures, sound, and videos that the website contains.
     b. site's capabilities to enable commercial transactions.
     c. degree the site is linked to other sites.
     d. layout of the site.
     e. ways the site enables user-to-user communication.

17. A website designer who is concerned about having the right links to other sites available for visitors to the site being designed, is concerned about:
     a. community.
     b. commerce.
     c. content.
     d. communication.
     e. connection.

18. The _____ of a website refers to its aesthetic appeal and functional look and feel reflected in site layout and design.
     a. content
     b. community
     c. commerce
     d. context
     e. customization

19. Half.com is an Internet source for new and used books, videos, and CDs that are sold at about half the price you would find at full-price retailers. If a book you desire is currently not available at the website, you can put the title on your wish list. As soon as someone lists the book for sale, half.com will e-mail you so you can buy it. Half.com's customer experience includes:
     a. convenience.
     b. connection.
     c. control.
     d. community.
     e. communication.

20. Which of the following profiles would most likely describe an online consumer?
     a. a 20-something high-school graduate earning $18,000 annually
     b. a 30-something college graduate with an annual income of $65,000
     c. a 50-something traditional housewife with an annual income under $35,000
     d. a 70-something retired postal worker receiving $45,000 in annual retirement benefits
     e. all of the above

21. Which of the following statements about online consumers is true?
     a. Online consumers are the subsegment of all Internet/Web users who employ this technology to research products and to make purchases.
     b. Fewer than 20 percent of Internet/Web users have ever even considered becoming online consumers.
     c. As a group, online consumers tend to be poorer than all Internet/Web users who employ this technology to research products and to make purchases.
     d. All Internet/Web users who employ this technology to research products and to make purchases are a subsegment of online consumers.
     e. As a group, online consumers tend to be less well-educated than the general U.S. population.

22. The largest online consumer lifestyle segment consists of:
     a. singles over the age of 60.
     b. teenagers.
     c. female who browse the internet but purchase in stores.
     d. males between the ages of 18 and 35.
     e. well-to-do grandparents.

23. Which of the online consumer lifestyle segments spends the most time online?
     a. ebivalent newbies
     b. click-and-mortar
     c. brand loyalists
     d. hooked, online, and single
     e. time-sensitive materialists

24. There are six general goods and services categories that dominate online consumer buying today and for the foreseeable future. Which of the following is an example of those categories?
     a. items for which audio or video demonstrations are important
     b. items for which product information is extremely important
     c. items that are regularly purchased and where convenience is very important
     d. highly standardized products for which information about price is important
     e. all of the above items

25. Which of the following product categories is expected to account for the largest proportion of total online consumer sales?
      a. travel reservations
      b. clothing and accessories
      c. food and beverages
      d. music and books
      e. ticket event sales

26. _____ are electronic shopping agents or robots that comb websites to compare prices and product or service features.
      a. Connectors
      b. Linking sites
      c. Permission marketers
      d. Bots
      e. Portals

27. Bots contribute to the convenience of online shopping because they:
      a. reduce time spent online.
      b. allow customers to make online comparisons of prices and product features.
      c. permit customers to design one-of-a-kind items that fit their specific needs.
      d. allow customers to engage in an electronic dialogue with marketers.
      e. offer customers almost any product or service they want.

28. Consumers typically refer to six reasons why they shop and buy online. Which of the following is NOT one of those reasons?
      a. content
      b. convenience
      c. control
      d. cost
      e. choice

29. Which of the following characteristics of online shopping contributes to its convenience?
      a. Customers don't have to fight traffic, find a parking space, walk long aisles, or stand in store check-out lines.
      b. Consumers can avail themselves of numerous websites for almost any product or service they want.
      c. Consumers who prefer one-of-a-kind items that fit their specific needs can create them online.
      d. Consumers can engage in an electronic dialogue with marketers.
      e. Consumers are in charge in the marketspace.

30. Too much emphasis on context can cause some computer systems to be slow about downloading a website. When this happens, it probably means the website designer forgot the:
      a. principles of transactional exchange.
      b. eight-second rule.
      c. 80/20 rule.
      d. Golden Rule.
      e. law of unforeseen consequences.

31. Online marketers believe consumers will abandon their efforts to enter and navigate a website if download takes longer than the customer thinks it should. When the customer is convinced the website takes too long to download, the site no longer offers the online consumer _____, one of the six reasons why people shop and buy online.
     a. choice
     b. cost
     c. convenience
     d. communication
     e. customerization

32. Consumers cite cost as one of the reasons they prefer to buy online because:
     a. shopping in the marketspace allows for easier price comparisons.
     b. the majority of the most popular items bought online can be purchased at the same price or cheaper than in retail stores.
     c. the time and effort of shopping is reduced.
     d. external search costs are lower.
     e. all the above.

33. Suppose you visit www.cdnow.com and purchase a Shania Twain CD. During your visit, you click on the Album Advisor feature, which instantly creates a list of other CDs that someone like you, who likes Shania Twain, might like. The Album Advisor has the greatest influence on which of the reasons consumers give for shopping online?
     a. convenience
     b. cost
     c. communication
     d. customization
     e. control

34. _____ can take the form of electronic junk mail or unsolicited email.
     a. Bots
     b. A web community
     c. A home page
     d. Spam
     e. Interstitials

35. Bolt.com is a popular online destination for people between the ages of 15 and 24. The main reason users come to this website is to communicate with their peers and voice their opinions through chat rooms, message boards, instant messaging, and polling. Topics of discussion range from school to music to dating. Bolt.com is an example of:
     a. spam.
     b. a shopping bot.
     c. a web community.
     d. interactive linking.
     e. a web cafe.

36. Viral marketing is an Internet/Web-enabled _____ strategy.
     a. pricing
     b. distribution
     c. promotion
     d. production
     e. product

37. In an online survey, La Senza, a Montreal-based apparel chain, asked women about their clothes. The query was part of an online survey designed to drive traffic to the company Web site, www.lasenza.com. The survey asked participants several multiple-choice questions and used the answers to describe the participant's personality style. Contestants, who sent the survey to at least five friends and got them to enter it, were then entered in a drawing to win a $300 personalized lingerie wardrobe. Names and information gathered were put into a database for later marketing efforts. This survey is an example of:
    a. opt-out marketing.
    b. customerization.
    c. viral marketing.
    d. niche marketing.
    e. permission marketing.

38. Internet/Web-enabled software permits _____, the practice of changing prices for products and services in real time in response to supply and demand conditions.
    a. equilibrium pricing
    b. illegal price fixing
    c. price lining
    d. price potentialities
    e. dynamic pricing

39. Portals help consumers exercise greater control over the online purchase decision process because a portal:
    a. is the means by which online consumers engage in electronic dialogue with marketers.
    b. gives online consumers access to information that enables them to make purchase decisions on their own terms and conditions.
    c. records an online consumer's visit to a website.
    d. contains information about online consumers' product preferences.
    e. all the above.

40. When a user subscribes to an online financial newsletter and provides all the requested information, he or she will be informed that the website will set a cookie and that it will not be necessary to register on the next visit. This means the:
    a. marketer will download a file onto the user's computer.
    b. user will be rewarded on his or her next visit.
    c. user will stay connected to the website in perpetuity.
    d. marketer will put the user's name and information in a public database.
    e. user cannot visit the site again unless invited.

41. Cookies represent a potential loss of privacy to online consumers because they:
    a. contain personal data, financial information, and consumers' credit card numbers.
    b. make a website user friendly.
    c. help marketers create customized product offerings that fit customers' expressed product preferences.
    d. allow online consumers to engage in interactive communication with marketers.
    e. none of the above.

42. Which of the following statements about online consumer shopping behavior is true?
    a. The busiest shopping day online is Wednesday.
    b. Consumers who go online are more likely to buy than to simply browse.
    c. There is typically very little online shopping during what is considered to be normal working hours.
    d. Saturday is the busiest shopping day for both online and traditional retailers.
    e. Users are just as likely to visit websites selling health and beauty aids and clothing whether they are at work or at home.

43. _____ is the blending of different communication and delivery channels that are mutually reinforcing in attracting, retaining, and building relationships with consumers who and ship and buy in the traditional marketplace and marketspace.
    a. Viral marketing
    b. Guerrilla marketing
    c. Multichannel marketing
    d. Integrated marketing communication
    e. Cross-transactional commerce

44. Two general applications of websites based on their intended purposes are:
    a. transformational and informational.
    b. informational and transactional.
    c. content-oriented and context-oriented.
    d. transactional and promotional.
    e. business and consumer.

45. The multichannel marketing multiplier refers to:
    a. the geometrically increasing costs associated with maintaining both a traditional retail outlet and a retail website.
    b. the increase in the number of browsers a retailer has when it uses dual distribution.
    c. how quickly store awareness increases as a result of a multichannel marketing strategy.
    d. the speed with which competitors enter the market when a retailer leaves one channel unused.
    e. an increase in spending as a result of a retailer being available in more than one channel.

46. _____ websites are essentially electronic storefronts.
    a. Promotional
    b. Transactional
    c. Informational
    d. E-commerce
    e. Transformational

47. Cisco Systems' website, Cisco Connection Online, generates about 60 percent of Cisco's sales. Cisco Connection Online is an example of a(n):
    a. promotional website.
    b. web community.
    c. transactional website.
    d. portal.
    e. information website.

48. Why do manufacturers of consumer products typically avoid using transactional websites?
    a. threat of channel conflict
    b. threat of losing channel control
    c. a highly influential channel champion
    d. loss of freedom to use dynamic pricing strategy
    e. all of the above

49. Maytag has created a website where potential customers can find the answers to the questions most asked during the appliance purchase process. Maytag uses a(n) _____ website.
    a. promotional
    b. transactional
    c. bot
    d. e-commerce
    e. transformational

50. Proctor & Gamble maintains separate websites for its leading brands to generate interest in and trial of its products and services. Proctor & Gamble uses:
    a. bot
    b. promotional
    c. transactional
    d. investor
    e. employee

ANSWER KEY

Answers to Questions & Problems

Interactivity, Individuality, and Customer Relationships in Marketspace

1. Choiceboards
2. Choiceboards
3. Collaborative filtering

Online Consumer Lifestyle Segmentation

1. Hunter-gathers
2. Click-and-mortar
3. Time-sensitive materialists
4. Hooked, online, and single
5. Brand loyalists
6. Ebivalent newbies

What and Why Consumers Buy Online

1. Choice
2. Communication
3. Customization
4. Cost
5. Control
6. Convenience

Answers to Sample Multiple Choice Questions

1. a p. 558; LO 1	14. c p. 562; LO 1	26. d p. 567; LO 4	38. e p. 570; LO 4
2. c p. 559; LO 1	15. b p. 562; LO 1	27. b p. 567; LO 4	39. b p. 570; LO 4
3. a p. 559; LO 1	16. a p. 562; LO 1	28. a p. 568; LO 4	40. a p. 570-571; LO 4
4. c p. 558; LO 1	17. e p. 562; LO 1	29. a p. 567; LO 4	41. a p. 570-571; LO 4
5. d p. 559; LO 1	18. d p. 562; LO 1	30. b p. 567; LO 4	42. a p. 571-572; LO 4
6. e p. 560; LO 1	19. e p. 563; LO 1	31. c p. 567; LO 4	43. c p. 572; LO 5
7. d p. 560; LO 1	20. b p. 565; LO 2	32. e p. 570; LO 4	44. d p. 573; LO 5
8. d p. 560; LO 1	21. a p. 564; LO 2	33. d p. 568; LO 4	45. e p. 573; LO 5
9. e p. 560; LO 1	22. c p. 565; LO 2	34. d p. 569; LO 4	46. b p. 573; LO 5
10. a p. 560; LO 1	23. d p. 565; LO 2	35. c p. 569; LO 4	47. c p. 573; LO 5
11. b p. 560; LO 1	24. e p. 566-567; LO 3	36. c p. 569; LO 4	48. a p. 574; LO 5
12. e p. 561; LO 1	25. a p. 567; LO 3	37. c p. 569-570; LO 4	49. a p. 574; LO 5
13. e p. 561; LO 1			50. b p. 574; LO 5

Note: LO indicates learning objective.

CHAPTER 22

PULLING IT ALL TOGETHER: THE STRATEGIC MARKETING PROCESS

Why is Chapter 22 important? This chapter brings together all of the marketing mix strategies examining their effective use in successfully meting the company's goals. It then looks into the planning and implementation of these strategies and the controls that make them more effective.

Strategic Marketing Process: The activities whereby an organization allocates its marketing mix resources to reach its target markets.

CHAPTER OUTLINE

I. MARKETING BASICS: DOING WHAT WORKS AND ALLOCATING RESOURCES

    A. Allocating Marketing Resources Using Sales Response Functions
        1. Maximizing incremental revenue minus incremental cost

    B. Allocating Marketing Resources in Practice
        1. Share points

    C. Resource Allocation and the Strategic Marketing Process

II. THE PLANNING PHASE OF THE STRATEGIC MARKETING PROCESS

    A. Variety of Marketing Plans
        1. Long range marketing plans
        2. Annual marketing plans

    B. Marketing Planning Frameworks: The Search for Growth
        1. Porter's generic business strategies
            a. cost leadership strategy
            b. differentiation strategy
            c. cost focus strategy
            d. differentiation focus strategy
        2. Profit enhancement options
            a. increase revenues
            b. decrease costs
            c. do both
        3. Multi-product synergies
            a. marketing synergies
                 i. market-product concentration
                 ii. market specialization
                 iii. product specialization
                 iv. selective specialization
                 v. full coverage
            b. R & D and manufacturing synergies

C. Some Planning & Strategy Lessons
   1. Guidelines for an effective marketing plan
      a. set measurable, achievable goals
      b. use a base of facts and valid assumptions
      c. utilize simple, but clear and specific, plans
      d. have complete and feasible plans
      e. make plans controllable and flexible
   2. Problems in marketing planning and strategy
      a. plans may be based on very poor assumptions about environmental factors
      b. planners and their plans may have lost sight of their customer's needs
      c. too much time and effort may be spent on data collection and writing the plans
      d. line operating managers often feel no sense of ownership in implementing the plans
   3. Balancing value and values in strategic marketing plans
      a. value-based planning
      b. value-driven strategies

III. THE IMPLEMENTATION PHASE OF THE STRATEGIC MARKETING PROCESS

   A. Increasing Emphasis on Marketing Implementation
   B. Improving Implementation of Marketing Programs
      1. Communicate goals and the means of achieving them
      2. Have a responsible program champion willing to act
      3. Reward successful program implementation
      4. Take action and avoid "paralysis by analysis"
      5. Foster open communication to surface the problem
      6. Schedule precise tasks, responsibilities and deadlines
         a. action item lists
            i. the task
            ii. name of person responsible for accomplishing task
            iii. the date by which the task is to be finished
         b. program schedules
            i. identify main tasks
            ii. determine the time to complete each task
            iii. arranging activities to meet deadline
            iv. assigning responsibilities to complete each task

   B Organizing for Marketing
      1. Line versus staff and divisional groups
         a. line positions
         b. staff positions
         c. divisional groupings
            i. product line groupings
            ii. functional groupings
            iii. geographical groupings
            iv. market-based groupings
      2. Role of product manager

IV. THE CONTROL PHASE OF THE STRATEGIC MARKETING PROCESS

    A. Marketing Control Process
          1. Measuring results
          2. Taking marketing actions

    B. Sales Analysis
          1. customer characteristics
          2. product characteristics
          3. geographic region
          4. order size
          5. price or discount class
          6. commission to sales representative

    C. Profitability Analysis and ROI Marketing

You should be able to place these key terms in the outline and be able to discuss them.

action item list	**geographical groupings**	**ROI marketing**
cost focus (generic) strategy	**line positions**	**sales analysis**
cost leadership (generic) strategy	**market-based groupings**	**sales component analysis**
differentiation (generic) strategy	**product line groupings**	**sales response function**
differentiation focus (generic) strategy	**product or program champion**	**share points**
functional groupings	**profitability analysis**	**staff positions**
generic business strategy		

QUESTIONS & PROBLEMS

ALLOCATING MARKETING RESOURCES IN PRACTICE

Many firms use share points or percentage points as the basis of comparison to allocate marketing resources effectively.

List the three important types of information a marketing manager must estimate in order to make resource allocation decisions using share points:

1._____

2._____

3._____

Marketing managers must decide how much it would take (in time, money, energy) in order to achieve an additional market share point. This is especially important in companies that have multiple businesses within their own company, since the effort required to gain an additional point in one area may not be the same as the effort required to gain a percentage point in another.

THE PLANNING PHASE OF THE STRATEGIC MARKETING PROCESS

Annual marketing plans deal with the marketing goals and strategies for a product, product line, or entire firm for a single year, whereas long-range marketing plans cover from two to five years into the future.

Identify the following as annual marketing plans or long-range marketing plans:

1. Ford's introduction of the small Lincoln sport utility vehicle, the Aviator._____
_____

2. Fuddrucker's plans to enter the Mexican food fast food market at all their locations by the year 2005.
_____

3. Pepsi's rollout of their new corporate colors._____

4. General Motors plan for additional new models of Cadillac to appeal to younger buyers._____
_____

MARKET-PRODUCT SYNERGIES

Marketing synergies can act as a framework for relating market segments to products offered or potential marketing actions by a firm. This type of evaluation suggests several alternative strategies. These are:

Market-product concentration
Market specialization
Product specialization
Selective specialization
Full coverage

Indicate which marketing strategies are being used by the following products:

1. Kellogg's—cereals_____

2. Dr. Pepper—soft drinks_____

3. Kraft Foods—food_____

4. Hewlett Packard—printers_____

5. Netscape_____

GUIDELINES OF AN EFFECTIVE MARKETING PLAN

"Plans are nothing; planning is everything." - Dwight D. Eisenhower

List the five basic elements for effective market planning and plans:

1._____

2._____

3._____

4._____

5._____

PROBLEMS IN MARKETING PLANNING AND STRATEGY

List four common areas where problems can occur in the planning phase of a firm's strategic marketing process:

1._____

2._____

3._____

4._____

THE IMPLEMENTATION PHASE OF THE STRATEGIC MARKETING PROCESS

No magic formula exists to guarantee effective implementation of marketing plans. In fact, the answer seems to be equal parts of good management skills and practices.

List six guidelines for improving program implementation:

1._____

2._____

3._____

4._____

5._____

6._____

ORGANIZING FOR MARKETING

What are the major differences between line positions and staff positions?_____
_____

There are four commonly used organizational groupings:

Product line groupings
Functional groupings
Geographical groupings
Market-based groupings

Match the correct term to the statements listed below:

1. Organization based on the different business activities performed with in the firm, such as marketing, finance, and manufacturing._____

2. Organization based upon assigning responsibility for a specific type of customer to a given unit.
_____

3. Organization based on the geographic region, for example, in terms of sales territory or responsibility.
_____

4. Organization based on specific product offerings._____

CAN YOU PASS THE TEST?
Sample Multiple Choice Questions

1. A _____ is a unique strength relative to competitors, often based on quality, time, cost, or innovation.
      a. distinctive parity
      b. sustainable dominance
      c. synergistic edge
      d. market dominance
      e. competitive advantage

2. A marketing manager would use the sales response function to:
      a. mentor organizational change.
      b. determine job descriptions for new marketing positions.
      c. compare the expense of marketing effort to the marketing results obtained.
      d. validate the timeliness of the organizational mission statement.
      e. create line and staff positions within the marketing department.

3. The relationship of annual marketing effort to annual sales revenue is assumed to be an S-shaped curve because the sales response function shows:
      a. that when demand diminishes, production costs rise.
      b. an additional $1 of marketing effort results in a far greater increases of sales revenue in the mid-range than at either end.
      c. the point at which total revenue and total cost are equal.
      d. decreasing costs as a result of marketing economies of scale.
      e. increasing costs as a result of the attempt to gain additional market share.

4. General Mills does extensive analysis using share points. The marketing manager for Wheaties wants to increase market share by 5 percent. Before allocating resources, General Mills must know:
      a. the current market share of Wheaties.
      b. the revenues associated with each point of market share.
      c. the contribution to profit for each share point.
      d. whether the addition of a new product will cannibalize other products in the line.
      e. all of the above.

5. When using share points to make marketing resource allocation decisions, marketing managers must estimate all of the following EXCEPT:
      a. corporate return on investment.
      b. market share for the product.
      c. revenues associated with each point of market share.
      d. the contribution to overhead and profit (or gross margin) of each share point.
      e. possible cannibalization effects on other products in the line.

6. Step 1 of the planning phase of the strategic marketing process is to:
      a. develop a marketing mix.
      b. conduct a situation analysis.
      c. estimate revenues in order to develop a budget.
      d. select target markets.
      e. determine positioning strategy.

7. Marketing plans that cover marketing activities from two to five years into the future are called:
   a. generic marketing strategies.
   b. long-range strategic plans.
   c. marketing strategies.
   d. long-range marketing plans.
   e. marketing tactics.

8. For which of the following industries is long-range planning most likely to go beyond five years?
   a. steel industry
   b. movie industry
   c. construction industry
   d. restaurant industry
   e. toy industry

9. Wal-Mart's sophisticated systems of regional warehouses and electronic data interchange with its suppliers has led to huge cost savings. It is following a:
   a. positioning strategy
   b. differentiation strategy
   c. cost leadership strategy
   d. cost focus strategy
   e. differentiation focus strategy

10. Vokswagen has achieved success targeting the "nostalgia segment," 35- to 55-year-old baby boomers, with its technology-laden New Beetle. Volkswagen is using a:
   a. differentiation strategy.
   b. cost leadership strategy.
   c. cost focus strategy.
   d. a diversification strategy.
   e. differentiation focus strategy.

11. Annual marketing plans:
   a. sequence the details of day-to-day planning implementation of a product strategy for an entire year.
   b. deal with marketing goals and strategies for a product, product line, or entire firm for a single year.
   c. forecast anticipated revenue for each year during a two to five year period.
   d. deal with marketing goals and strategies for a product, product line, or entire firm for two to five years.
   e. state results sought (such as sales, profits, market share, etc.) quantified for each year for a period of two to five years.

12. A _____ requires innovation and significant points of difference in product offerings, brand image, higher quality, advanced technology, or superior service in a relatively broad array of market segments.
   a. market aggregation strategy
   b. differentiation strategy
   c. cost leadership strategy
   d. cost focus strategy
   e. differentiation focus strategy

13. Southwest Airlines has successfully offered low fares between very restricted pairs of cities. It is using a:
      a. cost focus strategy.
      b. differentiation focus strategy.
      c. cost leadership strategy.
      d. differentiation strategy.
      e. positioning strategy.

14. A generic business strategy is:
      a. one that describes the day-to-day activities needed to implement a product strategy.
      b. a marketing program that deals with marketing goals and strategies for a product, product line, or entire firm for a single year.
      c. a general statement of results sought.
      d. a marketing program that deals with marketing goals and strategies for a product, product line, or entire firm for two to five years.
      e. one that can be adopted by any firm, regardless of the product or industry involved, to achieve a competitive advantage.

15. Based on relative competitive scope (broad target to narrow target) and source of competitive advantage (lower cost to differentiation), Porter's four generic business strategies are cost leadership, differentiation, cost focus, and:
      a. price leadership.
      b. diversification.
      c. quality focus.
      d. differentiation focus.
      e. reactive.

16. In the 1920s, the Ford Motor Company dominated the automotive industry. Henry Ford's low priced, mass produced Model T, available in only one color and with few options, was selling like hot cakes to car buyers. In order to combat Ford's success, General Motors offered automobiles in a variety of colors and with special features that were designed to fit the specific needs and wants of individual car buyers in many different segments of the market. By employing a _____ business strategy, General Motors developed a position that was very distinct from that of the Ford Motor Company.
      a. cost leadership strategy
      b. cost focus strategy
      c. differentiation strategy
      d. differentiation focus strategy
      e. innovation strategy

17. Ads for Wolverine boots and shoes emphasize the boots' comfort and ruggedness, with a company has high level of quality maintained since Wolverine started making footwear in 1883. Wolverine uses a(n) _____ strategy.
      a. cost leadership
      b. cost focus
      c. innovation
      d. differentiation focus
      e. market aggregation

18. America Online (AOL) acquired Time Warner and General Mills acquired Pillsbury to get:
    a. value-based marketing.
    b. a high sales response function.
    c. synergies.
    d. new retail outlets.
    e. value-added efficiency.

19. Walt Disney Co. pursued a _____ strategy following the success of the original Disneyland by expanding to Orlando, Tokyo, and Paris.
    a. market development
    b. product development
    c. differentiation
    d. diversification
    e. differentiation focus

20. Which of the following is an advantage inherent in the use of market-product grids?
    a. A market-product grid identifies potential supply-chain opportunities.
    b. A market-product grid highlights potential synergies.
    c. A market-product grid shows potential revenue losses caused by cannibalism.
    d. A market-product grid identifies potential advertising appeals.
    e. All of the above are advantages inherent in the use of market-product grids.

21. Which marketing strategy focuses its efforts on a single product line and market segment?
    a. full coverage
    b. market specialization
    c. product specialization
    d. selective specialization
    e. market-product concentration

22. Which marketing strategy involves targeting separate product lines for unique separate segments?
    a. full coverage
    b. market specialization
    c. product specialization
    d. selective specialization
    e. market-product concentration

23. _____ of marketing plans requires that people at all levels in the firm understand what, when, and how they are to accomplish their tasks.
    a. Downsizing
    b. The acculturation
    c. Effective execution
    d. A feasibility projection
    e. The hierarchical development

24. When developing a marketing plan, a business should:
    a. set measurable, achievable goals.
    b. utilize simple, but clear and specific, plans.
    c. make plans controllable and flexible.
    d. use a base of facts and valid assumptions.
    e. all of the above.

25. Two important trends likely to influence the strategic marketing process in the future are value-driven strategies and:
        a. value-based planning.
        b. e-planning.
        c. minimal inventory holding.
        d. outsourcing.
        e. more benchmarking.

26. Value-based planning combines marketing planning ideas and financial planning techniques to assess how much a division or a strategic business unit (SBU) contributes to:
        a. benchmarking efforts.
        b. realizing important societal needs.
        c. the elimination of cannibalization.
        d. the price of a company's stock (or shareholder wealth).
        e. downsizing.

27. _____ incorporate concerns for ethics, integrity, employee health and safety, and environmental safeguards with more common corporate values such as growth, profitability, customer service and quality.
        a. Value-driven strategies
        b. Value-based plans
        c. Value analyses
        d. Market audits
        e. Value-added marketing tactics

28. Most of the failures of dot.com companies can be traced to:
        a. good planning and implementation, but poor controls.
        b. poor planning and poor implementation.
        c. good planning but poor implementation.
        d. poor planning that could not be helped by good implementation.
        e. a lack of control systems.

29. As the marketing manager for gizmos at Acme Products Inc., you notice sales have been below expectations. Based on the results of a customer satisfaction survey recently conducted, you discover consumers want Acme gizmos to have more features, which will make them a better value relative to comparable offerings by competitors. However, on the positive side, customers stated Acme gizmos were (1) widely available in sufficient quantities, (2) made with high quality materials, (3) sold by knowledgeable salespeople at the appropriate retail outlets where they would shop for gizmos, and (4) the average response time for the toll-free telephone hot-line for customer questions and complaints was significantly less than expected. Based on this information, you should conclude Acme used:
        a. an appropriate marketing strategy and effective implementation.
        b. an inappropriate marketing strategy but effective implementation.
        c. an appropriate marketing strategy but ineffective implementation.
        d. an inappropriate marketing strategy and ineffective implementation.
        e. an appropriate marketing strategy and effective control.

30. A _____ is a person within a firm who is able and willing to cut red tape and move a product or program forward.
        a. channel captain
        b. marketing mediator
        c. program director
        d. product champion
        e. program facilitator

31. To improve the implementation of the strategic marketing process, a company should:
    a. have a program champion.
    b. communicate goals and the means of achieving them.
    c. foster open communication to foster problem discovery.
    d. reward successful program implementation.
    e. do all of the above.

32. Saturn's management and employees avoided the pitfalls associated with the "NIH syndrome" by:
    a. using a no-increase-in-hiring policy.
    b. using a sequential process of manufacturing design.
    c. studying cars made by other manufacturers to find product ideas that could be used with the saturn.
    d. avoiding the use of benchmarking.
    e. consciously avoiding any comparisons with japanese automakers.

33. The _____ has three columns—the task, the name of the person who is to perform the task, and the date when the task should be completed.
    a. Gantt chart
    b. PERT chart
    c. job specification
    d. job description
    e. action item list

34. Program schedules:
    a. are similar to action item lists.
    b. show the relationships through time of the various tasks to be accomplished.
    c. can be done using gantt charts.
    d. require that sequential and concurrent tasks be identified.
    e. are accurately described by all of the above.

35. People in _____ positions have the responsibility to advise people in line positions but cannot issue them direct orders.
    a. staff
    b. line
    c. stakeholder
    d. management
    e. supervisory

36. Those in staff positions have the authority and responsibility to advise people in line positions:
    a. and can recommend salary and benefit adjustments for them.
    b. but cannot issue direct orders to them.
    c. but must clear all such communication with their superiors.
    d. and must clear all such communication with the corporate human resources department.
    e. but cannot fraternize with them.

37. A company that uses an organizational structure based on _____ uses product line groupings.
    a. product offerings
    b. areas such as marketing, finance, and r&d
    c. areas of geographic location
    d. method of distribution
    e. specific types of customers

38. Pillsbury organizes by _____ groupings in which a unit is responsible for specific product offerings.
    a. market-based
    b. competitor-based
    c. supply-based
    d. functional
    e. product line

39. An organizational structure that is based on specific customer segments, such as the banking, health care, or manufacturing segments, is using:
    a. product line grouping.
    b. geographical grouping.
    c. functional grouping.
    d. matrix organization
    e. market-based grouping.

40. Within DuPoint's textile fiber department, there is a separate product manager for rayon, acetate, orlon, nylon, and Dacron. Each product manager is responsible for selling to the various markets in which the textile could be used such as clothing, furniture, or floor coverings. Its other product divisions have similar structures. DuPont uses _____ to organize the company.
    a. product line groupings
    b. geographical groupings
    c. functional groupings
    d. matrix organization
    e. market-based groupings

41. A category manager:
    a. is a job title that is no longer used.
    b. is a staff position.
    c. is only found in businesses that are organized according to market-based groupings.
    d. has profit-and-loss responsibility for an entire product line.
    e. plans, implements, and controls the annual plans for the single product for which he or she is responsible.

42. Colgate moved from brand management (Colgate toothpaste) to category management (toothpaste product line). Under Colgate's new system, a category manager would have:
    a. completely different duties from the brand manager.
    b. profit and loss responsibility for all toothpaste products.
    c. to use persuasion as opposed to direct authority to get any goals achieved.
    d. no authority over functions that affects toothpaste products except marketing.
    e. no authority on international toothpaste product sales.

43. Which of the following statements describes a disadvantage of the product manager system?
    a. Product managers are strong advocates for their assigned product.
    b. Product managers tend to remain in the same position for an extended period of time.
    c. Even though product managers have major responsibilities, they have relatively little direct authority.
    d. Product managers are considered line personnel and therefore have little control over decision-making.
    e. Product managers do not assume profit and loss responsibility for their brand.

44. A marketing manger uses management by exception to:
    a. take over responsibilities no one else can handle.
    b. schedule concurrent and sequential activities using the NIH model.
    c. identify results that deviate from plans to diagnose their causes and take new actions.
    d. delete from the line any product that fails to have both marketing and production economies of scale with the existing line.
    e. all of the above.

45. The control phase of the strategic marketing process includes all of the following activities EXCEPT:
    a. establishing quantified goals to be measured.
    b. measuring the results against the quantified goals.
    c. comparing goals and results to identify deviations.
    d. identifying the causes of deviations.
    e. formulating new marketing plans and actions.

46. The purpose of sales analysis is to:
    a. enable the marketing manager to measure the profitability of the firm's products, customer groups, etc.
    b. spotlight the behavior of controllable costs and indicate the contribution to profit of a specific marketing factor.
    c. trace sales revenues to their sources such as specific products, sales territories, or customers.
    d. allocate resources that balance incremental returns of an action against incremental costs.
    e. use the firm's sales records to compare actual results with sales goals and identify areas of strength and weakness.

47. A sales component analysis is also called a:
    a. sales situational analysis.
    b. microsales analysis.
    c. macromarketing audit.
    d. marketing audit.
    e. profitability analysis.

48. When engaged in a _____, a marketing manager might use the 80/20 rule to identify the 20 percent of customers that generate 80 percent of revenue and profits to find more like them.
    a. social audit
    b. marketing audit
    c. situation audit
    d. microsales analysis
    e. profitability analysis

49. A marketing manager could use a profitability analysis to:
    a. measure the profitability of the firm's products, customer groups, sales territories, channels of distribution, and order sizes..
    b. spotlight the behavior of controllable costs and indicate the contribution to profit of a specific marketing factor.
    c. trace sales revenues to their sources such as specific products, sales territories, or customers.
    d. allocate resources that balance incremental returns of an action against incremental costs.
    e. use the firm's sales records to compare actual results with sales goals, and identify areas of strength and weakness.

50. _____ uses computer models to analyze data.
   a. sales analysis
   b. strategic plan
   c. ROI marketing
   d. corporate survey
   e. sales component analysis

ANSWER KEY

Answers to Questions & Problems

Allocating Marketing Resources in Practice

1. Market share of the product
2. Revenues associated with each point of market share
3. Contribution to overhead and profit of each share point

Market-Product Synergies

1. Market specialization
2. Product specialization
3. Full coverage
4. Market-product specialization
5. Selective specialization

Guidelines for an Effective Marketing Plan

1. Measurable, achievable objectives
2. A base of valid assumptions
3. Simple, clear, and specific plans
4. Complete and feasible plans
5. Controllable and flexible plans

Problems in Marketing Planning and Strategy

1. Plans may be based on very poor assumptions about environmental factors
2. Planners and their plans may have lost sight of their customers needs
3. Too much time and effort may be spent on data collection and writing the plan.
4. Line operating managers often feel no sense of ownership in implementing the plans.

The Implementation Phase of the Strategic Marketing Process

1. Communicate goals and the means of achieving them.
2. Have a responsible program champion willing to act.
3. Reward successful program implementation.
4. Take action and avoid "paralysis by analysis."
5. Foster open communication to surface the problems.
6. Schedule precise tasks, responsibilities, and deadlines.

Organizing for Marketing

1. Functional groupings
2. Market-based groupings
3. Geographical groupings
4. Product line groupings

Answers to Sample Multiple Choice Questions

1. e p. 582; LO 1	14. e p. 588; LO 2	26. d p. 595-596; LO 3	38. e p. 601; LO 5
2. c p. 584-585; LO 1	15. d p. 589; LO 2	27. a p. 596; LO 3	39. e p. 601; LO 5
3. b p. 584; LO 1	16. c p. 590; LO 2	28. b p. 596; LO 3	40. d p. 601; LO 5
4. e p. 585; LO 1	17. d p. 590; LO 2	29. b p. 596; LO 3	41. d p. 601; LO 5
5. a p. 585; LO 1	18. c p. 592; LO 2	30. d p. 598; LO 3	42. b p. 601; LO 5
6. b p. 586; LO 1	19. a p. 590; LO 2	31. e p. 598-600; LO 3	43. c p. 602; LO 5
7. d p. 587; LO 3	20. b p. 591; LO 2	32. c p. 599; LO 3	44. c p. 602; LO 6
8. a p. 587; LO 3	21. e p. 592; LO 2	33. e p. 599; LO 4	45. a p. 602; LO 6
9. c p. 589; LO 2	22. d p. 592; LO 2	34. e p. 599; LO 4	46. e p. 603; LO 6
10. e p. 590; LO 2	23. c p. 594; LO 3	35. a p. 601; LO 5	47. b p. 603; LO 6
11. b p. 587; LO 3	24. d p. 594; LO 3	36. b p. 601; LO 5	48. e p. 604; LO 6
12. b p. 589; LO 2	25. a p. 595-596; LO 3	37. a p. 601; LO 5	49. a p. 604; LO 6
13. a p. 589-590; LO 2			50. c p. 604; LO 6

Note: LO indicates learning objective.

FLASH CARDS

customer value	customer relationship management (CRM)
environmental factors	exchange
macromarketing	market
marketing	marketing concept
marketing mix	marketing orientation

The process of identifying prospective buyers, understanding them intimately, and developing favorable long-term perceptions of the organization and its offerings so that buyers will choose them in the marketplace.

The unique combination of benefits received by targeted buyers that includes quality, price, convenience, on-time delivery, and both before-sale and after-sale service.

The trade of things of value between buyer and seller so that each is better off after the trade.

The uncontrollable factors involving social, economic, technological, competitive, and regulatory forces.

People with the desire and ability to buy a specific product.

The study of the aggregate flow of a nation's goods and services to benefit society.

The idea that an organization should (1) strive to satisfy the needs of consumers while (2) also trying to achieve the organization's goals.

An organizational function and a set of processes for creating, communicating, and delivering value to customers and for managing customer relationships in ways that benefit the organization and its stakeholders.

When an organization focuses its efforts on(1)continuously collecting information about customers' needs and competitors' capabilities, (2) sharing this information across departments, and (3) using the information to create customer value.

The marketing manager's controllable factors of product, price, promotion, and place he or she can take to solve a marketing problem.

marketing program	micromarketing
organizational buyers	relationship marketing
societal marketing concept	target market
ultimate consumers	utility
benchmarking	business unit

A plan that integrates the marketing mix to provide a good, service, or idea to prospective consumers.	Units such as manufacturers, retailers, or government agencies that buy goods and services for their own use or for resale.
How an organization directs its marketing activities and allocates its organization directs its marketing resources to benefit its customers.	The view that an organization should discover and satisfy the needs of its customers in a way that also provides for society's well-being.
Linking the organization to its individual customers, employees, suppliers, and other partners for their mutual long-term benefits.	One or more specific groups of potential consumers toward which an organization directs its marketing program.
People who use the goods and services purchased for a household; sometimes also called ultimate users.	Discovering how others do something better than your own firm so you can imitate or leapfrog competition.
The benefits or customer value received by users of the product.	Element of a firm that markets a set of related products to a clearly defined group of customers.

business unit level	competencies
competitive advantage	corporate level
cross functional team	functional level
goals	marketing plan
market share	marketing strategy

Level at which business unit managers set directions for their products and markets.

An organization's special capabilities, including skills, technologies, and resources that distinguish it from other organizations.

Level at which top management directs overall strategy for the entire organization.

A unique strength relative to competitors, often based on quality, time, cost, or innovation.

Level at which groups of specialists create value for the organization.

A small number of people from different departments in an organization who are mutually accountable to a common set of performance goals.

A written statement identifying the target market, specific marketing goals, the budget, and tinting for the marketing plan A roadmap for the marketing activities of an organization for a Specified future period of time, such as one year or five years.

A targeted level of performance to be achieved, often by a specific time.

The means by which a marketing goal is to be achieved, characterized by (1) a specified target market and (2) a marketing program to reach it.

The ratio of sales revenue of the firm to the total sales revenue of all firms in the industry, including the firm itself.

marketing tactics	mission
objectives	organizational culture
points of difference	profit
quality	situation analysis
stakeholders	strategic marketing process

A statement of the organization's scope.	The detailed day-to-day operational decisions essential to the overall success of marketing strategies.
Targeted levels of performance to be achieved, often by a specific time.	A system of shared attitudes and behaviors held by the employees that distinguish an organization from others.
A business firm's reward for the risk it undertakes in offering a product for sale; the money left over after a firm's total expenses are subtracted from its total revenues.	Those characteristics of a product that make it superior to competitive substitutes.
Taking stock of where the firm or product has been recently, where it is now, and where it is headed in terms of the organization's plans and the external factors and trends affecting it.	Those features and characteristics of a product that influence its ability to satisfy customer needs.
The activities whereby an organization allocates its marketing mix resources to reach its target markets.	The people who are affected by what the company does and hoe well it performs.

SWOT analysis	baby boomers
barriers to entry	blended family
competition	consumerism
culture	demographics
discretionary income	disposable income

The generation of children born between 1946 and 1965.	An acronym describing an organization's appraisal of its internal strengths and weaknesses and its external opportunities and threats.
Two families from prior marriages merged into a single household as spouses remarry.	Business practices or conditions that make it difficult for a new firm to enter the market.
A movement to increase the influence, power, and rights of consumers in dealing with institutions.	The set of alternative firms that could provide a product to satisfy a specific market's needs.
A description of the population according to selected characteristics such as age, sex, ethnicity, income, and occupation.	The sets of values, ideas, and attitudes of a homogeneous group of people that are transmitted from one generation to the next.
The money a consumer has left after taxes to use for food, shelter, and clothing.	The money that remains after taxes and necessities have been paid for.

economy	electronic commerce
environmental scanning	extranets
Generation X	Generation Y
gross income	intranet
marketspace	multi-cultural marketing

Any activity that uses some form of electronic communication in the inventory, exchange, advertisement, distribution, and payment of goods and services.	The income, expenditures, and resources that affect the cost of running a business and household.
An Internet/Web-based network that permits secure business-to-business communications between a manufacturer and its suppliers, distributors, and sometimes other partners.	The process of acquiring information on events occurring outside the company and interpreting potential trends.
The generation of Americans born after 1976. Also described as the baby boomlet, or the Net Generation.	The 17 percent of the population born between 1965 and 1976.
An Internet-based network used within the boundaries of an organization.	The total amount of money earned in one year by a person, family, or household.
Combinations of the marketing mix that reflect the unique attitudes, ancestry, communication preferences, and lifestyles of different races.	An information- and communication-based electronic exchange environment mostly occupied by sophisticated computer and telecommunication technologies and digitized offerings

regulation	self-regulation
social forces	value consciousness
cause marketing	caveat emptor
code of ethics	Consumer Bill of Rights
economic espionage	ethics

An industry policing itself rather than relying on government controls.

Restrictions state and federal laws place on business with regard to the conduct of its activities.

The concern for obtaining the best quality, features, and performance of a product to reduce purchasing costs.

The demographic characteristics of the population and is values.

A Latin term that means "let the buyer beware."

Tying the charitable contributions of a firm directly to the customer revenues produced through the promotion of one of its products.

The rights of consumers in the exchange process including the right to safety, to be informed, to choose, and to be heard.

A formal statement of ethical principles and rules of conduct.

The moral principles and values that govern the actions and decisions of an individual or group.

The Clandestine collection of trade secrets or proprietary information about a company's competitors.

green marketing	ISO 14000
laws	moral idealism
social audit	social responsibility
sustainable development	utilitarianism
whistleblowers	attitudes

Worldwide standards for environmental quality and green marketing practices.	Marketing efforts to produce, promote, and reclaim environmentally sensitive products.
A personal moral philosophy that considers certain individual rights or duties as universal regardless of the outcome.	Society's values and standards that are enforceable in the courts.
The idea that organizations are part of a larger society and are accountable to society for their actions.	A systematic assessment of a firm's objectives, strategies, and performance in the domain of social responsibility.
A personal moral philosophy that focuses on the "greatest good for the greatest number" by assessing the costs and benefits of the consequences of ethical behavior.	The practice of conducting business in a way that protects the natural environment while making economic progress.
Learned predisposition to respond to an object or class of objects in a consistent manner.	Employees who report unethical or illegal actions of their employers.

beliefs	brand loyalty
cognitive dissonance	consumer behavior
consumer socialization	evaluative criteria
consideration set	family life cycle
involvement	learning

A favorable attitude toward and consistent purchase of a single brand over time.

A consumer's subjective perception of how well a product or brand performs on different attributes; these are based on personal experience, advertising, and discussions with other people.

Actions of a person to purchase and use products and services, including the mental and social processes that precede and follow these actions.

The feeling of post-purchase psychological tension or anxiety a consumer often experiences.

Both the objective and subjective attributes of a brand important to consumers when evaluating different brands or products.

The process by which people acquire the skills, knowledge, and attitudes necessary to function as consumers.

The concept that each family progresses through a number of distinct phases, each of which is associated with identifiable purchasing behaviors.

The group of brands a consumer would consider acceptable out of the set of brands in the product class of which he or she is aware.

Those behaviors that result from (1) repeated experience and (2) thinking.

The personal, social, and economic significance of the purchase to the consumer.

motivation	lifestyle
opinion leaders	perceived risk
perception	personality
purchase decision process	reference group
self-concept	situational influences

A mode of living that is identified by how people spend their time and resources (activities), what they consider important in their environment (interests), and what they think of themselves and the world around them (opinions).

Motivation is the energizing force that causes behavior that satisfies a need.

The anxieties felt because the consumer cannot anticipate the outcome but sees that there might be negative consequences.

Individuals who exert direct or indirect social influence over others.

A person's consistent behaviors or responses to recurring situations.

The process by which an individual selects, organizes, and interprets information to create a meaningful picture of the world.

People to whom a person turns as a standard of self-appraisal or source of personal standards.

Steps or stages a buyer passes through in making choices about which products to buy.☐

A situation's effect on the nature and scope of the decision process. These include(1) the purchase task, (2) social surroundings, (3) physical surroundings,(4) temporal effects, and (5) antecedent states.

The way people see themselves and the way they believe others see them.

social classes	subcultures
subliminal perception	word of mouth
bidder's list	business marketing
buy classes	buying center
derived demand	e-marketplaces

Subgroups within the larger or national culture with unique values, ideas, and attitudes.	The relatively permanent and homogeneous divisions in a society of people or families sharing similar values, lifestyles, interests, and behavior.
People influencing each other during their face-to-face conversations.	Means that a person sees or hears messages without being aware of them.
The marketing of goods and services to commercial enterprises, governments, and other profit and not-for-profit organizations for use in the creation of goods and services that they then produce and market to other business customers as well as individuals and ultimate consumers.	A list of firms believed to be qualified to supply a given item.
The group of persons within an organization who participate in the buying process and share common goals, risks, and knowledge important to that process.	Groups of three specific buying situations organizations face: new buy, straight rebuy, and modified rebuy.
Online trading communities that bring together buyers and supplier organizations.	Sales of a product (typically industrial) that result from the sales of another item (often consumer).

government units	industrial firm
ISO 9000	make-buy decision
North American Industry Classification System (NAICS)	organizational buyers
organizational buying behavior	organizational buying criteria
reciprocity	reseller

An organizational buyer that in some way reprocesses a good or service it buys before selling it again.	The federal, state, and local agencies that buy goods and services for the constituents they serve.
An evaluation of whether a product or its parts will be purchased from outside suppliers or built by the firm.	International standards for registration and certification of a manufacturer's quality management and quality assurance system.
Units such as manufacturers, retailers, or government agencies that buy goods and services for their own use or for resale.	A system for classifying organizations on the basis of major activity or the major good or service provided used by the three NAFTA countries--Canada, Mexico, and the United States.
The objective attributes of the supplier's products and services and the capabilities of the supplier itself.	The decision-making process that organizations use to establish the need for products and identify, evaluate, and choose among alternative brands and suppliers.
An industrial buying practice in which two organizations agree to purchase products from each other.	A wholesaler or retailer that buys physical products and resells them again without any processing.

reverse auction	reverse marketing
supply partnership	traditional auction
value analysis	back translation
balance of trade	consumer ethnocentrism
countertrade	cross-cultural analysis

The effort by organizational buyers to build relationships that shape suppliers' products, services, and capabilities to fit a buyer's needs and those of its customers.

A buyer communicates a need for a product or service and would-be suppliers are invited to bid in competition with each other.

A systematic appraisal of the design, quality, and performance requirements of a product to reduce purchasing costs.

A relationship between an organizational buyer and its supplier created to adopt mutually beneficial efforts to lower the cost and/or increase value delivered to the ultimate consumer.

The practice of retranslating a word or phrase into the original language by a different interpreter to catch errors.

A systematic appraisal of the design, quality, and performance of a product to reduce purchasing costs.

The tendency to believe that it is inappropriate, indeed immoral, to purchase foreign-made products.

The difference between the monetary value of a nation's exports and imports.

The study of similarities and differences between consumers in two or more nations or societies

Using barter rather than money in making international sales.

cultural symbols	currency exchange rate
customs	direct investment
dumping	Economic Espionage Act
exporting	Foreign Corrupt Practices Act
global brand	global competition

The price of one country's currency expressed in terms of another country's currency.

Things that represent ideas and concepts. □

In global marketing, a domestic firm actually investing in and owning a foreign subsidiary or division.

Norms and expectations about the way people do things in a specific country.

A law that makes the theft of trade secrets a federal crime in the United States.

When a firm sells a product in a foreign country below its domestic price.

A law that makes it a crime for U.S. corporations to bribe an official of a foreign government or political party to obtain or retain business in a foreign country.

Producing goods in one country then selling them in another country.

A competitive situation that exists when firms originate, produce, and market their products and services worldwide.

A brand marketed under the same name in multiple countries with similar and centrally coordinated marketing programs.

global consumers	global marketing strategy
gray market	gross domestic product
joint venture	multi-domestic marketing strategy
protectionism	quota
semiotics	strategic alliances

The practice of standardizing marketing activities when there are cultural similarities, and adapting them when cultures differ.	Customer groups living in many countries or regions of the world who have similar needs or seek similar features and benefits from products and services.
The monetary value of all goods and services produced in a country during one year.	A situation in which products are sold through unauthorized channels of distribution; also called parallel importing.
A firm's worldwide marketing strategy that offers as many different product variations, brand names, and advertising programs as countries in which it does business.	In international trade, an arrangement in which a foreign company and a local firm invest together to create a local business.
In international marketing, a restriction placed on the amount of a product allowed to enter or leave a country.	The practice of shielding one or more industries within a country's economy from foreign competition through the use of tariffs or quotas.
Agreements between two or more independent firms to cooperate for the purpose of achieving common goals.	The field of study that examines the correspondence between symbols and their role in the assignment of meaning for people.

tariff	values
World Trade Organization	constraints
data	data mining
decision	information technology
marketing research	measures of success

The beliefs of a person or culture; when applied to pricing, the ratio of perceived quality to price (Value = Perceived benefits/Price).	In international marketing, a government tax on goods or services entering a country.
The restrictions, such as time and money, placed on potential solutions by the nature and importance of the problem.	An institution that sets rules governing trade among its members through a panel of experts.
The extraction of hidden predictive information from large databases.	The facts and figures pertinent to the problem, composed of primary and secondary data.
Involves designing and managing computer and communication networks to provide an information system to satisfy an organization's needs for data storage, processing, and access.	A conscious choice from among two or more alternatives.
Criteria or standards used in evaluating proposed solutions to the problem.	The process of defining a marketing problem and opportunity, systematically collecting and analyzing information, and recommending actions to improve an organization's marketing activities.

non-probability sampling	observational data
primary data	probability sampling
questionnaire data	sampling
secondary data	statistical inference
80/20 rule	direct forecast

Facts and figures obtained by watching, either mechanically or in person, how people actually behave.	Using arbitrary judgments to select the sample so that the chance of selecting a particular element may be unknown or zero.
Using precise rules to select the sample such that each element of the population has a specific known chance of being selected.	Facts and figures that are newly collected for the project.
Selecting representative elements from a population.	Facts and figures obtained by asking people about their attitudes, awareness, intentions, and behaviors.
Drawing conclusions about a population from a sample taken from that population.	Facts and figures that have already been recorded before the project at hand.
An estimate of the value to be forecast without the use of intervening steps.	The principle that 80 percent of sales (and costs) are generated by 20 percent of the items or customers, and vice versa, thus suggesting priorities.

lost-horse forecast	market potential
market segments	market-product grid
perceptual map	product positioning
product repositioning	sales forecast
sales force survey forecast	survey of buyers' intentions forecast

Maximum total sales of a product by all firms to a segment under specified environmental conditions and marketing efforts of the firms (also called industry potential).	Starting with the last known value of the item being forecast, listing the factors that could affect the forecast, assessing whether they have a positive or negative impact, and making the final forecast.
Framework for relating market segments to products offered or potential marketing actions by a firm.	The groups that result from the process of market segmentation; these groups ideally (1) have common needs and (2) will respond similarly to a marketing action.
The place an offering occupies in a consumer's mind with regard to important attributes relative to competitive offerings.	A graph displaying consumers' perceptions of product attributes across two or more dimensions.
What one firm expects to sell under specified conditions for the uncontrollable and controllable factors that affect the forecast.	Changing the place an offering occupies in a consumer's mind relative to competitive products.
A method of forecasting sales that involves asking prospective customers whether they are likely to buy the product or service during some future time period.	Asking the firm's salespeople to estimate sales during a coming period.

trend extrapolation	synergy
consumer goods	convenience goods
usage rate	business analysis
business goods	commercialization
consumer goods	convenience goods
development	failure fees

The increased customer value achieved through performing organizational functions more efficiently.	Extending a pattern observed in past data into the future.
Involves specifying the features of the product and the marketing strategy needed to commercialize it and making necessary financial projections.	Refers to quantity consumed or patronage during a specific period, and varies significantly among different customer groups.
☐The final phase of the new-product process.	Products used in the production of other items for ultimate consumers.
Items that the consumer purchases frequently and with a minimum of shopping effort.	Products purchased by the ultimate consumer.
A penalty payment made to retailers by manufacturers if a new product does not reach predetermined sales levels	Phase of the new product process in which the idea on paper is turned into a prototype; includes manufacturing and laboratory and consumer tests.

idea generation	market testing
new-product process	new-product strategy development
product	product line
product mix	production goods
protocol	screening and evaluation

A phase of the new product process, in which prospective consumers are exposed to actual products under realistic purchase conditions to see if they will buy.

A phase of the new product process, in which a firm develops a pool of concepts as candidates for new products.

The phase of the new-product process in which a firm defines the role of new products in terms of overall corporate objectives.

The sequence of activities a firm uses to identify business opportunities and convert them to a saleable good or service. There are seven steps: new-product strategy, idea generation, screening and evaluation, business analysis, development, testing, and commercialization.

A group of products closely related because they satisfy a class of needs, are used together, are sold to the same customer group, are distributed through the same outlets, or fall within a given price range.

A good, service, or idea consisting of a bundle of tangible and intangible attributes that satisfies consumers and is received in exchange for money or other unit of value.

Products used in the manufacturing of other items that become part of the final product.

The number of product lines offered by a company.

The phase of the new product process in which a firm uses internal and external evaluations to eliminate ideas that warrant no further development effort.

In the new product development process, an early statement that identifies a well-defined target market; specifies customers' needs, wants, and preferences; and states what the product will be and do.

shopping goods	Six Sigma
slotting fee	specialty goods
support goods	unsought goods
brand equity	brand name
brand personality	branding

A means to "delight the customer" by achieving quality through a highly disciplined process to focus on developing and delivering near-perfect products and services.

Products for which the consumer will compare several alternatives on various criteria.

Products that a consumer will make a special effort to search out and buy.

Payment by a manufacturer to place a new product on a retailer's shelf.

Items that the consumer either does not know about or knows about but does not initially want.

Items used to assist in the production of other goods.

Any word or device (design, shape, sound, or color) that is used to distinguish one company's products from a competitor's.

The added value a given brand name provides a product.

Activity in which an organization uses a name, phrase, design, or symbol, or a combination of these, to identify its products and distinguish them from those of a competitor.

A set of human characteristics associated with a brand name.

co-branding	downsizing
label	brand licensing
	market modification
mixed branding	multibranding

The practice of reducing the content of package without changing package size and maintaining or increasing the package price.

The pairing of two brand names of two manufacturers on a single product.

A contractual agreement where by a company allows another firm to use its brand name, patent, trade secret, or other property for a royalty or fee.

An integral part of the package that typically identifies the product or brand, who made it, where and when it was made, how it is to be used, and package contents and ingredients.

Attempts to increase product usage by creating new-use situations or finding new customers.

A manufacturer's branding strategy in which a distinct name is given to each of its products.

A branding strategy in which the company may market products under their own name and that of a reseller

multi-product branding	packaging
private branding	product class
product form	product life cycle
product modification	trade name
trademark	trading down

The container in which a product is offered for sale and on which information is communicated.	A branding strategy in which a company uses one name for all products; also called blanket or family branding.
An entire product category or industry. product counterfeiting Low cost copies of a popular brand, not manufactured by the original producer.	When a company manufactures products that are sold under the name of a wholesaler or retailer.
The life of a product over four stages: introduction, growth, maturity, and decline.	Variations of a product within a product class.
The commercial name under which a company does business.	Strategies of altering a product characteristic, such as quality, performance, or appearance.
Reducing the number of features, quality, or price of a product.	Legal identification of a company's exclusive rights to use a brand name or trade name.

trading up	warranty
capacity management	customer contact audit
four I's of service	gap analysis
idle production capacity	internal marketing
off-peak pricing	service continuum

A statement indicating the liability of the manufacturer for product deficiencies.

Adding value to a product by including more features or higher quality materials.

A flow chart of the points of Interaction between a consumer and a service provider.

Managing the demand for a service so that it is available to consumers.

An evaluation tool that compares expectations about a particular service to the actual experience a consumer has with the service.

Four unique elements to services: intangibility, inconsistency, inseparability, and inventory.

The notion that a service organization must focus on its employees, of internal market, before successful programs can be directed at customers.

A situation where a service provider is available but there is no demand.

A range from the tangible to the intangible or good-dominant to service-dominant offerings available in the marketplace.

Charging different prices during different times of the day or days of the week to reflect variations in demand for the service.

services	average revenue(AR)
barter	break-even analysis
break-even chart	break-even point (BEP)
demand curve	demand factors
fixed cost(FC)	marginal analysis

The average amount of money received for selling one unit of a product.

Intangible items such as airline trips, financial advice, or telephone calls that an organization provides to consumers in exchange for money or something else of value.

An analysis of the relationship between total revenue and total cost to determine profitability at various levels of output.

The practice of exchanging goods and services for other goods and services rather than for money.

Quantity at which total revenue and total cost are equal and beyond which profit occurs.

A graphic presentation of a break-even analysis.

Factors that determine the strength of consumers' willingness and ability to pay for goods and services.

The summation of points representing the maximum quantity of a product consumers will buy at different price levels.

☐ Principle of allocating resources that balances incremental revenues of an action against incremental costs.

Factors that determine the strength of consumers' willingness and ability to pay for goods and services.

marginal cost(MC)	marginal revenue(MR)
price elasticity of demand	price(P)
pricing constraints	pricing objectives
profit equation	total cost(TC)
total revenue(TR)	Unit variable cost(UVC)

The change in total revenue obtained by selling one additional unit.	The change in total cost that results from producing and marketing one additional unit.
The money or other considerations exchanged for the purchase or use of the product, idea, or service.	The percentage change in quantity demanded relative to a percentage change in price.
Goals that specify the role of price in an organization's marketing and strategic plans.	Factors that limit a firm's latitude in the price it may set.
The total expense a firm incurs in producing and marketing a product, which includes fixed cost and variable cost; in physical distribution decisions, the sum of all applicable costs	Profit = Total revenue-Total cost.
The total amount of money received from the sale of a product.	Variable cost expressed on a per unit basis.

value pricing	value
variable cost(VC)	
	above-, at-, or below-market pricing
basing-point pricing	bundle pricing
cost-plus pricing	customary pricing

Specifically, value can be defined as the ratio of perceived quality to price (Value = Perceived benefits/Price).	The practice of simultaneously increasing service and product benefits and decreasing price.
	An expense of the firm that varies directly with the quantity of product produced and sold.
Pricing based on what the market price is.	
The marketing of two or more products in a single "package" price.	Selecting one or more geographic locations (basing point) from which the list price for products plus freight expenses are charged to buyers.
A method of pricing based on a product's tradition, standardized channel of distribution, or other competitive factors.	The practice of summing the total unit cost of providing a product or service and adding a specific amount to the cost to arrive at a price.

everyday low pricing	experience curve pricing
flexible-price policy	FOB origin pricing
loss-leader pricing	odd-even pricing
one-price policy	penetration pricing
predatory pricing	prestige pricing

A method of pricing where price often falls following the reduction of costs associated with the firm's experience in producing or selling a product.

The practice of replacing promotional allowances given to retailers with lower manufacturer list prices.

A method of pricing where the title of goods passes to the buyer at the point of loading.

Offering the same product and quantities to similar customers, but at different prices.

Setting prices a few dollars or cents under an even number, such as $19.95.

Deliberately pricing a product below its customary price to attract attention to it.

Pricing a product low in order to discourage competition from entering the market.

Selling products at a low price to injure or eliminate a competitor Clayton Act as amended by the Robinson-Patman Act prohibits this action.

Setting a high price so that status-conscious consumers will be attracted to the product.

The practice of charging a very low price for a product with the intent of driving competitors out of business.

price discrimination	price fixing
price lining	price war
product line pricing	promotional allowance
quantity discounts	skimming pricing
standard markup pricing	target pricing

A conspiracy among firms to set prices for a product.	The practice of charging different prices to different buyers for goods of like grade and quality.
Successive price cutting by competitors to increase or maintain their unit sales or market share.	Setting the price of a line of products at a number of different specific pricing points.
The cash payment or extra amount of "free goods" awarded sellers in the channel of distribution for undertaking certain advertising or selling activities to promote a product.	Reductions in unit costs for a larger order quantity.
A high initial price attached to a product to help a company recover the cost of development.	Setting prices by adding a fixed percentage to the cost of all items in a specific product class
The practice of deliberately adjusting the composition and features of a product to achieve the target price to consumers.	Setting prices by adding a fixed percentage to the cost of all items in a specific product class

target profit pricing	target return-on-investment pricing
target return-on-sales pricing	uniform delivered pricing
yield management pricing	brokers
channel captain	channel conflict
channel partnership	direct channel

Setting a price to achieve a return-on-investment target.

Setting a price based on an annual specific dollar target volume of profit.

A geographical pricing practice where the price the seller quotes includes all transportation costs.

Setting a price to achieve a profit that is a specified percentage of the sales volume.

Channel intermediaries that do not take title to merchandise and make their profits from commissions and fees by negotiating contracts or deals between buyers and sellers.

The charging of different prices to maximize revenue for a set amount of capacity al a given time.

Arises when one channel member believes another channel member is engaged in behavior that prevents it from achieving its goals.

A marketing channel member that coordinates, directs, and supports other channel members; may be a manufacturer, wholesaler, or retailer.

A marketing channel where a producer and ultimate consumers deal directly with each other.

Agreements and procedures among channel members for ordering and physically distributing a producer's product through the channel to the ultimate consumer.

direct marketing channels	**disintermediation**
dual distribution	**electronic marketing channel**
exclusive distribution	**franchising**
indirect channel	**industrial distributor**
intensive distribution	**manufacturer's agents**

The practice whereby a channel member bypasses another member and sells or buys products direct.

Allow consumers to buy products by interacting with various advertising media without a face-to-face meeting with a salesperson.

Employ the Internet to make goods and services available for consumption or use by consumers or industrial buyers.

An arrangement by which a firm reaches buyers by employing two or more different types of channels for the same basic product.

The contractual agreement between a parent company and an individual or firm that allows the franchisee to operate a certain type of business under an established name and according to specific rules.

A distribution strategy whereby a producer sells its products or services in only one retail outlet in a specific geographical area.

A specific type of intermediary between producers and consumers that generally sells, stocks, and delivers a full product assortment.

A marketing channel where intermediaries are situated between the producer and consumers.

Individuals or firms that work for several producers and carry noncompetitive, complementary merchandise in an exclusive territory; also called manufacturer's representatives.

A distribution strategy whereby a producer sells products or services in as many outlets as possible in a geographic area.

marketing channel	merchant wholesalers
selective distribution	selling agent
strategic channel alliances	vertical marketing systems
customer service	efficient consumer response
electronic data interchange (EFI)	just-in-time (JIT) concept

Independently owned firms that take title to the merchandise they handle.

People and firms involved in the process of making a product or service available for use or consumption by consumers or industrial users.

A person or firm that represents a single producer and is responsible for all marketing functions of that producer.

A distribution strategy whereby a producer sells its products in a few retail outlets in a specific geographical area.

Professionally managed and centrally coordinated marketing channels designed to achieve channel economies and maximum marketing impact.

A practice whereby one firm's marketing channel is used to sell another firm's products.

An inventory management system designed to reduce the retailer's lead-time for receiving merchandise.

The ability of a logistics system to satisfy users in terms of time, dependability, communications, and convenience.

An inventory supply system that operates with very low inventories and requires fast, on-time delivery.

Combine proprietary computer and telecommunication technologies to exchange electronic invoices, payments, and information among suppliers, manufacturers, and retailers.

lead time	logistics
logistics management	materials handling
quick response	reverse logistics
supply chain	supply chain management
third-party logistics providers	total logistics cost

Those activities that focus on getting the right amount of the right products to the right place at the right time at the lowest possible cost.	Lag from ordering an item until it is received and ready for use.
Moving goods over short distances into, within, and out of warehouses and manufacturing plants. □	The practice organizing the cost-effective flow of raw materials, in-process inventory, finished goods, and related information from point-of-origin to point-of-consumption to satisfy customer requirements.
The process of reclaiming recyclable and reusable materials, returns and reworks from the point-of-consumption to use for repair, remanufacturing, or disposal.	An inventory management system designed to reduce the retailer's lead time for receiving merchandise.
The integration and organization of information and logistic activities across firms in a supply chain for the purpose of creating and delivering goods and services that provide value to customers.	A sequence of firms that perform activities required to create and deliver a good or service to consumers or industrial users.
Expenses associated with transportation, materials handling and warehousing, inventory, stockouts, and order processing.	Firms that perform most or all of the logistics functions that manufacturers, suppliers, and distributors would normally perform themselves.

vendor-managed inventory	breadth of product line
category management	central business district
community shopping center	depth of product line
form of ownership	hypermarket
intertype competition	level of service

The variety of different items a store or wholesaler carries.	An inventory management system whereby the supplier determines the product amount and assortment a customer (such as a retailer) needs and automatically delivers the appropriate items.
The oldest retail setting; the community's downtown area.	An approach to managing the assortment of merchandise in which a manager is assigned the responsibility for selecting all products that consumers in a market segment might view as substitutes for each other, with the objective of maximizing sales and profits in the category.
The assortment of each item a store or wholesaler carries.	A retail location that typically has one primary store (usually a department store branch) and 20 to 40 smaller outlets and serves a population base of about 100,000.
A large store (over 200,000 square feet) offering a mix of food products and general merchandise.	Who owns a retail outlet. Alternatives are independent, corporate chain, cooperative, or franchise.
The degree of service provided to the customer by the retailer: self, limited, or full.	Competition between very dissimilar types of retail outlets.

merchandise line	multi-channel retailers
off-price retailing	power center
regional shopping centers	retail positioning matrix
retail life cycle	retailing
retailing mix	scrambled merchandising

Utilize and integrate a combination of traditional store formats and non-store formats such as catalogs, television, and online retailing.	The number of different types of products and the assortment a store carries.
Large strip malls with multiple anchor (or national stores), a convenient location, and a supermarket.	Selling brand name merchandise at lower than regular prices.□
A framework for positioning retail outlets in terms of breadth of product line and value added.□	Suburban malls with up to 100 stores that typically draw customers from a 5- to I0-mile radius, usually containing one or two anchor stores.
All the activities that are involved in selling, renting, and providing goods and services to ultimate consumers for personal, family, or household use.	The process of growth and decline that retail outlets, like products, experience.
Offering several unrelated product lines in a single retail store.	The strategic components that a retailer manages, including goods and services, physical distribution, and communication tactics.

shrinkage	strip location
telemarketing	wheel of retailing
advertising	all-you-can-afford budgeting
channel of communication	communication
competitive parity budgeting	decoding

A cluster of stores that serves people who live within a 5- to 10-minute drive in a population base of under 30,000.

A term used by retailers to describe theft of merchandise by customers and employees.

A concept that describes how new retail outlets enter the market as low-status, low-margin stores and gradually add embellishments that raise their prices and status. They now face a new low-status, low–margin operator, and the cycle starts to repeat itself.

Involves the use of the telephone to interact with and sell directly to consumers.

Allocating funds to promotion only after all other budget items are covered.

Any paid form of nonpersonal communication about an organization, good, service, or idea by an identified sponsor.

The process of conveying a message to others. Six elements--a source, a message, a channel of communication, a receiver, and the processes of encoding and decoding—are required for communication to occur.

The means (e.g., a salesperson, advertising media, or public relations tools) of conveying a message to a receiver.

The process of having the receiver take a set of symbols, the message, and transform them back to an abstract idea.

Matching the competitors' absolute level of spending or the proportion per point of market share.

direct marketing	direct orders
encoding	feedback
field of experience	heirarchy of effects
integrated marketing communications	lead generation
message	noise

A promotional alternative that uses direct communication with consumers to generate a response in the form of an order, a request for further information, or a visit to a retail outlet.

A promotional alternative that uses direct communication with consumers to generate a response in the form of an order, a request for further information, or a visit to a retail outlet.

The communication flow from receiver back to sender; indicates whether the message was decoded and understood as intended.

The process of having the sender transform an abstract idea into a set of symbols

The sequence of stages a prospective buyer goes through from initial awareness of a product to eventual action (either trial or adoption of the product. The stages include awareness, interest, evaluation, trial, and adoption.

A person's understanding and knowledge; to communicate effectively, a sender and a receiver must have a mutually shared field of experience.

The result of direct marketing offer designed to generate interest in a product or a service, and a request for additional information.

The concept of designing marketing communications programs that coordinate all promotional activities-advertising, personal selling, sales promotion, and public relations-- to provide a consistent message across all audiences.

Extraneous factors that work against effective communication by distorting a message or the feedback received.

The information sent by a source to a receiver in the communications process.

objective and task budgeting	percentage of sales budgeting
personal selling	promotional mix
public relations	publicity
pull strategy	push strategy
receivers	response

A budgeting approach whereby the company (1) determines its promotion objectives, (2) outlines the tasks to accomplish these objectives, and (3) determines the promotion cost of performing those tasks.

Allocating funds to advertising as a percentage of past or anticipated sales, in terms of either dollars or units sold.

The combination of one or more of the promotional elements a firm uses to communicate with consumers. The promotional elements include: advertising, personal selling, sales promotion, and publicity.

The two-way flow of communication between a buyer and seller, often in a face-to-face encounter, designed to influence a person's or group's purchase decision. □

A nonpersonal, indirectly paid presentation of an organization, good, or service.

A form of communication management that seeks to influence the feelings, opinions, or beliefs held by customers, stockholders, suppliers, employees, and other publics about a company and its products or services.

Directing the promotional mix to channel members or intermediaries to gain their cooperation in ordering and stocking a product.

Directing the promotional mix at ultimate consumers to encourage them to ask the retailer for the product.

(1) In behavioral learning, the action taken by a consumer to satisfy a drive. (2) In the feed back loop, the impact the message had on the receiver's knowledge, attitudes, or behaviors.

The consumers who read, hear, or see the message sent by a source in the communication process.

sales promotion	source
traffic generation	advertising
consumer-oriented sales promotion	cooperative advertising
cost per thousand (CPM)	frequency
full-service agency	gross rating points (GRPs)

A company or person who has information to convey.	A short-term inducement of value offered to arouse interest in buying a good or service.
Any paid form of non-personal communication about an organization, good, service, or idea by an identified sponsor.	The outcome of a direct marketing offer designed to motivate people to visit a business.
Advertising programs in which a manufacturer pays a percentage of the retailer's local advertising expense for advertising the manufacturer's products.	Sales tools used to support a company's advertising and personal selling efforts directed to ultimate consumers; examples include coupons, sweepstakes, and trading stamps.
The average number of times a person in the target audience is exposed to a message or advertisement.	The cost of reaching 1,000 individuals or households with an advertising message in a given medium.
A reference number for advertisers, created by multiplying reach (expressed as a percentage) by frequency.	An advertising agency providing a complete range of services, including market research, media selection, copy development, artwork, and production.

infomercials	in-house agency
institutional advertisement	limited-service agency
posttests	pretests
product advertisements	product placement
publicity tools	rating (TV or radio)

A company's own advertising staff which may provide full services or a limited range of services.	Program length advertisements, often 30 minutes long, that take an educational approach to communicating with potential customers.
An agency that specializes in one aspect of the advertising process such as providing creative services to develop the advertising copy or buying previously unpurchased media space.	Advertisements designed to build goodwill or an image for an organization, rather than promote a specific good or service.
Tests conducted before an advertisement is placed to determine whether it communicates the intended message or to select between alternative versions of an advertisement.	Tests conducted after an advertisement has been shown to the target audience to determine whether it has accomplished its intended purpose.
Advertising media alternative in which the manufacturer pays for the privilege of having a brand name product used in a movie.	Advertisements that focus on selling a good or service and take three forms: (I)pioneering (or informational), (2) competitive (or persuasive), and (3) reminder.
The percentage of households in a market that are tuned to a particular TV show or radio station.	Methods of obtaining nonpersonal presentation of an organization, good, or service without direct cost. Examples include news releases, news conferences, and public service announcements.

reach	trade-oriented sales promotions
account management policies	adaptive selling
consultative selling	emotional intelligence
formula selling presentation	major account management
missionary salespeople	need-satisfaction presentation

Sales tools used to support a company's advertising and personal selling efforts directed to wholesalers, distributors, or retailers. Three common approaches are allowances, cooperative advertising, and salesforce training.	The number of different people or households exposed to an advertisement.
A need-satisfaction sales presentation involving adjusting the presentation to fit the selling situation.	Policies that specify whom salespeople should contact, what kinds of selling and customer service activities should be engaged in, and how these activities should be carried out.
The ability to understand one's own emotions and the emotions of people with whom one interacts on a daily basis.	A need-satisfaction sales presentation where the salesperson focuses on problem definition and serves as an expert on problem recognition.
The practice of using team selling to focus on important customers to build mutually beneficial long-term, cooperative relationships.	The selling format that consists of providing information in an accurate, thorough, and step-by-step manner to persuade the prospect to buy.
A selling format that emphasizes probing and listening by the salesperson to identify needs and interests of perspective buyers.	Sales support personnel who do not directly solicit orders but rather concentrate on performing promotional activities and introducing new products.

order getter	order taker
partnership selling	personal selling
personal selling process	relationship selling
sales engineer	sales management
sales plan	sales quota

A salesperson who processes routine orders and reorders for products that have already been sold by the company.	A salesperson who sells in a conventional sense and engages in identifying prospective customers, providing customers with information, persuading customers to buy, closing sales, and following on customer experience with product or service.
The two-way flow of communication between a buyer and seller, often in a face-to-face encounter, designed to influence a person's or group's purchase decision.	The practice whereby buyers and sellers combine their expertise and resources to create customized solutions, commit to joint planning, and share customer, competitive, and company information for their mutual benefit, and ultimately the customer.
The practice of building ties to customers based on a salesperson's attention and commitment to customer needs over time.	Sales activities occurring before and after the sale itself, consisting of six stages: (1) prospecting, (2) pre-approach, (3) approach, (4) presentation, (5) close, and (6) follow-up.
Planning, implementing, and controlling the personal selling effort of the firm.	A salesperson who specializes in identifying, analyzing, and solving customer problems and who brings technological expertise to the selling situations, but does not actually sell goods and services.
Specific goals assigned to a salesperson, sales team, branch sales office, or sales district for a stated time period.	A statement describing what is to be achieved and where and how the selling effort of salespeople is to be deployed.

salesforce automation	stimulus-response presentation
team selling	workload method
blog	bots
choiceboard	collaborative filtering
cookies	customer experience

A selling format that assumes the prospect will buy if given the appropriate stimulus by a salesperson.

The use of technology designed to make the sales function more effective and efficient.☐

A formula-based method for determining the size of a sales force that integrates the number of customers served, call frequency, call length, and available time to arrive at a sales force size.

Using a group of professionals in selling to and servicing major customers.

Electronic shopping agents or robots that comb Web sites to compare prices and product or service features.

A web page that serves as a publicly assessable personal journal for an individual.

A process that automatically groups people with similar buying intentions, preferences, and behaviors and predicts future purchases.

An interactive, Internet/Web-enabled system that allows individual customers to design their own products and services.

The sum total of interactions that a customer has with a company's website.

Computer files that a marketer can download onto the computer of an online shopper who visits the marketer's Web site.

customerization	**dynamic pricing**
eight-second rule	**interactive marketing**
multi-channel marketing	**online consumers**
permission marketing	**personalization**
portals	**spam**

The practice of changing prices for products and services in real time in response to supply and demand conditions.	The growing practice of not only customizing a product or service bur also personalizing the marketing and overall shopping and buying interaction for each customer.
Buyer-seller electronic communications in a computer-mediated environment in which the buyer controls the kind and amount of information received from the seller.	Customers will abandon their efforts to enter and navigate a website if download time exceeds 8 seconds.
The sub-segment of all Internet/web users who employ this technology to research products and services and make purchases.	The blending of different communication and delivery channels that are mutually reinforcing in attracting, retaining, and building relationships with consumers.
The consumer-initiated practice of generating content on a marketer's website that is customer tailored to an individual's specific needs and preferences.	The solicitation of a consumer's consent (called "opt-in")to receive email and advertising based on personal data supplied by the consumer.
Electronic junk mail or unsolicited email.	Electronic gateways to the World Wide Web that supply a broad array of news and entertainment, information resources and shopping services.

viral marketing	web communities
action item list	cost focus strategy
cost leadership strategy	differentiation focus strategy
differentiation strategy	functional groupings
generic business strategy	geographical groupings

Web sites that cater to a particular group of individuals who share a common interest.	An Internet/Web-enabled promotional strategy that encourages users to forward marketer-initiated message to others via email.
Involves controlling expenses and, in turn, lowering prices, in a narrow range of market segments.	An aid to implementing a market plan, consisting of three columns: (1) the task, (2) the person responsible for completing that task, and (3) the date to finish the task.
Using significant points of difference in the firm's offerings to reach one or only a few market segments.	Using a serious commitment to reducing expenses that, in turn, lowers the price of the items sold□in a wide range of market segments.
Organizational groupings in which a unit is subdivided according to the different business activities within a firm, such as manufacturing, marketing, and finance.	Using innovation and significant points of difference in product offerings, higher quality, advanced technology, or superior service in a wide range of market segments.
Organization groupings in which a unit is subdivided according to geographical location.	Strategy that can be adapted by any firm, regardless of the product or industry involved, to achieve a competitive advantage.

line positions	market-based groupings
product line groupings	profitability analysis
ROI marketing	sales analysis
sales component analysis	sales response function
share points	staff positions

Organizational groupings that assign responsibility for a specific type of customer to a unit.	People in line positions, such as group marketing managers, have the authority and responsibility to issue orders to the people who report to them, such as marketing managers.
A means of measuring the profitability of the firm's products, customer groups, sales territories, channels of distribution, and order sizes.	Organizational groupings in which a unit is responsible for specific product offerings.
A tool for controlling marketing programs where sales records are used to compare actual results with sales goals and to identify strengths and weaknesses.	A tool for controlling marketing programs using the applications of modern measurement technologies and contemporary organizational design to understand, quantify, and optimize marketing spending.
The relationship between the expense of marketing effort and the marketing results obtained. Measures of marketing results include sales revenue. profit, units sold, and level of awareness.□	A tool for controlling marketing programs that traces sales revenues to their sources such as specific products, sales territories, or customers.
People in staff positions have the authority and responsibility to advise people in the line positions but cannot issue direct orders to them.	Percentage points of market share; often used as the common basis of comparison to allocate marketing resources effectively.